Language and Literacy in Bilingual Children

Child Language and Child Development: Multilingual-Multicultural Perspectives

Series Editor: Professor Li Wei, *University of Newcastle-upon-Tyne, UK*
Editorial Advisors: Professor Gina Conti-Ramsden, *University of Manchester, UK*
Professor Kevin Durkin, *The University of Western Australia*
Professor Susan Ervin-Tripp, *University of California, Berkeley, USA*
Professor Jean Berko Gleason, *Boston University, USA*
Professor Brian MacWhinney, *Carnegie Mellon University, USA*

Children are brought up in diverse yet specific cultural environments; they are engaged from birth in socially meaningful and appropriate activities; their development is affected by an array of social forces. This book series is a response to the need for a comprehensive and interdisciplinary documentation of up-to-date research on child language and child development from a multilingual and multicultural perspective. Publications from the series will cover language development of bilingual and multilingual children, acquisition of languages other than English, cultural variations in child rearing practices, cognitive development of children in multicultural environments, speech and language disorders in bilingual children and children speaking languages other than English, and education and healthcare for children speaking non-standard or non-native varieties of English. The series will be of particular interest to linguists, psychologists, speech and language therapists, and teachers, as well as to other practitioners and professionals working with children of multilingual and multicultural backgrounds.

Other Books in the Series
Culture-Specific Language Styles: The Development of Oral Narrative and Literacy
    Masahiko Minami

Other Books of Interest
The Care and Education of a Deaf Child: A Book for Parents
    Pamela Knight and Ruth Swanwick
The Care and Education of Young Bilinguals: An Introduction to Professionals
    Colin Baker
Child-Rearing in Ethnic Minorities
    J.S. Dosanjh and Paul A.S. Ghuman
Cross-linguistic Influence in Third Language Acquisition
    J. Cenoz, B. Hufeisen and U. Jessner (eds)
Dyslexia: A Parents' and Teachers' Guide
    Trevor Payne and Elizabeth Turner
Foundations of Bilingual Education and Bilingualism
    Colin Baker
Encyclopedia of Bilingualism and Bilingual Education
    Colin Baker and Sylvia Prys Jones
Multicultural Children in the Early Years
    P. Woods, M. Boyle and N. Hubbard
Working with Bilingual Children
    M.K. Verma, K.P. Corrigan and S. Firth (eds)
Young Bilingual Children in Nursery School
    Linda Thompson

Please contact us for the latest book information:
Multilingual Matters, Frankfurt Lodge, Clevedon Hall,
Victoria Road, Clevedon BS21 7HH, England
http://www.multilingual-matters.com

CHILD LANGUAGE AND CHILD DEVELOPMENT 2
Series Editor: Li Wei

Language and Literacy in Bilingual Children

Edited by
D. Kimbrough Oller and Rebecca E. Eilers

MULTILINGUAL MATTERS LTD
Clevedon • Buffalo • Toronto • Sydney

Library of Congress Cataloging in Publication Data
Language and Literacy in Bilingual Children/Edited by D. Kimbrough Oller and
Rebecca E. Eilers
Child Language and Child Development: 2
Includes bibliographical references and index.
1. Bilingualism in children. 2. Children–Language. I. Oller, D. Kimbrough.
II. Eilers, Rebecca E. III. Series
P115.2.L35 2002
404'.2'083–dc21   2001044538

British Library Cataloguing in Publication Data
A catalogue entry for this book is available from the British Library.

ISBN 1-85359-571-3 (hbk)
ISBN 1-85359-570-5 (pbk)

Multilingual Matters Ltd
UK: Frankfurt Lodge, Clevedon Hall, Victoria Road, Clevedon BS21 7HH.
USA: UTP, 2250 Military Road, Tonawanda, NY 14150, USA.
Canada: UTP, 5201 Dufferin Street, North York, Ontario M3H 5T8, Canada.
Australia: Footprint Books, Unit 4/92a Mona Vale Road, Mona Vale, NSW 2103, Australia.

Typeset by Archetype-IT Ltd (http://www.archetype-it.com).
Printed and bound in Great Britain by the Cromwell Press Ltd.

Contents

Acknowledgements

The research reported in this volume was supported by a grant from the National Institutes of Health (5R01 HD30762) to D. Kimbrough Oller (PI) and Rebecca E. Eilers (Co-PI). Sincere thanks go to the Dade County Public Schools for their cooperation and collaboration in the effort. We also offer our thanks for insights and helpful suggestions to reviewers of and advisors to various portions of this work: Katsura Aoyama, Yuko Butler, Annick De Houwer, Jill de Villiers, Kenji Hakuta, and Erika Hoff.

Part 1

Background

Chapter 1

Assessing the Effects of Bilingualism: A Background

D. KIMBROUGH OLLER and BARBARA ZURER PEARSON

Monolingualism, Multilingualism, Culture and Politics

Multilingualism is all around us. Even in the United States, where a single language is clearly predominant, there are hundreds of languages spoken, both indigenous ones that predate the arrival of Europeans, and a vast array of languages from around the world. Yet the United States may be atypical in its possession of a single language to which immigrant populations as well as surviving indigenous ones have tended to assimilate with remarkable rapidity (Grosjean, 1982). The nations of the world often do not have a single predominant language, and even when they do, there are often other strong pretenders to the title. In India, the world's second most populous nation, the five most widely spoken languages (Hindi, Urdu, Telugu, Marathi, and Tamil) all have more than 30 million speakers, but none of these languages is spoken by as much as a quarter of the population. In fact there are more than 200 languages in India, and it is typical for individuals, especially in urban areas, to speak several of them (Khubchandani, 1978; Southworth, 1980).

It is hard to estimate how many people worldwide are multilingual, although it is known that in practically every country in the world, people utilize more than one language in daily discourse. It is also hard to know whether the speaking of multiple languages was typical of prehistoric humans, but it is so common in modern times that it would be problematical to justify the assumption that the culturally pristine condition of our species is a monolingual one. The human organism is enormously adaptable, and multilingualism is one of the conspicuous signs of that gift.

The tendency of American institutions (whether officially or unofficially) to press everyone in the nation to speak English and to offer education in other languages only with reluctance (Hakuta, 1986) is viewed

3

as a significant anomaly by many educated people from around the world, people who often view the fluent command of foreign languages as a requirement of a proper education. People around the world appear to experience a mixture of skepticism and envy in recognizing that Americans are often proudly monolingual. After all, English (especially American English) has swept the globe as the world's predominant *lingua franca* in both commercial and academic realms over the past few decades.

In the context of the obvious potency of American English as a medium of exchange that increasingly displays both social adaptability and prestige worldwide, it is surprising to witness the widespread, home-grown expressions of fear that the USA may be vulnerable to 'balkanization' due to the effects of many languages in our midst. The 'English-Only' movement (for commentary see Padilla *et al.*, 1991) is merely the most recent of these expressions. Nor did official pressure to assert the dominance of English begin in reaction to the Bilingual Education Act of the Johnson Administration, a body of legislation designed, ironically, not to encourage bilingualism, but to hasten the accomplishment of the transition to English in children of non-English linguistic heritage. But since the late 1960s when the Johnson Administration's efforts began to take hold by establishing federally-sponsored bilingual programs of instruction for children with limited proficiency in English, there has emerged particular political pressure to reassert a reigning role for English.

The goal of the research in bilingualism to be reported in this volume is undeniably inspired in part by the political debate over the role of English and other languages in education in the USA. In the sometimes vicious disputation, there reside critical, though sometimes inexplicit questions of theoretical as well as practical interest.

(1) Does bilingualism, in and of itself, cause educational or cognitive harm to children?
(2) The first question can be turned on its head: does bilingualism, in and of itself, *enrich* children educationally or cognitively?

It may be that the answers to such questions depend in part upon the way we frame the questions, and upon what we view as desirable goals of education. The research upon which this volume is based began with the recognition that there are multiple ways to assess the effects of bilingualism. Oral skill in both languages is relevant to a comprehensive and evenhanded assessment. So are literacy and other academic capabilities in both languages. Yet very little research in the United States has addressed abilities in both languages of any bilingual group either in the oral realm or in literacy. The effects of knowing and being educated in more than one language may be different depending upon the age at which the learning of a second language is initiated, the type of educational approach that is used, and the social background of the learner (for discussion, see Meyer & Fienberg, 1992). Research has rarely been conducted to address such issues systematically and comprehensively. Furthermore, the multivariate nature of the issues produces a circumstance where any study yields complex interpretations and potentially important ambiguities. So it is not clear that there are simple answers to general questions about effects of bilingualism. Yet much public opinion in the USA has been influenced by expectations that there are straightforward, negative effects.

Background on the Evidence Regarding Effects of Bilingualism

Among those who fear that English might be lost in America amidst a sea of immigrant languages, there resides an abiding opinion that children should be educated in English alone, no matter what their language background before they began school in America. Advocacy in behalf of education by English immersion is often justified by easily documented demographic patterns of school performance on English-language and general measures presumed to reflect intelligence. Language minority students in the United States often show weaknesses on intelligence tests and on achievement tests in oral English, reading in English, and in other academic realms. This lack of success is of particular concern with respect to the large Spanish-language minority. The academic gap contributes to alarming dropout statistics among Hispanic students (Fernandez et al., 1989; Hirano-Nakanishi, 1986; Velez, 1989). The gap is clearly evident in evaluation of tests administered in English (Frase et al., 1999), but even when tested in Spanish, children from Spanish-speaking homes appear to achieve below monolingual norms, about one year below in elementary school, two years in 8th grade, and three years in 12th grade (De La Rosa & Maw, 1990; Goldenberg & Gallimore, 1991; Orfield, 1986).

The claim that bilingual children of many language backgrounds show academic or intellectual deficiencies was widespread through most of the 20th century (cf. Barke, 1933; Dunn, 1987; Jones & Stewart, 1951; Kittel, 1959; Macnamara, 1967; Saer, 1923; Smith, 1923; Yoshioka, 1929). The studies purporting to demonstrate such deficiencies typically showed a correlation between bilingual status and low scores on academic or intelligence tests.

The causes of these apparent deficiencies demand evaluation. Could the problem reside in bilingualism *per se*? Might the bilingual child be hampered by the extra cognitive/linguistic burden imposed by multiple language learning? It has been argued that 'time on task' (Porter, 1990;

Rossell & Baker, 1996) in learning is a primary factor in success, and that dilution of time on task for each language in bilingual education causes bilingual students to be overburdened and consequently to be at risk for school failure. In accord with the reasoning, it might be thought that children in bilingual education who are allowed to speak and learn in their first language may fail to acquire English quickly or fully, and as a result, may emerge ill-prepared for further education or for employment in English, the primary language of the society.

In the USA, the key facts that have been invoked to support this reasoning have long been based upon the well-documented tendency of Hispanic-American children to perform poorly on various tests of achievement when compared with monolingual children (Dunn, 1987; Fernández & Nielsen, 1986; Smith, 1995; White & Vanneaman, 1995). This result, however, may not mean what it has often been interpreted to mean. While it is true that the average Hispanic child scores below the mean for the nation on academic tests, it is also true that the average Hispanic child in the United States is of lower socio-economic status than the average child as measured across the entire population. A substantial proportion of Hispanic children, especially in the past, were born into poverty. In studies comparing academic performance of Hispanic children of low socio-economic status with non-Hispanic children of similar socioeconomic status, Hispanic children do not trail academically (Lambert, 1981; Peal & Lambert, 1962). These results suggest that poor academic performance could be the result of factors other than bilingualism (cf. August & Hakuta, 1997). A variety of factors could be involved since poverty is common in language-minority students, and poverty is associated with low educational levels in parents, poor nutrition, domestic violence, a sense of diminished status and self-worth, and lower levels of linguistic stimulation than are available to children of higher socioeconomic status. Children can fail in school for many reasons, and those who enter school at an academic disadvantage, either through lack of knowledge at entry, lack of sociocultural support from the family for learning, or through effects of prejudice (social or ethnic) may be at risk for failure to thrive in school (Hart & Risley, 1981; 1992; Osborn, 1968).

In fact many bilingual children do well in school. A thorough analysis of the evidence on educational and linguistic outcomes for children educated in two languages yields a complex picture that suggests bilingual education is sometimes advantageous. Based in part on the results of the Canadian studies of bilingualism through French immersion in elementary school for children from English-speaking homes (Hart & Lapkin, 1989; Lambert & Tucker, 1972; Lapkin *et al.*, 1980; Swain & Lapkin, 1991), it appears that, for some children, successful adaptation to the needs of bilingualism may produce academic and social advantages in comparison with monolingual peers.

It is important to note that for the past 30 years there have been a spate of investigations suggesting that bilingual children (and adults) actually possess significant and consistent advantages over monolinguals on a variety of metalinguistic and/or cognitive tasks. It has been posited that in order for the child to reach a threshold point of command for both languages, a variety of general cognitive and metalinguistic capabilities must be mastered, capabilities that monolinguals may be able to forego, or may not need to develop so soon or to the same extent (Cummins, 1979). Although both results and opinions about the validity of the empirical claims vary (for commentary see Hakuta & Diaz, 1985), specific capabilities that have been reported to be superior in bilinguals or superior in balanced bilinguals as opposed to partial bilinguals include metalinguistic capabilities related to the 'word concept' (Ben-Zeev, 1977, 1984; Bialystok, 1988; Cummins, 1978) and sometimes grammaticality judgments (Galambos & Goldin-Meadow, 1990; Galambos & Hakuta, 1988), as well as explanations and scientific formulations (Kessler & Quinn, 1980; Rosenblum & Pinker, 1983) and a variety of non-verbal capabilities (Ben-Zeev, 1984; Bialystok, 1992; Bialystok & Majumder, 1998; Hakuta, 1987; Peal & Lambert, 1962). Bialystok (1999) has particularly emphasized that bilingual advantages are often associated with tasks requiring metalinguistic 'control' or selective attention as opposed to 'analysis' (see also Butler, 2000). These findings encourage further evaluation of relatively good performance and relatively poor performance of bilingual children in academic domains.

Variables that Should be Controlled in Bilingual Education Research

The children in the Canadian studies were often of relatively high socioeconomic status. One possibility that we have entertained is that the apparent ability of children in the Canadian studies to profit from the bilingual experience may be the result of other advantages associated with their social backgrounds. Perhaps the children in the Canadian investigations received more academic attention at home than would have been available to children of lower socio-economic status. Perhaps they had more books to read at home. Perhaps they were physically healthier. Perhaps they had an especially positive opinion about their own cultural backgrounds. Perhaps this constellation of advantages (along with others known to be associated with high socio-economic status) made it possible for the Canadian participants in the studies to profit from the opportunities presented by bilingualism. Conversely, it could be that children who begin education at a disadvantage (because of less academic attention, fewer books to read at home, poorer physical health and so on) might find bilingualism more difficult to attain fully.

This reasoning suggests that circumstances surrounding language learning and the resources available to children for acquiring knowledge of the world could play critical roles in educational outcome. This thinking has helped to structure the design of certain aspects of the work represented here.

Bilingualism might be expected to produce positive effects for children whose social advantages are high while producing negative effects for children whose social advantages are low. In the prior literature assessing effects of bilingualism, direct evidence to address these possibilities is hard to come by.

The failure of incorporation of the socio-economic status (SES) factor in much of the previous work on the effects of bilingualism is not the only serious flaw in that body of research. Perhaps most important among the commonly missing components in research in the United States has been thorough evaluation of the abilities of children in both languages. In general, research on bilingual education has simply not included the *dependent variable* of home language skill. Without it we cannot develop a comprehensive perspective on the knowledge of bilingual children, either academic or non-academic. Furthermore, up to the present, we have had little basis for gauging the effect of the extent to which children of limited English proficiency (LEP) have knowledge of English *when they come to school*. Retrospective research, the standard approach in past work on bilingual education, has generally not provided access to information about the level of exposure children experience to each language outside of school. Extent of English knowledge at entry to school could play a critical role in achievement of oral capability and literacy (see Cummins, 1979) and needs to be evaluated as an *independent variable*. Finally, it is possible that the *method* by which children are educated at school in the home language and in English could play a major role (either through a main effect or through an interaction with other factors) in how bilingualism affects children's learning. There has been extensive research on this topic, but future efforts are needed to integrate work on educational method more thoroughly with evaluation of socio-economic status and language spoken at home, and the work needs to include dependent variables for knowledge of both the home language and English.

The Importance of Assessing Both Languages

The failure of most prior research on bilingualism in the United States to address directly the knowledge of children in both languages represents an interpretive limitation of monumental proportions. This limitation can be viewed from both the standpoint of specific linguistic knowledge and from the standpoint of more general cognition. To illustrate the points, let us refer briefly to a key prior study on receptive vocabulary development in Hispanic children from our own laboratories (Umbel *et al.*, 1992), although many of the same points could be made based on evidence from other studies. In this study, children in Miami schools were tested for vocabulary knowledge. Outcomes suggested that these children, of generally above average socio-economic status, had vocabulary levels in English that were slightly below the mean for the norming sample (composed overwhelmingly of monolingual children with average socio-economic status) even after several years of schooling in English. At first blush, the results in English might be taken to suggest that the children were indeed harmed by bilingual experience, since their socio-economic status would have predicted better performance than was obtained. The first-blush conclusion is doubly worrisome because the test in question, the Peabody Picture Vocabulary Test (Dunn & Dunn, 1981), has been widely, though erroneously, interpreted as an intelligence test within schools. The relatively low scores of bilingual children on the test leave the unfortunate (and empirically unjustified) impression that bilingualism might have harmed not only the linguistic capability of the children but also their intellectual capacity.

The thoughtful reader will notice that this conclusion unjustifiably ignores the fact that the children may have had substantial knowledge in Spanish of words they did not know in English. An even-handed assessment of the vocabulary outcome would need to balance any lack of knowledge in the one language against knowledge in the other, which has its own value as a communicative medium. Even though this logic may seem compelling and unavoidable, bilingual children's academic abilities in school are often judged without any attempt to seek a balance of information regarding knowledge in the home language to supplement information on knowledge of English. It is perhaps even more notable that much *research on bilingualism* has been done without any attempt to assess knowledge of the home language. It seems clear that the decision to ignore knowledge of the home language has been driven by the political assumption that English should play a primary role in the USA, rather than by academic or cognitive considerations.

The study by Umbel *et al.* (1992) was designed to address Spanish and English knowledge in similar ways. Assessment in Spanish for the children studied by Umbel *et al.*, however, also showed scores slightly below the mean for the norming sample on the Spanish version of the same test (Dunn *et al.*, 1986). Again at first blush, one might be inclined to conclude that requirements of learning two languages produced relatively inadequate knowledge of two languages, and insofar as each evaluation might be taken (although improperly) as an intelligence test, the results might be interpreted to show that the bilingual children were harmed intellectually by the fact that they knew two languages.

The Distributed Characteristic of Bilingual Knowledge

Additional evidence, however, shows that such a conclusion would be ill-considered. It was noted in the research that children often knew both words of a translation pair (English 'dog' and Spanish 'perro', for example), but that the vocabulary knowledge did not always cross the language barrier; some words appeared to be known in one language but not the other and vice versa. After selecting all the items on both tests that constituted translation equivalent pairs and after correcting for chance performance in both cases, it was shown that bilingual children had statistically reliable vocabulary knowledge in each language that was disjunct from that in the other. Put another way, the children reliably knew some words in English that they did not know in Spanish and vice versa. This 'distributed characteristic' of bilingual knowledge implies that vocabulary knowledge is broader than can be assessed by looking at either language alone. The distributed characteristic is perfectly predictable based on the different life circumstances that commonly require bilingual individuals to speak one language or the other. Some words are learned in one language but not the other, because those words tend to be used in situations where one language, but not the other is the medium of exchange.

Adult bilinguals confirm the existence of the distributed characteristic. For example, the automobile shop may be a place where English is spoken, and consequently an individual may know the vocabulary of engines, drive-trains, axles, and so on primarily in English. The same individual may speak Spanish in the home, and consequently the vocabulary of the kitchen, with its pots, whisks, and range-tops may be known only or primarily in Spanish. The distributed pattern is viewed as both appropriate and somewhat inevitable given the pattern of living experienced by the individual.

The distributed characteristic of vocabulary knowledge across two languages is the basis for a critically important re-evaluation of the first-blush conclusions mentioned above. The relatively low vocabulary scores in both languages for the children that were studied cannot be taken to mean that the children had low vocabulary knowledge overall, because neither test was capable of assessing the totality of their vocabulary capabilities. Some combination of scores might be developed, but additional norming work would be required to interpret vocabulary knowledge in bilingual children. In the meantime, the best that can be said is that relatively low scores for bilingual children on vocabulary tests normed primarily on monolingual children cannot be taken to mean that bilingual children have poor vocabulary knowledge overall. At present we cannot be sure that bilingual children do not actually exceed monolinguals in the realm of 'conceptual vocabulary' (a term that is intended to encompass all mappings of words to concepts in the lexicons of both languages) (Pearson & Fernández, 1994). Early evaluations on conceptual vocabulary knowledge suggest that bilingual children may lexically map just as much of the conceptual world as monolingual children do, while having 'total vocabularies' (a term intended to encompass the total number of words in the two languages) that outstrip those of monolingual children (Pearson & Fernández, 1994; Pearson et al., 1995).

While there is much left to be learned from research, there is an irrefutable conclusion to draw from these studies: it is impossible to evaluate the knowledge of bilingual children, either from the standpoint of linguistic issues or from the standpoint of intelligence, in the absence of evaluation of both languages. The examples presented here have been taken from existing information on receptive vocabulary knowledge, but evaluation of both languages may be equally important in other realms including both production vocabulary and higher order linguistic functions such as morphology and syntax. The ability to command certain complex morphological or syntactic resources may be more well-developed in English than in Spanish and vice versa, and the distributed ability to use such devices from the two languages may be conditioned, as with vocabulary, by differing circumstances of language learning. Thus, an individual bilingual child may come to command some structures more effectively in one language than in the other based on more intensive early experience with the need for those structures. For example, if children are accustomed to being read to and told stories in Spanish at home, they may become competent in Spanish in the use of certain syntactic structures that are common in the story-telling modality. When the children enter school in English, they may be less competent in interpretation or use of similar structures in English. At the same time, formal classroom language, which includes some of its own syntactic forms appropriate for giving instructions to groups of children, for example, may be learned in English more quickly during early school years than in Spanish. In this way, bilingual children may come to have knowledge of some syntactic structures more fully in one language than the other and vice versa, during the early school years. The differences between bilingual and monolingual abilities to command such syntactic structures would presumably abate as years pass and bilingual children have further opportunity to be exposed sufficiently to all the types of syntactic structure that occur in both languages.

It is also true that bilingual children must come to command certain syntactic functions in Spanish that do not _exist_ in English (consider the morpho-syntactic function of gender in nouns, for example), and other functions in English that do not exist (or do not function in such a general manner) in Spanish (the mass-count distinction, for example). Since the bilingual child must learn these special syntactic devices in both languages, it is possible that it will take longer for them to be learned in each language than for a monolingual child, whose task is of lesser magnitude.

Carrying this reasoning further, we can speculate that even in the early years of learning, the bilingual child may actually command _more_ syntactic resources _in toto_ than the monolingual, since there is simply more to learn about syntax when learning two languages. Consequently, relatively low performance by bilinguals on general linguistic evaluations normed primarily on monolinguals could suggest the existence of distributed capabilities across two languages, rather than a general academic or linguistic weakness. It is not at all clear how to compare standardized test scores (especially early in the process of acquisition of the two languages) across monolingual and bilingual learners because the science of evaluation has not reached a point that allows adjustment of scores to take account of the distributed characteristic of learning in young bilinguals.

Limitations of ability on particular features of syntax or domains of vocabulary for each language may be particularly notable during the early years in school for children who start school with much more knowledge of Spanish than English, and who reverse that pattern during the elementary school years. As one language wanes and the other is acquired, it is logical to expect that both will show certain deficiencies during the process; this 'subtractive' pattern of learning over the early school years is well-recognized in the USA, where assimilation to English is a powerful trend among immigrant children (Veltman, 1983b). If we are to evaluate bilingual children's knowledge, then it is clear that there is no way to do it without evaluating their knowledge in Spanish as well as English.

The Role of First-language Instruction in Bilingual Education: The Interdependence Hypothesis

The study of bilingualism is commonly motivated by interest in determining the optimal method of education. Here again, a focus on both languages is potentially crucial. There is notable research and theory supporting the idea that the manner in which knowledge is instilled and maintained in the first language as well as the second language may play a key role in the attainment of academic skills in bilingual children. Cummins' (1984) interdependence hypothesis suggests that the level of ability in the second language (for children who begin learning a second language in school, and where the second language is the primary language of the host society) is partly a function of ability in the first language. Consequently, a strong foundation in the first may facilitate second language development, which in turn may facilitate educational success, even in the second language.

Although research on 'home-language' training has been sparse, evidence is mounting that schooling in a first language may, in the long term, foster successful language and literacy development in the second language. Young Navahos at the Rock Point School who learned to read first in Navaho trailed their English-learning peers in 2nd grade. But by 5th grade, these students were within six months of their grade level norms in English reading, while their peers in English-only programs, despite greater exposure to English, had an average reading level of 3rd grade (Rosier & Farella, 1976; Vorih & Rosier, 1978). Likewise Skutnabb-Kangas and Toukomaa (1976) found that young Finns in Sweden who learned to read Finnish in Finland before emigrating performed better in reading Swedish than Finns who emigrated before preschool or at the start of school. Similar advantages for early literacy training in a first language are reported for the Carpinteria, California Spanish-language preschool (Cummins, 1984), and for Mexican-Americans in a first-language maintenance program, K-2 (Medina & Escamilla, 1992). Other studies from around the world offer similar suggestions that first-language training may be important to ultimate success in the second language (Gale et al., 1978).

The George Mason research team directed by Collier and Thomas (Collier, 1987, 1989) has provided analysis on how many years of English schooling it took for immigrant children (about half of whom were Asian, one-quarter of whom were Hispanic, one-quarter from other groups) to 'catch up' with monolingual English peers in academic performance in English. One conclusion of the work was that children starting in English schooling at ages 8–11 (after significant schooling in the first language had already occurred) took fewer years to catch up than children starting at 5–7 (after little or no training in the first language). An implication is that very early second language training may be relatively ineffective, and that consolidation of home language knowledge (through ages corresponding to first or second grade) may establish a basis upon which second language training can proceed with greater facility.

The results of the studies indicating academic advantages of home-language instruction in the elementary years suggest that the home language provides a basis for general academic learning. The results suggest that children at risk for academic failure due to the short-term linguistic disadvantages of limited English proficiency (LEP) may be able to overcome the risk if their disadvantages are minimized and their existing language skills are utilized for the purposes of content matter instruction during the crucial early periods of schooling that lay foundations for literacy and other academic skills. A bilingual approach to education, where a substantial proportion of training is provided in the home language for LEP children may: (1) have the effect of maintaining children's confidence through early school years, while a second-language immersion approach may damage self-esteem by subjecting children to early failure and frustration; (2) foster more substantial long-term learning in children because certain fundamental academic skills may be acquired earlier and may form the basis for more rapid and early academic progress, while immersion may limit children's access to academic fundamentals as they struggle to understand what is being said in class; and (3) as Cummins suggests, the bilingual approach may assist children in learning English, while immersion approaches may hinder English acquisition by requiring children to learn English from a more limited linguistic base, slowing the process and leaving children behind in both linguistic and academic skills.

Two-way Bilingual Education

An intriguing approach to bilingual education, one that attempts to create a balance based on the Cummins interdependence hypothesis, works by fostering first-language learning directly, while encouraging learning of the second language early. This 'two-way' approach requires that content instruction (in math, social studies, language, arts, etc.) be segmented into components implemented roughly equally in each language. Half-day blocks of content are taught in one language, followed by half-day blocks in the other language. Much of the learning of language in the two-way approach is presumed to be embedded in the learning of subject matter rather than in direct language instruction.

One of the key points of rationale for two-way education is that the division of instruction into separate half-day long periods may give children the opportunity to gain momentum in the use of each language. The instruction in the first language (henceforth in this volume we shall consider circumstances where the first language is always Spanish) is assumed, in this approach, to begin in Kindergarten (K) or early elementary school by offering a basis upon which children can gain confidence, learning rapidly, acquiring a sense of what school is about in terms of etiquette and procedure, and forming an early base of academic knowledge. Activities in the second language (henceforth, English) are expected to show slower initial progress (because the children often begin with little knowledge of English), but also fewer general problems of socialization and procedure, because the children have the opportunity to acquire an understanding of how the classroom is supposed to work while they are in the Spanish segment of each day at school.

The practical idea is that by learning how school works and how to engage in study in Spanish, children gain a foothold on how to do it in English, even though they may (for the first year or so) understand relatively little of what transpires linguistically in the English portion of the day. As their knowledge of English grows, the difference in performance in the two languages should abate, according to this reasoning, and this growth of ability in English should be accompanied by maintenance (rather than replacement) of Spanish knowledge along with a sense of linguistic and social competence. A crucial element of this reasoning is that two-way education may minimize the presumed frustration and sense of defeat that children with LEP may experience early in an English immersion experience in school where they do not understand even simple instructions from teachers about classroom procedure. If children with LEP fail to learn the basics of reading and mathematics by the middle of elementary school when monolingual English-speaking children are beginning to accelerate into independent reading and academic reasoning, the children with LEP may fall far enough behind that they can never catch up. The two-way approach aims to ensure that even if children from Spanish-speaking homes are behind monolingual peers in English by middle elementary school, they are not behind (or at least not far behind) in academic learning in general.

Another notable potential advantage of the two-way approach is that it is expected to help preserve facility in the home language. Instead of giving up Spanish in order to learn English (the pattern of learning in school that is most commonly observed in Hispanic children in the United States), children are expected to continue expanding their capabilities in Spanish while they acquire English. The presumed result is a child literate in both languages and capable of future employment in either or both. The potential international commercial benefits of having a population that is trained well in both languages has not escaped notice.

While the two-way approach has its theoretical and practical merits, first-language instruction as a means to develop second language and academic skills has not been widely implemented in the United States, partly due to the unfavorable recommendation of a widely-cited review of the literature on bilingual education done for the Department of Education by Baker and de Kanter (Baker & de Kanter, 1981, 1983). The authors found the evidence favoring education in two languages inconclusive. It should be noted that the research reviewed was heavily focused upon outcomes in English, and gave little attention to the effects of bilingual education on the maintenance of skills in Spanish. Similarly, two recent research reports form the New York City schools showed disappointing results for bilingual education with a large home language component (Mujica, 1995; Torres & Fischer-Wylie, 1990). In the context of such outcomes the number of two-way programs implemented nationally has been restricted. Only 261 were listed in a national survey of the Center for Applied Linguistics (Christian, 2000).

At the same time, the studies mentioned were fraught with design limitations (for example, lack of control for socio-economic status and language spoken at home), and their conclusions are of uncertain value with regard to English oral and academic skills and of little value, if any, with regard to Spanish language skills. In response to the need for further evidence, other research has compared academic outcomes in English immersion, early-exit bilingual and late-exit bilingual programs in a four-year national study of 2300 children by Ramírez and colleagues (Ramírez *et al.*, 1991a, b, c, and reviewed in Meyer & Fienberg, 1992). Late-exit programs were those that continued first-language training even after students became relatively proficient in English. Evidence on late-exit programs included data from two-way education programs as well as data from other programs where children were given specific home-language training but not content matter training in the home language. In early-exit programs, children were trained to a minimal standard of English knowledge by teachers capable of providing home-language support, and then the children were promptly moved into English immersion.

The work provides a body of evidence indicating that academic outcomes (as judged by language and academic scores on the Comprehensive Test of Basic Skills) *in English* by the third grade were in general comparable for children in the three program types; thus, it seems possible that children in the bilingual programs (both early and late-exit) may have obtained the benefit of Spanish literacy development without loss in English language or literacy. But Spanish skills were not directly assessed. Growth curves of linguistic and academic learning in English from first to third grade showed the children in the late-exit programs (the ones with the most first-language instruction) to exceed those of the other programs. Additional evidence from the study compared late-exit programs with greater or lesser amounts of first-language training; these comparisons suggested that children with the highest proportion of Spanish-language training had the highest growth rates. Of special interest was the fact that the Miami-Dade County late-exit group in the study achieved scores that were comparable to national norms. Again, however, the studies did not address the effect of bilingual education on Spanish skills.

In an unpublished analysis of early effects of programs utilizing home language training, Thomas and Collier (in preparation, summary was provided on request) have reviewed results on 42,000 children from numerous databases, including the results of the Ramírez report and a number of others. The preliminary outcomes, compared in terms of type of training in the first and second language, suggest that: (1) children who have substantial training in the home language (usually Spanish) during early elementary school reap substantial advantages in academic subjects in English by late elementary or middle school when compared with children who have little or no home language training; and (2) substantial home language training in the elementary years lays foundations upon which advantages continue to accrue through high school, long after home language training has been supplanted by English only (and see Medina *et al.*, 1985). In general the results suggest advantages of 'late-exit' from home language training, and more generally, advantages of two-way training over English immersion training. And again, the studies focus on outcomes in English, but they have largely left out consideration of the potentially important effects of two-way education on children's knowledge of the home language.

The Need for Additional Evidence Regarding Early Bilingualism and Home-language Instruction

The Ramírez study and the analysis of Thomas and Collier provide the most important current empirically-based sources on the linguistic and academic effects of first-language education for American Hispanic children, but the findings leave key questions unanswered. The studies have focused almost exclusively on the performance of children in English, while giving little if any attention to the effects on Spanish, maintenance of which could have important long-term consequences for individuals in terms of self-confidence, educational opportunity, and employability.

Furthermore, interpretation of the results of former investigations is hampered by potentially important differences among the programs studied with respect to educational methodology at differing sites (e.g. mainstreaming occurred early in some, late in others, amount of Spanish training varied even within program type, etc.), duration of program assessment (long or short term), and by the lack of proactive selection of social and linguistic characteristics of children in the schools selected for investigation. Additional variables (beyond educational method) that may have strongly influenced the academic performance of the children studied include, in particular, socio-economic status (SES) and language spoken at home (LSH); both these variables have been highlighted by Dulay and Burt (1978) and Zappert and Cruz (1977) as being of potentially critical importance.

The population studied by Ramírez *et al.* was overwhelmingly of Low SES: over 85% of the children came from families reporting yearly incomes of less than $20,000, and 44% reported incomes less than $10,000; the pattern of Low SES typified all three program groups. Analysis of covariance suggested some SES effects in the study. However, the limited range of SES available inhibited the power of the evaluation to clarify the complex role that SES may play in educational and linguistic outcome. Other studies suggest the role of SES may be very important (for reviews, see Deutsch, 1967; White, 1981) .

Several mechanisms may be reflected by the SES variable, which is widely recognized as playing a key role in language acquisition (Hoff-Ginsberg, 1998; Hoff-Ginsberg & Tardif, 1995; Snow, 1995). Children of Low SES might be expected to have educational disadvantages associated with lack of educational materials at home (e.g. books, computers or other intellectually stimulating materials), parental expertise regarding educational matters, physical (e.g. nutritional) or emotional support. In addition, there could be attitudinal disadvantages owing to lower self-esteem in the Low SES child who enters school and finds that other children have nicer clothes, better lunch boxes, and so on. There are very substantial SES differences among children in public schools in the USA, and such differences are found in the schools in Miami to be evaluated here (see Chapter 2).

It seems likely that a language minority child who faces adapting to school and learning academic material in an unfamiliar language may be doubly disadvantaged by Low SES. At the same time, the language minority child who is not disadvantaged in SES may be insulated from the primary effects of linguistic disadvantage and, consequently, may not necessitate a late-exit two-way treatment in order to perform adequately in academics. Existing studies (including those of Ramírez *et al.* and Thomas & Collier) simply do not make clear how SES may interact with educational methods in producing academic outcomes.

With regard to language spoken at home (LSH), a similar limitation on interpretation of the Ramírez *et al.* study is discernible. Over 85% of the parents in the study reported using only or primarily Spanish in parent-to-parent conversation, and 79% reported speaking only or primarily in Spanish to their children. Consequently, the study appears to have been heavily weighted towards evaluation of children in a sequential language-learning circumstance rather than in a simultaneous one. The results reviewed by Thomas and Collier do not allow unambiguous evaluation of the simultaneous / sequential learning factor, because the work has been, to the point of this writing, published only in a preliminary form that does not specify subject characteristics.

Simultaneous learning of English and Spanish from the first year of life in Hispanic children may play a key role in educational outcome. This expectation is based in part upon the assumption that simultaneous learners have stronger English skills at the point of entry to the school system than sequential learners. Furthermore, the expectation is consistent with the idea that social attitudes about language may influence learning in bilingual children. Lambert (1977) has emphasized the potential importance of attitudes toward language in educational outcomes. He has characterized two forms of sequential bilingualism, 'additive' and 'subtractive'. With the additive form, positive values are attributed to the two languages, and education in one language does not constitute a threat against the other. Like additive bilingualism, simultaneous learning of both languages may foster a sense of positive value for both languages. Subtractive bilingualism occurs when the first language is not valued outside the home. Under these circumstances, the language of the economically and culturally more prestigious group tends to replace the minority language during early school years. Since the first language of children whose bilingualism is subtractive regresses while they are acquiring the second language, children are required during an unspecified time period to have less than native skills in both languages. Negative academic effects are hypothesized to result from low levels of skill in both languages. Such negative effects would presumably not accrue in the case of simultaneous bilingualism, assuming that positive attitudes are attributed to both languages and assuming that English is well-established by school age. Thus, the simultaneous bilingual child would presumably not be at a disadvantage in English-only schooling (see review in Hakuta, 1986).

Some children educated in language immersion settings do extremely well academically, as indicated by the experience of the studies conducted in Canada with children whose English-speaking parents chose to enroll them in special programs providing content subject education in French during elementary school (Barik & Swain, 1976a; Peal & Lambert, 1962). Yet the circumstances in the Canadian immersion studies may have been critically different from those in most of American research on immersion education. Although language immersion programs seemed not to have produced special benefits in Ramírez' subjects, for example, it seems likely that children in such programs may have undergone a subtractive experience while the children in the Canadian studies appear to have undergone an additive experience.

Furthermore, the children in the Canadian studies may have been of higher SES than the children in the Ramírez study. The Canadian parents might have been able to provide the children with additional resources allowing the children to capitalize on the opportunities provided by bilingualism. This support may be crucial in helping children to manage the extra cognitive/linguistic requirements that an additional language may impose.

Bilingualism: Theoretically, Empirically, Politically

Bilingualism is a fact of life in the United States as it is elsewhere. Immigration is a fact of life, and no amount of pressure in behalf of English-language assimilation can undo the fact that many children come to school with limited proficiency in English. It is necessary, from a practical standpoint, to begin reasoning about optimal educational and research strategies from this point, where children have a cultural heritage that cannot be negated without harm, and where they enter the educational arena with a language other than English that may be their primary means of discourse.

If we wish to understand the effects bilingual education has on children who begin school with LEP, then it will be necessary to compare children with LEP who are educated bilingually (in two-way approaches) to other children with LEP who are educated in immersion. Further, we will need to control for factors such as socio-economic status and language spoken at home. The standard of monolingual English children represents another point of comparison for the LEP groups, a point of comparison that is useful for different reasons that may shed light on general effects of bilingualism. Again, however, it is critical to control for socio-economic status. Finally, if we are truly interested in the effects of bilingual education, we cannot allow investigation to be conducted in the absence of thorough evaluation of the effects of the method on the maintenance and learning of oral and academic skills in the home language. All matters that are assessed in English for bilingual children need to be evaluated in Spanish as well.

The ideal approach to study of such a question would be an experimental one with random assignment of children to groups of training, language experience and socio-economic status. Of course, in practice, no such experiment is possible. The best alternative, in our opinion, is one that seeks proactively to locate children who happen to fit into various categories of socio-economic status, language spoken at home and educational method and to study them prospectively and systematically after they have been located.

The question of how bilingualism affects cognition and education cannot be answered fully in a single study. But well-controlled investigation can help to improve our reasoning on a topic that has been addressed often on the basis of anecdotally-inspired fears that bilingualism and bilingual education are inherently damaging to children. Through further systematic investigation, it may be possible to determine that bilingual education yields relative advantages or disadvantages depending on social, linguistic and/or educational variables. By ensuring that the evaluation provides a comprehensive view of skills children develop in *both* languages, it should be possible to broaden substantially the discussion of bilingualism and bilingual education.

Chapter 2

An Integrated Approach to Evaluating Effects of Bilingualism in Miami School Children: The Study Design

D. KIMBROUGH OLLER and REBECCA E. EILERS

A Multi-factor Study of Bilingual Education

The studies published in this volume are the product of research conducted during the mid to late 1990s in Miami, Florida, under a grant from the National Institutes of Child Health and Human Development (NICHD). In one sense the effort was opportunistic, having been formulated and pursued in Miami, where a unique setting afforded the opportunity to evaluate bilingual education in significant new ways. The fact that socio-economically well-balanced groups of Hispanic and non-Hispanic school children were easily located in South Florida, and well-established public bilingual education programs were likewise available provided the ingredients for an integrated analysis of critical variables.

The opportunistic effort was based also upon the presence in South Florida during the 1990s of a group of collaborating scholars who were all trained in and deeply committed to empirical research on language acquisition in both English and Spanish. The Bilingualism Study Group[1] was formed around these interests and provided the administrative frame around which much of the work was conducted at the University of Miami, at Florida International University and in the Miami-Dade County Public Schools.

In accord with the reasoning outlined in Chapter 1, the participants in the project built upon the foundations of prior work in perception of speech by Spanish- and English-learning infants (Eilers *et al.*, 1979; Eilers *et al.*, 1982), phonological development in Spanish- and English-learning and bilingual infants and children (Eilers *et al.*, 1984; Oller & Eilers, 1982, 1983;

Oller *et al.*, 1997; Pearson *et al.*, 1995), vocabulary development in bilingual children (Fernández *et al.*, 1992; Pearson *et al.*, 1993b; Umbel *et al.*, 1992), semantic and syntactic development in Spanish- and English-learning and bilingual children (Gathercole, 1989; Gathercole & Hasson, 1995; Gathercole, 1997; Gathercole & Min, 1997; Gathercole & Montes, 1997), language choice among bilingual Hispanic teenagers (Pearson & McGee, 1993), and performance in college and on college entrance examinations by Hispanic students (Pearson, 1993). The collaborators established a broad effort designed to evaluate linguistic and academic effects of bilingualism in school children. The work was intended in part to assess educational practices that may enhance performance of bilingual children in school. Two categories of factors were deemed critical in addressing the role of bilingualism: first, it was taken to be necessary to evaluate the capabilities and backgrounds of bilingual children in *both* their languages, and second, it was deemed crucial that social and educational variables be systematically controlled (for discussion of this crucial issue see Meyer & Fienberg, 1992).

Accordingly, the dependent variables of study were:

(1) English oral language and academic performance, and
(2) Spanish oral language and academic performance.

Also in accord with the reasoning, the selected independent variables were:

(1) socio-economic status (SES),
(2) language spoken at home (LSH), and
(3) instructional method at school (IMS).

The effort was pursued largely within a single investigation, wherein schools and children were located and assigned to design categories before outcomes were assessed. Bilingual children were tested in both English and Spanish throughout the study. For certain comparison purposes monolingual English-speaking children were tested in English, and for two comparisons, monolingual Spanish-speaking children were tested as well.

The Advantage of Studying Bilingualism in Miami

The Miami metropolitan area (Miami-Dade County) provided a unique setting within which such an effort could be pursued. About half the population of the metropolitan area was Hispanic. Unlike Hispanic bilingual populations in other parts of the United States, the entire range of socio-economic strata could be found in substantial numbers among the Miami Latin community, which included particularly strong economic and political components. The Cuban-Americans, who made up over 60% of Miami

Hispanics, controlled large sectors of the banking industry, media, and government. In particular, the main strata of Hispanic society in Miami compared favorably in income and educational attainment opportunity with mainstream America (Boswell & Curtis, 1983; Pérez, 1986), while they concurrently retained the use of the Spanish language to a greater degree than Latin groups of different national origins (Nielsen & Fernández, 1982).

The importance of this socio-economic diversity as a foundation for the research conducted here can be seen in the fact that key prior studies of bilingual education have been conducted in the absence of the possibility of matching for socio-economic status across subject groups. Moreover, the sampling of Hispanic children has typically been heavily biased toward the lower socio-economic strata. For example, consider what is perhaps the most highly regarded empirical work on bilingual education (Ramírez *et al.*, 1991b), an effort focusing on educational strategies with Hispanic children in a multisite study that encompassed schools in a variety of states. In this work, the socio-economic status of families who participated was predominantly low (85% had incomes of less than $20,000 per year). Furthermore, the families were heavily biased toward OSH ('Only Spanish at Home'), and 85% reported no English in the home. This imbalance is reflective of national patterns for families whose children have limited English proficiency. In Miami school children, on the other hand, the patterns of income and socio-economic status showed no disadvantage in Hispanic groups compared with non-Hispanics, white or black, based on data gathered in multi-school studies of language acquisition (Fernández *et al.*, 1992; Umbel *et al.*, 1992). The community also included Hispanic families with a wide range of language capabilities, extending from monolingualism in Spanish to balanced bilingualism to monolingualism in English.

Bilingual Education Programs in Miami

In addition to the advantages of socio-economic and linguistic diversity in the community, Miami also presented advantages in terms of public educational settings. The metropolitan area was the site of one of the most well-established two-way bilingual schools in the nation, Coral Way Elementary, initiated in 1963, and a more recent school (operating as a two-way program since 1990), Marjory Stoneman Douglas Elementary, organized on the Coral Way model. At the time of our study, both schools, in accord with a two-way approach, educated children in Spanish 40% of the day and in English 60%,[2] a pattern that was maintained from Kindergarten (5–6 year-olds) through 5th grade (10–11 year-olds). Fifth grade was the highest grade level at which two-way education was implemented. The two schools, enrolling over 1000 students each, were essentially neighborhood-based, drawing 97% of their students from their own geographic boundaries. Because it was possible to select students whose performance in these two-way schools was of interest and whose demographic characteristics were appropriate to the design of the study, we were able substantially to limit the problem of subject 'self-selection', a factor that can hamper generalizability of results. In a variety of previous studies (especially from the Canadian 'immersion' programs, see Hakuta, 1986) students have entered programs voluntarily or based upon parental choice, and they thus represented an indeterminate spectrum of factors such as socio-economic status or multiple language use at home. In addition to the two-way schools, Miami offered many socio-economically similar public schools that educated Hispanic children in an English immersion approach. Four schools utilizing an English immersion approach and four schools with a large proportion of monolingual English children were selected for comparison with the two-way schools as explained below.

It bears explaining that the definition of the notion 'two-way school' has varied over the near half-century of its usage. The study reported here pertains to two particular schools that meet one of the key criteria that has always been invoked in defining two-way schools, namely that participant children be taught content matter in two languages during separate near half-day portions of each school day. Thus the programs at Coral Way and Marjory Stoneman Douglas were based on a long-standing tradition, and Coral Way has long been acknowledged as an exemplary two-way program. At the same time, there is a recent trend that invokes an additional criterion, namely that a minimal proportion of the participants in a two-way program must be representatives of the majority language (the Center for Applied Linguistics, for example, added this criterion to its definition of 'two-way immersion' for its national survey as of the year 2000). In fact, it is not clear whether either Coral Way or Marjory Stoneman Douglas should be treated as having met this additional criterion, either as of the year 2000 or during the period of the research in the mid 1990s. During the time of the research, well over 90% of the children in both programs were Hispanic, and Spanish was spoken at least some of the time in many, perhaps the great majority of the homes by parents and grandparents, and in all the homes of 'bilingual' children that were specifically selected for study within the targeted schools. At the same time, the children themselves might have met the language-majority criterion, because, as indicated in Chapter 3, most children in the programs spoke primarily English, at least when speaking to peers at school, regardless of their family backgrounds. Additional evidence to be presented in Chapters 4–11 will offer a perspective on the extent of command that children in the programs had of both English and Spanish. These issues may be important in the interpretation of the results of the present work, because both research and theory suggest that a critical factor in the achievement of native or near-native command of a language is consistent interaction with native-speaking peers (Hart & Lapkin, 1989; Lambert, 1977, 1981; Lambert & Tucker, 1972; Veltman, 1983a).

When the term 'two-way' is used to refer to the programs at Coral Way and Marjory Stoneman Douglas in this volume, it is done with full recognition of the fact that there is ambiguity about whether the schools technically meet all the criteria that have sometimes been invoked in the utilization of the term. Results based on the particular pattern of two-way education studied here may not be entirely generalizable to other settings, but the schools chosen did represent an important focus of inquiry since they provided the opportunity to evaluate bilingual education in a well-established, economically thriving immigrant community. Hereafter in this volume, the term 'Two-way' will be capitalized when referring to the particular programs under study. The terms referring to the bilingual 'English Immersion' programs as well as the 'Monolingual English' programs that will be compared will likewise be capitalized.

Miami thus offered all the combinations of social class, language background, and educational program necessary to evaluate key factors that are expected to influence academic success in bilingual children. Furthermore, the Miami-Dade County Public School system constituted an enormous (the fourth largest nationally) single district, with students drawn from a total population exceeding 1.8 million. At the time of initiation of the study reported here, the system had 187 elementary schools (for children 5 to 10 years old) with 154,000 students at the elementary level.

The district was administered by a long-standing, elected board of education, which appointed its superintendent and staff. The district had a long-term and strong relationship with its teachers' union, the United Teachers of Dade. The system was widely regarded as a model for metropolitan school administration in circumstances of multi-ethnicity. The centralization of authority in the district afforded the opportunity for relatively large-scale studies across schools that could be verified to be well-matched. A key factor in this opportunity was the existence in the district of standardized testing of students as well as regular monitoring of demographic factors, all recorded in the system's Demographics Manual.

Through an excellent relationship between the University of Miami's Bilingualism Study Group and the Miami-Dade County Public Schools and through use of the 1990 US Census database for each school neighborhood in the district, it was possible to select well-matched Two-way, English Immersion, and Monolingual English (ME) schools, to select within those schools children that met rigorous socio-economic status (SES) and lan-

The Core Design
(replicated at Kindergarten (K), 2nd, and 5th grade)

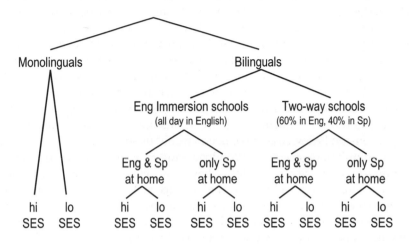

Total N = 952

Figure 2.1 Core Design

guage spoken at home (LSH) criteria, and subsequently to administer a wide variety of standardized tests of language and literacy in both English and Spanish to children so selected at Kindergarten (K, 5 year olds), 2nd (7 year olds) and 5th (10 year olds) grade (see Figure 2.1).

Standardized Tests

The work reported here, with only minor exceptions to be detailed as they appear in subsequent chapters, was conducted with a common group of children over a four-year period within what will be referred to as the 'Core Design' (see below). All the children participating in the Core Design were given a battery of standardized tests of oral language and academic performance. The Woodcock-Johnson/Woodcock-Muñoz battery was selected to constitute the primary group of standardized tests. It was the only available major educational test covering a broad range of subcategories of knowledge applicable at the elementary school level with full norming in both English (Woodcock, 1991) and Spanish (Woodcock & Muñoz-Sandoval, 1995a). The battery had the advantage of psychometric soundness and substantial breadth, providing well-motivated standardized scores allowing comparison among groups of children from a variety of backgrounds.

As a supplement to the Woodcock-Johnson and Woodcock-Muñoz, the children in the Core Design were also tested for receptive vocabulary on the well-standardized and widely-used Peabody Picture Vocabulary Test (PPVT) (Dunn & Dunn, 1981) and its Spanish equivalent, the Test de Vocabulario en Imágenes Peabody (TVIP) (Dunn et al., 1986). Research on vocabulary knowledge in bilingual children has been extensive, including a number of studies from our own laboratories (Fernández et al., 1992; Pearson & Fernández, 1994; Pearson et al., 1993a, b; Pearson et al., 1995; Umbel, 1991, January; Umbel et al., 1992). However, such research has provided only sketchy information regarding the possible effects of first-language training in school and of SES. Furthermore, relationships between production and comprehension knowledge have been largely unstudied.

The English versions of the Woodcock and PPVT were based on samples carefully chosen to be representative based on US Census data. The tests utilized standard American English. The Woodcock-Muñoz battery for Spanish as well as the TVIP were both constructed to be as dialect-independent as possible, selecting vocabulary and other structures that tend to be relatively universal in both New World and Old World versions of Spanish. The tests were normed with New World monolingual speakers from Mexico and Puerto Rico in both cases, and with additional speakers from Central and South America in the case of the Woodcock-Muñoz battery.

Probe Evaluations

In addition to taking the standardized tests, a substantial subset of the children participated in a series of 'probe' evaluations based upon non-standardized procedures developed and/or adapted by the participating scholars. In this way, the work sought to address gaps in previous studies of bilingual education regarding evaluation of linguistic variables that have recently been shown to play significant roles in academic success. The investigation of narrative skills and their relation with literacy has included studies of typically developing and language-impaired monolingual children (Bamberg, 1987; de Villiers, 1991; Hedberg & Westby, 1993; Hemphill et al., 1991). It is now widely believed that much of the linguistic growth that children experience in elementary school years occurs at a level beyond individual sentences in the creation and understanding of extended discourse or 'texts'. Insightful analytical frameworks (Halliday & Hasan, 1976; Labov, 1972; Labov & Waletzky, 1967; Stein & Glenn, 1979) have aided description. Such frameworks have been applied in cross-linguistic research on narrative in a wide variety of languages (summarized by Berman & Slobin, 1994). The outcomes of such research are intriguing in suggesting a linguistic basis for complex reading skills. The work of Barbara Pearson, reported here in Chapter 7, is among the first to begin to assess the role of bilingualism in the development of control over the linguistic devices of narrative.

Furthermore, an extensive set of probe studies has been conducted by Virginia Mueller Gathercole on morpho-syntactic knowledge in Spanish/English bilingual and monolingual children in both languages focusing on differences in syntactic devices across the languages. Chapters 8–10 address: (1) the English mass/count distinction and how bilingual and monolingual English-speaking children treat it; (2) the Spanish gender distinction and how bilingual and monolingual Spanish-speaking children treat it; and (3) the phenomenon of 'that-trace', a structure involving sentential complements implemented in fundamentally different ways in the two languages, studied here in terms of its control by bilingual and monolingual children in both languages. The results provide fundamental new indications of both strengths and weaknesses in bilingual children's command of subtleties in their languages and offer perspectives on the relative performance of bilingual children compared with monolingual peers.

An additional probe evaluation presented in Chapter 11 addresses the fact that learning to read has been hypothesized to require a minimum level of 'phonological awareness' (Liberman et al., 1989). There has been very little research on phonological awareness in bilingual children (however, see Bialystok, 1991; Bruck & Gennessee, 1995; Rubin & Turner, 1989), even though it seems possible that learning multiple languages could have a sensitizing effect, focusing children's attention on sounds and their functions in different settings. Neither the possible existence of phonological sensitization nor the possibility that first-language education might foster it had been considered in previous work. An early report on the work conducted by the collaborating team of the present work (Oller et al., 1998) described a new tool for phonological awareness research that was developed and evaluated with bilingual and monolingual children. The tool allows testing of children's abilities to perform 'phonological translation', a skill that has been shown in this work to differentiate clearly between monolingual and bilingual children and to provide a clear measure of development. A primary goal of the work is to assess the possibility that phonological translation fosters phonological awareness in bilingual children and thereby enhances reading capabilities.

Test Scheduling

All the children in the study were tested in sessions conducted at their schools. Each child was taken to a separate room or isolated space for testing on the Woodcock-Johnson/Woodcock-Muñoz and PPVT/TVIP. In each language, the standardized tests were administered to each child in two 30–40 minute sessions, with one session per day. Because bilingual children were tested in both Spanish and English, four such sessions were required to complete data collection for each bilingual child. Bilingual children completed one language's sessions before beginning the other language's sessions. Of the 704 bilingual children, 354 (50.3%) received the English battery first. Systematic counterbalancing was used throughout the study when appropriate.

The probe evaluations were not conducted with all the children, but a sample (to be described in each relevant chapter in this volume) was selected as necessary for each study. The probe evaluations were conducted during a fifth session of comparable duration to the regular sessions.

Test Administrators

The test administrators were all fluently bilingual in English and Spanish. Each tester was selected specifically to meet a high standard of capability in both languages. The coordinator of the testing (Umbel) was herself a balanced English–Spanish bilingual of Cuban heritage, having grown up in an English-speaking area of South Florida. She selected individuals to perform the testing if and only if they had native or near-native command of both languages, and evidenced no English accent in Spanish, nor Spanish accent in English. All testers had grown up speaking both languages. The dialects of the testers in both English and Spanish were distinctly 'New World', with a notable Caribbean flavor in Spanish, to match the language exposure that the children in the study experienced at home. Similarly the English dialects of the speakers were typical of native English speakers in modern Miami. There were eight testers. To the extent possible given the need to travel efficiently to and from schools (the schools were located all over Miami-Dade County), the testers were assigned to test individuals from as many cells as possible and as evenly as possible across the cells of the research design.

Overview of the Core Design

Since random assignment of subjects to groups was not feasible,[3] we selected both bilingual (Spanish/English) and monolingual (English) subjects proactively to fit preset categories of SES (high and low, or High SES and Low SES) and LSH (where bilinguals are exposed to either only Spanish [OSH] or English and Spanish [ESH] nearly equally in the home). Such subject selectivity is rare in educational research, and especially in research on bilingualism. The success of subject selection depended on a long-term, close relationship with the Dade County Public Schools. It capitalized on the availability in Miami of a large demographic base of Hispanic and non-Hispanic families of all the relevant SES and LSH categories.

The current work was based on reasoning drawn in part from Cummins' interdependence hypothesis (Cummins, 1984), from Lambert's distinction between 'additive' and 'subtractive' learning (Lambert, 1977), and from empirical evidence suggesting that differences in SES may modify the impact of bilingualism on academic and linguistic outcomes (Lambert & Tucker, 1972). We posed the possibility that bilingualism might impose undue burdens of learning on children who enter school at a disadvantage (due to Low SES for example), but might present opportunities for enhancement for children entering school in a position of social advantage.

Core Design and Matching of Schools

The research within the Core Design included variables as indicated in Figure 2.1. Nine hundred and fifty-two subjects were tested (704 Spanish–English bilinguals, 248 English monolinguals). Because the intent of the research was to examine not only the effects of bilingualism and school instructional variables (English Immersion vs. Two-way) on language and literacy, but also the effects of SES on outcome, careful preparation was made for selecting and matching schools on demographic variables.

The Dade County Public School (DCPS) Demographics Manual (including a variety of demographic and test information on every school in the system) was used to screen potential elementary schools for percent of children with limited English proficiency (LEP), eligibility for school lunch programs, classroom size, teacher experience and advanced degrees, ethnic mix and school-wide achievement scores. The data in the Manual were used to find potential matches for the two Two-way schools in the Dade County system. Accordingly, a pool of potential schools was chosen in which English Immersion was the instructional strategy and most students were of Hispanic origin, many with limited English proficiency. These schools were selected because they provided a range of SES while they matched the Two-way schools on the other relevant variables mentioned above. In addition, schools in which less than half the students were from homes in which Spanish was spoken, were chosen on the basis of the same educational, achievement and SES criteria. These latter schools were designated as Monolingual English (ME) schools and the students of interest were those whose home language was exclusively English.

The selected school boundary maps were superimposed on CD ROM-based 1990 US Census maps to obtain identification of Census blocks within the school boundaries in order further to verify the adequacy of the ethnic and socio-economic matching of districts. Variables examined from

Table 2.1 School matching based on Dade County Public Schools Manual Data

	% Hispanic	% LEP	FTE/child in thousands of dollars	SAT math scores at K and 1st grade
Two-way (2 schools)	92.5 (90–95)	38.5 (37–40)	3.48 (3.0–3.8)	67 (63–71)
English Immersion (4 schools)	93.7 (90–95)	36.7 (31–37)	3.58 (2.9–4.0)	67 (63–67)
Monolingual English (4 schools)	40 (18–50)	12.7 (3–20)	3.41 (3.0–3.8)	65 (57–69)

the census data included parents' country of origin, age at entry to the USA, native country, parents' educational level, parents' occupation, languages spoken in home, number of bedrooms in the home and whether the home was rented or owned. These data were then used to select from the eligible schools, four of each type (Monolingual English and English Immersion), that best matched the range of SES and ethnicity found in the Two-way schools. Table 2.1 provides key data on the matching of schools. In particular, we selected Two-way and English Immersion schools that were matched on the percentage of students who were Hispanic and on the percentage deemed to have LEP. In this way we hoped to ensure relative similarity in the amount of exposure to Spanish and English for children in the schools. Monolingual English schools could not be matched to the predominantly Hispanic schools on these factors (a matter which will be taken up below), but were matched on expenditure per student (FTE) and on school performance on a standardized test of mathematics for students in (Kindergarten) K and 1st grade. Mathematics scores were selected for matching since it was presumed they would be more free of language-bias than any other available measure. Matching for scores at K and 1st grade was intended to maximize the power of the investigation to detect effects of program type, which if they occurred, would presumably accumulate across time for children in the programs. It was reasoned that if one program was superior to another, children with similar capabilities at early grade levels would be seen to differ at later grade levels based on the program in which they studied.

Subject Selection

Subject selection within the matched schools began with the distribution of a consent form and a questionnaire (see Table 2.2) to all K, 2nd and 5th

Table 2.2 Immigration demographics for all bilingual families in the sixties

VAR	G	111	112	121	122	211	212	221	222
MUS	K	21.9	22.7	12.9	24.0	16.5	24.6	10.1	18.3
	2	24.4	24.7	14.9	26.1	20.4	24.3	13.8	22.5
	5	25.5	27.5	17.9	27.3	23.6	19.7	14.7	24.5
FUS	K	22.3	23.0	14.9	20.7	18.0	22.0	11.6	20.8
	2	24.7	22.8	16.2	20.5	20.2	24.9	14.6	21.5
	5	23.9	28.9	20.1	27.3	27.3	22.3	14.3	20.0
%USF	K	6	35	8	19	5	33	21	41
	2	3	16	16	27	5	27	13	35
	5	5	13	16	15	17	0	19	33
%CNF	K	68	57	55	58	43	44	24	29
	2	76	64	41	39	60	54	39	42
	5	81	74	62	73	66	67	54	33
%OF	K	25	8	36	23	52	22	55	29
	2	21	16	43	33	35	19	48	23
	5	14	13	22	11	17	33	27	33
%USM	K	25	46	5	46	9	26	0	35
	2	17	28	3	44	15	31	0	19
	5	9	22	6	23	17	0	4	11
%CNM	K	50	42	31	42	43	59	21	29
	2	65	56	37	28	50	54	32	58
	5	86	74	56	69	67	67	46	33
%OM	K	25	11	64	11	48	15	79	35
	2	17	16	59	28	35	15	68	23
	5	5	4	37	8	17	33	50	55

Codes: digit one = IMs (Instructional Method in School):
              1 = English Immersion, 2 = Two-way
         digit two = SES (socio-economic status):
              1 = LSES (low), 2 = HSES (high)
         digit three = LSH (Language spoken at home):
              1 = OSH (Only Spanish, at home), 2 = ESH (English and Spanish, at home)

Key:
   FUS number of years father in US
   MUS number of years mother in US
   %USF Percentage of fathers born in US
   %CNF Percentage of fathers born in Cuba
   %OF Percentage of fathers born in other countries
   %USM Percentage of mothers born in US
   %CNM Percentage of mothers born in Cuba
   %OM Percentage of mothers born in other countries

graders. The questionnaire probed issues such as languages and language proficiency in the home, parents' educational history and occupation both in the home country and in the USA, family income, parents' aspirations for their children's level of schooling and estimates of the likelihood that these aspirations would be met, number of children and adults living at home, country of origin and duration of life in the USA.

All prospective subjects were required to have been born in the USA (to help avoid differential effects of immigration status), and to have had one of two language histories, either a reported equal exposure to English and Spanish in the home (ESH) before K or only Spanish in the home prior to K (OSH). Subjects who met these criteria were further divided into SES categories based on parents' educational level, family income and parental occupations. Categorization of children regarding exposure to English and Spanish as well as SES was based on the questionnaires filled out by parents prior to subject selection. A final criterion for entry to the subject pool was that children had to have been educated in only one method throughout elementary school. Thus children in the Two-way programs at all grade levels (K, 2nd and 5th) had to have been in school in Two-way programs since the beginning of K. Likewise children selected for the project to represent English Immersion programs had to have been in English Immersion programs since the beginning of K.

Thus the full Core Design called for children from High and Low SES categories and from both English Immersion and Two-way schools, and from OSH and ESH language backgrounds. In addition, monolingual English-speaking children who met the SES requirements were recruited from matching schools.

The research team's ability to match groups to the ultimate ideal was limited by where children in the various language groupings could be found. The controlling circumstance was that presented by the Two-way schools. There were only two such schools operating from K to 5th grade, and consequently, the ideal arrangement would have been one in which all other selected schools displayed demographic patterns matching those of the Two-way schools. Matching was not a problem with regard to such variables as socio-economic status of families in these neighborhood schools. All the schools were, on average, middle-class, and demographics presented here support that conclusion. However, the ethnic distribution was substantially imbalanced across the schools as evidenced by the fact that Two-way and English Immersion children were drawn from schools where over 90% of children were Hispanic, and more than 30% of the children in all such schools selected for study were categorized formally as having LEP. The 90% Hispanic distribution for the English Immersion schools that were selected was dictated by the fact that *both* Two-way schools in the Dade County system showed this pattern.

As a result, in both English Immersion and Two-way schools, children were exposed to peers who in the great majority of cases spoke two languages, while very few of them spoke English as a first language, and virtually none monolingually. In contrast, monolingual children were drawn from schools in which English was predominant, and where most children spoke (and went to school in) English only. Both the children and the schools meeting this monolingual requirement are referred to here as ME (Monolingual English). The imbalance was dictated by the fact that sufficient numbers of ME children in the Two-way and English Immersion schools could not be located in order to fill out the design we sought to evaluate. Consequently the great majority of ME children came from ME schools where only a small proportion of children were deemed LEP and where the majority were non-Hispanic.

In spite of the fact that children in both Two-way and English Immersion schools were largely Hispanic, and that many had LEP, Hispanic children tended to speak English to each other (see Chapter 3). A substantial amount of the communication, especially in the early elementary years, was necessarily negotiated in non-native English. Learning English and learning to read in English may be an especially difficult task for children who lack exposure to English monolingual peers. As noted earlier, a key principle of second language acquisition is that children rarely achieve native abilities in a language in which they do not have native-speaking peers (Brown, 1980; Lambert, 1981; Veltman, 1983a). It is consequently important to acknowledge that the bilingual children studied here may not have been in the optimal environment to produce linguistic and academic success in English during the elementary school years. Consequently, the comparison of monolingual and bilingual children's performance in English needs to be considered in the light of the unavoidable paucity of monolingual English-speaking peers for children in the Two-way and English Immersion schools.

Moreover, just as the lack of monolingual English-speaking peers might limit the success of bilingual children in English, so could the relative lack of monolingual Spanish-speaking peers limit their success in Spanish. The overall pattern of language use noted in the children in this study shows overwhelming favoritism to English (see Chapter 3). Consequently, even children who began school with substantial knowledge of Spanish showed diminishing commitment to Spanish outside the Spanish-speaking classroom. Consequently individual children in the bilingual schools not only spoke less Spanish but also heard less of it. It is possible that this pattern produced a generalized reduction in the potency of the Spanish peer environment for the children.

On the one hand, it might be argued that given this pattern, perhaps Miami was not the ideal site for the natural experiment we conducted. There is good reason to moderate such concern in light of the common facts of immigration and neighborhood life. The bilingual circumstance we have evaluated represents a typical one with regard to peer language exposure. Immigrant children, both in the USA and elsewhere, often grow up in communities where a home language is in the process of replacement (over a period of a few generations) by a host language (Fishman, 1966; Glazer, 1966; Haugen, 1972; Huls & Van de Mond, 1992; Smolicz, 1992; Veltman, 1983b). The bilingualism that exists in that context does not always persist, and especially in the USA, it is well-known that the host language tends to overwhelm immigrant languages within two generations or so (and see Chapter 3). It is the transition period for an immigrant language that to a substantial extent creates the circumstance of interest, and the natural experiment conducted here evaluates an apparently common pattern of language learning and use (Fase _et al._, 1992) within just such a circumstance. At the same time, the results on language learning that we report here cannot be generalized to, for example, circumstances in which individual immigrant families raise children in a host community where the great majority of the children's peers are native speakers of the host language, and where the only speakers of the home language to which the children are exposed are themselves native speakers of the home language.

In addition, it should be noted that since participants were required to have been born in the USA, it is possible that their Spanish command may have been more limited than that of many other Hispanic children within the schools in question. The limitation was imposed in order to maintain a practicable sample size for the research design – if individuals with variable numbers of years in the USA had been included, it would have been important to analyze that issue as a variable, and to do so with substantial statistical power would have required increasing the number of subjects greatly.

Characteristics of the Study Population

Based on the questionnaire data, it was determined that High SES families selected for the study were characterized by fathers and mothers with a mean of from 14.1–15.6 years of education across the Core Design groups (see Table 2.3). The High SES families had professional and white collar and management occupations. Low SES families had a mean of 10.5–12.7 years

Table 2.3 Parents' educational level (years of schooling)

	SES	LSH	Mother		Father	
			Mean	SD	Mean	SD
Eng Imm Bilinguals	hi	OSH	14.31	2.09	14.11	2.84
		ESH	14.51	2.24	14.51	2.68
	lo	OSH	11.28	2.85	10.46	3.68
		ESH	12.73	1.46	12.01	1.51
2-way Bilinguals	hi	OSH	15.11	2.52	15.52	2.78
		ESH	15.17	2.06	14.49	2.59
	lo	OSH	11.52	3.29	11.14	3.51
		ESH	12.58	2.27	12.06	2.21
Monolinguals	hi	Eng	15.57	2.30	15.61	2.81
	lo	Eng	12.52	1.77	12.38	2.10

Table 2.4 Parents' language proficiency (1 = lo, 3 = hi)

	SES	LSH	Mother's English		Father's English		Mother's Spanish		Father's Spanish	
			Mean	SD	Mean	SD	Mean	SD	Mean	SD
Eng Imm Bilinguals	hi	OSH	2.65	0.55	2.35	0.72	2.87	0.34	2.92	0.31
		ESH	2.91	0.32	2.84	0.39	2.72	0.50	2.78	0.49
	lo	OSH	1.43	0.68	1.55	0.80	2.79	0.41	2.70	0.55
		ESH	2.80	0.46	2.34	0.80	2.70	0.54	2.70	0.57
2-way Bilinguals	hi	OSH	2.35	0.73	2.37	0.72	2.95	0.22	2.91	0.33
		ESH	2.79	0.49	2.68	0.54	2.81	0.40	2.72	0.55
	lo	OSH	1.40	0.65	1.56	0.70	2.78	0.44	2.75	0.46
		ESH	2.70	0.52	2.47	0.74	2.67	0.57	2.69	0.60
Mono-linguals	hi	Eng	2.99	0.08	3.00	0.00	1.22	0.49	1.31	0.62
	lo	Eng	2.97	0.17	2.89	0.41	1.17	0.44	1.28	0.63

of education across IMS, which often included vocational training. When asked to rate their English proficiency (see Table 2.4), all High SES and all ESH groups (including both mothers and fathers) rated themselves as quite proficient in English (with group means of 2.3 or higher on a 3 point scale). The groups indicating low English proficiency (those who were both Low SES and OSH) also reported themselves to be relatively recent immigrants (see Table 2.5); they had been living in the USA for an average of 13.1 to 16.9

Table 2.5 Parents' years residing in the USA

	SES	LSH	Mother		Father	
			Mean	SD	Mean	SD
Eng Imm Bilinguals	hi	OSH	24.21	9.85	23.43	10.04
		ESH	26.21	7.95	25.27	7.85
	lo	OSH	15.23	7.23	16.88	8.41
		ESH	26.00	9.71	23.08	12.42
2-way Bilinguals	hi	OSH	20.49	9.96	20.92	11.51
		ESH	24.45	8.39	22.86	9.92
	lo	OSH	13.13	6.29	13.84	6.27
		ESH	22.81	7.90	20.85	9.01
Mono-linguals	hi	Eng	15.38	10.78	22.48	12.27
	lo	Eng	18.29	12.92	21.92	13.51

years, across the groups. All other bilingual groups reported more than 20 years of parental residence in the USA. Among the monolingual mothers, quite a few were native speakers of English who had immigrated from locations other than Latin America, especially from the English-speaking Caribbean; this fact explains the relatively low mean years in the USA for the monolingual English-speaking mothers. All groups rated themselves as very proficient in Spanish except the monolingual English groups who professed to knowing essentially no Spanish. The OSH and ESH children differed sharply in the age at which their parents reported the children had begun to learn English (Table 2.6).

Between 38 and 53% of bilingual parents across various groups born outside the USA were born in Cuba, with 5th graders having the greatest number of Cuban-born parents, a pattern that is consistent with the general change that occurred in Miami toward the end of the 20th century, away from primarily Cuban immigration, and toward more balanced immigration from a variety of Latin American countries (see Table 2.2). Between 29 and 33% of parents were born outside of the USA but not in Cuba. These parents immigrated principally from Guatemala, Nicaragua, Chile, Peru and Colombia. No notable differences existed among the groups (either monolingual or bilingual) with regard to the number of adults in the home (slightly over two) nor the number of children in the home (average of two to three). Finally, children in OSH homes were reported to start learning English at reliably older ages than children from ESH homes. All the parents in the study rated high school, college and graduate school to be important for their children's future. There was only a small tendency for

Table 2.6 Age that children began English acquisition (years)

	SES	LSH	Age of English	
			Mean	SD
Eng Imm Bilinguals	hi	OSH	3.75	1.23
		ESH	1.23	1.28
	lo	OSH	3.90	1.55
		ESH	1.34	1.23
2-way Bilinguals	hi	OSH	3.33	1.44
		ESH	1.17	1.34
	lo	OSH	4.39	1.25
		ESH	1.24	1.26
Monolinguals	hi	Eng	0.08	0.27
	lo	Eng	0.48	0.72

Low SES parents to indicate a reduced likelihood of their children's attaining post high school degrees.

Special Educational and Demographic Conditions to be Considered in Interpretation

A few words are in order about the specific methods of training in the Two-way and English Immersion programs studied here, because programs so-described are not identical in other parts of the country. The key issue is that even the English Immersion programs studied here involved some classroom exposure to Spanish for children who entered school without substantial command of English. Special programs of instruction were provided to hasten the transition to English; thus children were as quickly as possible moved from classes with some Spanish support to classes where no such support was available, viz. to classes in English-only. During the K year in particular, LEP children had extensive work with ESOL-trained (English for Speakers of Other Languages) instructors. Most, though not all of this instruction, was conducted in English (see Chapter 3). As children progressed in the acquisition of English, they were expeditiously moved into higher 'levels' of English instruction, and by the end of

K in most cases and by the end of 1st grade in others, children were no longer involved in ESOL.

This sort of program is referred to in the work of Ramírez *et al.* (1991b) as being characterized by 'early exit' from structures involving native-language support. The presence of ESOL instruction creates only a slight complication in the design of this natural experiment, because the English Immersion programs clearly did not involve exclusive training in English. The complication is minimal because of the overwhelming predominance of English in the teacher communications to children in ESOL (see Chapter 3).

There remains another wrinkle to consider in the present design. Even after exit from ESOL, the children in English Immersion programs typically had one period per day (approximately 10% of the day) that was devoted to special experiences in the native language (in the parlance of the Dade County Public Schools at the time, this program was often referred to as BSHL, Basic Skills in the Home Language[4]). The class was conducted by a native speaker of Spanish. Consequently, the contrast in classroom exposure to Spanish between the Two-way programs and the English Immersion programs in the studies conducted here was notable, but far from absolute. According to the administrative protocol, children in the Two-way programs should have had about 40% of their educational experiences in Spanish, while children in the English Immersion programs should have had about 10% of their experiences in Spanish after the first grade. Results reported from deep description research in Chapter 3 support the idea that the administrative protocol was well-implemented.

Notes

1. The BSG was very active from the mid 1980s through 1998, directed by D.K. Oller and Barbara Pearson.
2. The reason for the imbalance is that mathematics was taught in English only. The remainder of school days was split equally, yielding the 40/60 arrangement.
3. The National Research Council's investigation (Meyer & Fienberg, 1992) assessing evaluation studies in bilingual education repeatedly expressed the interest of scholars in establishing random assignment studies. However, the panel of authors acknowledged that it was unlikely such an educational study could be conducted on any substantial scale for ethical and political reasons. Familial commitments to beliefs about the value of particular educational approaches are not easily modified, and if, in the course of a training study, parents choose to advocate a change for their children, it is not in the power of research scientists (nor should it be under our system of laws) to prevent them from making the change.
4. Such programs were also sometimes called 'Spanish-S' (Spanish for Spanish Speakers). Hereafter in this volume 'BSHL' will be used as a proxy for both BSHL and Spanish-S.

Part 2

Overall Results on Language Use and Standardized Test Performance

Chapter 3

Bilingualism and Cultural Assimilation in Miami Hispanic Children

REBECCA E. EILERS, D. KIMBROUGH OLLER and
ALAN B. COBO-LEWIS

Languages Spoken in School: Characteristics of the Subject Population and School Environment

The Core Design outlined in Chapter 2 is predicated upon the existence of two types of bilingual education in Miami. Empirical support is required to show that the Two-way and English Immersion classes provided education according to the presumed language-usage patterns. The present chapter reports on the evaluation of language use patterns in the classrooms that were studied. In the course of that language usage evaluation, we took the opportunity to study a related question that sheds light upon the nature of bilingualism in Miami. In accord with the broadened scope of study, the focus included both language usage of teachers in the formal circumstances of the classroom, as well as children's language usage with both teachers and peers. This latter evaluation yielded a surprising pattern given the seeming power of Spanish as a medium of communication in Miami. Spanish is extremely prominent in public life in all of South Florida, and its prestige is high. The community has been governed primarily by Hispanic people for many years. Yet, as we shall see, Hispanic children in Miami showed strong signs of rejecting Spanish in circumstances where they had a choice to speak either language.

The Tendency Toward Assimilation and Language Shift in the USA

The pattern of peer language use reported here does not appear to be at all unique to Miami. Widely expressed fears that languages other than English are challenging the majority language and creating a balkanization of culture in the United States are not supportable empirically. There is a remarkable amount of evidence in support of an opposite conclusion. In fact,

43

the culture of the United States has been notably effective in fostering assimilation to English as the primary, and ultimately the only language of its inhabitants. The tendency toward English language assimilation in the USA applies to the great majority of languages. Spanish has offered no exception to the pattern (Hakuta, 1994). The role of English and other languages in immigrant families was considered directly and in detail in a broad scale evaluation with over 10,000 subjects aged 14–26 years and living in the USA (Veltman, 1983b). Parents of the subjects spoke various languages other than English at home. Results indicated that for both individuals with Spanish-language background, and for individuals of other minority-language backgrounds, neither used the minority language as much as half the time with their peers, and it was deemed unlikely that many of the individuals evaluated would speak the minority-language at home in the future.

For a wide variety of immigrant groups, including Germans in the Midwest, Italians and eastern Europeans in the east, and Latin Americans in the south and southwest, it appears that within a two- to three-generation time frame, the home language is typically lost in favor of English (Grosjean, 1982; Southworth, 1980). Consider Veltman's conclusion about the strength of language assimilation in the USA:

> These findings oblige us to conclude that there is a great deal of intergenerational language shift. Not only is English bilingualism unstable; all forms of minority language use appear to be unstable in the United States. The data everywhere suggest that children are more anglicized than their parents . . . moving inexorably toward English monolingualism. The rate is very rapid . . . the only type of adaptation which seemed possible [in light of the data] . . . was one in which English bilingualism was successfully transmitted to the succeeding generation . . . no form of minority language use is so transmitted. (Veltman, 1983b: 140)

The Presumed Role of Linguistic Freedom

The reasons for this rapid language shift may be in part associated with a particularly effective environment for assimilation in the USA. Rapid language assimilation has not commonly been assumed by theorists to require suppression of immigrant languages nor explicitly to require promoting the learning of English. On the contrary, the emphasis in speculations about the power of English assimilation in America has been on the tendency of the American environment to leave language use open to the individual and the community. In circumstances where there has been no prohibition against maintenance of the culture of origin, it is assumed that immigrants have perceived little threat to their identities and consequently have been more open to seeking the advantages, both culturally and economically, that are offered by the English-speaking community. Contrasts are drawn between the relatively strong assimilation seen in the USA compared with the long-term maintenance of relatively separate (and somewhat physically segregated) language groups in Belgium, Switzerland, or Spain, for example. The languages of minorities in the USA, in the words of Glazer (1966): '... shriveled in the air of freedom while they had apparently flourished under adversity in Europe' (Glazer, 1966: 361).

Southworth (1980: 123) argues that 'threatened identity' is the primary factor in language maintenance. The Québecois French culture provides a noteworthy example where pressures to merge with the more numerous English-speaking Canadian culture have been resisted mightily and where a sense of threatened identity appears to have been an important factor in an often oppositional relationship regarding language usage. The Québecois have clearly intended to maintain their culture, and their French language is viewed as a key part of it.

Another particularly noteworthy case of language maintenance in the face of pressure and in many cases in the face of open hostility is that of Catalan in twentieth century Spain. During the Franco years, the speaking of the Catalan language was largely forbidden, but if anything, the result was an entrenchment among the Catalonian people, who insisted on speaking Catalan when they could do it without penalty. They commonly managed through the years of suppression to maintain a strong commitment to their language, even among the young. The oppositional character of the relationship between Castile and Catalonia seemed to encourage maintenance of language differences.

In the USA by contrast, immigrant communities usually do not experience such strong opposition in the opinion of theorists who have studied language shift. Consider the reasoning of Fishman (1966: 29) regarding the history of immigration to the USA:

> There was no apparent logical opposition between the ethnicity of incoming immigrants and the ideology of America. Individually and collectively, immigrants could accept the latter without consciously denying the former. However, once they accepted the goals and values of Americans, the immigrants were already on the road to accepting their life-styles, their customs, and their language.

To say that the USA has been characterized through its history by *relative* openness with regard to language usage is not, of course, to say that there have not been important cases of active suppression. The examples are numerous, from deliberate separation of slave families to prevent contact among individuals of the same language backgrounds, to a ban on speaking German in certain Midwestern areas during World War II, to prohibitions against teaching or speaking of French in schools in Maine (a pattern that persisted until the 1960s), to widespread interdictions against the speaking of Amerind languages even in reservation schools into the middle of the 20th century. One might add to the list the suppression of American Sign Language usage among the culturally deaf in many public and private schools until relatively recent times. Still, observers conclude that in the USA by and large, language freedom has been more the rule than the exception, with increasing linguistic liberty in recent times, and the result has been a sense of openness that has in the long run supported linguistic assimilation.

Other Examples of Linguistic Assimilation Tendencies in Immigrant Communities

Modern Sweden seems to offer similar evidence of the paradoxical effect that openness to linguistic diversity seems to produce. One observer remarks with regard to immigrant communities in Sweden that:

> ... one can hardly imagine a more idyllic, socialist, positive support for immigrants to maintain their original mother tongue. In fact, this is not happening ... An amazing 94% of children, both of whose parents [of non Swedish heritage] were born in Sweden, always speak Swedish with either of the parents. (Paulston, 1992: 65)

Just as in the American case, Turkish, Finnish and other immigrant children in Sweden do not appear to maintain a command of their home languages for long:

> The very liberal Swedish educational language policies of mother tongue instruction will not succeed in bringing about L1 [Language number one, the home language] maintenance and will at most contribute to a few generations of bilingualism before complete shift to Swedish. (Paulston, 1992: 71)

Similar outcomes are seen in the cases of other immigrant groups in northern Europe. For example in the Netherlands among the numerous immigrants from Turkey: '... parents push the maintenance of the Turkish language, whereas the children tend to favour Dutch' (Huls & Van de Mond, 1992: 113).

English in Australia has played a role similar to the one it has in the USA. Polish, Welsh and German immigrant children appear quickly to adopt English as their primary language (Döpke, 1988; Smolicz, 1992). The futures of languages other than English appear to be 'far from secure'

(Smolicz, 1992: 300) since children seem to move quickly toward English, and immigrant parents often seem to give up on attempts to maintain the home language in the context of strong resistance from children. Smolicz (1992: 301) refers to 'Australia's continual suspicion of linguistic pluralism . . .', a pattern of concern that seems to parallel that of the American English-Only movement, and to be built upon a similar misconception about the likely effects of prohibiting the speaking of foreign languages. The evidence suggests, ironically, that if one's goal is to limit linguistic pluralism, the most effective approach in cases of immigration to a country with a well-established dominant language, may be to foster linguistic freedom and allow the immigrant families to choose.

Other Factors Influencing Language Shift

While linguistic openness of nations to immigrant groups may be a major factor in language shift, there appear to be others as well. Economic and social communication factors may play important roles. Often the motivation for immigration appears to be primarily economic. In all the cases mentioned above where language shift has occurred rapidly, it is reasonable to speculate that economic motivation may have played a substantial role in driving the tendency to shift. In the context of such motivation there are cases of strong language shift that seem to be occurring among cultures that are not in a relationship of host to immigrant, but rather represent cultures that have been in contact for many generations. For example, in Morocco, Berber is now 'rapidly being lost' (Bentahila & Davies, 1992: 203) after more than a thousand years of contact with Arabic.

> Factors such as increased communications and travel, the mass media, especially television, [and] extensive migration from rural areas have all encouraged the spread of Arabic, and bilingualism in turn frequently leads to the abandonment of Berber. Among 180 families we surveyed, in which the youngest generation had lost Berber entirely, the commonest pattern of shift was for bilingualism to be retained over two generations, which ensures that at any time children have at least one language in common with their grandparents; but cases where only one generation is effectively bilingual, the next failing to learn Berber or acquiring only limited comprehension skills, are also commonplace. (Bentahila & Davies, 1992: 198)

Factors influencing language shift in general have been outlined by Haugen (1972). One of his conclusions offers an interesting comment on the tendency for bilingualism to represent an intermediate stage in language shift, as in the case of Berber and Arabic in Morocco. The idea is that bilingualism can be relatively stable in a community as long as it is not shared across too much of the community. At some point in the spread of bilingualism, it becomes so general that it loses its reason for existing (Haugen, 1969). If everyone or nearly everyone in a community can speak the same languages well, it becomes unnecessary to maintain both. Bilingualism thus appears often to constitute a temporary condition for communities. One of the two languages, if it is perceived as predominant, will tend to take over as bilingualism becomes widespread. Fase *et al.* (1992: 5) summarized the situation this way:

> . . . when migration is followed by more or less permanent settlement, and both sides choose for integration rather than segregation, members of the minority group almost unavoidably shift towards the use of the dominant language in most of their contacts with the dominant group.

The study of language shift has produced many examples of relatively rapid linguistic assimilation. But it would be a mistake to assume that language shift is inevitable in all circumstances. Sometimes communities do not choose cultural integration. Southworth (1980) emphasizes that the pattern of attrition leading to home language loss in two to three generations as seen in the United States is far from universal, and relatively permanent bilingualism or multilingualism often occurs in circumstances that differ from those described above. India provides particularly poignant examples, especially in urban settings, where large groups of speakers of multiple languages can be found, having existed for many generations.

The Miami Situation

The assessment of bilingualism in Miami presents a peculiar case. Because the community is more than half Hispanic, because both economically and politically the power structure has long been primarily Hispanic, and because there has been notable hostility from the relatively small Anglo community toward the idea of Spanish dominance, one might imagine that the ideal arrangement is in place for the appearance of a cultural island of permanent American Hispanism in South Florida with Spanish as the primary language. No other area of the USA appears so well-suited to such a possibility. It even seems plausible that Spanish/English bilingualism, according to this reasoning, could be a temporary stage of history before Spanish, not English would assume the clearly dominant role. The establishment of such a permanent island of Spanish is feared by many Miami Anglos in spite of the history of Spanish language assimilation in other parts of the country. The present report offers an empirical perspective on the pattern of language usage in Miami school children, and by implication a perspective on the prospects for Spanish as a cultural medium in Miami's future.

Goals of the Deep Description

The research reported in this chapter offers perspectives on two points. First it provides deep description of key variables regarding language use in the schools and especially language use in classrooms by teachers; these are variables that pertain to all the subsequently reported studies (Chapters 4–11). The goal is to verify that the patterns of language use specified for each Instructional Method in School (IMS) were implemented in the schools as expected. Second, the research reports on patterns of language use by the children, and thus offers a portrait of the process of language maintenance and/or assimilation as it appears to have occurred among the children studied here.

Methods

Members of the project staff of the Bilingualism Study Group, the same individuals who tested children in both standardized and probe evaluations described in Chapter 2, made systematic observations of classroom and hallway conversations in the schools selected for study. All the project staff members were thoroughly competent speakers of both English and Spanish in the dialects with which the children were familiar. The method of observation consisted of a staff member taking a seat or standing unobtrusively in the classroom or hallway where observations were to be made with a clipboard and a scoring sheet. The task was to indicate the language spoken for every utterance (typically every sentence, but sentence fragments were accepted as utterances if they constituted conversational turns spoken in intelligible words) occurring within conversations and lectures within the observer's focus. When multiple conversations occurred simultaneously, the observer simply focused on one at a time, and the choice of which conversation to consider was made on the basis of which speakers were most clearly audible to the observer.

It should be noted here that while the classrooms observed were the same ones from which the subjects were drawn, the question pursued concerned the language spoken by *all* the children and teachers within the observers' earshot. Because the observers made no effort to be positioned in any special location with regard to children who were specific subjects of the research, the data to be reported in this chapter simply represent a random sampling of the linguistic environment in the classes where the subjects were being schooled as well as in the hallways between class

Table 3.1 Number of sessions for each situational category

English Immersion Classrooms	23
Two-way English Classrooms	26
Two-way Spanish Classrooms	25
Monolingual English Classrooms	21
English Immersion Hallways	49
Two-way Hallways	25
ESOL Basic Classrooms	40
ESOL Advanced Classrooms	38
BSHL Classrooms	18

periods. The specific subjects enrolled in the research project were typical socio-economically and linguistically of children in these classes. This sampling of utterances from subjects of the research as well as other children in the same classrooms applied both to observations taken during classes and in the hallways. During hallway observations, the staff made a special effort to follow classes as they moved as groups from one place to another, since it was of interest to evaluate peer language usage by grade and class type.

The scoring sheet included spaces for check marks indicating the language (English, Spanish or Mixed) in which each utterance was spoken under each of four interlocutor categories (Teacher to Class, Teacher to Individual Child, Individual Child to Teacher, and Individual Child to Individual Child). All four interlocutor categories were coded in formal classroom observations, but only the Individual Child to Individual Child category was coded for the hallway observations.

There were 265 observation sessions. At each grade level there were nine situational observation categories based on school-type and context (see Table 3.1). Within each situational category and each age level, all sessions were conducted with different teachers, no individual classroom type was sampled more than once, and to the extent possible, the number of schools from which samples were taken was also maximized. The goal was to collect at least 100 utterances in each session. Over 31,000 utterances were coded, with an average of 119 per session. Utterances that were coded occurred in the following average numbers within interlocutor categories: Teacher to Class, 42 per session; Teacher to Individual Child, 23; Individual Child to Teacher, 22; and Individual Child to Individual Child, 32.

A breakdown on numbers of sessions by situational category is provided in Table 3.1. Two-way classes were observed both during designated English sessions and designated Spanish sessions. ESOL (English for

Table 3.2 Number of sessions for each grade level

Kindergarten-Early	44
Kindergarten-Late	53
First Grade	58
Second Grade	61
Fifth Grade	49

Speakers of Other Languages) classes were studied in order to provide a perspective on the role of Spanish and English in classes designed to 'transition' children from Spanish to English. The great majority of students in the schools under study spent not more than one year in ESOL classes, which consisted of one class period (10% of the class day). It was assumed that the great majority of communication in ESOL classes (at least when teachers were the speakers) would be in English, but the use of Spanish as a bridging mechanism in ESOL was always a possibility. Consequently, it seemed important to evaluate the amount of Spanish exposure children may have gotten in ESOL classes. While the children we studied based on the design in Chapter 2 were typically in ESOL only for the K or at latest 1st grade year, we also took samples of ESOL classes for children in higher grades (2nd and 5th) in order to provide supplementary information on the nature of language shift across age. Children who were in ESOL classes after K were typically children not born in the USA (and consequently not candidates for enrollment in the research project in general). BSHL (Basic Skills in the Home Language) classes were also studied in order to provide verification for the use of Spanish in the daily classroom experience among children in the English Immersion schools, where approximately 10% of classroom time was in BSHL for the students enrolled in the research project.

Sessions were conducted at K, 2nd and 5th grade in accord with the Core Design presented in Chapter 2. In addition, however, we assessed 1st grade classes in the same schools, to account for the possibility of especially rapid changes in English and Spanish usage during the first two or three years of schooling. Furthermore, to evaluate the question even more thoroughly, we broke the K evaluations down into first (early) and second (late) semester assessments. The number of sessions at each grade level is presented in Table 3.2.

The number of sessions for each situational category at each age level was at least three in all cases but one (K-early BSHL was not sampled). There were 45 such possible session types in the evaluation, based on five ages times nine situational categories. The cases involving three or four sessions were: 1st grade English Immersion (3), K-early English Immersion (4), 1st grade Monolingual English (4), K-early Monolingual English (4), K-late Monolingual English (3), K-late BSHL (3), 5th grade ESOL Advanced (3). For all other cases (37 of them) at least five different classes (with five different teachers) were evaluated for each situational category at each age level.

The observations were found to be easy to make with confidence, and pairs of observers in the same classrooms working in pilot efforts found that they rarely disagreed about the categorization of utterances as Spanish, English or Mixed. Following the pilot tests, the availability of audio-tapes and corresponding transcripts for many of the sessions provided an opportunity to evaluate the reliability of the live observations. Many of the sessions transcribed (in fact the bulk of all sessions) were associated with 99–100% usage of either English or Spanish. In all such cases (21 sessions), where the original live coding yielded an evaluation proportion of 99–100% for the Teacher speaking to the Class in the designated language of instruction, transcripts of tape recordings (produced by bilingual staff members other than the ones who did the classroom observations and without reference to the on-line coding results), also yielded a judgment of 99–100% usage of the designated language. The nearly perfect alignment of teachers' language use and class type (English or Spanish) could be thought to trivialize the observational reliability among coders, since the task of observation in such cases was obviously easy. In seven cases, however, the Teacher to Class language usage percentages were lower, with values based on the live classroom observations ranging from 62–97% appropriate language use. The Pearson correlations between these observation percentages and those based on the tape-transcripts was 0.92. The average discrepancy between the two percentages was less than 0.04, indicating a high level of observational reliability.

Results

Monolingual schools

The Monolingual English (ME) schools were monitored in classroom observations, but yielded virtually no indication of usage of Spanish, even though many of the children in the classrooms (although not the children selected for study under the Core Design) came from homes where Spanish was sometimes or often spoken. Almost 100% of utterances observed were in English in all four interlocutor categories (Teacher to Class, Teacher to Student, Student to Teacher, and Student to Student), and at all age levels (K-early, K-late, 1st, 2nd and 5th), and consequently, no effort has been made to report data in detail on language usage for the ME schools, and no further analysis was conducted on language usage in the ME schools.

Mixed utterances

While both languages were spoken often in the bilingual schools, fewer than 1% of utterances were mixed (including words from both Spanish and English; words of very similar or identical form in both languages were ignored in the determination) in any of the four interlocutor categories. Also only miniscule numbers of mixed utterances occurred at any age level, for both classroom and hallway data. Consequently no analysis was performed on utterances in the mixed category. (Note that mixed utterances were apparently more common among these children in other circumstances; see Chapter 7's discussion of narratives produced by the children).

Teacher to Class communications

Figure 3.1 provides a breakdown of languages spoken in all situational categories for both regular classes and BSHL (Basic Skills in the Home Language) classes. Note first the large open circles, representing the proportions of English utterances produced by teachers when speaking to their

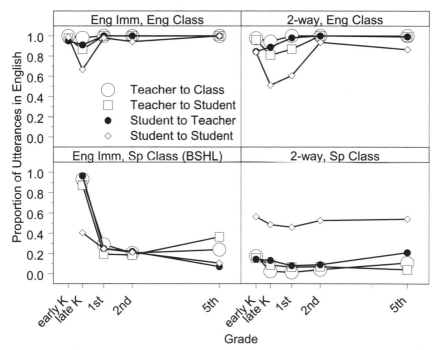

Figure 3.1 Regular and BSHL classrooms

classes as a whole. The English Immersion classes in English (representing 90% of the classroom school day for children in English Immersion) were expected to be conducted in English, and as can be seen, almost every utterance was produced as expected, in English, with exceptions limited primarily to the late K sessions, and even there, 98% of utterances were in English. The English-designated classes, occurring during 60% of the school day for Two-way schools, also showed overwhelming English usage by the teachers when speaking to classes, with not less than 94% of utterances in English at any age level. In contrast, but also in accord with the administrative prescription, the Spanish-designated classes in the Two-way schools (representing 40% of the classroom school day for children in Two-way programs) showed 95% or more usage of Spanish for three of the five ages and more than 80% usage at the other two (early-K, 83%, and 5th grade, 89%).

BSHL classes, designed to provide Hispanic children in English Immersion programs with formal experience in the home language, were offered during not more than 10% of the school day for individual students. The proportion of Spanish used by teachers speaking to classes was consistently lower than in Two-way Spanish-designated classes. In fact, for K sessions (the data represent only three late-K sessions) the BSHL experience was not implemented according to protocol, and the great bulk of teacher utterances (93%) were produced in English. In 1st, 2nd and 5th grades, on the other hand, the proportion of English utterances by teachers to classes was down to 20–29%, in basic conformity with the intended usage of language according to the administrative plan. The lack of aggressive Spanish instruction in BSHL at K may reflect the school system's general approach to home language education. In this approach it appears a compromise was struck between forces favoring English-only education and forces favoring some Spanish-language instruction. The general compromise favored English strongly, but allowed some Spanish instruction in limited proportions but only after children were already well-immersed in English. The existence of Two-way programs in the school system (but only very limited numbers of them) represented a further aspect of the same compromise.

Teacher to Student communications

Figure 3.1 also shows that when teachers spoke in class to individual students (observe the small open squares), the pattern of language usage was very similar to that seen for teacher to class communications. Again, the overwhelming proportion of utterances at each age level was in the appropriate language for each category of classroom, with the exception of the BSHL Kindergarten sessions (13% Spanish). The BSHL programs also seemed to be only marginally in conformity with the designated language protocol in the 5th grade classes, with 36% of utterances occurring in English.

There was an apparent tendency for more Teacher to Student than Teacher to Class communications in Spanish for the English-designated classes, in late-K for English Immersion (13% compared to 2%) and in both late-K (19% compared to 6%) and 1st grade for Two-way English (13% compared to 0%). This pattern of teachers speaking to students in Spanish occasionally in early elementary English-designated classes may have reflected an attempt by teachers to try to recapture or maintain the attention of individual children whom they presumed had failed to understand certain communications in English.

Individual Child to Teacher

The children also appeared to cooperate very substantially with the protocols. In every category and at every age except BSHL Kindergarten (only 4% Spanish), it was found that at least 75% of utterances produced in class to teachers by students conformed to the language prescriptions. In fact in many of the situational categories, the proportion of utterances by individual children speaking to teachers in the appropriate language exceeded 90%.

Student to Student in class

During the classroom sessions, children often spoke to each other. Most of these communications were also produced in the prescribed language. Students in English Immersion classes spoke to each other in English more than 90% of the time at all grades except K-late (67%). Likewise the same children spoke Spanish to each other in BSHL classes at least 75% of the time except at K (60%). Students in Two-way English-designated classes also conformed to the language prescriptions in their peer communications, speaking in English more than 80% of the time at K-early, 2nd and 5th grades. However, quite a bit of Spanish was used between students in the Two-way programs in English-designated classes at late K (39%) and first grade (49%). For Spanish-designated classes, the pattern of language usage among students more strongly violated the classroom language prescription and applied across the entire age range. Approximately 50% of communications occurred in English, student to student, across all age levels in the Two-way programs, even though Spanish was the designated classroom language.

Student to Student in hallways

In the hallways of both Two-way and English Immersion schools, communications among students at each age level presented a pattern of less

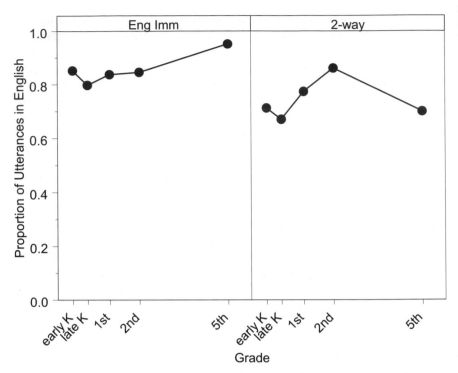

Figure 3.2 Proportion of utterances in English as a function of instructional method

than 35% Spanish usage at all age levels, as seen in Figure 3.2. Somewhat more Spanish was used in the Two-way schools than in the English Immersion schools in all grades other than 2nd.

ESOL classes

In order to provide a full picture of the usage of language and the tendencies of children across time, ESOL classes in the schools were also studied. It is important to note that the composition of these classes was typical of the students who were enrolled in the study only for the K-early and K-late levels. Hispanic students who entered the schools we studied in K (as all the children in the language and literacy studies did) and who also had Limited English Proficiency at the beginning of schooling were assigned to ESOL classes for one class session per day (about 10% of the classroom day). These students were usually 'transitioned' out of ESOL by the 1st grade. Students who were in ESOL classes at the 2nd grade or above were most frequently students who had been born abroad and were rela-

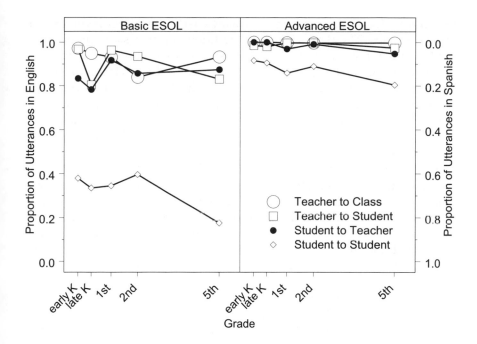

Figure 3.3 Language usage in ESOL classes

tively recent arrivals in the USA, and consequently were ineligible to participate in our language and literacy studies. Still, the data on ESOL classes offers additional perspective on the language environment of the students in the study, and supplies particularly useful indications about approximately 10% of the K experience for many of the children in the studies.

As seen in Figure 3.3, the data are broken down into two subheadings, Basic and Advanced ESOL, in accord with the DCPS system of categorization. Each child was designated as being in Level 1, 2, 3 or 4. On graduation from Level 4, children were treated as ready for content-matter classes in English only. Since ESOL classes were usually composed of combinations of children from higher and lower levels, we simply split the sessions such that classes composed exclusively of children categorized as ESOL 3 or 4 were called 'Advanced' while 1 or 2 were called 'Basic'.

The communications from teachers in ESOL classes, whether to the classes as a whole or to individual students, were largely in English, in accord with the administrative expectation. The proportion of English usage by the teachers in communications both to the classes as a whole and to individual students in the classes was at least 95% at all age levels for Advanced classes. The Basic classes in the English Immersion schools were implemented in English for more than 80% of utterances at all grades.

Individual Child to Teacher communications in ESOL classes of all varieties were also predominantly in English, with 90–100% English communications for Advanced ESOL classes. The Basic ESOL classes also showed a strong pattern of English speech by students to teachers, with more than 80% of all utterances in English at all grade levels except K, where the proportion approached 80%.

Student to Student communications in the Basic ESOL classes offered the most notable exception to the general tendency for the English language to be dominant in the schools in circumstances where English was encouraged by administrative prescription. Spanish accounted for more than half the utterances (60% to more than 80% depending on grade level) for students talking to each other in ESOL Basic classes at all age levels. The pattern contrasts strongly with the Student to Student speech in Advanced ESOL classes where 80 to 90% of utterances were in English.

The differentiated pattern of Student to Student communication in the Basic vs Advanced ESOL classes seems to be in accord, at least to some extent, with the differentiated pattern of teacher speech. While teachers in both Basic and Advanced classes spoke primarily in English, the tendency was much stronger in the Advanced classes. It seems likely that the teachers adapted in their attempt to draw children toward English in such a way that they tended to utilize Spanish as a bridge more commonly for the children who were less able to speak English, namely those in the Basic classes.

Discussion

Concordance between administrative plan and implementation of educational approaches

The Core Design presumes a substantial differentiation of language usage in English Immersion and Two-way schools. In general during the period of our study, the administrative plan with regard to the two types of schools can be summarized as follows: (1) at least 90% of the classroom language input from teachers to children in English Immersion schools was presumed to be in English; (2) the 10% Spanish input to children in the English Immersion schools was presumed to occur in BSHL (Basic Skills in the Home Language) classes; (3) the split of language input in Two-way schools was expected to be 40% (Spanish) vs 60% (English), with the class day split into English classes and Spanish classes accordingly; and (4) ESOL classes were expected to be conducted in English for both types of schools. Of course the administrative plan with regard to Monolingual English schools was such that students of monolingual English background could be expected to hear English nearly 100% of the time in classes.

The results of the 'deep description' research reported above confirm that the basic characteristics of the administrative design were implemented admirably. Teachers spoke to children and children spoke to teachers according to the administrative protocol in overwhelming proportions, with one apparent exception. Kindergarten BSHL was apparently not implemented in Spanish, but this pattern was corrected in 1st grade and thereafter. The presumable violation of expectation may have resulted in less Spanish input than expected for children in English Immersion schools in the K year. Still, it is unclear that the apparent paucity of Spanish input at K in BSHL represented a notable or important violation of administrative intent. All the children in the BSHL classes were in English Immersion schools where the plan was to impose a rapid transition to English. Consequently it may have been that BSHL classes were simply not emphasized until after the K year. In any case this is a small point in the context of massive evidence showing that the basic administrative plan in both English Immersion and Two-way schools was implemented rigorously for most circumstances within the Dade County Public Schools.

The students responded to the language usage protocols in ways that fundamentally supported the administrative prescription as long as the children were speaking to the teachers. Consequently it can be concluded that students were neatly influenced by the protocols, speaking to teachers in the language the teachers used to address them.

The results appear then to support the key assumption of the Core Design. Two-way schools appear to have presented a great deal more Spanish instruction than the English Immersion schools, as intended. English Immersion schools proportionally presented much more English. The planned comparisons across schools, then, are justified insofar as they are predicated upon the expectation that the Two-way schools under study were designed in terms of language of instruction to foster bilingualism strongly while English Immersion schools were primarily intended to foster linguistic assimilation to English. At the same time, it is important to acknowledge the fact that the differentiation between the two types of programs was not as complete as one might have wished for given the purposes of the research. The perfect test of the basic hypotheses would presumably have required 50% Spanish in Two-way programs and 0% in English Immersion programs. Still, the Dade County Public School system, with its relatively uniform application of programs across the entire district, offered perhaps as clean an example of a natural experiment in this area as one could have hoped to find.

Language usage by the children and the pattern of cultural assimilation

While Teacher to Class and Teacher to Student communications offer a clearly confirmatory perspective on the effective implementation of educational strategies, an additional perspective on the effects of the strategies is provided by peer communications within those contexts. Student to Student language usage patterns also offer a perspective on the tendency toward linguistic maintenance or linguistic assimilation in the children that were studied.

In most cases children spoke to each other in class according to the same patterns that were seen for their communications to teachers. A major exception was in the Two-way Spanish-designated classes where students spoke to each other half the time in English across the entire age range. This salient exception to the pattern of language usage given the situational agenda suggests the possibility that the students were generally inclined to speak English more than Spanish – notice that the Two-way children were much *less* likely to speak Spanish when English was on the agenda. Also children in English Immersion classes showed no strong tendency to switch to Spanish when speaking to each other in English-designated regular classes. In one case where a switch from Spanish to English would have been possible, BSHL classes, a switch to English did not commonly occur. The fact that English Immersion children (the children for whom BSHL classes were provided) did not speak much English to each other during BSHL classes may have been the result of a sort of novelty or starvation effect: their BSHL classes represented a very small proportion of their school experience, and if Spanish was a significant part of their lives (even if less significant than English), it may have felt comfortable to let the Spanish inclination reveal itself at least for the short period daily when they were encouraged to speak Spanish in class.

Results from the ESOL classes presented a pattern that differed by level. The predominant language in Student to Student communications in the Basic level classes across all ages was Spanish even though English was the presumed target language. To understand the discrepancy between this pattern and the general pattern of English dominance in other classes, it should be noted that children in the Basic ESOL classes (at all age levels) were selected for those classes precisely because they spoke extremely little English, and they were moved up to Advanced ESOL as soon as their English usage improved. Children in Advanced ESOL showed the more common pattern of English dominance even in Student to Student communications at all grade levels, even though they too were only at a very early level in the process of learning English.

Student to Student communications outside the classroom

Outside of class, when no administratively imposed language protocol was in effect, the opportunity to evaluate the children's language choice was maximally available. In this case the issue of language maintenance and language assimilation could be directly evaluated. The data showed that regardless of the school-type and regardless of age, children spoke predominantly in English to each other. At every age student-to-student communication in the hallways occurred at least twice as often in English as in Spanish. Perhaps the most notable feature of this pattern is that it began in the *first semester of K* when many (perhaps most) of the children in these primarily Hispanic schools may have been experiencing their very first encouragement to speak English. Many of them at that point were not only categorized as having Limited English Proficiency, but were thought to be effectively monolingual in Spanish.

It is worthwhile considering the logical possibility that the method of data collection resulted in selective sampling from children who were already particularly competent in English. Observers recorded the utterances that occurred in the hallways, and these utterances could have been produced by only a subset of the children. In accord with this possibility the primarily Spanish-speaking children may have been intimidated by the environment of English Immersion schooling and so may have been inhibited from speaking in the hallways. Such a pattern of unintended selectivity in sampling might help account for the pattern seen in the English Immersion schools, but it is hard to see how it could have biased the results in the Two-way schools where children were encouraged to speak Spanish nearly half the day, and where, in spite of the encouragement, a strong pattern of favoritism to English also showed up in the hallways during the first semester of K. Moreover, it is hard to imagine that unintended selectivity in sampling could account for the strong and consistent patterns of English preference in the hallways among the older children in both types of schools. All in all, it seems an inescapable conclusion that what was seen in the research was not an illusion, but was in fact the crisp image of a populace of Hispanic children choosing to speak English.

The pattern of English dominance in the children's chosen communications matched the impressions of all the projects' observers and seemed to confirm reports from many teachers and parents. Also for many prior years of research on bilingualism and on language acquisition more generally in Miami, the Bilingualism Study Group project members were confronted with lamentations from Hispanic parents about the difficulty of maintaining any knowledge of Spanish in their offspring. Hispanic children were reported by their parents to refuse to respond in Spanish at home, to speak only English with their friends, and in fact to be incapable in many circumstances of speaking Spanish well even if they tried. Anglo members of the community have expressed fear that Spanish is taking over in Miami, but Hispanic members of the community, viewing the matter from up close, have seen a different pattern. The results of this investigation seem to confirm the fears of the Hispanic parents.

The public perception of the power of Hispanic culture in Miami is correct insofar as it recognizes political influence and wealth. No Hispanic community in America can match that of the Miami community in these domains. However, the public perception is often misguided, it appears, in drawing the conclusion that the relatively common use of Spanish among adults in public life in Miami is likely to persist into the next generation. Evidence of this untenable public perception is to be found in comments on the street as well as in the most respected issues of the public press. As an example, consider an article in *The New York Times* by Peter T. Kilborn on January 16, 2000 titled 'Custody Case is Overshadowing Shift Among Cuban Immigrants', an article focused on the now famous international custody battle over the Cuban child, Elián González, and emphasizing that younger Cuban Americans recently show opinions that often differ from those of the older generation with regard to Fidel Castro, the president of Communist Cuba. The article focused on an apparent cultural shift in politics in Miami, but it implied that other aspects of the 'emphatically Cuban' culture of Little Havana have remained stable. One way the author chose to emphasize the presumed cultural stability was through the claim that Little Havana was a place where 'third-generation children speak Spanish at home' (p. 13). Perhaps the author found individual cases supporting this claim, but it appears he drew his general conclusion too quickly. In fact, in light of the present results and those of other studies on language shift in Miami (see e.g. Pearson & McGee, 1993), the conclusion appears to be egregiously misleading. The author may also have been influenced by the common usage of Spanish among adults on Little Havana streets. He may have been unaware that much of the Spanish on Miami streets is a function of recent and continuing immigration rather than of language maintenance across generations born in the USA.

The results of the present work suggest that the claim that third-generation children speak Spanish at home is founded primarily on supposition and not upon fact. To assess the claim, it is important first to note that there were few third-generation Cuban children to be found in Miami during the period of this study, since the major wave of immigration began in the late 1950s. If a generation is assumed to be 20 years in duration, then the first generation from the major immigration was born during the 1960s and 1970s, the second generation only began in the late 1970s, and the third could not have begun to any significant extent until this study's data collection had been completed (the research was conducted in the mid 1990s). The great bulk of children selected for the studies were clearly first-generation themselves, since the overwhelming majority of their parents were born in Latin America (see Chapter 2, Table 2.2). A smaller proportion were second-generation and at most a very small proportion were third-generation. While we know that among first and second-generation Hispanic children in Miami many were encouraged by their parents to speak Spanish at home, the outcome was not as the parents had hoped, and the children appeared to choose to speak English. Projecting forward from this trend, and recognizing the similarity with other well-documented patterns of English assimilation in the USA, it is hard to see how there will be much at all left of Spanish in the Miami community by the third generation of Cuban-Americans. Only through continued immigration can the role of Spanish be expected to continue to be significant.

This pattern of language loss is the one that has been seen clearly in prior studies in the USA, perhaps the most broad-scale of which was conducted by Veltman (1983b). English usually seems to take over in immigrant communities virtually completely within two or three generations, with exceptions that pertain exclusively to communities that severely isolate themselves from the mainstream (e.g. the Pennsylvania Dutch, see Fishman et al., 1985). The speculation that Miami might present a new kind of exception, founded on economic and political power of Spanish as well as excellent commercial connections to Latin America, appears to have been proven groundless. In spite of the prominence of Latin culture, Spanish appears to be dying in Miami.

Chapter 4

Effects of Bilingualism and Bilingual Education on Oral and Written English Skills: A Multifactor Study of Standardized Test Outcomes

ALAN B. COBO-LEWIS, BARBARA ZURER PEARSON,
REBECCA E. EILERS and VIVIAN C. UMBEL

A Multivariate Investigation of Bilingualism

Assessing effects of bilingualism in education requires a broad approach focusing on a variety of factors that may influence learning in both literacy and oral language. Variations among school programs and demographic factors conspire to limit the interpretations that can be drawn from previous studies of bilingualism. An ideal solution to the study of bilingualism would require a true experimental design (or a series of such designs), in which the important factors would be deliberately manipulated. Of course, such a comprehensive experimental design would be both impractical and unethical. However, the large, socio-economically diverse population of Dade County, Florida, presented educational opportunities including both English Immersion and Two-way education in the public schools, a fortuitous circumstance that afforded the possibility of conducting a pseudo-experiment in which the effects of most critical variables on academic and linguistic outcomes could be examined.

Chapters 1, 2 and 3 provide background rationale and deep description of the language environment in which children in the study reported here were immersed from the mid to late 1990s when the data were collected. The present chapter recounts results on English literacy and oral language for the standardized tests that were administered. Chapter 5 reports results for Spanish language and literacy, and Chapter 6 details the relationships between patterns of results for individual children across the two languages.

The rationale for the present investigation as detailed in Chapter 1 focuses on the fact that in order to compare the efficacy of differing approaches to bilingual education, there is need for study of both languages and also for selectivity regarding programs and students to be evaluated. It is critical to ensure that:

- programs be well-matched for factors such as ethnicity, educational expenditure per student, and standardized test performance; and
- children selected for evaluation be well-matched for socio-economic status (SES) and language spoken at home (LSH).

As indicated in the design figure (Chapter 2, Figure 2.1), the independent variables of interest included Lingualism (Monolingual or Bilingual), Instructional Method in the School (IMS, Two-way or English Immersion), Language(s) Spoken at Home (LSH, only Spanish at home [OSH], or both English and Spanish at home [ESH]), Socio-economic Status (SES, High or Low), and Grade Level (Kindergarten, 2nd or 5th). IMS and LSH factors applied only to bilingual children, as monolingual children perforce experience English Immersion and speak only English at home. Preselection of subjects on the LSH and SES factors was deemed critical in order to ensure that comparisons across Lingualism groups could be done in 'matched' subgroups. All standardized tests were administered *after* subjects were carefully assigned to groups according to strict criteria detailed in Chapter 2. The IMS factor required prematching of schools on a variety of demographic variables. Data reported in Chapter 2 confirm that all the selected schools showed similar patterns of educational expenditure per student and standardized test performance at K and 1st grade. Further, the schools administering bilingual education programs (either English Immersion or Two-way) showed similar ethnic distributions and degrees of Limited English Proficiency (LEP) among their students. Data reported in Chapter 3 focus on deep description verifying that programs of instruction were implemented consistent with official descriptions of the programs.

Evaluation of the Effects of Educational Method

The IMS variable is of particular interest. In America at the turn of the millennium there are two broad classes of education for children who are either bilingual or have LEP. English Immersion education programs, where English instruction is the focus and where little if any education is conducted in the home language, predominate in the United States. Two-way education programs, sometimes called 'bilingual education' (although the term 'bilingual education' is often applied to programs that do not follow a two-way method), invest significant portions of the school day delivering content courses in the home language, and other portions in the host language (in this case, English). Two-way education is relatively rare, as indicated in a survey maintained by the Center for Applied Linguistics (Christian, 2000), which shows 261 extant programs of which 240 are in English and Spanish.

There is great variety of implementation within both English immersion and two-way approaches. English immersion without special support for LEP students is illegal in the United States, but English immersion programs still differ on several dimensions. For example, LEP students can be taught in special classes that include no English monolinguals, or in classes with high proportions of native English-speaking peers. Language teaching can also be provided by adjustments of regular classroom activities, or by 'pulling out' children from their regular classrooms for supplementary instruction supported by the home language. Some English immersion programs use 'controlled English', in which new features of the language are introduced in a specific, deliberate fashion, with a goal of facilitating rapid English acquisition, while others introduce English as dictated by other curricular goals.

Two-way education programs can also be distinguished on several dimensions. Like English immersion programs, two-way programs can be directed only at LEP or bilingual students, or at a mixture of language-minority and language-majority students. The research reported here focused on bilingual schools where the vast majority of students were Hispanic, but where most of the students appeared to speak English preferentially to peers (see Chapter 3). Consequently, in the two-way programs evaluated here, the participating children were bilingual, but English-biased, while at the same time being overwhelmingly Hispanic. Thus they might be deemed 'language-majority' or 'language-minority' depending upon definitional criteria. In addition, two-way programs differ on the proportion of the school day devoted to home language instruction. While the Miami programs studied here were 40/60 (60% English), other programs seek a 50/50 pattern, and still others vary in relative proportion year to year.

While the schools under study here provided clear differentiation between the Two-way and English Immersion approaches, it is clear that the pattern of education and exposure to language in the schools was notable. The 40/60 split represents one notable feature of the Two-way programs. Another notable feature is that for both Two-way and English Immersion schools selected for study, well over 90% of students were of Hispanic origin. Since the children typically learned English in school while maintaining some degree of Spanish proficiency (either with or without significant support for Spanish in the classrooms), they showed varying degrees of bilingualism and varying degrees of proficiency in both languages. It was rare for the children to interact in school with monolingual peers, in either language, simply because there appeared to be few monolingual peers to be found in these schools.

Questions To Be Evaluated

Chapters 1 and 2 provide background supporting several key questions to be addressed in the present research:

(1) What is the role of SES in performance of bilingual and monolingual children?
(2) Is there an interaction of factors such that bilingualism proves advantageous for children in circumstances of High SES, ESH and Two-way education, while proving disadvantageous for children in circumstances of Low SES, OSH and English Immersion education?
(3) What is the comparative performance of monolingual English children and bilingual children on English standardized tests?
(4) What is the comparative performance of bilingual children in English Immersion and Two-way programs?
(5) What role does LSH play in bilingual performance?
(6) What role do the key factors of the design (IMS, SES and LSH) play in oral language as opposed to literacy?
(7) Assuming bilingual children's performance changes with respect to monolingual children's performance across time, what rate of change is observed?

Method

Participants

Data were collected from 952 elementary-school students in the Dade County Public School system. Demographic information on the sample is presented in Chapter 2.

Design

A pseudo-experimental design (see Figure 2.1) was followed, with children selected on the basis of Grade in school (332 kindergartners, 306 2nd graders, 314 5th graders), SES (485 middle SES, 467 Low SES), and Lingualism (704 bilinguals, 248 monolinguals). Among the monolinguals, 218 came from schools with predominantly English-speaking peers, and 30 came from schools with predominantly bilingual peers. Among the bilinguals, 355 were enrolled in English Immersion education, and 349 were enrolled in Two-way education. Also among the bilinguals, 333 had ESH, and 371 had OSH. The design was as balanced as possible, with two predominant exceptions. One exception was unfortunate but unavoidable given the demographics of schools in Miami: it was not possible to find many monolingual English-speakers from schools with predominantly bilingual peers. The other exception was intentional: bilinguals outnumbered monolinguals because the design included several variables (IMS predominant among them) that applied only to bilinguals; more bilinguals than monolinguals were therefore required to adequately populate all the cells in the design.

Dependent measures

Nine standardized tests were selected to evaluate oral language, reading, and writing skills. All students were administered the Word Attack, Letter–Word Identification, Passage Comprehension, and Dictation tests from the Woodcock-Johnson Psycho-Educational Battery – Revised (Woodcock & Johnson, 1989), the Picture Vocabulary, Verbal Analogies, and Oral Vocabulary tests from the Woodcock Language Proficiency Battery (Woodcock, 1991), and the Peabody Picture Vocabulary Test – Revised (PPVT, Dunn & Dunn, 1981). In addition, bilingual students were administered Spanish versions of these same tests (Dunn *et al.*, 1986; Woodcock & Muñoz-Sandoval, 1995b). A major reason for the selection of the Woodcock-Johnson battery and the PPVT was that there exist normed versions of these tests in both English and Spanish.

Descriptions of tests

The standardized tests were categorized as pertaining to either oral language or literacy. The literacy subtests were further subdivided into those pertaining to reading vs writing.

Tests of oral language. Four of the standardized tests measure oral language. The first, Picture Vocabulary, is a straightforward picture naming exercise measuring expressive vocabulary. For each item, the child is presented with a picture of an object and asked by the examiner to name it. The Peabody Picture Vocabulary Test, on the other hand, measures receptive vocabulary. The child is presented with a plate containing pictures of four objects and is required to point to the named object for each item. Each plate of four pictures is used to test for a single word. Oral Vocabulary is the third vocabulary test in the language test subgroup. The child is asked to say a word with the opposite meaning of an orally presented target word, or in the case of the subsection on synonyms, to name another word to replace the target. The final test in the language battery is Verbal Analogies. It follows a familiar standard format of the following form: 'Scissors is to cut as pencil is to _____'. The Verbal Analogies subtest is the only language test used here that requires more than vocabulary knowledge.

Each of the oral language tests has a basal rule and a ceiling rule. Each has suggested starting points consistent with grade or age expectations. The four tests have transparent face validity with each having items at the lowest end (Kindergarten [K] for the present study's purposes) that are good exemplars of the test as a whole.

Tests of reading. Three tests of reading are included in the Woodcock-Johnson battery. The Letter–Word Identification test requires the child to read individual letters at the lowest levels and increasingly more difficult words as the test progresses. In each case, a single letter or word is presented per item. Kindergartners start with the identification of isolated letters and may not proceed to the items containing words unless they can identify letters. Only those children whose raw score is 10 or above on Letter–Word Identification are eligible to take the Word Attack test. Children who do not identify letters well enough to achieve a 10, receive an automatic raw score of zero for Word Attack. (Not surprisingly, many students received a score of zero on Word Attack. Consequently, the standard deviations for Word Attack scores in the present study were very low in K – see Table 4.2.) The Word Attack test requires children to read isolated pseudo-words composed in accord with English phonotactics. The words are arranged from simple to complex in terms of length and the variety of phonotactic rules needed for decoding. The Passage Comprehension test utilizes 'Cloze' style items. Children are required to fill in a blank in a short passage. The blank requires a narrow range of items. Straying from this range results in a semantically or syntactically ill-formed response that is considered incorrect. Accompanying each of the first 10 items on the test is an illustration that may cue the child to the correct response if the child can read the passage. Beyond the first 10 items, no illustrations are used and the only clues are the context provided by the passage itself.

As with the test of oral language, the tests of reading have procedures for determining basal and ceiling scores. The face validity of the tests changes dramatically by grade or age level. At the K level (ages 5–6), the tests represent, at best, prereading or reading readiness skills, and provide little if any differentiation among children from different language backgrounds, as indicated by the outcome of the evaluations. In the case of Passage Comprehension, even 2nd graders receive visual prompts to support understanding, while 5th grade readers do not receive this support. The lack of reading knowledge by children in all the experimental groups at K (and lack of differentiation among groups based on language background) led to special treatment of K data in the subsequently reported analyses.

Tests of writing. Two tests of writing were administered, Dictation and Proofing. At the K level, Dictation involves writing one's name and transcribing in either lower- or uppercase a few isolated letters of the alphabet.

At the 2nd grade level, children are presented with simple words to 'spell' in written form. In some cases the test departs from 'dictation'. Item 11, for instance, on the English version calls for 'writing the word that means more than one man'. As the test progresses, there is a mixture of items that involve 'spelling' more and more advanced vocabulary, knowledge of irregular plurals, and technical writing knowledge (e.g. 'write an asterisk'). Thus it is not apparent that the Dictation test possesses internal conceptual consistency, and the problems of interpretation that this presents are particularly notable at K. At K, the Proofing test is administered (as is the Word-Attack test) only if the child receives a raw score of 10 or more on the battery's Letter–Word Identification test. Otherwise, the child receives a raw score of zero on Proofing, yielding a standard score of 100 for children through 63 months of age. (In the present research 99% of the Kindergartners received a raw score of 0 on Proofing, and 92% received a standard score of 100.) Consequently, the standard deviations of Proofing scores were very low at K – see Table 4.2.) For 2nd graders, the Proofing test begins with simple sentences that have embedded orthographic errors. Corrections are needed for capitalization, punctuation, spelling, and grammatical errors. The child is asked to locate and correct the errors orally. The test uses a basal and ceiling rule for scoring.

Overall comparison of oral language and literacy tests

The tests administered in this research were selected because they have substantial stature and have been broadly utilized in educational research and because they are normed for both English- and Spanish-speaking children. However, no test of language or literacy can be applied across ages without some interpretive difficulties since language and literacy abilities change not just in degree but in type across time. It is consequently important to be mindful of limitations in test interpretation. Overall, it can be said that the literacy tests show notable changes in what they address and how they address it across time. At K, some of the literacy evaluations proved in this research to be insensitive to differences in language background of children, in part because the tests only measure 'prereading' skills that are relatively common across the languages. Also, the way the tests are constructed, kindergartners are commonly expected to receive zero raw scores on some of the tests, a fact that leads to unavoidable statistical limitations associated with lack of variance. At 2nd and 5th grades the literacy tests prove more consistent in concept and implementation than at K, and the expected variability in test scores required for typical statistical evaluation is obtained.

The oral language tests tend to be more sensitive and show greater face validity than the literacy tests, and this difference is especially obvious at K.

Even at K, for instance, the tests of vocabulary measure concrete vocabulary knowledge directly. Further, the formats for the tests remain identical from K through 5th grade, and consequently statistical evaluation across all ages is more straightforward than with the literacy tests.

Test administration. In each language, the tests were administered to each child in two 30–40 minute sessions, with one session per day. Because bilingual children were tested in both Spanish and English, four such sessions were required to complete their data collection. Bilingual children completed one language's sessions before beginning the other language's sessions. Of the 704 bilingual children, 354 (50.3%) were tested in English first. Test administrators were thoroughly bilingual in English and Spanish.

Results

Analysis structure

For all analyses reported in the current chapter, the dependent variables were standardized scores (mean of 100 and standard deviation of 15 at each age for norming samples). To evaluate differences among group means, the data were analyzed via eight-way multivariate analysis of variance (MANOVA), with seven between-subjects factors and one within-subjects factor. Three between-subjects factors were fully crossed with one another: SES (high vs low), Grade (K, 2nd, or 5th), and Lingualism (bilingual vs monolingual). In addition, three between-subjects factors nested within Lingualism – IMS (Instructional Method at School), LSH (Language Spoken at Home), and First Language Tested – applied only to bilingual children. IMS contrasted bilinguals attending English Immersion and Two-way schools, and LSH contrasted bilinguals who had ESH and bilinguals who had OSH. First Language, nested within Lingualism, contrasted bilinguals who took the English vs the Spanish battery first (this factor was merely used to test potential effects of counterbalancing). Another factor that was not included in the rationale for the study, but that was implemented out of practical necessity, was the factor Peer, also nested within Lingualism; it contrasted monolinguals in Monolingual English (ME) schools (the great bulk of the monolinguals) and those in bilingual schools (a small proportion of the monolinguals). In the former schools the peer environment was mostly monolingual, while in the latter it was mostly bilingual. Because the design was not balanced with respect to the factor Peer, it was deemed important to estimate potential effects of peer type on the outcomes for monolingual children. Given the somewhat unbalanced design, all between-subjects effects were calculated using Type III sums of squares.

The eighth factor in the MANOVA was the within-subjects factor Test. This factor had nine levels, for it coded the nine standardized tests (eight Woodcock-Johnson subtests, plus the Peabody Picture Vocabulary Test [PPVT]) administered to each child. Statistical tests involving the Test factor were conducted via F approximations (or exact Fs) corresponding to Pillai's trace statistic.

The design described above yields a total of 77 effects. Assuming statistical independence among these effects, the customary comparisonwise alpha rate of 0.05 would have yielded a groupwise Type I error rate > 98%, and was therefore judged too liberal. Tests of main effects and interactions therefore used a comparisonwise alpha rate of 0.01. Under the null hypothesis, this would yield an expected value of 0.77 Type I errors. If all 77 comparisons were statistically independent, then no more than two Type I errors would be made with > 95% certainty, and no more than three Type I errors would be made with > 99% certainty.

The large sample size (N = 952) afforded excellent statistical power. Where the MANOVA yielded significant results involving the Test factor, they were followed up via *post hoc* examination of partial interactions with orthogonal single-degree-of-freedom contrasts, with corrections for the eight effects thus examined in each follow-up.[1] These contrasts are best understood with reference to Figure 4.1, which diagrams the hierarchy by which the nine tests were classified.[2] Where appropriate, significant effects in the MANOVA were also followed up by examining effects in univariate ANOVAs applied to each test individually, with corrections for examining nine effects groupwise.

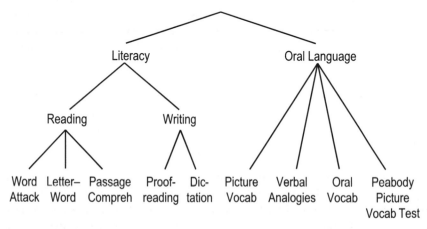

Figure 4.1 Nine standardized tests of language, and the hierarchy by which they were classified

Table 4.1 Results of MANOVA of English Standardized Scores

Source	$\eta 2$	df_{num}	F	$\eta 2$	df_{denom}	df_{num}	F
				Between-subjects effects		Interactions with test	
				0.492	887	8	107.370****
SES	0.107	1	106.941****	0.055	887	8	6.402****
Grade	0.074	2	35.59****	0.263	1776	16	~39.585****
Ling	0.057	1	54.006****	0.106	887	8	13.177****
Peer within Ling	0.000	1	0.265	0.010	887	8	1.166
IMS within Ling	0.002	1	2.231	0.038	887	8	4.388****
LSH within Ling	0.041	1	38.613****	0.075	887	8	8.992****
1st within Ling	0.010	1	8.867**	0.026	887	8	2.933**
SES × Grade	0.002	2	1.104	0.013	1776	16	~1.470
SES × Ling	0.003	1	2.929	0.015	887	8	1.680
SES × Peer	0.001	1	1.213	0.017	887	8	1.874
SES × IMS	0.000	1	0.294	0.013	887	8	1.430
SES × LSH	0.008	1	7.111**	0.025	887	8	2.841**
SES × 1st	0.000	1	0.329	0.005	887	8	0.518
Grade × Ling	0.002	2	0.818	0.023	1776	16	~2.592***
Grade × Peer	0.001	2	0.62	0.008	1776	16	~0.840
Grade × IMS	0.005	2	2.456	0.032	1776	16	~3.648****
Grade × LSH	0.002	2	1.094	0.030	1776	16	~3.427****
Grade × 1st	0.003	2	1.287	0.016	1776	16	~1.782
IMS × LSH	0.000	1	0.022	0.007	887	8	0.750
IMS × 1st	0.001	1	1.19	0.013	887	8	1.497
LSH × 1st	0.000	1	0.042	0.003	887	8	0.348
SES × Grade × Ling	0.000	2	0.099	0.004	1776	16	~0.463
SES × Grade × Peer	0.002	2	0.723	0.004	1776	16	~0.427
SES × Grade × IMS	0.000	2	0.046	0.011	1776	16	~1.265
SES × Grade × LSH	0.002	2	0.949	0.012	1776	16	~1.327
SES × Grade × 1st	0.004	2	1.583	0.011	1776	16	~1.214
SES × IMS × LSH	0.000	1	0.217	0.010	887	8	1.171
SES × IMS × 1st	0.000	1	0.143	0.002	887	8	0.193
SES × LSH × 1st	0.000	1	0.062	0.009	887	8	1.008
Grade × IMS × LSH	0.000	2	0.051	0.009	1776	16	~0.955
Grade × IMS × 1st	0.000	2	0.14	0.009	1776	16	~0.995
Grade × LSH × 1st	0.003	2	1.173	0.017	1776	16	~1.887
IMS × LSH × 1st	0.000	1	0.061	0.019	887	8	2.127
SES × Grade × IMS × LSH	0.001	2	0.234	0.008	1776	16	~0.886

Table 4.1 *(cont.)* Results of MANOVA of English Standardized Scores

SES × Grade × IMS × 1st	0.005	2	2.177	0.008	1776	16	~0.907
SES × Grade × LSH × 1st	0.004	2	1.656	0.008	1776	16	~0.890
SES × IMS × LSH × 1st	0.003	1	2.851	0.004	887	8	0.488
Grade × IMS × LSH × 1st	0.002	2	0.872	0.010	1776	16	~1.119

Asterisks indicate comparisonwise *p*s (*p* < 0.05 not indicated, **p < 0.01, ***p < 0.001, ****p<0.0001).
Approximate *F* ratios indicated by ~.
Ling indicates Lingualism.
1st indicates First Language Tested.
All between-subjects effects have 894 denominator degrees of freedom.
The main effect of Test (*F* = 107.370) is the first effect listed on the right side of the table (formally equivalent to the 'Intercept × Test interaction').

Table 4.1 presents a summary of the MANOVA results. Table 4.2 shows means and standard deviations for all groups in the design.

Main effect of Test

As expected, the main effect of Test was significant, indicating that different tests yielded different average performance when pooled across other factors. Because the interest in the Test effect is contingent on its interaction with other factors in the design, this main effect is not plotted separately. It can be examined by reference to other figures that plot two-way interactions with Test (e.g. Figure 4.2).

Socio-economic status

As expected, the main effect of SES was significant, as was the SES × Test interaction. Follow-up tests revealed that the effect was carried by a significant interaction of SES with the contrast of literacy vs oral language (*p* < 0.001), of SES with the contrast of Letter–Word vs Word Attack (*p* < 0.01), and of SES with reading vs writing tests (*p* < 0.05). Although univariate tests revealed that SES was significant for each test (*p*s < 0.0001), the effect was indeed strongest for Picture Vocabulary (9.6 points) and PPVT (10.8 points), both of which test oral language, as well as for Letter–Word (8.6 points). This is illustrated in Figure 4.2, whose most obvious feature is that High SES children outperformed Low SES children on each test (by 7.2 points, averaged across test).

Grade

The main effect of Grade and the Grade × Test interaction were both sig-

Table 4.2 Means and standard deviations

Grade	Ling & IMS	LSH	SES	n	Word Attack		Letter-Word		Passage comp		Proofing		Dictation		Picture vocab		Verbal analogies		Oral vocab		PPVT	
					M	SD	M	SD	M	SD	M	SD	M	SD	M	SD	M	SD	M	SD	M	SD
K	Eng Imm	Sp	hi	28	97	13	94	17	100	13	100	1	99	15	74	21	90	13	99	12	77	16
			lo	36	92	7	80	12	92	10	99	2	89	13	61	17	89	16	88	13	63	20
		Sp&Eng	hi	33	95	8	92	12	94	13	100	2	99	10	82	14	97	14	99	13	80	14
			lo	28	92	6	90	8	92	13	100	5	98	13	75	15	93	13	96	13	82	14
	Two-way	Sp	hi	29	98	10	93	12	100	13	100	1	99	9	68	17	88	13	91	11	68	16
			lo	38	96	8	79	16	97	12	99	3	85	13	50	13	79	12	81	13	50	12
		Sp&Eng	hi	34	93	6	90	12	93	9	100	0	98	9	77	14	91	13	96	13	79	16
			lo	25	93	8	84	12	91	12	98	5	95	11	75	16	87	14	92	14	70	15
	Mono-ling	Eng	hi	43	93	7	95	11	97	11	100	0	102	9	96	19	100	12	105	13	96	15
			lo	38	94	7	90	10	95	12	99	3	100	8	86	16	93	16	97	13	83	17
2nd	Eng Imm	Sp	hi	30	104	15	109	15	102	10	97	13	98	8	82	18	93	10	91	11	80	16
			lo	32	99	15	98	16	94	12	91	12	92	9	71	15	86	10	85	9	65	17
		Sp&Eng	hi	29	106	17	111	14	107	12	101	16	101	10	93	13	98	11	97	10	90	13
			lo	21	98	18	99	19	101	12	93	13	95	13	83	16	92	10	91	13	81	10
	Two-way	Sp	hi	24	105	18	108	18	103	14	100	13	99	13	81	15	95	12	91	10	87	17
			lo	31	98	14	101	19	97	14	90	14	89	14	62	16	85	11	84	10	68	20
		Sp&Eng	hi	31	111	16	114	14	107	12	102	14	102	10	86	16	99	13	94	12	88	16
			lo	29	103	18	106	20	101	14	97	16	95	11	80	17	92	12	92	10	81	16
	Mono-ling	Eng	hi	47	112	17	117	15	117	13	109	14	105	11	106	12	109	11	107	14	105	11
			lo	32	93	13	100	15	103	17	97	14	96	10	95	13	98	10	93	12	92	17

Table 4.2 (*cont.*) Means and standard deviations

Grade	Ling & IMS	LSH	SES	n	Word Attack		Letter-Word		Passage comp		Proofing		Dictation		Picture vocab		Verbal analogies		Oral vocab		PPVT	
					M	SD	M	SD	M	SD	M	SD	M	SD	M	SD	M	SD	M	SD	M	SD
5th	Eng Imm	Sp	hi	28	109	21	109	19	101	13	101	13	94	13	88	17	98	18	99	16	93	12
			lo	33	97	19	100	18	93	14	94	16	88	12	82	13	91	14	90	10	87	15
		Sp& Eng	hi	29	106	17	110	16	102	14	102	13	95	10	94	12	105	17	101	15	96	15
			lo	28	101	19	105	18	96	12	99	14	92	12	89	12	96	14	95	14	90	16
	Two-way	Sp	hi	29	108	18	112	11	98	9	97	9	92	8	89	9	96	13	99	12	96	16
			lo	33	101	16	106	15	92	9	95	11	87	10	77	11	90	11	87	8	79	10
		Sp& Eng	hi	20	111	18	117	14	100	13	101	11	92	8	90	10	97	15	100	15	96	15
			lo	26	107	15	109	11	95	10	92	11	90	8	85	12	92	10	96	12	88	15
	Mono-ling	Eng	hi	51	108	16	113	14	107	11	105	12	96	13	100	11	106	15	106	14	105	15
			lo	37	103	17	107	14	101	9	99	14	93	8	90	12	94	10	95	12	93	13

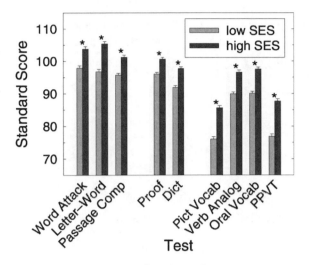

Figure 4.2 Standard score on each subtest, by socio-economic status (SES). Bars represent unweighted means, and error bars represent standard errors. Asterisks indicate significant univariate effects of SES

nificant despite the fact that standardized scores were analyzed. Because of the overriding importance of the other between-subjects factors, the Grade and Grade × Test effects should not be interpreted in isolation, but rather in the context of the Grade × Lingualism × Test, Grade × IMS × Test, and Grade × LSH × Test effects, discussed below.

Lingualism

The main effect of Lingualism was significant, as was the Lingualism × Test interaction. Figure 4.3 illustrates these effects. The Lingualism × Test interaction was carried by the following partial interactions: (1) Lingualism interacted with the contrast of literacy vs oral language, $p < .0001$. This indicates that monolinguals enjoyed an especially large advantage in oral language, as Figure 4.3 illustrates in the large monolingual-bilingual difference for Picture Vocabulary, Verbal Analogies, Oral Vocabulary, and PPVT (average of 11.6 points across these four tests). (2) Lingualism interacted with the contrast of Picture Vocabulary vs Verbal Analogies and Oral Vocabulary, $p < .0001$, as can be seen in the especially large (14.9-point) advantage of monolinguals in the Picture Vocabulary test. (3) Lingualism interacted with the contrast of the phonics-oriented tests (Letter–Word and Word Attack) vs Passage Comprehension, $p < 0.001$, as Figure 4.3 illustrates

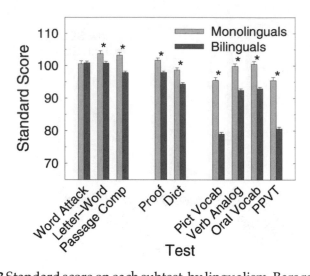

Figure 4.3 Standard score on each subtest, by lingualism. Bars represent unweighted means, and error bars represent standard errors. Asterisks indicate significant univariate differences between monolinguals and bilinguals

that among the tests of reading, only Passage Comprehension showed a reliable Lingualism effect (a pattern that persisted when excluding the K data, for which the literacy tests have questionable face validity). (4) Lingualism interacted with the contrast of Letter–Word vs Word Attack, as Figure 4.3 illustrates that Word Attack was the only test not exhibiting a Lingualism effect. (All other univariate tests of Lingualism were significant.) To summarize, oral language tests showed the largest Lingualism effects, writing tests showed moderate Lingualism effects, and reading tests showed somewhat smaller effects (with Word Attack showing no Lingualism effect).

There was also a significant Grade × Lingualism × Test interaction, $p < 0.0006$. This was carried by a significant partial interaction of Grade × Lingualism with the contrast of Picture Vocabulary vs Verbal Analogies and Oral Vocabulary, $p < 0.01$. In the univariate follow-ups, the Grade × Lingualism effect was significant only for Picture Vocabulary, $p < 0.01$. As illustrated in Figure 4.4, at later grades, the gap between bilinguals and monolinguals narrowed in the test (Picture Vocabulary) where they showed the largest deficit in K.

If the K data are excluded from attention in the five literacy tests (which have questionable validity for kindergartners), then the univariate Grade × Lingualism effect is rendered significant for Passage Comprehension and

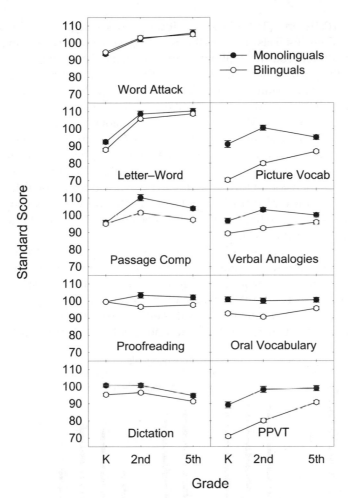

Figure 4.4 Standard score on each subtest, by lingualism and grade. Points represent unweighted means, and error bars represent standard errors

Dictation ($ps < 0.05$), for which a gap that opened by 2nd grade closes slightly by 5th grade.

Instructional Method in the School

The IMS × Test interaction was significant. The interaction was carried by significant partial interactions of IMS with the contrast of (1) oral language vs literacy, $p < 0.0001$, and (2) reading vs writing, $p < 0.001$. Figure 4.5 illustrates these effects. (Figure 4.5 also re-plots the monolingual scores from 4.3, in order to compare differences among bilinguals in the context of monolingual performance.) As the partial interactions indicate, the figure suggests that English Immersion bilinguals outperformed Two-way bilinguals (when data were pooled across all three grade levels) in tests of English oral language (3.1-point advantage across Picture Vocabulary, Verbal Analogies, Oral Vocabulary, and PPVT), performed similarly in tests of writing (0.9-point advantage across Proofing and Dictation), but were outscored by Two-way bilinguals on tests of reading (1.6-point disadvantage across Word Attack, Letter–Word, and Passage Comprehension). However, univariate evaluations of the IMS effect were significant only for Picture Vocabulary ($p < 0.01$) and Verbal Analogies ($p < 0.05$), the tests for which the English Immersion bilinguals had the largest advantage (4.3 and 3.1 points, respectively).

The two-way interaction of IMS × Test can be interpreted in the context of a significant three-way interaction of Grade × IMS × Test. This was carried by a significant partial interaction of Grade × IMS with the contrast of the reading tests (Letter–Word and Word Attack) vs Passage Comprehension, $p < 0.01$. Figure 4.6 illustrates this effect. (To put the IMS effects in context, Figure 4.6 also re-plots the monolingual data from Figure 4.4.)

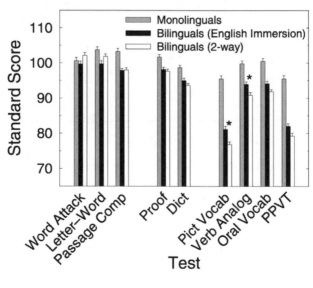

Figure 4.5 Standard score on each subtest, by Lingualism and Instructional Method in School. Bars represent unweighted means, and error bars represent standard errors. Asterisks indicate significant univariate differences between bilinguals in English Immersion schools and those in Two-way schools.

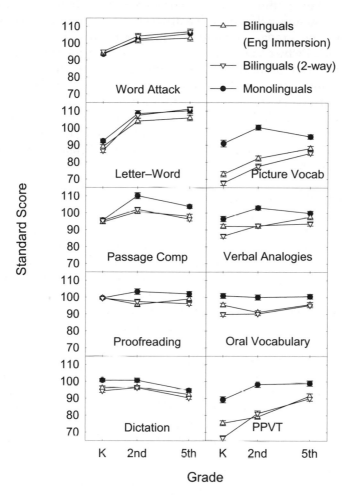

Figure 4.6 Standard score on each subtest, by Lingualism, Instructional Method in School, and Grade. Points represent unweighted means, and error bars represent standard errors

Letter–Word and Word Attack both showed Two-way children gaining a slight advantage over English Immersion children as they left K and progressed through 2nd and 5th grade, whereas Passage Comprehension showed English Immersion children gaining a slight advantage over Two-way children. In light of the questionable face validity of these tests at K, the relevant comparison occurs at 2nd and 5th grades; as the tests gained validity, the differences between Two-way and English Immersion children emerged. However, these effects were small, and examination of the univariate follow-ups tells a story that differs from the one presented by the data pooled across grades: the Grade × IMS interaction was significant only for the Peabody Picture Vocabulary Test, $p < 0.01$. Figure 4.6 illustrates that in K, this is the test that shows the largest advantage for English Immersion children. Because any advantage for English Immersion children is effectively extinguished by 2nd grade (save for Picture Vocabulary), this causes an interaction for PPVT. Overall, Figure 4.6 suggests the following interpretation of the Grade × IMS × Test interaction: whereas English Immersion children had some advantage in K, this difference had essentially dissipated by the later grades.

Language Spoken at Home

The main effect of LSH was significant, as was the LSH × Test interaction. This was carried by significant partial interactions of LSH with the contrast of (1) literacy vs oral language, $p < 0.0001$, (2) Picture Vocabulary vs Verbal Analogies and Oral Vocabulary, $p < 0.0001$, and (3) Letter–Word vs Word Attack, $p < 0.05$. Figure 4.7 illustrates these effects. (For comparison, Figure 4.7 also re-plots the monolingual data from Figure 4.3.) Consistent with the partial interactions, the figure suggests that the tendency of bilinguals who had ESH to outperform those who had OSH was strongest in tests of oral language (7.4-point advantage, averaged across the four oral-language tests). This was especially true for Picture Vocabulary, where those who had ESH held a 10.3-point advantage. In univariate follow-ups, the advantage for children who had ESH was statistically reliable for all tests of oral language ($ps < .0001$); for other tests, the effect was statistically reliable only for Dictation ($p < .001$) and Letter–Word ($p < .05$), where children who had ESH showed a 3.4- and 3.2-point advantage, respectively.

There was also a significant three-way interaction of Grade × LSH × Test. This was carried by partial interactions of the Grade × LSH effect with the contrasts of (1) literacy vs oral language ($p < 0.01$), (2) reading vs writing ($p < 0.05$), and (3) reading tests (Letter–Word and Word Attack) vs Passage Comprehension ($p < 0.05$). Figure 4.8 illustrates these effects (and also re-plots the monolingual data from Figure 4.4), and suggests that the first partial interaction arises because Picture Vocabulary and PPVT, both of which test oral language, had almost identical effects whereby the advantage experienced by ESH bilinguals systematically decreased from K through 5th grade. The second and third partial interactions probably arise from the fact that Passage Comprehension exhibits a peculiar interaction. When the univariate follow-ups were examined, a significant Grade × LSH effect was found for Picture Vocabulary and PPVT ($ps < 0.05$) and for

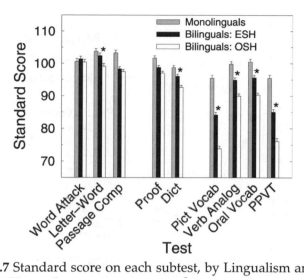

Figure 4.7 Standard score on each subtest, by Lingualism and Language Spoken at Home. Bars represent unweighted means, and error bars represent standard errors. Asterisks indicate significant univariate differences between bilinguals speaking English and Spanish at home and those speaking only Spanish at home

Passage Comprehension ($p < 0.001$). The univariate interactions for Picture Vocabulary and PPVT confirm that scores of children with OSH tended at later grades to approach the scores of their peers with ESH. The univariate interaction for Passage Comprehension might appear puzzling: Figure 4.8 suggests that in K, bilinguals with OSH may have had a slight advantage over bilinguals with ESH, but that in 2nd grade the pattern was reversed. Still, Passage Comprehension has questionable validity in K. When the K data were excluded, the univariate Grade × LSH effect for Passage Comprehension evaporated.

SES × LSH

There was a significant two-way interaction of SES × LSH and a significant three-way interaction of SES × LSH × Test. Figure 4.9 illustrates these effects, showing that the advantage of bilinguals with ESH over those with OSH was greater for Low SES children than for High SES children. The three-way interaction was carried by significant partial interactions of the SES × LSH effect with the contrast of Proofing vs Dictation, $p < 0.01$, which illustrates that among the contrasts tested, the Proofing and Dictation showed the most divergence in the extent to which they exhibited that SES × LSH effect (Dictation showed a moderate effect, but Proofing showed

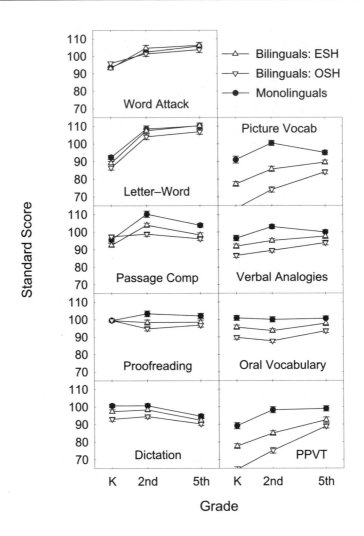

Figure 4.8 Standard score on each subtest, by Lingualism, Language Spoken at Home, and Grade. Points represent unweighted means, and error bars represent standard errors

none). In univariate follow-ups, the SES × LSH effect was significant for Picture Vocabulary ($p < 0.05$), PPVT ($p < 0.001$), Oral Vocabulary ($p < 0.05$), and Dictation ($p < 0.05$); the SES × LSH interaction was of greatest magnitude for these four tests.

The SES × LSH interaction shows that the advantage of bilinguals with

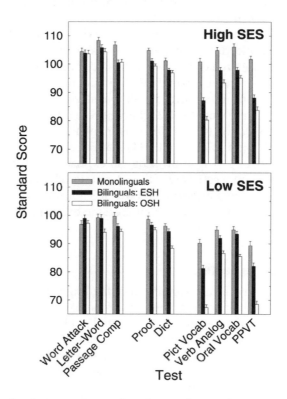

Figure 4.9 Standard score on each subtest, by socio-economic status, lingualism, and language spoken at home. Bars represent unweighted means, and error bars represent standard errors

ESH over those with OSH was larger for Low SES than for High SES children. The result is consistent with the fact that parents of children in the Low SES/OSH category rated themselves as substantially less proficient in English than parents of children in the High SES/OSH (Chapter 2). Whereas all parents of children in the OSH category deemed their households to include little or no English, the actual amounts of English may have varied in accord with the English proficiency of the parents. Conversations with parents and children in the study suggested that many Low SES families may have spoken only Spanish to their children because of their low proficiency in English, whereas High SES families who spoke only Spanish to their children may have done so out of choice. Thus, in some High SES families who endeavoured to speak only Spanish to their children, there may have been some additional English input, leaking through in moments of inattention.

The SES × LSH interaction can be viewed as representing an imperfection in subject selection (which was inevitable given the demographics of the schools at the time of the research, since families claiming to use only Spanish at home tended strongly to differ in English proficiency as a function of SES), but it should be emphasized that the effects of this imperfection, while statistically reliable, were minimal in magnitude. The SES × LSH interaction ($\eta^2 = 0.008$) was smaller in magnitude than both the SES ($\eta^2 = 0.107$) and LSH ($\eta^2 = 0.041$) main effects. If the above interpretation is correct (implying more English exposure in the High SES/OSH groups), then a better estimate of the advantage of ESH bilinguals would be obtained by confining attention to Low SES households. Averaging across tests, this would have the effect of increasing the estimate of the LSH effect from 4.4 points to 6.3 points.

First Language Tested

Bilinguals were administered either the English or the Spanish battery first, in a counterbalanced arrangement. There was a significant main effect of First Language Tested and a significant First Language Tested × Test interaction. Bilinguals who took the English battery first did somewhat better than did those who took the Spanish battery first. On average, students tested first in English outperformed those tested first in Spanish by 2.1 points. In univariate follow-ups, the effect was significant for Proofing, $p < 0.01$, and for Dictation, $p < 0.05$, for which the difference was 3.0 and 2.6 points, respectively. All plots and analyses control for these small, unexpected effects.

The test effects reflect the influence of order of test administration in English and Spanish. The tests were counterbalanced to make it possible to control for the possibility that if a child took the battery first in one language, then it might inflate the child's scores in the other, because of the opportunity to practice a version of the test in the first tested language. Surprisingly, the result did not suggest a practice effect: in eight out of nine English tests, bilinguals who took the English battery first outscored in English those who took the Spanish battery first. This unanticipated result provokes interesting cognitive and linguistic questions about how one language might have interfered with the other language, or how children might have, for instance, lost interest in the second version of the test, as a result of a fatigue or boredom effect. In addition, the effect may have important practical implications, for one would not wish to artificially deflate a bilingual's score on an English-language test by testing too soon after administering a Spanish-language version of a test. However, it should be emphasized that the effect is very small: averaged across the nine tests, there was only a 2.1-point difference between bilinguals who took the English battery first and those who took the Spanish battery first, and the biggest difference across cells of the design was only 3.0 points.

Discussion

Superior performance by children of High SES

The present study disentangled effects of SES from those of bilingualism, and confirmed that SES had a large effect on patterns of literacy attainment, and an especially large effect on oral language. As anticipated, children from High SES homes did better in English on a wide variety of tasks. The advantages of High SES applied to all of the standardized tests and to both monolingual and bilingual children, and were of substantial magnitude; on the average scores for High SES children were 7.2 points or nearly half a standard deviation higher than those for Low SES children. While the differences varied somewhat by grade level, throughout the design, scores favored the High SES groups notably. Such an outcome is not surprising in light of prior results suggesting that linguistic development is correlated positively with SES (Hart & Risley, 1981, 1992).

Lack of four-way interaction among IMS, SES, LSH and Grade

An important inspiration for the research project reported on here was found in the idea that there might exist an important interaction between bilingualism and factors that appear to predispose a child to success in school. In short, the idea was that children might profit from the opportunities presented by bilingualism in conditions of advantage, but suffer from burdens of extra learning required by bilingualism in conditions of disadvantage. While there are a number of ways such an idea might play out, the research team posited a four-way interaction among IMS, SES, LSH and Grade. It was speculated that children from High SES homes and from homes where both English and Spanish was spoken would profit from Two-way education (and would be expected to be firmly bilingual in both oral and written language by 5th grade). At the same time, it was speculated that children from Low SES homes and from homes where Spanish-only was spoken, might suffer under the demands of two languages and profit relatively little or not at all from Two-way education. Consistent with this reasoning, it was hypothesized that High SES children who spoke English and Spanish at home might be poised to take particular advantage of bilingualism, because the home environment might provide sufficient support to allow the children to learn two language systems simultaneously.

Conversely, Two-way education might be disadvantageous to Low SES children, whose home environments might be less likely to provide support for academics and literacy.

Thus, an IMS × SES × LSH × Grade interaction was predicted such that High SES children who spoke English and Spanish at home and who were enrolled in Two-way education would do especially well by the 5th grade, possibly even outperforming monolinguals. Such an effect did not obtain (see Tables 4.1 and 4.2). The data instead exhibited an SES effect that was more straightforward, with High SES children substantially outperforming Low SES children. The advantage of High SES children was most pronounced in oral language.

The idea that inspired the interest in a possible interaction of social factors and bilingualism cannot, however, be entirely excluded based on this evidence. The results suggest that under the circumstances evaluated here, the predicted interaction does not obtain for English acquisition in elementary school, but it is necessary to evaluate Spanish outcomes independently (see Chapter 5). Furthermore, changes of circumstance might change the outcome even in English. It may be important, for example, that children in English Immersion programs experienced approximately 10% of their school day in Spanish (in the BSHL programs, see Chapter 3). While this 10/90 split of the school day provided substantially less Spanish input than the 40/60 arrangement that occurred in the Two-way programs, it appears that the English Immersion efforts of the Miami-Dade County system succeeded in providing significant support in the home language as will be seen based on data in Chapter 5. If it is true that children in the English Immersion programs profited significantly from exposure to the home language in school, it is possible that the anticipated interaction of IMS × SES × LSH × Grade could have been obscured. This reasoning suggests the desirability of a study where English Immersion is implemented in a 0/100 pattern and where Two-way programs are implemented in a 50/50 pattern, maximizing the difference between language exposure of children in the two instructional methods.

There is a further complication that imposes limits on the conclusions that can be arrived at from the fact that the predicted interaction did not obtain: the peer environments of the children in both the English Immersion and Two-way schools may not have included many native speakers in either English or Spanish. Well over 90% of children in these schools were Hispanic, but the typical pattern of language learning in these schools involved usage of both English and Spanish. Observations of the research team suggested that few of the children in these schools showed full native proficiency in either language. It has been suggested that native-speaking peers provide a key environment for the attainment of native competency in language learning (Brown, 1980; Genessee, 1987; Hart & Lapkin, 1989; Lambert, 1981; Lambert & Tucker, 1972). While the naturalistic experiment presented in this volume may provide evidence on a very common pattern of school experience for bilingual children in the USA (one where the great majority of peers appear to be non-native speakers), it is not clear that the results represent the optimal environment for bilingual learning. If the lack of native speaking peers did play a significant role in the outcomes here, it is unclear whether that same factor might have confounded the anticipated interaction of IMS × SES × LSH × Grade. It is simply not clear what role peer language input may have played in the results.

A final concern regarding the interpretation of the lack of the anticipated interaction is based upon the fact that the participating bilingual children were all born in the USA and educated either in English Immersion or in Two-way approaches from K. While it is a matter worthy of further empirical investigation to evaluate skills of children born outside the USA and/or educated partially in Spanish before beginning to be educated in English, there is evidence suggesting that there may be advantages, at least under some circumstances to early home language education, and to initiating second-language instruction only after several years of schooling that establish the home language firmly (see Chapter 1). The anticipated interaction could conceivably occur in comparisons involving foreign born children who begin school in English at, for example, the 2nd grade. Again it is not clear what role the restriction of subject selection to individuals born in the USA may have played in the results.

Monolingual advantages in English

Controlling for SES frees other effects from the potential interpretational difficulties engendered by SES confounds. One effect thereby revealed in the present study is that of Lingualism. Even when SES was taken into account, monolinguals outperformed bilinguals in oral language in English. The differences were large in K (over 13 points) and 2nd grade (nearly 15 points, approaching a full standard deviation of the test scores), but diminished notably by 5th grade (to fewer than 7 points or less than half a standard deviation). A major factor in this difference appears to be limited English vocabulary in bilinguals, presumably engendered by less exposure to English, and perhaps less exposure to natively spoken English, especially by peers. This interpretation appears to be supported by the narrowing gap between monolinguals and bilinguals in the 5th grade, presumably as bilinguals gained more exposure to English. The reading and writing tests, on which vocabulary appears to have played a smaller part, showed smaller differences or no differences between monolinguals and bilinguals for all three grades (with an average of less than a quarter of a standard deviation at 5th grade).

An additional factor that needs to be considered in interpreting the apparent advantage of monolinguals in English, especially on oral language, is what has been termed the 'distributed characteristic' (Chapter 1) of bilingual knowledge. It is known that bilingual children have distributed knowledge, that is, knowledge in one language that they do not have in the other, and vice versa. For example, they know words in each language that they do not know in the other (Umbel *et al.*, 1992), and it seems likely that this distributed pattern of knowledge applies in other domains, such as syntax. When a bilingual child scores below monolingual levels on a standardized test in English, normed primarily with English monolinguals, it is not clear how much of the difference might be attributed to errors that the bilingual child makes in English, but would not make if the test were administered in Spanish. According to this reasoning, bilingual children may have general conceptual and linguistic capabilities that surpass those manifest in their scores on English tests.

This problem of interpretation of test scores in English is inherent in comparing monolingual and bilingual performance on language tests and cannot be resolved by simply testing in Spanish, because the distributed characteristic affects outcomes in Spanish also. The problem occurs when testing either language, and we have no method of correcting scores to account for the differences so that monolingual and bilingual outcomes can be compared in a generally equitable fashion. If such a method existed, uniting the benefits of complementary knowledge of each of the languages in bilingual children, it could show that bilingual children have vocabulary and syntactic capabilities that equal or exceed those of monolingual children. What can be said from the present research is that the bilingual children did not score as well as their monolingual English counterparts in English.

Another interpretive difficulty in comparing monolingual and bilingual performance in the present study is associated with the peer language arrangement in the schools that were studied. The concerns of interpretation here are similar to those expressed in the discussion above regarding the lack of an IMS × SES × LSH × Grade interaction: since there appear to have been few native English-speaking peers in the bilingual schools, it is possible that the children's English language acquisition may have been negatively affected. The way to test this possibility would be to run studies directly comparing bilingual schools with small and large proportions of native English-speaking children. Miami did not present such possibilities in Two-way programs, and consequently it was impossible to manipulate the peer factor within the study.

Similarly, the fact that children participating in the study were selected only if they were born in the USA may present an important interpretive limitation. Children born in foreign countries and having been educated partially in Spanish (and having established a strong linguistic base) before beginning school in Miami might have performed better in English than those evaluated here.

The effect of instructional method in bilingual education

It is not uncommon in the USA for the public and many educators to express interest in the educational use and acquisition of only one language, English, in elementary school. However, documenting an effect of Lingualism that favors monolingual children on tests of English language and literacy does not imply that Hispanic children should be educated 'monolingually', that is, by English Immersion, even from the standpoint of an interest in English outcomes. No amount of school intervention can change the fact that some children come from Spanish-only or bilingual homes, and many enter school with severely limited English proficiency. The research suggests that children from such homes cannot be converted into monolinguals with the same English skills as lifelong monolinguals simply by putting them into English Immersion elementary schools of the sort that were available in Miami during the research project. These were clearly good schools, but they did not yield perfectly monolingual-like competence for typical bilingual children in English by 5th grade.

The ideal instructional method for bilingual children can only be determined empirically. This study's design included two bilingual groups, one in English Immersion and one in Two-way education. Because of careful matching on demographic characteristics, the study's design allowed as close an approximation as was feasible of an experimental evaluation of Instructional Method in the Schools. By careful socio-economic and linguistic matching, the study avoided the problems of possible self-selection that complicate the interpretation of certain important prior studies attempting to assess effects of program type on educational outcome (Lambert & Tucker, 1972; Swain, 1979).

The results did not show durable advantages for English language knowledge based upon English Immersion instruction, but they showed that on the English battery, K children in English Immersion programs tended to outperform those in Two-way programs on oral language in English. By analogy with the discussion of Lingualism effects, the pattern appears to be attributable substantially to more limited English vocabulary in children in Two-way programs at K, a deficit presumably engendered by their more limited exposure to English during the first year of schooling. However, the oral language advantage experienced by children in English

Immersion programs was less than a point at 2nd grade and was 2 points (around 1/7 of a standard deviation) at 5th grade, and these differences from performance of Two-way children were not statistically reliable. The results suggest that there may be short-term advantages to English Immersion for the learning of oral English, but that the advantages may disappear in elementary school. A reminder may be worthwhile at this point: the relative value of the two educational methods for oral language cannot be assessed entirely on the basis of outcomes in English. If children in Two-way education gain advantages in Spanish over their English Immersion peers, these too need to be considered (see Chapter 5).

The tests of literacy also did not support the English Immersion approach. In fact, across all the literacy tests Two-way education produced slightly (though statistically unreliably) higher mean scores than English Immersion at all grade levels. This tendency masked a very slight advantage of English Immersion over Two-way education in writing and Passage Comprehension, and a somewhat larger advantage of Two-way education on the phonics tests (Word Attack and Letter–Word). The face validity of the Word Attack and Letter–Word tests is questionable at K where the reading tests did not distinguish between monolinguals and bilinguals nor between English and Spanish reading skills. This lack of distinctive performance may owe to the fact that the reading tests are largely simple alphabetic assessments at K, and English and Spanish alphabets are very similar derivations of the same Roman orthography. The slight advantage that bilinguals in Two-way education enjoyed emerged in 2nd grade, as the tests acquired face validity and language specificity. The largest advantage of Two-way children on the phonics tests occurred at 5th grade, where they outscored the English Immersion children by more than 4 points (an advantage that was twice as large as the one held by English Immersion children on the writing and Passage Comprehension tests at the same age). The performance of the children in Two-way schools actually exceeded (though not statistically reliably) that of monolingual children on the phonics tests at 2nd and 5th grade.

The relatively good performance of students in Two-way education in the phonics tests, especially in later grades, could be the result of training in Spanish, where the orthographic system is related to the phonemic system in a relatively simple way, unlike English, where spelling is extremely complicated. Two-way children, by receiving instruction in Spanish literacy, where phonics is relatively easy, may have been provided a bridge toward phonics in English, where the task is more difficult. Ultimately they might have done better in English phonics because the instruction in Spanish provided them with confidence or consistent frames of reference for phonics. If this interpretation is correct, then it may have implications beyond those associated with bilingualism, for it suggests support for step-by-step phonics-oriented instruction in the teaching of reading skills.

Of course there are other possibilities to explain the fact that students in Two-way programs did particularly well in reading. One possibility concerns phonological awareness, a factor that has been speculated to be enhanced by bilingual experience with phonological translation. Evidence in Chapter 11 is consistent with the possibility that bilingual children may, through their common requirement to translate phonologically, acquire a special awareness that might aid them in the learning of phonics.

However the results are viewed, they do not provide general support for English Immersion as an alternative to Two-way education for bilingual children, even if one considers outcomes in English alone. Differences between the two approaches beyond K appear to be minimal and mixed for English outcomes.

Effects of LSH

On the English battery discussed in the present chapter, bilinguals with English and Spanish at home (ESH) outperformed those with only Spanish at home (OSH). As seen in effects of Lingualism and IMS, this difference was largest on tests of oral language (where children with ESH enjoyed an advantage in scores of over 7 points or nearly half a standard deviation, compared to only a 2 point advantage on literacy tests). Again, the difference appears likely attributable to the more limited exposure to English by those children with OSH. As seen in the Lingualism and IMS effects, the oral-language advantage of bilinguals with ESH over those with OSH dissipated in the later grades (from over 9.5 points at K to less than 4.5 at 5th grade), presumably because the children with low English exposure gained more experience with English as they progressed through school. Data reported in Chapter 3 suggest strongly that all the children were being exposed primarily to English in peer interactions (though it appears this may not have been natively spoken English) since English appeared to be the preferred language of peer conversation even for children with LEP. Consequently the strongest effects of exposure to OSH were seen in the youngest children. These findings are broadly consistent with previous results that have highlighted the importance of LSH (Dulay & Burt, 1978; Zappert & Cruz, 1977).

It should be noted that children classified as having OSH may have actually experienced some English in the home. Chapter 2 explains that all the selected children were born in the USA and that assignment into the ESH group versus the OSH group was based on whether or not parents reported that they spoke any English to their children *in the earliest years of life*. The age of first exposure to English was 3.8 years for the OSH group. While this is notably later than for the ESH group, it does predate entry to K. Thus, the effects of LSH may well have been diluted by the difficulty of identifying large numbers of children from purely monolingual Spanish homes. The possible dilution suggests that the LSH effects that are reported here may represent conservative estimates of possible effects of LSH in more extreme cases of early monolingual exposure.

Effects of the study variables on oral language versus literacy

In the English-language battery considered in the present chapter, the advantage of High SES children over Low SES children was largest for tests of oral language. Similarly, the advantage of monolingual English-speaking children over bilingual children was largest for tests of oral language. Furthermore, the advantage of bilinguals with ESH over those with OSH was also largest for tests of oral language. A recurring theme is that performance in oral language measures appear to have been more affected by variations on the dimensions of study than literacy was. This may have occurred because oral language is learned to a great extent outside of school, but reading and writing tend to be much more dependent on school-based instruction. Thus, in reading and writing, school may function as a 'great equalizer', minimizing the effects of extra-scholastic variables on children's performance. Oral language is learned in school, in the home, and in the community. Literacy, though not taught exclusively in the schools, is much more heavily dependent on school-based instruction than it is on extra-scholastic influences.

Rate of acquisition of competence in English by bilinguals

How quickly did bilinguals approach the performance of monolinguals on tests of English proficiency? In prior research on rate of gain in education, the metric of the Normal Curve Equivalent has been utilized as a standard (Tallmadge & Wood, 1976). The NCE is a linear transformation of a standardized score in which the scale's mean is 50 and the scale's standard deviation is 21.06. NCEs thus convey essentially the same information as standardized scores, but are rescaled to mimic the percentile metric with which many interpreters are more familiar. The mean and standard deviation of the NCE scale are chosen so that NCE and standardized scores are equivalent for scores of 1, 50, and 99.

According to retrospective research surveying standardized test results obtained for a large number of programs in bilingual education, bilingual students in strong-to-moderate-quality educational programs can be expected to gain 4–6 NCEs per year (~1/4 standard deviation per year (Thomas & Collier, 1997)). The results of the Thomas and Collier investigations are founded on the assumption that bilinguals can be expected to start out with a 25–30 NCE gap relative to their monolingual peers (Thomas & Collier, 1997). On most tests, the bilinguals in the present study started out scoring much closer to the monolinguals than has been seen in the Thomas and Collier results. Since the tests here were intended to evaluate language specific knowledge, the lack of strong differentiation between monolingual English children and children with both OSH and ESH at K on literacy assessments suggests that the tests were incompatible with an evaluation such as that conducted by Thomas and Collier. Exceptions were Picture Vocabulary and PPVT, which were much stronger psychometrically when utilized across all three grade levels, and for which the bilinguals started out up to 35 NCEs behind the monolingual peers; on these two tests, the students did achieve the anticipated gain of 4–6 NCEs/year. Another factor that may again be important is that all the students in the present study were born in the USA. Their starting scores in K in English may, thus, have been higher than those for children born outside the USA, and consequently their gains year-by-year with respect to monolingual peers may have been less notable.

Given the psychometric limitations of a number of the tests administered here, especially at K, and given that the children were all born in the USA, evaluation of NCE gains across time should be approached with caution. With this proviso in mind, we report the following comparisons of English Immersion and Two-way program results: Averaged across all nine tests, bilinguals in English Immersion programs made progress of approximately 0.5 NCEs per year, and bilinguals in Two-way education made progress of approximately 1 NCE per year. At 5th grade, bilinguals in English Immersion programs were approximately 6 NCEs behind monolinguals, and bilinguals in Two-way education programs were approximately 7 NCEs behind monolinguals, averaging across all nine tests. However, as discussed above in the analysis of group means, there were differences in performance among subtests: Bilingual 5th graders in English Immersion were 5–7 NCEs behind monolingual 5th graders for reading, writing, and vocabulary tests; in contrast, bilingual 5th graders in Two-way programs were 8–10 NCEs behind monolingual 5th graders in writing and vocabulary tests, but were about 1 NCE ahead of monolinguals on reading tests.

The present research focused entirely upon elementary school. Projecting results into the future for the children evaluated here is speculative. Still, it is possible, based on the present results, that many bilingual children would eventually catch up with or even surpass monolingual peers in English language knowledge. The Thomas and Collier results suggest that such outcomes are common for children whose education is two-way through elementary school.

Summary

This study's pseudo-experimental design permits one to assess effects of a variety of variables in educational and linguistic outcomes for bilingual children. It was confirmed that socio-economic status plays a consistent role in influencing language outcome in bilinguals. Interactions of SES with other factors were largely absent, save for the small-to-moderate interaction with Language Spoken at Home. LSH has not been widely assessed in previous studies, and the fact that it produced a solid main effect in the present research indicates that this factor exerts considerable influence on English-language outcomes. The extra-scholastic factors of SES and LSH affected oral language more than literacy, and consequently it can be said that reading and writing achievement appeared to depend on schooling more strongly than did oral language.

English Immersion education appeared to have a short-term advantage over Two-way education in K on oral language tests. Beyond K, however, the two education strategies for bilingual children appeared to produce largely comparable outcomes. Monolinguals outperformed bilinguals in English, although the gap between monolinguals and bilinguals in both types of educational programs did tend to narrow across grade. Still, bilinguals tended to lag behind monolingual peers even at 5th grade on most tests. It is unclear how much of this gap might be bridged if it were feasible to adjust scores to account for the 'distributed characteristic' of bilingual learning, the characteristic by which the children in the study may have achieved mastery for some linguistic and or academic information in Spanish only. Further it is unclear whether bilingual children might have performed substantially better in English had their educational settings included substantial numbers of native English-speaking peers.

Of course investigations of English performance alone offer an incomplete picture of language proficiency in bilingual children, as well as an incomplete picture of the influence of scholastic and extra-scholastic factors that influence learning in the two languages. Investigations using standardized tests of Spanish performance are the topic of the next chapter.

Notes

1. Post hoc tests applied the Holm procedure with the Dunn-Šidák correction (e.g. Kirk, 1995). The Dunn-Šidák correction is a more accurate version of a Bonferroni-type correction, and the Holm procedure adjusts the comparisonwise p for each comparison in such a way as to yield a more powerful test while still maintaining groupwise p at the specified level. All *post hoc* tests used a groupwise alpha rate of 0.05.
2. One contrast compared the five literacy tests against the four tests of oral language. Within literacy, another contrast compared the three reading tests against the two writing tests. Within reading, one contrast compared the two

phonics tests (Word Attack and Letter–Word) against Passage Comprehension. Another contrast compared Word Attack against Letter–Word. To examine differences between the two writing tests, a contrast compared Proofing against Dictation. Finally, three contrasts are required to distinguish among the four tests of oral language. One compared the Peabody Picture Vocabulary Test against the other three tests, all of which are drawn from the Woodcock-Johnson battery. Another compared Picture Vocabulary (the straightforward picture naming test) against Verbal Analogies and Oral Vocabulary. The last contrast compared Verbal Analogies against Oral Vocabulary.

Chapter 5

Effects of Bilingualism and Bilingual Education on Oral and Written Spanish Skills: A Multifactor Study of Standardized Test Outcomes

ALAN B. COBO-LEWIS, BARBARA ZURER PEARSON,
REBECCA E. EILERS and VIVIAN C. UMBEL

The Crucial Role of Evaluating Knowledge of the Home Language

In studies of bilingual education in the USA, it has been routine to evaluate capabilities of children as they acquire English, and to focus attention on English alone. Even the important research of Ramírez and colleagues (Ramírez *et al.*, 1991b) was limited to evaluation of English skills. Yet it is clear that understanding the effects of education on bilingual children, whether in English Immersion or Two-way approaches, requires evaluation of the competency of children in both the home language and the language of the host community.

The present research was constructed with the goal of evaluating both languages thoroughly from the outset. Standardized tests in both English and Spanish were thus administered to all the bilingual children. This chapter reports results of the standardized tests in Spanish.

Questions to be evaluated

Just as it is true that English-language performance may be affected by multiple factors, so is it true that Spanish skills may be multiply influenced. Outcomes may depend on the type of skills being assessed, the child's age, as well as socio-economic and environmental factors that affect the child's linguistic and academic performance. We were interested in interrelationships among language skills at two different levels of analysis. In the current chapter, we addressed the question of how the Core Design variables affected performance on standardized tests of Spanish. In Chapter 6 the extent to which English and Spanish skills cohered in oral language and literacy is examined. Specifically, the questions addressed in the current chapter are:

(1) What was the role of SES in Spanish performance?
(2) What was the comparative Spanish language performance of bilingual children in English Immersion and Two-way educational programs?
(3) What role did Language Spoken at Home (LSH) play in Spanish proficiency?
(4) Did SES, LSH and Instructional Methods in School (IMS) interact, conferring an advantage on High SES children in whose homes both languages were spoken and who attended Two-way schools?
(5) What role did IMS, SES and LSH play in oral language vs literacy for Spanish language attainment?
(6) How well did bilingual children perform with respect to monolingual Spanish norms?

Method

Participants, measures, variables

The participants, test procedures and design (see Figure 2.1 in Chapter 2) are described in Chapter 4. In addition to the nine measures of written and oral language in English, the same skills were assessed in Spanish (Dunn *et al.*, 1986; Woodcock & Muñoz-Sandoval, 1995a). As in Chapter 4, the dependent variables were standard scores (mean of 100 and standard deviation of 15 at each age in the test's norming sample).

Analysis of Spanish group means

To evaluate differences among group means, the Spanish data were analyzed via six-way multivariate analysis of variance (MANOVA), with five fully crossed between-subjects factors and one within-subjects factor. The between-subjects factors were socio-economic status or SES (High vs Low), Grade (K, 2nd, or 5th), Instructional Method in School or IMS (English Immersion vs Two-way), Language Spoken at Home or LSH (ESH vs OSH), and First Language Tested (English battery administered first vs Spanish battery administered first). There were unequal numbers of subjects per cell (see Chapter 2), and all between-subjects effects were calculated using Type III sums of squares.

The sixth factor in the MANOVA was the within-subjects factor Test. This factor had nine levels, for it coded among the nine standardized Spanish tests (eight Woodcock-Muñoz subtests, plus the Test de vocabulario en imágenes Peabody (TVIP)) administered to each child. Statistical tests

Table 5.1 Results of MANOVA of Spanish standardized scores

Source	η^2	df_{num}	F	η^2	df_{denom}	df_{num}	F
		Between-Subjects Effects			Interactions with Test		
				0.795	649	8	314.941****
SES	0.003	1	1.690	0.094	649	8	8.380****
Grade	0.117	2	43.341****	0.481	1300	16	~75.426****
IMS	0.111	1	81.907****	0.116	649	8	10.694****
LSH	0.042	1	28.587****	0.107	649	8	9.732****
1st	0.005	1	3.400	0.033	649	8	2.797**
SES × Grade	0.001	2	0.266	0.017	1300	16	~1.382
SES × IMS	0.000	1	0.074	0.028	649	8	2.344
SES × LSH	0.004	1	2.407	0.020	649	8	1.662
SES × 1st	0.000	1	0.107	0.004	649	8	0.324
Grade × IMS	0.052	2	18.116****	0.045	1300	16	~3.853****
Grade × LSH	0.000	2	0.101	0.022	1300	16	~1.827
Grade × 1st	0.002	2	0.616	0.025	1300	16	~2.093**
IMS × LSH	0.001	1	0.586	0.018	649	8	1.448
IMS × 1st	0.003	1	1.797	0.003	649	8	0.285
LSH × 1st	0.000	1	0.253	0.004	649	8	0.319
SES × Grade × IMS	0.003	2	0.999	0.018	1300	16	~1.453
SES × Grade × LSH	0.006	2	1.963	0.010	1300	16	~0.810
SES × Grade × 1st	0.001	2	0.338	0.011	1300	16	~0.903
SES × IMS × LSH	0.001	1	0.775	0.006	649	8	0.489
SES × IMS × 1st	0.001	1	0.564	0.007	649	8	0.571
SES × LSH × 1st	0.000	1	0.112	0.006	649	8	0.520
Grade × IMS × LSH	0.001	2	0.474	0.014	1300	16	~1.186
Grade × IMS × 1st	0.000	2	0.034	0.010	1300	16	~.838
Grade × LSH × 1st	0.002	2	0.708	0.019	1300	16	~1.596
IMS × LSH × 1st	0.001	1	0.979	0.022	649	8	1.822
SES × Grade × IMS × LSH	0.002	2	0.573	0.010	1300	16	~0.828
SES × Grade × IMS × 1st	0.012	2	4.050	0.009	1300	16	~0.712
SES × Grade × LSH × 1st	0.002	2	0.533	0.007	1300	16	~0.542
SES × IMS × LSH × 1st	0.001	1	0.741	0.012	649	8	0.966
Grade × IMS × LSH × 1st	0.004	2	1.287	0.014	1300	16	~1.149
SES × Grade × IMS × LSH × 1st	0.000	2	0.094	0.004	1300	16	~.347

involving the Test factor were conducted via F approximations (or exact Fs) corresponding to Pillai's trace statistic. The large sample size ($N = 704$ bilingual subjects) affords generally excellent statistical power, and many of the effects were of substantial magnitude.

The design described above yields a total of 63 effects. Assuming statistical independence among these effects, the customary comparisonwise alpha rate of 0.05 would have yielded a groupwise Type I error rate > 96% and was therefore rejected. Comparisons described below were based upon a comparisonwise alpha rate of 0.01. Under the null hypothesis, this would yield an expected value of 0.63 Type I errors. If all 63 comparisons were statistically independent, then no more than two Type I errors would be made with > 97% certainty, and no more than three Type I errors would be made with > 99% certainty.

Where the MANOVA yielded significant results involving the Test factor, they were followed up via *post hoc* examination of partial interactions with single-degree-of-freedom contrasts. These *post hoc* tests applied the Holm procedure with the Dunn-Šidák correction (e.g. Kirk, 1995; see also Note 1 in Chapter 4) to maintain groupwise alpha rate of 0.05. These contrasts are diagrammed in Chapter 4, Figure 4.1. Where appropriate, significant effects in the MANOVA were also followed up by examining effects in univariate ANOVAs applied to each test individually, with corrections for examining nine effects groupwise.

Results

Differences between English and Spanish norms on certain subtests at kindergarten

The psychometric properties of the English and Spanish versions of the standardized tests were comparable for all tests at 2nd and 5th grades. However, an important exception occurred at Kindergarten (K) where very large differences were observed between the English and Spanish Word Attack standardized scores. In the former case, the mean scores were in the mid 90s (Chapter 4, Table 4.2), while in the latter, the mean scores were below 50 (Table 5.2). Lest this apparent difference be misinterpreted, we hasten to focus on a psychometric oddity that is the source of this anomaly.

Notes to Table 5.1 (opposite): Asterisks indicate comparisonwise ps ($p < 0.05$ not indicated, **$p < 0.01$, ***$p < 0.001$, ****$p<0.0001$).
Approximate F ratios indicated by ~.
1st indicates First Language Tested.
All between-subjects effects have 656 denominator degrees of freedom.
The main effect of Test ($F = 314.491$) is the first effect listed on the right side of the table (formally equivalent to the 'Intercept × Test interaction').

Table 5.2 Means and standard deviations

Grade	IMS	LSH	SES	n	Word Attack M	Word Attack SD	Letter–Word M	Letter–Word SD	Passage comp M	Passage comp SD	Proofing M	Proofing SD	Dictation M	Dictation SD	Picture vocab M	Picture vocab SD	Verbal analogies M	Verbal analogies SD	Oral vocab M	Oral vocab SD	PPVT M	PPVT SD
K	Eng Imm	Sp	hi	28	48	18	78	7	82	19	96	1	89	9	62	17	88	18	88	16	91	18
			lo	36	48	16	76	15	82	13	96	3	87	9	77	22	91	19	96	16	98	11
		Sp& Eng	hi	33	51	23	79	13	75	16	96	2	88	8	52	13	85	19	84	16	86	17
			lo	28	47	9	80	15	74	10	96	1	87	9	52	12	86	18	86	15	85	22
	Two- way	Sp	hi	29	53	29	86	19	86	21	96	0	96	10	70	23	89	14	90	18	94	22
			lo	38	44	14	78	15	84	18	95	3	88	11	75	19	77	15	88	17	93	18
		Sp& Eng	hi	34	47	15	80	14	78	13	96	1	91	12	54	19	83	20	84	16	87	13
			lo	25	46	10	80	15	79	18	95	4	87	10	60	16	81	20	83	17	88	14
2nd	Eng Imm	Sp	hi	30	95	12	101	22	86	13	80	8	78	11	55	21	87	10	76	15	86	9
			lo	32	94	21	98	31	82	22	83	8	78	16	69	22	87	12	81	12	93	11
		Sp& Eng	hi	29	97	15	102	24	86	18	84	12	83	13	54	18	84	15	71	11	85	15
			lo	21	88	21	85	22	77	19	77	10	75	16	56	23	80	14	67	21	88	13
	Two- way	Sp	hi	24	106	15	120	28	94	17	91	12	92	18	76	28	97	10	83	24	98	17
			lo	31	109	23	121	30	95	16	88	12	89	14	81	27	93	9	92	17	97	13
		Sp& Eng	hi	31	114	16	130	22	98	9	89	8	94	10	59	19	95	9	79	12	92	14
			lo	29	106	20	117	28	87	15	87	12	89	14	57	22	93	13	77	17	91	13
5th	Eng Imm	Sp	hi	28	103	21	118	28	84	13	78	15	81	13	66	22	89	8	79	12	87	18
			lo	33	93	24	103	32	80	18	76	20	75	15	75	22	87	9	86	16	92	16
		Sp& Eng	hi	29	91	17	103	22	80	12	76	15	77	11	57	20	87	8	75	15	81	19
			lo	28	88	21	95	27	77	14	73	15	71	15	65	22	83	14	73	17	80	19
	Two- way	Sp	hi	29	109	14	127	15	87	8	83	13	87	12	77	18	89	9	84	15	103	18
			lo	33	110	15	129	22	88	6	85	15	84	10	83	17	90	6	93	13	92	13
		Sp& Eng	hi	20	109	16	126	26	85	8	79	14	85	6	73	19	88	6	82	14	99	17
			lo	26	109	10	128	19	86	7	82	11	82	7	73	24	89	10	86	16	87	19

In both English and Spanish, children who scored below a criterion level on Letter–Word Identification automatically received raw scores of 0 on both Proofing and Word Attack subtests, in accord with instructions of the Woodcock-Johnson scoring manual (on the assumption that such students would likely have very limited or nil capabilities for Proofing and Word Attack). For the sample of children studied here, the procedure yielded K standardized scores for these two subtests in English of 90–100 along with standard deviations that were extremely low, because so many students were given raw scores of 0 when they failed to meet criterion, and because the 0's were translated across a substantial age range into standard scores of 100 for the English test, in accord with data from the original norming sample. In Spanish, the same procedure resulted in Proofing means in K that were similar to those for English and also produced low standard deviations corresponding, as in the English tests, to large numbers of automatically assigned 0 raw scores along with a typical assignment of standard scores of 100 when raw scores were 0 at a variety of ages. In Word Attack, however, the K means in Spanish were dramatically reduced (so that they were about 50 points lower than in English, with standard deviations ranging from 9 to 18) due to differences in the data from norming samples in English and Spanish. Computation of standard scores based on the norming sample data in Spanish resulted in a wide range of low standard scores (rather than consistent assignment of 100) when the raw score was 0 and a consequent major reduction in standard scores compared to the English case for K.

One way to understand the problem is to recognize it as the result of a 'floor effect'. The psychometric properties of tests can be expected to be poor at extreme values. In this case the psychometric anomalies of the floor effect resulted in the Kindergartners' mean standard scores for the Spanish sample being very low. Recall from Chapter 4, however, that the literacy tests have questionable face validity in K in any event. As in Chapter 4, this led us to provide a special treatment of Kindergarten data in the subsequently reported analyses.

Test main effect

The main effect of Test was significant ($p < 0.0001$). This indicates that pooled across all other factors, different tests yielded different average performance patterns. Such differences are not of primary concern here, but merely constitute a background for interpretation of other, more germane factors regarding possible group differences. Because Test interacted with several factors of more substantial interest (see Table 5.1), it can be examined by reference to other figures that plot interactions with Test (e.g. Figure 5.1).

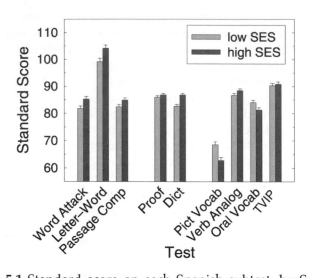

Figure 5.1 Standard score on each Spanish subtest, by Socio-economic status (SES). Bars represent unweighted means, and error bars represent standard errors.

Socio-economic Status

In the data on Spanish performance, a main effect for SES was not obtained. This contrasts sharply with the English data, which showed a strong SES main effect. The SES × Test interaction was, however, significant ($p < 0.0001$), and is illustrated in Figure 5.1. There was a significant partial interaction of SES with the contrast of oral language vs literacy ($p < 0.0001$): for only two tests of oral language did High SES children outperform Low SES children, whereas there was a High SES advantage for all literacy tests. (The High SES advantage in literacy averaged 3.2 points, though it was significant only for Letter–Word [5.0 points, $p < 0.05$] and Dictation [4.2 points, $p < 0.0001$], and the High SES advantage became non-significant in Letter–Word when excluding the K data, for which the literacy tests are of questionable face validity). There was also a significant partial interaction of SES with the Proofreading vs Dictation contrast ($p < 0.001$), since the SES effect was not significant for Proofreading but was significant for Dictation ($p < 0.0001$). Low SES children showed an advantage over High SES children in Picture and Oral Vocabulary as illustrated by a significant partial interaction of SES with the contrast of Picture Vocabulary vs Verbal Analogies and Oral Vocabulary ($p < 0.001$). Picture Vocabulary had the largest SES effect among all the tests (5.7 points), with Low SES children outperforming High SES children ($p < $

0.01). There was also a significant partial interaction of SES with the contrast of Verbal Analogies vs Oral Vocabulary ($p < 0.001$): High SES children non-significantly outperformed Low SES children in Verbal Analogies, but Low SES children non-significantly outperformed High SES children in Oral Vocabulary. Finally, there was a significant partial interaction of SES with the contrast of TVIP versus the other test of oral language ($p < 0.05$), merely indicating that there was essentially no SES effect for TVIP (Low SES scores within 0.5 points of High SES scores), whereas two of the other three tests of oral language exhibited at least trends favoring Low SES children.

Grade

The main effect of Grade was significant ($p < 0.0001$) as was the Grade × Test interaction ($p < 0.0001$). There were partial interactions between Grade and each 1-df contrast among Tests ($ps < 0.01$). Univariate evaluations of the Grade effect were significant for each test except TVIP (other $ps < 0.01$). Figure 5.2 plots the pattern of results, and shows that scores differed across grades for all tests but the TVIP. Among the tests of reading, Letter–Word and Word Attack showed very large gains from far below norms at K to at or above norms at 2nd grade, with Letter–Word showing additional gain from 2nd grade to 5th grade; Passage Comprehension showed no consistent gain, with scores remaining well below norms. (Recall that the extremely poor Word Attack performance at K is attributable to how the Spanish version of the Woodcock treated raw Word Attack scores of 0, which resulted automatically when children scored below criterion in Letter–Word. If the literacy data are excluded at K, where they have questionable face validity, then the univariate Grade effect for Word Attack becomes non-significant, indicating the Grade effect in Word Attack was caused solely by the anomalously low means at K. The univariate Grade effects for the other literacy tests remained significant when the K data were excluded.) The tests of writing both showed decreasing standard scores across Grade. Among the tests of oral language, TVIP and Verbal Analogies did not show substantial change, Oral Vocabulary showed a drop after K, and Picture Vocabulary showed a slow climb across Grade from a large deficit in K.

Instructional Method in the School

The main effect of IMS was significant ($p < 0.0001$) as was the IMS × Test interaction ($p < 0.0001$). This was carried by significant partial interactions of IMS for all contrasts *except* those of (1) TVIP vs the Woodcock-Muñoz tests of oral language, and (2) Verbal Analogies vs Oral Vocabulary (other

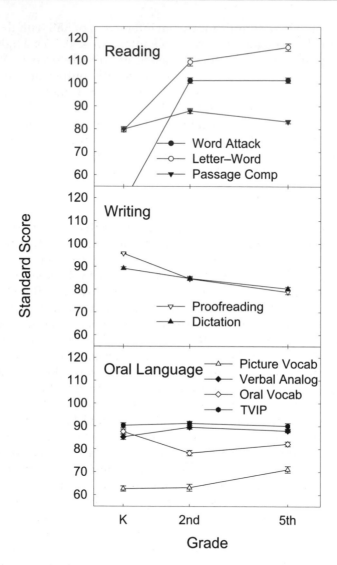

Figure 5.2 Standard score on each Spanish subtest, by Grade. Data points represent unweighted means, and error bars represent standard errors

$ps < 0.01$). Figure 5.3 illustrates these effects. Children in Two-way education significantly outperformed those in English Immersion in every test but Verbal Analogies (other $ps < 0.0001$). The effect was especially large

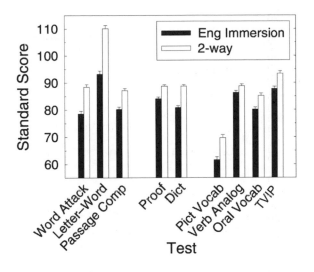

Figure 5.3 Standard score on each Spanish subtest, by IMS. Bars represent unweighted means, and error bars represent standard errors

for Word Attack and Letter–Word (9.9 and 16.9 point differences, respectively). The advantage of Two-way education in univariate evaluations of each literacy subtest remained significant when the K data were excluded.

The main effect of IMS and the IMS × Test interaction should be interpreted in the context of their interactions with Grade, illustrated in Figure 5.4. Specifically, the Grade × IMS interaction was significant ($p < 0.0001$) as was the Grade × IMS × Test interaction ($p < 0.0001$). The three-way interaction was carried by a significant partial interaction of Grade × IMS with the contrast of (1) reading vs writing ($p < 0.01$) and (2) Letter–Word and Word Attack vs Passage Comprehension ($p < 0.0001$). In univariate follow-ups, the Grade × IMS effect was significant for all but Passage Comprehension and Picture Vocabulary tests (other $ps < 0.05$). For Word Attack and Letter–Word, children in Two-way education started out even with those in English Immersion programs, but jumped far ahead by 2nd grade (difference of 15.0 and 25.3 points, respectively), maintaining the large advantage in 5th grade (difference of 15.3 and 22.7 points, respectively). For these two tests, both groups started out below norms in K (though recall the explanation for the anomalous Word Attack scores); in 2nd and 5th grade, the English Immersion group remained below norms, but the Two-way group exceeded norms. In the writing tests (Proofreading and Dictation), both groups remained below norms, but the children in English Immersion

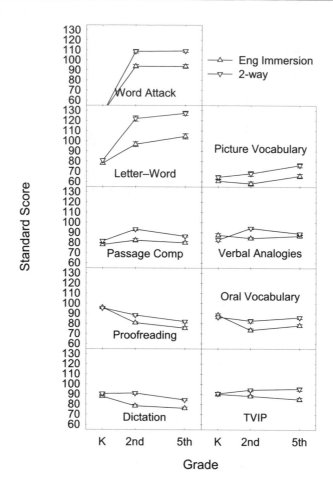

Figure 5.4 Standard score on each Spanish subtest, by Grade and IMS. Data points represent unweighted means, and error bars represent standard errors

slipped farther behind than those in Two-way education (the average gap between English Immersion and Two-way being 10.1 points in 2nd grade and 7.3 points in 5th grade). In the tests of oral language as well, children in both groups remained below norms, though the difference between English Immersion and Two-way children widened for children beyond K: in K, there was a 0.5 point difference favoring those in English Immersion, but in 2nd and 5th grade, there was an average difference of 8.8 and 7.8 points, respectively, favoring those in Two-way education.

Language Spoken at Home

The main of effect of LSH was significant ($p < 0.0001$) as was the LSH ×
Test interaction ($p < 0.0001$). This was carried by significant partial interactions of LSH with the contrast of (1) oral language vs literacy ($p < 0.0001$), (2)
Picture Vocabulary vs Verbal Analogies and Oral Vocabulary ($p < 0.0001$),
and (3) Verbal Analogies vs Oral Vocabulary ($p < 0.001$). Figure 5.5 illustrates these effects. Bilinguals with OSH outperformed those in with ESH.
To clarify the demographic difference between the two LSH groups, recall
that a requirement for inclusion in the OSH group was that the parents
report speaking only Spanish at home at least through K age. Thus, mixing
of languages may have occurred in the homes of children in the OSH group
after K.

As the partial interactions indicate, the tendency for children in the OSH
group to outperform those in the ESH group was strongest in tests of oral
language (7.3 point advantage, averaged across the four oral-language tests).
This was especially true for Picture Vocabulary, where those with OSH held
a 12.6 point advantage. In univariate follow-ups, the advantage for children
in the OSH group was statistically reliable for three of four oral language
tests: Picture Vocabulary, Oral Vocabulary, and TVIP ($ps < 0.0001$). Among
literacy tests, the effect was statistically reliable only for Passage Compre-

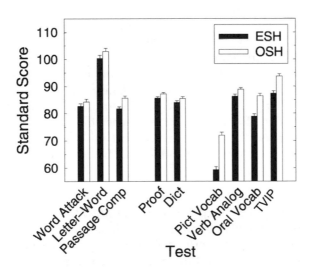

Figure 5.5 Standard score on each Spanish subtest, by LSH. Bars represent
unweighted means, and error bars represent standard errors

hension ($p < 0.01$), though even that effect was rendered non-significant when the K data were excluded on the grounds of poor face validity.

First Language Tested

As with the English data there was a small First Language Tested × Test interaction ($p < 0.005$). The First Language Tested × Test interaction was carried by a partial interaction of the First Language Tested factor with the contrast of Letter–Word and Word Attack vs Passage Comprehension ($p < 0.05$), though only for Verbal Analogies did the univariate follow-ups show a significant effect of First Language Tested ($p < 0.01$). There tended to be an advantage to being tested first in English, but the advantage depended on the test. Some tests showed little or no advantage, and the largest advantage was 4.3 points (for Letter–Word, but $p > 0.07$). The effect for Verbal Analogies was 3.2 points.

In the case of both Spanish and English testing, being tested in English first carried a small advantage on some of the tests. The reason for this outcome is unclear. It may be that English-first testing primed Spanish performance while Spanish-first testing did not have that effect or even led to boredom or fatigue for English tests. Perhaps both practice/priming and fatigue played roles in test performance, but to different extents for the different languages. The difference could also be sociological. English appears to be the language with the greater status even among small children, and they may have attached more importance to the tasks performed in English first and less importance to the tasks performed in Spanish first. In any case the effects of test order were relatively small and not consistent across tests.

There was also a First Language Tested × Grade × Test interaction, ($p < 0.007$). There were no significant partial interactions of First Language Tested × Grade with any 1-df contrast involving Test. Univariate follow-ups revealed a significant First Language Tested × Grade interaction for Passage Comprehension ($p < 0.05$) that disappeared ($p > 0.88$) when the K data were excluded on the grounds of poor face validity. In any event, the First Language Tested × Grade × Test interaction was small and will not be discussed further.

Discussion

The complex role of SES in Spanish competency

The role of SES in Spanish performance differed from that in English. In standardized tests of English performance, SES had a large influence, with High SES children outscoring Low SES children, especially in oral language (Chapter 4). In Spanish, no main effect of SES was found, but High SES children generally outscored Low SES children on reading and writing measures. However, in Spanish, instead of this advantage being magnified in oral language as it was in English, two of four tests (Picture Vocabulary and Oral Vocabulary) showed strong opposite effects, i.e. Low SES children outperformed High SES children. This reversal may reflect a difference in linguistic environment for Low SES vs High SES homes in cases where Spanish was reported as the only language spoken at home. Low SES children whose parents reported that they spoke only Spanish at home (OSH) may have received less English input than High SES children whose parents reported OSH, for the High SES parents may have been more likely to speak only Spanish at home by choice, rather than by necessity. OSH/Low SES families may have spoken Spanish to their children because it was the only language in which they were fluent. Clear support for this possibility is found in the parent report data. High SES/OSH parents reported much greater competency in English (about 2.5 on a three-point scale) than Low SES/OSH parents (about 1.5 on the same scale) as seen in Chapter 2, Table 2.4.

Accordingly the Low SES parents may have naturally restricted their children's exposure to English language media (TV, radio and videos) and conversation because they did not themselves understand English well. Given the parents' low English proficiency, the language environment of the child was presumably heavily Spanish. On the other hand, more English exposure may have occurred from English media and conversation in homes where English was understood with facility (namely in High SES/OSH). Thus the Low SES advantage for oral Spanish language may have been the product of time on task in the home. Low SES children may have been exposed to more Spanish than their High SES counterparts with OSH. This effect contrasts, however, with the results on the standardized tests in English, where time on task appeared to have had relatively discernible effects at K but little or no effect for older children.

The critical role of IMS in Spanish language attainment

This study collected data from children in English Immersion and Two-way schools carefully matched on demographic characteristics, thus allowing, as close as feasible, an approximation to an experimental test of the effect of IMS. In particular, because neighborhood schools were utilized, the study does not suffer from problems of subject self-selection that complicate the interpretation of the important Canadian studies on effects of bilingual education (see e.g. Lambert & Tucker, 1972; Swain, 1979). Recall from Chapter 4 that in English, bilinguals in English Immersion programs tended to outperform those in Two-way programs, especially in oral language, but that this effect was nullified or reversed in simple reading tests in English (Letter–Word and Word Attack). Furthermore, the disadvantages experienced by children in Two-way programs dissipated in the later grades, presumably because any effect of greater English exposure for the children in English Immersion in K was nullified over time.

The results in Spanish were quite different. Here, children in Two-way education programs outperformed those in English Immersion on a variety of tests, and by amounts that were much larger at 2nd and 5th grade than at K, suggesting that the greater Spanish-language exposure in school assisted the Two-way children. Consistent with the English-language results, the advantage of Two-way children was especially large for Letter–Word and Word Attack (persisting, importantly, when the questionable K literacy data were excluded). These tests of basic reading seem to have measured skills that readily transferred across languages. This point is addressed further in Chapter 6 where interrelationships among test scores and individual differences are examined.

Although scores on most tests were very similar at K for children in the two program types, children in English Immersion programs fell behind those in Two-way programs for Spanish-language by 2nd grade, and tended to remain far behind in 5th grade. This effect is unsurprising, and can be regarded as an indication that Spanish instruction was much more effective in the Two-way schools in the current study. Thus Two-way instruction had a clear and convincing advantage over English Immersion for Spanish language and literacy even though English Immersion was supplemented with a Spanish language study period (about 10% of the school day) and students received continued support for Spanish at home.

The magnitude of the advantage held by Two-way students in Spanish is notable. In contrast to the English language and literacy outcomes, where all differences were minimal by 5th grade, the scores in Spanish language and literacy suggest clear and educationally important differences by 5th grade. Averaging across all the tests at 5th grade, the Two-way children were ahead of their English Immersion counterparts by about 10 points (or two-thirds of a standard deviation) on the Spanish tests. For the oral language tests, the 5th grade Two-way children were ahead by more than half a standard deviation, a difference that was more than three times as large as the statistically non-reliable difference favoring English Immersion children on English oral language tests. For literacy tests, the difference was even greater than on oral language tests, favoring the Two-way children in Spanish (by nearly 12 points, or ¾ of a standard deviation). While no important advantage occurred on the standardized tests in English for children in English Immersion, there was a substantial advantage on the standardized tests in Spanish for children in Two-way programs.

LSH strongly affects Spanish language and literacy

When tested in Spanish, bilinguals with OSH outperformed (by 4.4

points) those with ESH, especially on tests of oral language (by 7.25 points). We attribute this effect, which complements that observed in English (Chapter 4), to the lower exposure to Spanish by those children with ESH. Our findings add to previous results that highlighted the importance of LSH for English-language performance (Dulay & Burt, 1978; Zappert & Cruz, 1977). Not surprisingly, time of exposure in the home to the language being learned seems to be an important factor in attaining oral competence at least under some circumstances. At the same time the effect of time of exposure is complicated and appears commonly to wane as children grow up and progress through school.

Lack of the hypothesized 4-way interaction among IMS, SES, LSH, and Grade

As with the data on English attainment, the hypothesized interaction did not occur. At the outset of the project it was hypothesized that children from High SES and with ESH might profit most from Two-way education. Conversely it was posited that children from Low SES homes with OSH would profit least in Two-way schools. For these children the added burdens of English learning might have been expected to subtract from Spanish achievement.

In fact, the data suggested that children from Low SES homes where only Spanish was spoken may have profited most in Spanish from Two-way schools. By 5th grade, the Low SES children with OSH were more than three points ahead of their High SES counterparts with ESH. While the difference was small and not statistically reliable, it went in the opposite direction of the original hypothesis.

Monolingual/bilingual comparisons

The study conducted here included no monolingual Spanish comparison group for the standardized tests. However, the tests themselves provide norms for monolingual Spanish speakers. The standardized scores have a mean for the norming sample of 100 and a standard deviation of 15. Based on these values as reference points, it can be said that at K, the children in the Miami sample began school far behind norming samples in Spanish (by 20 points or 1.33 standard deviations) across the nine tests. This condition of apparent disadvantage characterized all groups, even including the children with OSH (where the deficit was more than a full standard deviation at K). Even on such a straightforward task as Picture Vocabulary (a simple naming task), K children with OSH showed performance nearly two standard deviations below the mean for the norming sample.

This outcome suggests that the 'bilingual' children came to school with notable deficits in Spanish competency. They also seemed more inclined to speak English than Spanish to each other even in K (see Chapter 3). The results suggest that in spite of parental reports, the children had already begun the process of linguistic assimilation to English well before entry to school. The weakness in Spanish might further suggest, in some instances at least, discrepancies between the Spanish the children were exposed to and the varieties of Spanish upon which the test was based. It is perhaps important once again to emphasize that all the children selected for study were born in the USA. Children born in other countries, and having spoken only Spanish prior to entry to school, might have shown a substantially higher level of Spanish knowledge at K.

The tendency to begin school trailing with respect to Spanish norms does not of course mean that the children did not have significant Spanish knowledge in both IMS groups. Furthermore, Two-way education provided a springboard for the children to begin catching up with their monolingual peers. While the children were at nearly a 20-point disadvantage across all the Spanish tests at K, the deficit had been trimmed to only seven points (about half a standard deviation) by 5th grade for the Two-way children. The pattern was in fact quite different for oral language and literacy tests, however. While even the Two-way children continued to trail norms substantially in Spanish oral language at 5th grade (by nearly a standard deviation), their literacy performance was identical to that of the norming sample, i.e. they showed no deficits in literacy relative to monolingual Spanish children. The best performance was on the Letter–Word and Word Attack tests where the Two-way children substantially exceeded norms (by more than 1½ standard deviations on the Letter–Word test). It was suggested in Chapter 4 that the particularly good performance of Two-way children on these same tests in English (where they outperformed the monolingual comparison group by a small but non-reliable margin) may have been the result of training with the phonetically transparent orthography of Spanish. It can be reasoned that perhaps children learn phonics most easily when they have many examples of words to read that include simple mappings of orthography to speech sounds, as in Spanish. It was speculated in Chapter 4 that learning to read in the more simple orthography of Spanish might provide a bridge to the more difficult task of phonetic to orthographic mapping in English. The excellent performance of the Two-way children in Spanish, however, suggests that the bridge may work both ways. One possibility is that Spanish training may help with phonics learning initially, but perhaps at a later point, the more difficult tasks of English phonics provide a basis upon which to firm up the general capability for phonetic/orthographic mapping, a process that could improve performance across the board, even in Spanish.

Yet another possibility remains to explain the high performance of Two-way students in phonics. Bilingual children, and perhaps especially children who are schooled in two languages, may have a special kind of phonological awareness that is both nurtured by the special schooling, and at the same time contributes to reading performance. This special kind of phonological awareness may be a product of phonological translation, a natural process of language usage in bilingual speakers who are routinely required to translate names and other words across the two languages that they speak. In Chapter 11 the nature of phonological translation and its possible role in the results presented here is explored.

Aside from the phonics tests, all the Spanish tests revealed deficits with respect to the norming sample for both Two-way and English Immersion children. To interpret these deficits appropriately it is necessary to make reference to all the same issues that were raised with regard to similar deficits in English in Chapter 4. In particular, the distributed characteristic of language knowledge in bilingual children imposes limits on our ability to draw general conclusions about linguistic competence from comparisons of scores for bilingual children with those for any monolingual sample. The bilingual child may have knowledge coded in English that supplements the knowledge the same child has in Spanish (Umbel *et al.*, 1992). Since Spanish testing cannot reveal that knowledge, it is not possible to know from testing in one language how much linguistic knowledge the child possesses. Testing in English does not solve the problem because the same difficulties obtain in reverse, and there is no known way to scale a combination score that would represent the knowledge in both languages while still permitting a valid comparison with any monolingual reference group (Pearson, 1998).

Other issues that should be taken into account in the interpretation of the Spanish performance of the children (and may limit generalizability of the findings) concern the peer environments and language backgrounds of the children. On the one hand, it is not clear that many of the peers of the children had full native competence as speakers of Spanish (or of English, for that matter). It appears that many (perhaps the great majority) of the children in these schools were in the process of assimilating to English, and may have possessed, consequently, less than full native competency in both languages (at least for some portion of their elementary school years). This possible lack of native-speaking peers could have limited the children's learning of Spanish.

Further, the fact that the children selected were all born in the USA may have been significant in limiting their competency in Spanish. Finally, it is also difficult to know what effect the different varieties of Spanish in the home may have had.

Effects of the study variables on oral language versus literacy

SES had a complicated effect for Spanish tests: proficiency in literacy was associated with High SES, but proficiency in oral language was associated with Low SES. In a manner similar to the English data, LSH had the greatest effect on oral language, but unlike the English data (where children with ESH did better), better performance was found for children with OSH. IMS had the greatest effect on literacy in Spanish, with children educated in Two-way programs substantially outperforming their English Immersion peers on measures of literacy after K. This last observation is consistent with the interpretation that schooling (not language in the home) is the primary determiner of literacy skills (as opposed to oral skills). This interpretation is consistent with that noted for English tests in Chapter 4.

In English testing, the strongest effects of SES, IMS, and LSH were manifested in measures of oral language. High SES, English Immersion, and ESH all produced benefits in English oral language performance to a greater extent than in English literacy. Though the patterning of the results was somewhat different for Spanish vs English, it is interesting to note that in each case, study variables tended to affect oral language or literacy in different ways. This observation suggests that the domains of language and literacy measured in this study are distinct domains and that the subtests which measure language and literacy tend to cohere. As with the English data, home language exposure tends to influence oral proficiency while school exposure tends to influence literacy.

Summary

The results of the present chapter indicate a major role for Language Spoken at Home and Instructional Method in the Schools for development of Spanish literacy and oral language proficiency. Children with a firm home language foundation in Spanish and who are given the opportunity to continue content learning in Spanish through Two-way education, continue to develop their Spanish skills to a greater extent than a cohort of similar children entering schools employing an English Immersion approach. The current chapter provides provocative evidence that Two-way education sustains and nurtures bilingualism, and together with Chapter 4, that the cost is small or nil in terms of English language attainment by the 5th grade. Taken as a whole, performance in 5th grade, when both Spanish and English are considered, is superior for children educated in Two-way schools.

It is thought provoking, however, to note that as a whole the children who began this study in homes where English and Spanish or only Spanish was spoken, fell below norms for monolingual children in both Spanish and English regardless of their method of instruction in school. These results may indicate general advantages of monolingual children within the languages they speak. However, one cannot rule out the possibility that the demographics of the Miami schools may have also played a role in the below norm performance of the bilingual children, since there appeared to be few native peers available for either language in the bilingual schools (but see comments on peer issues in Chapter 10). The results also need to be considered in light of the distributed characteristic of linguistic knowledge in bilinguals. The current study was cross-sectional and extended only to 5th grade. In most areas children gained on monolingual norms as they advanced through the grades. Further study will be needed to track the trajectory of these children throughout their educational experience.

Chapter 6

Interdependence of Spanish and English Knowledge in Language and Literacy Among Bilingual Children

ALAN B. COBO-LEWIS, REBECCA E. EILERS,
BARBARA ZURER PEARSON and VIVIAN C. UMBEL

The Interdependence Hypothesis

From studies of anglophone students attending French immersion schools in Ontario, it has been suggested that the bilingual experience encourages students to engage in 'incipient contrastive linguistics', supporting skills in both languages and helping to build vocabulary (Lambert & Tucker, 1972). Such thoughts and observations underlie the *interdependence hypothesis* (Cummins, 1984), which posits a core of skills common to both languages, such that learning in one language can advance learning in the other.

There is some evidence in support of the interdependence hypothesis. For example, 5th graders from anglophone families in Ontario French Immersion programs used proportionately more complex and compound-complex sentences than their monolingual peers (Swain & Wesche, 1975). In 6th grade, the bilingual students showed enhanced sensitivity to number marking and other grammatical forms such as double negatives, past tense forms, and erroneous pronoun usage in English (Harley *et al.*, 1986). But such interdependence seemed not to occur across all realms, for these students exhibited no special lexical advantage in the knowledge of French-English cognates (Harley et al., 1986). Indeed 1st graders in such programs lagged behind monolinguals in vocabulary (e.g. Barik & Swain, 1975; Barik & Swain, 1976b; Polich, 1974; Swain & Barik, 1976), a finding consistent with vocabulary knowledge assessment of bilingual children in the present study (Chapters 4–5). This vocabulary lag may, however, have been more apparent than real. Pearson and colleagues (1995) have shown that, at least in some cases, 'total conceptual vocabulary' in bilingual children may equal or exceed that of monolinguals. To assess conceptual vocabulary it is necessary that knowledge in both languages be taken into consideration. Some concepts can be named in one language but not the other and vice versa. Vocabulary knowledge is clearly distributed across languages with conceptual cognates occupying only a portion of total vocabulary knowledge. Children learn vocabulary in one language to which they may have no access in the other.

It has been suggested that there might be a threshold effect in bilingualism, especially sequential bilingualism: according to this idea, lower levels of competence in the first language may be associated with disadvantages in education, and higher levels of competence in the first language may be needed in order for positive effects to accrue (Cummins, 1979). Based on this hypothesis, Harley *et al.* (1986) contrasted the English skills of bilingual students from anglophone families with high French achievement against those with lower French achievement matched on IQ. Assessment of longitudinal data revealed a tendency for the low-French-achievement group to lag behind the high-French-achievement group in English vocabulary, reference skills, and punctuation. The results suggest an interdependence in which high level skills in one language support skills in the other.

Group Effects and Individual Differences

The literature suggests that interdependence between a bilingual's two languages is conditional. It may depend on the type of skills being assessed, the child's age, as well as socio-economic and environmental factors that affect the child's linguistic and academic performance. In the present chapter we examine the extent to which English and Spanish skills cohere in oral language and literacy. Specifically, the comprehensive assessment undertaken under the Core Design (Figure 2.1) for bilingual students' language skills in both English and Spanish afforded the opportunity to examine interrelationships among skills in the two languages and to look at the nature of individual differences in bilingual children. The study allowed the refinement and evaluation of certain ideas set forth in Cummins' (1984) interdependence hypothesis. This chapter and its analyses focus on the nature of interdependence that may exist in a diverse set of bilingual language learners. Specifically, the chapter addresses the following questions:

(1) Did children tend to show strength in one language if they showed strength in the other (interdependence) or did achievement in one language drain resources from the second (subtractive bilingualism)? More generally, was there a relationship between performance in the two languages?

(2) Were there sub-domains of language or literacy that were correlated across languages and others that seemed independent across languages?
(3) Did the main study variables, SES, LSH and IMS, influence performance across the two languages equivalently or were their effects language-specific?

The methods of study are detailed in Chapters 2 and 4. The present chapter focuses upon correlational analyses of the data acquired for Chapters 4 and 5.

Analysis of Residualized Standard Scores

Our first approach was to focus on individual differences among bilingual children. In order not to confound this important within-group variation with the between-group variation that was the topic of Chapters 4 and 5, residualized standard scores were analyzed. That is, for each of the 18 English and Spanish standardized tests separately, each child's standard score was subtracted from the group mean corresponding to the child's membership in a combination of socio-economic status (SES) × Instructional Method in the School (IMS) × Language Spoken at Home (LSH) × Grade × First Language Tested. Table 6.1 presents the correlation coefficients among the residualized standard scores. This correlation matrix was subjected to principal components analysis. Three factors had eigenvalues greater than one, and together accounted for 61% of the variance. These factors were submitted to varimax rotation with Kaiser normalization. Table 6.2 presents the factor loadings.

The correlations address several questions of theoretical interest. Did children tend to excel in one language at the expense of the other (cf. the idea of 'subtractive' bilingualism, from Lambert (1977))? That is, were high scores in one language systematically associated with low scores in the other (negative correlations)? Alternatively, did children tend to show similar scores in both languages, thus excelling in both or in neither (positive correlations)? Or, did children perform in each language independently (no reliable correlation)? The principal components analysis revealed that the situation was more complicated (and more interesting) than these questions imply. Nevertheless, the following points were clear: when compared to their peers in the same educational and demographic settings, the children did not tend to excel in one language at the expense of the other, for Table 6.1 displays no negative correlation, and only three loadings in Table 6.2 were negative (none more extreme than –0.05).

Did children tend to excel in both languages or in neither language? This answer depended on the realm of language evaluated. The principal com-

Table 6.1. Correlation Coefficients Among the 18 Residualized Standard Scores of Bilingual Children

		Word Attack		Letter–Word		Passage Comp		Proofing		Dictation		Picture vocabulary		Verbal analogies		Oral vocabulary		PPVT/TVIP	
		Eng	Sp	Eng	Sp	Eng	Sp	Eng	Sp	Eng	Sp	Eng	Sp	Eng	Sp	Eng	Sp	Eng	Sp
Word Attack	English																		
	Spanish	0.53																	
Letter–Word	English	0.72	0.56																
	Spanish	0.65	0.67	0.68															
Passage Comprehension	English	0.58	0.33	0.59	0.49														
	Spanish	0.41	0.44	0.42	0.50	0.44													
Proofreading	English	0.57	0.42	0.59	0.52	0.53	0.43												
	Spanish	0.50	0.45	0.51	0.57	0.39	0.44	0.55											
Dictation	English	0.51	0.38	0.69	0.52	0.53	0.35	0.57	0.42										
	Spanish	0.55	0.52	0.61	0.68	0.50	0.48	0.49	0.56	0.57									
Picture Vocabulary	English	0.25	0.18	0.40	0.19	0.32	0.12	0.28	0.14	0.44	0.22								
	Spanish	0.18	0.28	0.21	0.35	0.16	0.28	0.12	0.35	0.19	0.42	0.10							
Verbal Analogies	English	0.27	0.20	0.33	0.26	0.36	0.19	0.37	0.29	0.39	0.28	0.43	0.09						
	Spanish	0.15	0.21	0.22	0.24	0.19	0.26	0.22	0.27	0.30	0.30	0.21	0.34	0.45					
Oral Vocabulary	English	0.31	0.21	0.43	0.29	0.40	0.18	0.35	0.24	0.44	0.37	0.53	0.14	0.52	0.34				
	Spanish	0.18	0.28	0.24	0.34	0.18	0.25	0.18	0.35	0.24	0.43	0.10	0.55	0.19	0.44	0.31			
PPVT/TVIP	English	0.24	0.17	0.35	0.22	0.31	0.19	0.30	0.19	0.37	0.25	0.60	0.13	0.40	0.24	0.48	0.18		
	Spanish	0.17	0.22	0.27	0.29	0.21	0.30	0.20	0.34	0.25	0.41	0.18	0.50	0.22	0.39	0.28	0.47	0.33	

Notes. $N = 704$, $df = 679$. Two-tailed $p < 0.05$ when $r > 0.08$, $p < 0.01$ when $r > 0.10$, $p < 0.001$ when $r > 0.13$, $p < 0.0001$ when $r > 0.15$.

Table 6.2 Factor loadings from varimax-rotated principal component analysis of bilinguals' residualized standard scores

		Factor 1	Factor 2	Factor 3
Word Attack	English	0.82		–0.01
	Spanish	0.71		
Letter–Word	English	0.79	0.35	
	Spanish	0.82		0.25
Passage Comprehension	English	0.64	0.37	
	Spanish	0.61		0.28
Proofreading	English	0.70	0.32	
	Spanish	0.66		0.34
Dictation	English	0.61	0.48	
	Spanish	0.70		0.40
Picture Vocabulary	English		0.80	–0.00
	Spanish		–0.05	0.78
Verbal Analogies	English		0.69	
	Spanish		0.38	0.61
Oral Vocabulary	English		0.74	
	Spanish			0.78
PPVT/TVIP	English		0.74	
	Spanish			0.72
% of variance accounted for		29	17	15

Note. Factors were extracted whose eigenvalues were >1. Only loadings >0.25 or <0 are shown. Loadings >0.6 are set in boldface italic

ponents analysis revealed that literacy in this research tended to be a cross-language skill. Factor 1 can be interpreted as a literacy factor, on which all tests of reading and writing (Word Attack, Letter–Word, Passage Comprehension, Proofing, and Dictation) loaded highly, regardless of language. Thus, literacy skills did seem to be interdependent, as scores tended to covary in the two languages for individual children.

Oral language skills, on the other hand, tended not to cross the language boundary. Factor 2 can be interpreted as an English-specific language factor. The four oral language tests loaded highly on Factor 2, but only in English. Factor 3 can be interpreted as a Spanish-specific factor. The four oral language tests loaded highly on Factor 3, but only in Spanish. The oral language tests did not load on the cross-language Factor 1. The literacy tests other than Word Attack also loaded on the language-specific factors, though only moderately. In fact, the loadings of the literacy tests on the language-specific factors were of comparable magnitude to the loading of the Verbal Analogies Spanish test on the English-specific language factor. If attention is confined to loadings > 0.6 (boldface italic entries in Table 6.2), then Factors 2 and 3 are seen to represent primarily oral language. The one literacy test that loaded above 0.39 on Factors 2 and 3 was Dictation, which was the literacy test with greatest reliance on oral language skills.

Though the primarily oral language factors were language-specific, note that subtests from the opposite language did *not* load negatively on these factors: from the point of view of individual differences, oral language skills did not seem to be antagonistic between languages, though they did seem to be largely independent.

Another possibility to consider is that interdependence might occur in one circumstance of learning but not in another. To evaluate this possibility, the principal components analysis was repeated separately for students in English Immersion and Two-way education programs. In each of these cases, the results were essentially the same, with the corresponding factor loadings in the two groups correlating at no lower than 0.96. Furthermore, the principal components analysis was repeated separately for students with only Spanish at home (OSH), and those with both English and Spanish at home (ESH). Again, the results were essentially the same, with the corresponding factor loadings in the two groups correlating at no lower than 0.94.

In Chapters 4 and 5 it was noted that some of the literacy tests at Kindergarten (K) have questionable face validity and poor psychometric properties. The Word Attack test was particularly problematical, as its K properties differed markedly in English and Spanish. In analysis of residualized scores, this difficulty was curbed by the fact that residualized scores remove between-group differences in group means. Nevertheless, to verify that our conclusions did not depend on the K data, the main principal components analysis of residualized scores was redone after deleting the K data. The re-analysis essentially replicated the factor loadings of Table 6.2. The loadings for each of the three extracted factors correlated with the loadings on the corresponding factor in the original analysis at no lower than 0.98.

Direct Analysis of Standard Scores

The analyses of residualized scores made it possible to address two of the three questions posed for this chapter. But because residualized scores remove between-group differences, another approach was necessary to address the third question: whether the main study variables influenced performance across both languages equivalently or whether their effects were language-specific. Consequently, the correlations among unresidualized standard scores were also analyzed for the 18 English and Spanish standardized tests. Because these correlations necessarily confound between- and within-group variation, the resulting analyses are not independent of those in Chapters 4 and 5.

Recall that the literacy tests had questionable face validity and poor psychometric properties at K, and that the Word Attack test was particularly problematical, as its K properties differed markedly in English and Spanish (see Chapter 5). In the present analysis of unresidualized scores, the difficulty was manifest, as unresidualized scores maintained group differences and preserved what were essentially artifactual differences in English and Spanish Word Attack means at K. For this reason, the primary analysis of unresidualized scores excluded the K data. (For the sake of completeness, the unresidualized analyses with K data included were also run, and these analyses are referred to below where appropriate.)

Table 6.3 presents the correlation coefficients among the bilingual 2nd and 5th graders' standard scores for the 18 English and Spanish tests. The correlation matrix was submitted to principal components analysis. Three factors had eigenvalues greater than one, and together accounted for 70% of the variance. These factors were submitted to varimax rotation with Kaiser normalization. Table 6.4 presents the factor loadings. The same three factors extracted in the analyses of residualized scores were extracted in Table 6.4's analysis of unresidualized scores. As in the previous analyses, a Literacy factor crossed the language barrier, but oral language tests loaded only on language-specific factors. Whereas Word Attack did not load on the language-specific factors in the analysis of residualized scores, it loaded slightly on the language-specific factors in the analysis of unresidualized scores.

When the present analysis of unresidualized scores was repeated without excluding the K data (where it is clear that important anomalies occurred in psychometric properties of some of the tests), four factors were extracted. The two language-specific oral language factors persisted in representing primarily oral language for all four tests, but the cross-language literacy factor broke down into two cross-language factors, on one of which the Letter–Word and Word Attack tests loaded highly in each language, and on the other of which the other literacy tests loaded highly in each language. We attribute this breakdown of the literacy factor to problems with the poor psychometric properties of the tests especially at K and especially on the Word Attack test (which correlated with Letter–Word more highly than with any other test). Of course the fact that the literacy tests segregated

Table 6.3 Correlation coefficients among the standard scores for the 18 tests of English and Spanish performance in bilingual 2nd and 5th graders

		Word Attack		Letter-Word		Passage Comp		Proofing		Dictation		Picture vocabulary		Verbal analogies		Oral vocabulary		PPVT/TVIP	
		Eng	Sp	Eng	Sp	Eng	Sp	Eng	Sp	Eng	Sp	Eng	Sp	Eng	Sp	Eng	Sp	Eng	Sp
Word Attack	English																		
	Spanish	0.67																	
Letter–Word	English	0.81	0.68																
	Spanish	0.66	0.85	0.70															
Passage Comprehension	English	0.60	0.49	0.70	0.46														
	Spanish	0.54	0.71	0.62	0.73	0.55													
Proofreading	English	0.62	0.49	0.69	0.49	0.65	0.51												
	Spanish	0.49	0.59	0.52	0.61	0.44	0.61	0.48											
Dictation	English	0.60	0.47	0.68	0.47	0.72	0.52	0.72	0.49										
	Spanish	0.56	0.72	0.60	0.71	0.50	0.75	0.50	0.66	0.55									
Picture Vocabulary	English	0.35	0.15	0.45	0.12	0.46	0.12	0.43	0.07	0.43	0.16								
	Spanish	0.16	0.37	0.17	0.41	0.05	0.39	0.07	0.38	0.04	0.40	0.00							
Verbal Analogies	English	0.38	0.23	0.44	0.24	0.52	0.25	0.50	0.27	0.47	0.28	0.55	0.05						
	Spanish	0.26	0.39	0.32	0.44	0.34	0.49	0.34	0.47	0.32	0.50	0.18	0.42	0.38					
Oral Vocabulary	English	0.42	0.25	0.52	0.27	0.55	0.26	0.48	0.19	0.45	0.30	0.63	0.06	0.57	0.31				
	Spanish	0.18	0.39	0.22	0.43	0.11	0.45	0.14	0.43	0.09	0.43	–0.03	0.67	0.11	0.51	0.15			
PPVT/TVIP	English	0.36	0.21	0.46	0.24	0.46	0.20	0.43	0.12	0.39	0.25	0.71	0.09	0.53	0.24	0.64	0.09		
	Spanish	0.21	0.37	0.29	0.39	0.21	0.44	0.21	0.46	0.19	0.50	0.12	0.52	0.17	0.45	0.24	0.51	0.25	

Notes. $N = 453$, $df = 451$. Two-tailed $p < 0.05$ when $|r| > 0.09$, $p < 0.01$ when $|r| > 0.12$, $p < 0.001$ when $|r| > 0.15$, $p < 0.0001$ when $|r| > 0.18$

Table 6.4 Factor loadings from varimax rotated principal component analysis of bilingual 2nd and 5th graders' standard scores

		Factor 1	*Factor 2*	*Factor 3*
Word Attack	English	*0.79*	0.30	
	Spanish	*0.81*		0.34
Letter–Word	English	*0.79*	0.42	
	Spanish	*0.79*		0.40
Passage Comprehension	English	*0.65*	0.53	–0.00
	Spanish	*0.75*		0.43
Proofreading	English	*0.67*	0.48	
	Spanish	*0.66*		0.44
Dictation	English	*0.71*	0.45	–0.04
	Spanish	*0.72*		0.46
Picture Vocabulary	English		*0.86*	–0.02
	Spanish		–0.05	*0.83*
Verbal Analogies	English		*0.74*	
	Spanish	0.27	0.27	*0.64*
Oral Vocabulary	English		*0.81*	
	Spanish		–0.01	*0.83*
PPVT	English		*0.83*	
	Spanish			*0.74*
% of variance accounted for		31	21	18

Note. Factors were extracted whose eigenvalues were >1. Only loadings >0.25 or <0 are shown. Loadings >0.6 are set in boldface italic

in this way with regard to cross-language effect does not change the primary conclusion that is justified in all the analyses of residualized and unresidualized scores with and without including the K data: literacy skills crossed the language barrier in every case, whereas oral language skills were language-specific in every case. Thus, the extraction of cross-language literacy factor(s) and within-language oral factors was robust with respect to the mode of analysis.

The results in Table 6.3 include only a single negative correlation, and Table 6.4 displays only a few negative factor loadings, none with magnitude beyond –0.05. However, because the results of Tables 6.3 and 6.4 include between-group as well as within-group variation, it is worthwhile to take the opportunity to search for targeted between-group differences.

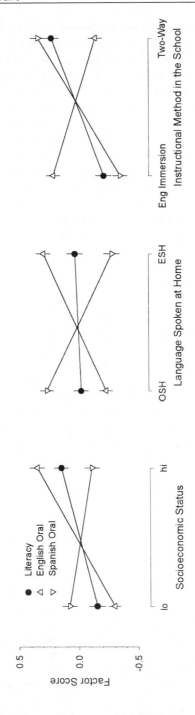

Figure 6.1 Unweighted mean factor scores on the three factors of Table 6.4's principal components analysis, by SES, Language Spoken at Home, and Instructional Method in the School. Error bars represent standard errors of the unweighted means

To accomplish this, factor scores for the three factors of Table 6.4 were calculated for each bilingual child, and the effects of SES, LSH, and IMS on these factor scores were examined. Figure 6.1 presents the results.

The first panel reveals that High SES children outperformed Low SES children in literacy, and this advantage obtained in *both* languages. (In an analysis where the K data were not excluded and two literacy factors were therefore extracted, the results were similar, but with SES having more influence on the phonics factor [Word Attack and Letter-Word] than on the other literacy factor.) Such an importance of SES is unsurprising, and was discussed in Chapters 4 and 5. High SES children also outperformed Low SES children in English oral language, though the High SES advantage was twice as large as for literacy. This difference is also unsurprising, and was discussed in Chapter 4. But in Spanish oral language, Low SES children outperformed High SES children. As in Chapter 5, we interpret the better performance of Low SES children in Spanish as reflecting more exposure to Spanish in the home, as parents in the Low SES households reported lower competency in English than in High SES households and may have spoken Spanish more frequently than in High SES households.

The second panel of Figure 6.1 reveals that LSH had little or no effect on literacy, and again the pattern was similar for the two languages. LSH did affect oral language, however, and the effects were language-specific. In English oral language, bilinguals with ESH outscored those with OSH. An effect of opposite direction and similar magnitude obtained in Spanish oral language: bilinguals with OSH outscored those with ESH. (In an analysis where the K data were not excluded and two literacy factors were therefore extracted, bilinguals with OSH showed a slight advantage on the phonics factor, and a very slight disadvantage on the other literacy factor, but even these LSH effects were slight. The LSH effect for the phonics factor was less than one-third, and the LSH for the other literacy factor was less than one-sixth of the LSH effects on oral language.) These results are also consistent with the interpretation that greater input levels in a language are correlated with higher levels of performance.

The third panel of Figure 6.1 reveals that bilinguals in Two-way educational programs outperformed those in English Immersion programs in literacy. (In an analysis where the K data were not excluded and two literacy factors were therefore extracted, this difference persisted, but was of larger magnitude for the phonics factor than for the other literacy factor.) Compared to their bilingual peers in English Immersion programs, bilinguals in Two-way educational programs performed more poorly in English oral language and performed better in Spanish oral language. Since Two-way programs exposed children to more Spanish and less English than English Immersion programs, it appears that this factor too is consistent with the interpretation that greater input levels were correlated with higher levels of performance.

General Discussion

Why might literacy skills have cohered across languages while oral language achievement seemed largely independent across languages? Part of the explanation may lie in the fact that reading and writing skills are dependent on language but not vice versa. Children learn to *speak* in the home and community. Reading and writing, on the other hand, are usually school-learned skills and as such depend on instruction rather than exposure to models of language at home. Different children have different levels of exposure to Spanish and English at home and through community participation, while they may have relatively more equal access to reading and writing through school instruction. School instruction may, then, create a natural tie between literacy in the two languages of bilingual children.

Another possibility suggested by Gathercole (see Chapters 8–10) with citations to the work of Bialystok and colleagues is that while oral skills are 'linguistic' in nature, literacy skills are 'metalinguistic' (Bialystok, 1991; Bialystok, 1999, Bialystok & Herman, 1999). In order to read, one must address language explicitly and form substantial awareness of its patterns. This process appears to have many general and language-independent characteristics. As a result, it may be that literacy in one language naturally tends to produce capabilities that transfer well to literacy acquisition in another. Linguistic capabilities, such as those manifest in oral language results, on the other hand, may be more language-specific and less subject to explicit language awareness.

In order to gain a perspective on whether the Core Design variables (Figure 2.1) influenced performance in the two languages equivalently, it is instructive to take account of results in Chapters 4 and 5, where results for all three main variables, IMS, LSH, and SES, are segregated by oral vs literacy outcomes. For IMS, Two-way education and English Immersion had different patterns of effect for literacy and oral language. Whereas IMS tended to have broadly similar literacy effects between English and Spanish, it had opposite oral language effects between English and Spanish (contrast the literacy and oral language scores in Figure 4.5 to those in Figure 5.3). Because oral language tests rely heavily on vocabulary, the contrasting effects of IMS on oral language could be explained by time on task (English Immersion children doing better in English, Two-way children better in Spanish). But the Two-way advantage in Spanish was larger than the English Immersion advantage in English. This could reflect a 'critical mass' or 'threshold' (Cummins, 1979; Marchman & Bates, 1994) effect where even

Two-way education provided sufficient English input to mitigate time on task effects, but where English Immersion supplied insufficient Spanish input to attain critical mass of input. The effects could also reflect greater exposure to setting-specific, especially school-relevant, vocabulary in Spanish for the children in Two-way education.

Two-way education affected literacy scores in the two languages in somewhat different ways with apparently larger positive effects in Spanish than in English. The frequency of input/critical mass explanation could also account for this imbalance. In addition, however, it may be that because Spanish is orthographically more regular than English, instruction in Spanish may have aided students in basic reading skills of the sort assessed by the Word Attack and Letter–Word tests. In this case, Two-way education might have had a strong positive effect on reading skills in Spanish (with its straightforward orthographic to phonetic mapping), but might have had a smaller effect on reading skills in English (with its complicated orthographic to phonetic mapping). Further support for this hypothesis might be obtained through evaluation of older subjects, for whom more sophisticated skills could be assessed. But even with the 2nd graders in the present work, this effect was observed in the Passage Comprehension scores: students in Two-way education dramatically outscored those in English Immersion in Spanish (see Chapter 5, Figure 5.4), and showed little or no difference in English (see Chapter 4, Figure 4.6). Considering 5th graders, for whom Passage Comprehension assessed more sophisticated skills, the same general pattern persisted (see Chapter 4, Figure 4.6, and Chapter 5, Figure 5.4).

Like IMS, LSH also had opposite oral language effects between English and Spanish tests (ESH better for English, OSH better for Spanish), and the hypotheses we propose to explain these effects are the same – time on task and/or setting specificity. But unlike IMS, LSH had opposite effects for the two languages in reading and writing. Note, however, that the LSH effects in reading and writing were smaller than the effects in oral language (see Chapter 4, Figure 4.7, and Chapter 5, Figure 5.5). Thus, time on task and/or setting specificity seemed to have a larger effect on oral language than on literacy.

The Spanish-language SES effects on oral language were also different from those obtained in literacy. In Spanish, Low SES children actually outscored High SES children on two of four oral language tests, but High SES children outscored Low SES children on all five tests of reading and writing (see Chapter 5, Figure 5.1). In contrast, in English, SES effects were consistent everywhere: High SES children always outscored Low SES children in English (see Chapter 4, Figure 4.2). Again, the results suggest that reading and writing were more influenced by school learning (or perhaps by the metalinguistic nature of literacy) than by other factors, and as a result, normal SES expectations obtained, i.e. High SES children generally outperformed Low SES children on these school-based tasks. In oral language, time on task in the language seemed to be more important and LSH seemed to be the determining factor for proficiency. However, the High SES advantage in English oral language exceeded the Low SES advantage in Spanish oral language (see first panel of Figure 6.1). This suggests that a possible role for typical SES influences should not be neglected even in oral language. In English oral language, the typical High SES advantage may have reinforced the apparent time-on-task effect of SES (associated with the fact that parents in Low SES homes reported lower competency in English), but in Spanish oral language, a High SES advantage apparently reduced but did not nullify the advantage of Low SES, where parents reported they had greater competency in Spanish (see Chapter 4, p. 83, section entitled SES × LSH).

Thus, LSH, IMS, and SES all showed substantial cross-language differences in oral language. In LSH and IMS, in particular, there was some trade-off between languages: more exposure to English (ESH and English Immersion conditions) improved English oral language, apparently at the expense of Spanish vocabulary. In the familiar standard score scale of Chapters 4 and 5, bilinguals with OSH scored an average of 7.4 points below those with ESH in English oral language, and scored an average of 7.3 above in Spanish oral language. Bilinguals in Two-way education scored an average of 3.1 points below (2.3 points below at 5th grade) those in English Immersion in English oral language, and scored an average of 5.3 points above (8 points above at 5th grade) in Spanish oral language.

Like the group effects seen in ANOVA from Chapters 4 and 5, the correlational results reflecting individual differences also failed to show cross-language coherence for oral language, either positive or negative, as seen in the principal components analysis of residualized standard scores (see Table 6.2). In fact, the low magnitude correlations for the individual differences evidently overwhelmed the time on task effects for LSH and IMS, as no negative association appeared even in the principal components analysis of unresidualized scores (see Table 6.4), and only a single cross-language correlation among unresidualized scores was negative at all (−0.05, see Table 6.3).

Though effects of LSH, IMS, and SES all showed substantial cross-language differences in oral language, they showed smaller cross-language differences in literacy. And for each language, IMS had somewhat different effects in reading than in writing. The latter phenomenon may offer an additional explanation for the separation between the tests of basic reading and the other literacy tests that occurred in the principal components analysis of unresidualized standard scores when the K data were included. But, neither phenomenon can explain the cross-language coherence of all five literacy scores in the principal components analysis of residualized standard scores (see Table 6.2). Thus, reading and writing appeared to be cross-language interdependent skills, both in their group effects and in their individual differences (Bialystok & Herman, 1999). Oral language skills, on the other hand, appeared to be independent in that proficiency could not be predicted across languages based on any of the data obtained in this research using standardized tests.

Perhaps the most significant conclusion that can be drawn from the correlational analyses is that there is no evidence for these children of any negative effects of competency in one language upon competency in the other. Furthermore, for literacy tests, there was positive interdependence. While such interdependence cannot prove that competence in one language fosters competence in the other, it does indicate that for these children there is no tendency for competence in one to inhibit competence in the other.

Summary

The principal component analyses lend support to the interdependence hypothesis (Cummins, 1984) with this important caveat: reading and writing skills were highly related between English and Spanish, but oral language skills were largely unrelated at the level of individual subjects. The results in oral language were consistent with those of Harley *et al.* (1986), who found little cross-language relationship in vocabulary. LSH, IMS and SES all showed substantial cross-language differences in oral language.

Part 3

Probe Studies on Complex Language Capabilities

Chapter 7

Narrative Competence among Monolingual and Bilingual School Children in Miami

BARBARA ZURER PEARSON

The narrative syntax project was designed to evaluate language and literacy development with a single task encompassing both domains. For this purpose, the children were asked to create a story, an extended discourse, which could be evaluated as a whole, but also as the sum of its parts. Thus, the children could demonstrate their strengths and weaknesses at several different levels at once.

Indeed, much of the language development in the ages between 5 and 10 is thought to take place at the level above the individual sentence (Karmiloff-Smith, 1986). That is, children by age 5 have demonstrated the use of the major syntactic structures of their language, but continue to expand the range and complexity of the uses to which those structures are put (Chomsky, 1969; Slobin, 1973). Perhaps the most important linguistic development in the early school period, then, is children's growing ability to create extended texts. They move from the local level of organizing words within a sentence to a global level, where they must organize sentences into a coherent, hierarchical discourse.

This development coincides at the start of school with learning to read. The child, through reading, is increasingly involved with texts longer than the typical conversational turn, and by the end of the elementary school period is expected to be able to write paragraph-length expositions and stories (Hunt, 1977). The sentences in those paragraphs individually contribute information to the whole, but they must also serve to direct the flow of information smoothly and cohesively across sentences. The linguistic devices which accomplish this task for the reader/writer are not usually new forms, but are recruited from the forms already at the child's disposal (Berman & Slobin, 1994) – notably the pronouns, determiners, adverbs, and conjunctions that can express the temporal, causal, and anaphoric connections between individual phrases.

As attested by the growth in the length of school texts in all subjects as children move up through the grades, the ability to work with longer and longer passages is a key element in academic success. To understand long texts, children must be able to interpret both the 'content' words and the 'function' words. Content words, roughly the nouns and verbs, provide 'information' on topics – 'steel', 'primate', 'evaporates'. Function words convey the relationships between content words, for example the prepositions 'to', 'without', or 'by' – something. Function words show the relations between propositions about the content words. They also signal which words give new information, say with an indefinite article or a full noun phrase, and which words must be interpreted anaphorically, that is with respect to what has come before in the passage. So, knowledge of function words and the grammatical structures they play a role in can be as crucial to understanding and creating texts as the content words that define the subject matter.

Children's ability to interpret these linguistic devices may be tested in reading through standard passage comprehension tasks (cf. Woodcock, 1991). In these tasks, some items are cloze-type questions which probe for a missing function word, thereby sending the child backward or forward in the passage to find the elements that constrain the options for that word. Even items which focus on a missing content word may require the reader to evaluate the relationships established by the conjunctions and prepositions present: ['Therefore, without _____, farmers must rely on wells.'] So typical passage comprehension scores are at least in part measures of children's ability to follow discourse markers embedded in texts.

Testing young children's literacy abilities productively, though, is more difficult. The mechanics of writing are still in the learning phase until middle elementary school, and so tests of children's early writing may underestimate their knowledge of how to structure a discourse. Fortunately, the oral genre of narrative has many features of written discourse (Chafe, 1980, 1982) and employs many of the same distinctive devices that will appear later in children's writing. Indeed, narrative development even at preschool has shown significant prediction of later literacy development (Snow & Dickinson, 1990; Torrance & Olson, 1984). Measurement of oral narrative ability, then, is a promising avenue for understanding children's growth in skills important for literacy.

Children from age 3 can generally be counted on to produce stories in response to a standard prompt. Their stories develop in interesting and measurable ways, especially from ages 5 to 10, in the creation of a unified plot structure, in the motivation of events through reference to internal states of the characters, and in the appreciation of the listener's needs for information which are different from the narrator's. From a discourse perspective, children's stories will provide increasingly more elements of the adult genre: especially, more setting of the scene, more problem-resolution sequences, and more complex and frequent narrator's comments on the action (Kemper, 1984). In terms of the development of discourse markers, children will show increasingly adequate contrast of indefinite and definite reference, less ambiguous pronoun reference, and more frequent and clearer expressions of emphasis (Kemper, 1984: 112). The patterns of that development have been explored in numerous studies, especially since Halliday and Hasan's (1976) groundbreaking work on cohesion. (See Berman & Slobin, 1994; Hedberg & Westby, 1993; Kemper, 1984; Peterson & McCabe, 1983, for syntheses of this literature.) Closely allied to discourse devices are advances with age in the narrative elements the children include in their stories. We see in Berman & Slobin (1994, chap. IIa) that older children's versions of their stories typically include more explicit references to cause and effect, more compound time referencing, and a more complex theory of other minds. So, simple stories like the 'Frog Story' used by Berman and Slobin, give children the opportunity to show evidence of their achievement of these cognitive developments known to be expanding during this age range.

At the same time, from a linguistic point of view, one can expect that as children approach age 10, their stories will become richer lexically and have more embedding syntactically (Karmiloff-Smith, 1986). The stories may contain more complex syntactic structures and more complex combinations of the structures. According to studies reviewed by Scott (1988: 60), post-modified noun-phrases, non-finite verbs, modal auxiliaries, and perfect tenses index increased complexity within clauses; across clauses, one sees an increase with age in the number of low-frequency conjunctions ('although', 'unless', etc.) and a greater density of syntactic units per sentence.

One goal in examining children's narratives, then, will be to evaluate the growth of discourse devices on the one hand, and on the other the specific linguistic structures which the extended narratives afford the opportunity to deploy. By separating the scoring of the stories into independent components and even subcomponents, we can examine the separate contribution of each element to more global measures of the children's growth. This is an especially useful framework for looking at stories from bilinguals, where greater dissociations between component language skills have been hypothesized to exist (Pearson *et al.*, 1996, October). It also provides an opportunity to isolate which elements appear to develop within the context of learning in a specific language, and which are tied to more general growth across languages (Cummins, 1984).

Using the full design at 2nd and 5th grades (Chapter 2), we could see which combinations of the study's factors – Lingualism, Socio-economic Status (SES), Instructional Method in School (IMS), Language Spoken at Home (LSH), and language of the story – are associated with greater or lesser growth in the two major dimensions outlined above. In addition, with stories in two languages from the same children, we were able to assess the degree to which growth in one language appeared to support or hinder the children's growth in the other language for the two domains of 'discourse' and 'language'.

The hypotheses to be tested were:

(1) Observed differences between bilinguals and monolinguals on a global measure of narrative ability in English will not be equally evidenced in the elements which make up the global measure.
(2) For bilinguals, Two-way instruction will enhance performance on narrative tasks in both languages.
(3) There will be a predictive relationship between narrative abilities children demonstrate in one language on comparable abilities in the other language.

Methods

Participants

The participants for the narrative study were a subset of the full design discussed in Chapter 2 (and below): there were 10 children each in the 8 bilingual groups, and 20 children each in the 2 monolingual groups at both 2nd and 5th grades, 240 children in all. The subject groups are displayed in Table 7.1.

To reiterate the key elements of the selection process (see Chapter 2), all the bilingual children were born in the United States. The OSH (Only Spanish at Home) children lived in homes where primarily Spanish was spoken at least until the child was age 5; the ESH (English and Spanish at Home) group children, in homes where English and Spanish were spoken approximately equally from the time of the child's birth. The bilingual children were in one of two types of schools: in English Immersion schools, instruction was all in English (except for an optional half-hour a day in Spanish); in Two-way schools, both languages were used as the medium of instruction; 60% of each day was taught in English and 40% in Spanish. (All the schools were 'neighborhood' schools; that is, almost no children chose the school because of the language policy.) The English monolinguals were all living in households where only one language was spoken and all but seven children were in schools with a majority of non-Hispanic peers. (The seven monolingual children in Spanish-peer schools were included in the analysis in Chapter 4, which showed no reliable difference between their

Table 7.1 Number of participants by group

	Bilingual							Monolingual	
	Eng. Imm. School				Two-way School				
	Hi-SES		Lo-SES		Hi		Lo		Hi	Lo
	OSH	ESH	OSH	ESH	OSH	ESH	OSH	ESH		
Grade 2	10	10	10	9	10	10	10	10	20	20
Grade 5	10	10	10	10	10	10	10	11	20	20

Notes: 2nd graders are ages 7and 8; 5th graders are 10 and 11

language achievement and the language achievement of the English-peer children.) Since one goal was to assess the effect of the two educational programs for the bilinguals, all children chosen for the study had been in the same educational program since kindergarten. Further, only children who had experienced the educational programs for at least two years were included. That is, this part of the study did not look at kindergartners.

All children in the narrative probe study (except two) participated in the full design (see Chapter 2). In addition to the narrative task, they were given the full set of eight Woodcock-Johnson oral and written language tests and the Peabody Picture Vocabulary tests, in both Spanish and English in counterbalanced order. All parents filled out an extensive demographic questionnaire. Additionally, many of the children in the narrative probe study also did the phonological translation (Chapter 11) and grammaticality judgment (Chapters 8–10) tasks, so a range of correlational analyses could be done. (The two children noted above as exceptions were selected for the study but were not given the Woodcock Battery because the cells matching their demographics had been filled before the narrative probe study began.)

The narrative probe study subgroups were constituted from the first 10 (or 20) children in each full design subgroup who were tested after the start of the narrative study in the middle of the second semester during which testing was conducted. There were some small adjustments for the balance between schools or occasional technical problems with the taping. In order to estimate how representative the smaller groups were of the groups from which they were drawn, mean scores on the Woodcock tests for the narrative probe study subgroups ($n = 10$ or 20) were compared to those for the subgroups in the larger design ($n = 30$ or $n = 40$, see Results, below).

The task

The children narrated the wordless picture book, *Frog, Where Are You?* by Mayer (1969). This book was chosen because it has been used successfully with grade-school children in many countries of the world, including the United States, Spain, and several of the Latin American countries where the Miami children's families came from. The book consists of 24 pictures depicting a little boy's search for a pet frog who escapes from the boy's room at the outset. The boy is aided in the search by his dog, whose adventures and misadventures complicate the story line. In the final pictures, the boy and the dog find a frog family and take one of the baby frogs home. (The book is reprinted in its entirety in Berman & Slobin, 1994, Appendix I.) The culture-specific story frames implicit in the book were explicated by anthropological linguist, D. Wilkins of the Max Planck Institute (quoted in Berman & Slobin, 1994: 21–22). The six or seven frames relevant for the story were judged consistent with the experiences of young children in all those parts of the world from which our subjects' families originated. The pictures are simple line drawings which are ambiguous enough to allow some legitimate differences of opinion about what is happening. The activities of the *two* major male protagonists make adequate pronoun reference and event sequencing quite tricky, even for adults. Finally, there are many more episodes than most people choose to include in their narrations, so although the story is somewhat constrained by the pictures, there is considerable variation in the children's renditions of it.

The stories were audio-taped individually in a quiet room in the children's school on one of the days when several subtests of the Woodcock Battery were also given and recorded. The seven testers were English–Spanish bilinguals recruited to have no non-native accent in either language. They were seven of the same eight research assistants who carried out the full design – standardized tests and other 'probe' studies – and thus were very familiar to the children whom they were recording. The children followed the standard protocol set out by Berman & Slobin (1994: 22), which eliminates any memory demand from the task. Children looked through the book to the end once and then again as they told the story, turning the pages at their own pace.

The bilinguals told the story in English one day and in Spanish another day. The order of the language was determined quasi-randomly for each child, and storytelling language and standardized testing language were maintained within testing sessions. Rendering of the story in the second language was usually a week or so after the first. Because the narrative study utilized only a subset of subjects from the full design, some imbalance was present in the order of testing. Hence, Language Order was included as a covariate in the analyses. The F-statistics are included under Control Variables in Results, below. Similarly, gender was not controlled for in the design. Therefore, gender was also included as a covariate and is reported below, under Control Variables.

As a final control variable, to evaluate the effect on the stories of having the bilinguals tell the story twice, 24 of the monolinguals also told the story a second time. Twelve monolingual English-speaking 2nd graders and twelve 5th graders, (half Low-SES and half High-SES), were asked to retell the story during another test session, one to two weeks after the first. The scores from the 24 Time–1 tellings were compared to the 24 Time–2 tellings with a paired-samples *t*-test and correlation. The *t*-statistic, *r*, and 95% confidence intervals for these analyses are also included under Control Variables in the Results, below.

Transcription procedures

The stories were transcribed by bilingual transcribers following the conventions outlined by Berman & Slobin (1994: 657–9), with one 'verbed clause' per line. (A verbed clause contains just one finite verb; it can be one word (a verb), or a whole sentence.) Standard orthography was used throughout; for unusual pronunciations, the child's production was spelled out phonetically in brackets. Ex: the cliff [clift]. All hesitations and false starts were included in curly brackets, {}. Unintelligible passages were marked as 'xxx'; less clear passages were enclosed in parentheses. The word-processed transcripts (without information as to group membership or grade) were printed with line numbers in a standard manner for the coding (described below). Then standard utterance delimiters were added, and the transcripts were put into CHAT format for analysis with the CHILDES programs (MacWhinney, 1995). (The stories are available through the CHILDES website at http://www.psy.cmu.edu/under frog corpora/miami.)

All the stories were listened to at least twice: 15% of the stories had two independent listenings in accordance with standard reliability procedures. The other 85% were given a non-independent second listening. That is, the second person had the transcription in front of her and listened only for disagreements. Stories averaged six discrepancies per 100 lines. Discrepancies between the transcribers or listeners were resolved by the author, resulting in a third listening when necessary.

Measures

The 400 stories were evaluated with a set of measures devised for the study that combined both analytical and holistic judgments. These measures incorporated the two broad areas outlined above. One primarily holistic set, the Story Score, looked at the child's ability to use a hierarchical story structure, maintain a clear flow of information, and include evaluative and metacognitive statements in recounting the events in the picturebook. The second, the Language Score, was a more analytical measure that examined the more purely linguistic aspects of the children's performances: counts of selected verb forms, conjunctions, adverbs, and the specialized noun vocabulary of the story.

There is not to our knowledge a recognized rubric – no 'answer key' – for scoring stories, but there is a wealth of descriptive information about this Frog Story in particular, which helps characterize the typical 3, 5, 9-year-old or adult response to it (Berman & Slobin, 1994, chap. IIa and Hoff-Ginsberg, 1997). By comparing elements reported for 'a few 5-year-olds and 90% of 9-year-olds' or 'a few 9's and a majority of the adults', we were able to assemble a developmental sequence for several elements of the domains noted above. For example, with respect to one key plot element, the frog's escape from the jar, according to Berman & Slobin (1994, p. 46), only 50% of the 4-year-olds, but 94% of the 9-year-olds used a 'mental predicate' to remark on the missing frog – 'the boy and the dog _saw_ or _discovered_ or _were upset_ that the frog was gone.' Likewise, 'only a few 5's but most of the 9's' began the story with some type of stereotypical story opener (p. 74). The older children were also more likely to give some background on events that might have led up to the first picture – on how the boy had come to have the frog, and so forth (p. 72). We used the elements described in Berman & Slobin (1994) as the basis for the two-pronged story metric. Our goal was to identify, separately for the two domains of narrative and linguistic development, which stories told by the children resembled a typical second-grader story and which were more or less advanced.

Using a model derived from gymnastics judging and portfolio evaluation (see Pearson, 1996, October, for the full rationale behind the measures), we retrofitted a descriptive framework capable of capturing the differences between the five best and five worst of the monolingual stories as judged holistically by a panel of educators and linguists. Monolingual stories were used in creating the rubric to help the panel focus on the story elements and not the language. (Based on the author's experiences training composition instructors, it was deemed too difficult, even for teachers, to keep surface-level language errors from coloring their overall evaluation of the discourse.)

The gymnastics judging model is especially apt for separating the judgment of a story's narrative elements from the judgment of its language. For each optional gymnastics routine on bars, beam, or floor exercise, the judge first counts the level of difficulty of all the moves and connections in the routine. By adding the values assigned each move (in the standard judging manual, which is always available), one arrives at the highest possible score for the particular routine performed – _if_ all the elements were executed perfectly. Then, one subtracts execution deductions according to a general table, also in the manual. One takes off so many points for a fall, so much for bending the arms, in an element or throughout. The execution deductions are subtracted from the 'value' of the routine to arrive at an overall score. Likewise, the metric that was devised partitioned the narrative or 'Story Score' into five areas – Story Elements, Sequencing, Reference to characters, Reference to internal states, and a quality of Engagement. The Language Score was divided into three areas: Complex Syntax, Lexicon, and Morphosyntactic Accuracy. The first two of these count elements present in the story; the last counts errors to be deducted. A summary of the categories with example passages from three stories is given below. A coding sheet is included in the Appendix to this chapter.

Summary on the Story and Language Scores

STORY SCORE	Possible points	Description of 'midpoint' score (6 or 3) for the 'average' 2nd grade story
Elements	12	a search story, including losing the frog, setting out in search, and finding a frog.
Sequence	12	sentence-by-sentence, picture-by-picture chain of events (little or no orientation, setting, summary).
Reference	6	use of indefinite article for first mentions; generally adequate pronoun antecedents (or use of 'thematic pronoun strategy' (Karmiloff-Smith, 1986), with some lapses.
Internal states	6	little reference to emotions, reactions, or thoughts of the characters.
Engagement	12	matter-of-fact tone; no 'literary' language
Total	48	
LANGUAGE SCORE		*Midpoint story generally correct, but unelaborated. A string of simple sentences, relatively correct.*
Complex Syntax	24	mostly simple verb phrases; points added for each occurrence, (up to 3) of modals or aspectual markings ('began to,' 'kept on'); (in Spanish, perfect tenses, subjunctive); across clauses, points given for conjunctions other than 'and then' ('y después'); bonus for noun or adjective clauses.
Lexicon	12	uses most of a set of 12 words, specific to the story: ('frog', 'jar', 'bees', 'beehive', etc.)
Morpho-syntactic accuracy	12	(errors deducted from 12) generally well-formed, a few non-prescriptive structures ('a owl,' 'there was bees')
Total	48	
NARRATIVE TOTAL	96	

At the 2nd grade level, all but the very lowest stories introduced the three main characters, related key events (while omitting others), and by the end resolved the search for the frog. The medium stories did so as a straightforward chronicle of events: 'this happened and then this happened and then this happened'. As indicated in the summary table, those stories were given the midpoint score on two of the scales of the Story Score: Frog Story 'Elements' and 'Sequence'. But the weaker stories lost points by getting side-tracked into details that did not advance the story or by lapsing into picture-description. The child could also lose points in the Reference category for failing to introduce one or more of the characters, or for losing track of clear reference when using pronouns (or at least not reserving the pronoun exclusively for the main character or 'thematic subject', as described by Karmiloff-Smith (1981)).

Example Second Grade Stories (Excerpts)

Note: Short pauses are indicated with '-' and longer pauses with '...' Words in curly brackets were judged to be retracings. The division into lines with one verbed clause per line follows the convention from Berman & Slobin (1994: 657–9).

Story Example 1 (Low Average)		
line	1	The dog – looked in – the bottle and looked at the frog. And the boy was sitting on a chair. And his – sock and his shirt was laying on the floor.
	5	And the light was on. And the window was opened . . . When – {the} the boy and the dog were sleeping - the frog – stuck his head out with his head an' his arm – out of the bottle.
Story Example 2 (High)		
line	1	One day a boy and his dog had found a frog. They kept him in the big jar. While the boy was asleep the frog climbed out of the jar
	5	and ran away. When the boy woke up the next morning he was very upset to see his frog missing. He searched everywhere.
	10	In boots . . . And he turned over tables.

Story Example 3 (High, Bilingual)		
line:	1	Once there was a little boy with his little dog. It was already night time. They were looking at the little frog. The little boy – and his dog went to sleep.
	5	The frog – wanted to go out to see {the w} the world. So he came out of the little – can. It was morning already. The puppy and the boy looked to the – can
	10	and saw {that there} that the frog was not there.

Stories that were above average included one or more of the following elements (noted by Berman & Slobin 1994: 82): short summary statements (either prospective or retrospective), comments on the reactions of the characters, clear articulation of the boy's goal (not just a description of his activities in pursuit of that goal), or, toward the end of the story, an explicit mention of the boy's misperception of the deer's antlers as sticks. This last element, for example, was reported by half of the adults in Berman & Slobin's Table 4 (p. 55), but by only a small percentage of school-age children. Then, based on the better stories in our sample, we also added a way for the children to earn credit for remarking on the boy's *lack* of success in the search, which must – like statements about internal states of the characters – be added by the child and not 'read' directly from a picture. We also added the possibility for extra credit to be earned in a category we called 'engagement'. Unlike the more strictly linguistic measures of language structures counted in the separate Language Score (discussed below), this column awarded 'narrative' credit for literary-like language – expressions that made the child's rendition more lively or engaging: using a refrain in the story, or direct speech, or even figures of speech. (The closest we found to that in this sample was stylistic word-order inversion, like 'the frog was nowhere to be found' or 'out popped an owl'.)

From the linguistic perspective, the stories that rated 'high' tended to have more subordination and greater specificity in the nouns and verbs used; the child would say 'deer' or 'antler' instead of 'the large animal with those sticks on his head'. The better stories also encoded more complex temporal and causal relations in their verb and adverb constructions. The Language Score tried to characterize how well the child handled the more advanced grammatical structures. The main thrust of the Language Score was to credit the children's performance for the language elements they demonstrated, not to penalize for mistakes, but it was not always possible to separate 'positive' and 'negative' scoring. Form errors inevitably had some impact on the Complex Syntax score, for example, because credit was given only when constructions were relatively well-formed. In lexical choice, as well, there were three levels of credit: +1 if the child used a keyword, zero if the concept was not referred to, and –0.5 if the child demonstrated that she did not know the word (saying 'flying things' for the bees, or 'that bee-thing' for the 'beehive').

In addition, a very salient characteristic of the bilinguals' stories (especially in Spanish), was the high number of morphosyntactic mistakes: the use of overregularizations, '*falled*' for 'fell', or the wrong form of an article '*el* ventana' for 'la ventana' [the window] or '*a* owl' instead of 'an owl'. (See also Martínez, 1993, on 'morphosyntactic erosion'.) In order to keep track of the incidence of such errors within the various bilingual subgroups and even among the monolinguals, a count of departures from morphosyntactic accuracy (MS Accuracy) was maintained. The Language Score Total was computed in two alternative ways, one based on only the positive qualities present in the language (Language Total 2, with only Complex Syntax and Lexicon), and another (Language Total 1) which also took into account the morphosyntactic errors, or elements that might draw sanction or correction from a monolingual adult (cf. Ochs, 1985). The tally of MS Accuracy is potentially problematic in both languages, but especially so in Spanish because there is not to our knowledge any well-defined framework for what is considered 'acceptable' in the adult varieties of Spanish spoken in Miami. Consultants disagreed as to whether the child should say 'cayó' or 'se cayó' ['he/she/it fell' or 'fell, reflexive'] when the boy or dog fell, as they did in almost every story. Pilot efforts to characterize the different varieties convinced us that while MS Accuracy was a useful index of 'exposure to literate Spanish', no conclusions could be drawn about a host of structures commonly accepted by Hispanic adults in Miami, whose grammatical status is beyond the scope of this paper.

The two scores, Story and Language, were not orthogonal, but they were distinct. For example, one element of the Complex Syntax score tracked how the child expressed the causes of events – including intentions. The expression of intentions was also counted in the Story Score, but the Language Score credit for this was more specific: it indicated that the child had made an explicit link *between clauses*. If a child got points for an intention structure in the Language Score, she would necessarily have credit in the Story Score as well, but the converse was not true. Likewise, the ability to express simultaneity is a key element in the foregrounding and backgrounding of actions, counted in a global way under 'Sequence' in the Story Store. In the Language Score, though, points were awarded only when the child used specific grammatical devices of the language: e.g. the conjunctions 'while' or 'mientras', some uses of 'when', or the present participle, as in 'he climbed up a rock, *calling* out to his frog'.

So, the child could get credit in the Story Score for elaborating an episode in several simple sentences, but would not get Language credit unless the sentences were also linked grammatically. The first score was more concerned with capturing the level of the child's conceptualization of the story and how it should be recounted – regardless of the level of language used. The Language Score, by contrast, focused more narrowly on the use of specific later-developing lexical and grammatical constructions.

Coding procedures and reliability

'Hand'-scoring. Using coding sheets for Story and Language Scores, stories were coded independently by two researchers who were 'blind' as to the identity and group membership or age of the child under consideration. Differences in the scoring were resolved by discussion, and a consensus score was reached.

As mentioned above under 'Task', a test-retest reliability scoring using the same procedure was performed for 30% of the monolinguals.

Machine-scoring. The CHILDES programs (MacWhinney, 1995) were used to characterize the quantitative aspects of the stories. A tally was made of length in words, clauses, and the sentence-like 't-units' (following the standard definition [Hunt, 1977], of a minimal terminable-unit, 'a single independent clause and all other clauses that . . . go with it so there will be no [dependent clauses] left over', p. 93). From those measures one can derive 'MLU' (mean length of utterance, here the number of words per t-unit) and a 'subordination index' (the mean number of clauses per t-unit). The number of different word-types in the story, as well as the number of types in the first 100 words, were also counted.

Analytic procedures

In all, there was in each language a summary score, Narrative Total, composed of a Story Score and a Language Score, which was comprised in turn of five and three subcomponents, respectively; finally there were eight variables from the CHILDES analysis. All were linked to the database with the standardized test scores and demographic information for each child (see Chapters 2–6). These 19 measures allowed the Frog Stories to be ranked from a variety of perspectives consistent with the main avenues of evaluation in the narrative literature discussed above. The three hypotheses specified above were evaluated in terms of both between- and within-subject questions, with subhypotheses as follows:

Between-subjects questions

H1.   How do monolinguals and bilinguals compare with respect to overall scores in English on the global measure of narrative ability? With respect to the specifically narrative aspects (Story Score and sub-components)? With respect to linguistic aspects (Language Score and subcomponents)?

H2.   How do bilinguals in English Immersion schools and Two-way schools compare to each other on the same sets of measures in English and in Spanish? Is the pattern different at 2nd and at 5th grade?

Within-subjects questions

H3.   Within subjects, how strong a prediction of ability in one language is given by ability demonstrated in the other? For the global measures of ability? For the subcomponents of the scores in each language? That is, beyond the demographic factors investigated, was there an influence of skills in a first language on learning in a second language (or of skills in the second on the first)?

Results

Summary of Frog Story Results

The patterns of results between the groups and across languages differed according to the measure being examined. For the Narrative Total scores in English there were main effects of SES, Grade, and Lingualism (monolingual versus bilingual), with a strong interaction of Grade and Lingualism. It is not surprising that there were grade effects, as these are non-standardized scores. However the grade effect was different for monolinguals (MLs) and bilinguals (BLs) with BLs showing relatively more improvement on these measures than MLs in this age range. That is, bilingual children's scores were significantly lower than MLs' at 2nd grade, but closer, and on many variables equal to MLs' at 5th grade. When the Narrative Total score was broken down into its component scores, ML-BL differences were quite small for the narrative and discourse elements, as captured in the Story Scores, but the differences were larger for the Language Scores.

Overall, most of the Hispanic children did better in English than in Spanish, with greater differences between languages on Language Scores than Story Scores. Only one of the 16 bilingual groups had higher mean scores in Spanish than in English: the Low-SES 2nd graders with only Spanish at home (OSH) and Spanish and English in the school (Two-way). The group with these same characteristics at 5th grade, though, appeared dominant in English.

Between bilingual groups, the patterns of effects from the factors nested within Lingualism were different in the two languages. In English, LSH showed a significant effect for Language Score (not Story), with the strongest effects seen in Lexicon and Morphosyntactic Accuracy (MS Accuracy). By contrast, in Spanish there was an LSH effect only in MS Accuracy and no other variable. Unlike in English, there was a significant effect of IMS on most measures in Spanish (but not on MS Accuracy). In Spanish, the Grade effect was strong on all measures (except MS Accuracy). Notably, SES showed no statistically reliable results for any Spanish variable studied.

Finally, between languages for the bilinguals, there was a strong prediction of ability in one language to ability in the other for some elements of the Narrative Total scores, but not for others. In particular, the narrative/discourse elements (Story Score) showed carry-over across languages while specific language elements (Language Score) did not. The degree of elaboration and embedding in complex sentences was similar across languages, but knowledge of vocabulary items and general well-formedness of sentences were not similar.

Descriptives

The descriptive statistics in Table 7.2 help define the information in the database.

One can see that as the monolingual children got older, the stories got a little shorter, and MLU went up. Since one sees that scores went up, one can infer that the older children were able to convey more information more efficiently.

The bilinguals' stories (Table 7.3) were shorter than the monolinguals' stories at 2nd grade, but similar at 5th grade. Whereas the monolingual

Table 7.2 Length of story, descriptive statistics (Monolinguals only) (40 children per grade)

		Mean	*Stdev.*	*Range*
2nd grade	# of words	324	(115)	167–605
	different words	109	(29)	63–174
	# of clauses	53	(17)	28–95
	MLU (mean length of utterance)	7.7	(1.2)	5.6–10.5
5th grade	# of words	259	(78)	68–448
	different words	98	(23)	41–157
	# of clauses	43	(12)	10–71
	MLU	8.4	(1.1)	5.7–10.5

Table 7.3 Length of story, descriptive statistics for English (Bilinguals) (40 children per school type per grade)

		Eng. Imm. Schools		Two-way Schools	
2nd grade	# of words	246	(78)	247	(70)
	different words	85	(20)	79	(17)
	# of clauses	43	(14)	41	(10.6)
	MLU	7.2	(1.1)	7.3	(1.1)
5th grade	# of words	269	(76)	309	(112)
	different words	97	(20)	106	(24)
	# of clauses	44	(12)	50	(16)
	MLU	8.3	(1.3)	8.9	(1.5)

Table7.4 Length of story, descriptive statistics for Spanish (Bilinguals) (40 children per school per grade)

		Eng. Imm. Schools		Two-way Schools	
2nd grade	# of words	248	(70)	217	(64)
	different words	76	(20)	74	(17)
	# of clauses	39	(13)	38	(11)
	MLU	6.6	(0.9)	6.9	(1.1)
5th grade	# of words	236	(80)	262	(84)
	different words	85	(20)	94	(22)
	# of clauses	42	(14)	46	(14)
	MLU	7.0	(1)	7.5	(1.3)

stories got shorter over this age range, the bilingual stories got longer. Both monolingual and bilingual groups experienced growth in MLU, but bilinguals showed more significant growth (ML: $F = 3.72$, $p = 0.058$; BL: $F = 42.4$, $p < 0.001$).

Comparing the English stories across IMS, we see the school types were similar in 2nd grade; in 5th grade the Two-way children's stories were longer and the sentences were somewhat more complex, according to the MLU measure ($F = 3.44$, $p = 0.065$).

The Spanish stories (Table 7.4) appeared similar across IMS at both grades, with a tendency for more complex sentences (or higher MLU) in the Two-way schools at 5th grade.

Table 7.5 includes the monolingual values at 2nd and 5th grade for the main elements of the Frog Story scoring.

Table 7.5 Selected Frog Story measures: Descriptive and inferential statistics (Monolinguals only)

		Mean	*Std.*	*Range*
2ND GRADE				
Story Total	**(of 48)**	28.2	(5.5)	20–43
Elements	(of 12)	6.7	(2.2)	3–12
Sequence	(of 12)	7.8	(1.3)	5–11
Internal	(of 6)	2.7	(1.2)	0–6
Language Total	**(of 50)**	34.4	(5.9)	21–45.5
Complex Syntax	(of 24)	16.7	(3.7)	11–23
Lexicon	(of 14)	9.1	(2.6)	4.5–14
MS Accuracy	(of 12)	8.6	(2.5)	2–12
Frog Total	**(of 98)**	62.6	(10.7)	45.5–85
(from CHILDES)				
Subordination Index		1.26	(0.17)	1.02–1.72
Type-token Ratio		0.35	(0.06)	0.24–0.47
5TH GRADE				
Story Total		30.1	(4.4)	23–44
Elements		7.6[a]	(1.9)	5–12
Sequence		8.8[b]	(1.1)	7–11
Internal		2.4	(1.3)	1–6
Language Total		37.3[c]	(4.2)	27–49.5
Complex Syntax		17.3	(3.1)	12–24
Lexicon		9.2[d]	(2.2)	3–13.5
MS Accuracy		10.7[e]	(1.2)	8 12
Frog Total		67.3[f]	(7.7)	53–93.5
(from CHILDES)				
Subordination Index		1.37[g]	(0.18)	1.08–1.78
Type-Token Ratio		0.39[h]	(0.06)	0.31–0.6

Notes (Significant effects):
[a] SES, $F = 6.35$, $p = 0.014$
[b] Grade, $F = 13.34$, $p < 0.001$
[c] SES, $F = 11.21$, $p = 0.001$; Grade, 6.68, $p = 0.012$
[d] SES, $F = 5.04$, $p = 0.028$
[e] SES, $F = 14.72$, $p < 0.001$; Grade, $F = 24.72$, $p < 0.001$; SES by Grade, $F = 5.81$, $p = 0.018$
[f] SES, $F = 8.18$, $p = 0.005$, Grade, $F = 5.48$, $p = 0.022$
[g] Grade, $F = 7.94$, $p = 0.006$
[h] Grade, $F = 9.03$, $p = 0.004$

Specific results from multivariate analysis of variance

To evaluate differences among group means, the data were analyzed via 6-way multivariate analysis of variance using Type III sums of squares (General Linear Model, SPSS 7.1 for Windows). Three between-subjects factors were fully crossed with one another: SES (high vs low), Grade (2nd or 5th, and Lingualism (bilingual vs monolingual). In addition, three between-subjects factors were nested within Lingualism – IMS (English Immersion or Two-way), LSH (OSH vs ESH), and Language Order (English 1st vs Spanish 1st).

The design yielded a total of 35 effects. To protect against inflation of Type I error rate, a Bonferroni correction was applied to yield a groupwise alpha of 0.05. As this corresponded to a very strict comparisonwise alpha of 0.0014 for the English scores (and 0.0033 for the bilingual-only comparisons with 15 effects [$2^4 - 1$]), some small effects due to Type II error might have been neglected. Nonetheless, the procedure resulted in many effects which remained statistically significant. (It should be added that for tests of simple effects, or *post hoc* comparisons involving only two groups – that is, in cases with only a single comparison – the Bonferroni groupwise correction was not used. Therefore, there may be some anomaly when F-statistics with Bonferroni correction were compared to those without the correction. In such cases the alpha value is explicitly stated so that appropriate caution can be used in comparing the simple effect to the original main effect.)

Tests of control variables: Language order, gender, and tester

As noted above in Methods, for the bilingual children, who told the story twice, the language order (English or Spanish first) was slightly unbalanced in the groups. There were 69 who told the story in English first and 91 in Spanish first. Therefore Language Order was included as a factor nested within Lingualism. For 15 of 16 dependent variables, Language Order yielded no significant main effect. For example, with Narrative Total, $F = 2.39, p = 0.123$; for Story Scores, $F = < 1, p = 0.4$. The single exception was for the English Lexicon scores, with no Bonferroni correction, $F = 7.46, p = 0.007$. In addition, Language Order entered into an interaction with SES and grade for Morphosyntactic Accuracy, again in English, such that the Low-SES children in the 5th grade spoke English more accurately in their stories (an average of 2 errors rather than 4) when they told the story in English first than when they told it in Spanish first. This difference was not evident for their High-SES classmates, nor was there an SES difference at 2nd grade. Language Order showed no significant effects for any of the Spanish measures. Still, it was included as a factor in all the analyses to insure that its contribution to the error term was correctly partitioned.

Similarly, gender was not controlled in the assignment of subjects, and in fact, there were 54% females in each of the three main groups, English Immersion bilinguals, Two-way bilinguals, and monolinguals. When gender was entered in the analysis as a covariate, it was not a significant factor for any dependent variable and thus was not included in any further analyses. Nor did Tester produce any significant effects.

A test for the effect of telling the story twice

To ascertain whether there was a practice effect from telling the same story twice one to two weeks apart, 24 monolinguals also repeated the story after a similar interval. The mean scores for the Time–1 and Time–2 tellings in English are found in Table 7.6.

The 24 Time–1 tellings were compared to the 24 Time–2 tellings with a paired-samples t-test, $t < 1$ (n.s.) for both Story and Language scores. Mean differences on the measures between tellings (for the whole group) were small, always less than 0.7 (compared to standard deviations around 6 points). Correlations between times of telling were 0.77 for the Story Scores, 0.76 for the Language Scores, and 0.8 for the two summed together (Narrative Total).

An additional check was made for stability with respect to three highly valued items in the Story Scores – the mention of a mental verb for the discovery of the missing frog (+2), mention of the boy's misperception of the deer's antlers as sticks, or similar misperception (+4), and the inclusion of more than one comment on the 'internal' state of the characters. Between

Table 7.6 Test-Retest Reliability: Story and Language Scores by time of telling and grade means (and standard deviations)

		N	(Time 1)	(Time 2)	t	95% Conf. Interval
Story Score						
All		24	29.17 (6.0)	29.17 (6.3)	0.0	±1.76
Grade	2	12	27.9 (6.6)	26.8 (5.6)		
	5	12	30.5 (5.4)	31.5 (6.2)		
Language Score						
All			35.6 (6.8)	36.3 (6.0)	–0.7	±1.88
Grade	2		34.1 (7.8)	34.0 (5.2)		
	5		37.2 (5.5)	38.6 (6.0)		
Narrative Total (Story + Language)						
All			64.8 (12.1)	65.4 (11.8)	–0.4	± 3.22

83% and 92% of the children were consistent across tellings. Of the three, four, and two children for each element, respectively, who were not consistent, there was an equal tendency to embellish the story more or elaborate it less in the second telling. There does not, then, appear to be significant systematic bias in the group scores as a result of telling the story twice. In addition, the lack of reliable differences on the Language Order variable helps confirm that there was no systematic bias according to which language the story was told in first.

Principal analyses

Table 7.7 shows the means and standard deviations for the 10 subgroups at each grade for Story, Language, and Narrative Total scores, in English and in Spanish.

Bilinguals' values on the Frog Story summary variables are shown in Figures 7.1 (English) and 7.2 (Spanish), for both 2nd and 5th grades. The scores are given separately for the eight bilingual subgroups at each grade, with the monolinguals' included for comparison in Figure 7.1.

In general, Story Scores in English were more consistent than Language Scores across the subgroups listed on the x-axis in Figure 7.1. The ML groups' Language Scores were higher than their Story Scores at both 2nd and 5th grade, but the same was true of BL groups only at 5th grade. ML Language Scores were dramatically better than BL at 2nd grade, but not at 5th grade.

In Spanish (Figure 7.2), Story Scores were better at 5th grade than 2nd grade, especially in the Two-way schools, and Language Scores were lower than Story Scores at both grades. Improvement in Language Scores

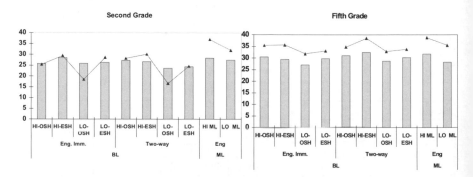

Figure 7.1 Story and Language Scores (English) (bars represent Story Scores; lines represent Language Scores)

Table 7.7 Descriptive statistics for Story, Language, and Narrative Total scores in English and Spanish by Grade, IMS, LSH, and SES

					Scores												
					English Story		English Language		English Total		Spanish Story		Spanish Language		Spanish Total	
Grade	IMS	LSH	SES	n	M	SD	M	SD	M	SD	M	SD	M	SD	M	SD
2nd	Eng Imm	OSH	hi	10	26	(3)	26	(4)	51	(6)	26	(5)	22	(6)	47	(10)
			lo	10	26	(3)	19	(6)	44	(7)	25	(3)	17	(7)	42	(8)
		ESH	hi	10	29	(5)	30	(5)	58	(8)	26	(5)	13	(9)	40	(13)
			lo	9	26	(4)	29	(5)	52	(7)	25	(4)	20	(11)	45	(14)
	Two-way	OSH	hi	10	27	(5)	28	(8)	56	(12)	28	(5)	20	(10)	48	(13)
			lo	10	24	(4)	17	(6)	40	(8)	24	(5)	22	(7)	46	(10)
		ESH	hi	10	27	(4)	30	(6)	57	(9)	27	(7)	19	(7)	46	(13)
			lo	10	24	(4)	25	(5)	49	(7)	26	(3)	16	(9)	42	(11)
	Mono-ling	Eng	hi	20	29	(5)	37	(5)	66	(9)						
			lo	20	28	(6)	32	(6)	60	(11)						
Grade	IMS	LSH	SES	n	M	SD	M	SD	M	SD	M	SD	M	SD	M	SD
5th	Eng Imm	OSH	hi	10	31	(4)	36	(4)	66	(7)	28	(4)	22	(7)	50	(10)
			lo	10	27	(4)	32	(6)	59	(9)	27	(6)	23	(10)	49	(11)
		ESH	hi	10	29	(5)	36	(6)	65	(9)	25	(5)	20	(8)	45	(10)
			lo	10	30	(3)	33	(9)	63	(11)	28	(4)	14	(11)	42	(14)
	Two-way	OSH	hi	10	31	(4)	35	(7)	66	(9)	30	(4)	22	(9)	51	(13)
			lo	10	29	(4)	33	(3)	62	(6)	29	(4)	27	(4)	56	(7)
		ESH	hi	10	33	(2)	39	(6)	71	(7)	33	(4)	25	(8)	58	(8)
			lo	11	30	(2)	34	(8)	64	(9)	29	(4)	25	(7)	55	(10)
	Mono-ling	Eng	hi	20	32	(5)	39	(4)	71	(8)						
			lo	20	29	(4)	36	(4)	64	(7)						

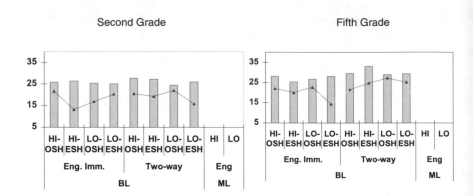

Figure 7.2 Story and Language Scores (Spanish) (bars represent Story Scores; lines represent Language Scores

across grades was found even in some English Immersion groups. The only subgroup whose Spanish Language Score was lower for the 5th graders than for the 2nd graders was the group with economic disadvantage and with the least Spanish input: Low-SES children in English Immersion Schools who had English and Spanish (hence less Spanish) in the home.

As described above, the six-way multivariate analysis of variance using Type III sums of squares was run first for the summary variables and then for the component scores. There were three fully crossed between-subjects factors: SES (high vs low), Grade (2nd vs 5th), and Lingualism (bilingual vs monolingual). In addition, three between-subjects factors were nested within Lingualism – IMS (English Immersion vs Two-way), LSH (OSH vs ESH), and Language Order (English 1st or Spanish 1st). A Bonferroni correction was applied to yield a groupwise alpha of 0.05 (comparison alpha = 0.0014).

Narrative Total score

Table 7.8 gives the Narrative Total values for the Monolinguals and the two groups of Bilinguals according to IMS. There were significant main effects of SES, Grade, and Lingualism, and an interaction of Grade by Lingualism (Table 7.9).

When the interactions were followed up with tests of simple effects (Table 7.10), the Grade effect was significant at both levels of Lingualism (ML: $F = 5.75$, $p = 0.022$; BL: $F = 93.94$, $p < 0.001$). However, the Lingualism effect was seen to diminish greatly from 2nd grade to 5th grade (Figure 7.3),

Table 7.8 Narrative Total Scores by Grade and IMS mean and (standard deviation)

Grade	English Immersion	Two-way	Monolingual English
2nd (7–8 years old)	51.5 (8.5)	50.5 (11.2)	62.5 (10.7)
5th (10–11 years old)	63.2 (9.1)	65.6 (8.6)	67.3 (7.7)

Table 7.9 Significant effects for Narrative Total score (English)

	F	p
SES	30.2	< 0.0001***
Grade	75.4	< 0.0001***
Lingualism	34.3	< 0.0001***
Grade by Ling	11.13	< 0.0010**

** $p < 0.01$, *** $p < 0.001$

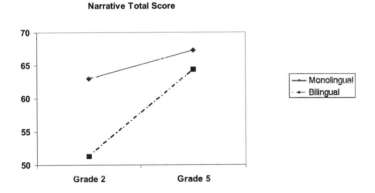

Figure 7.3 Narrative Total (English), Grade by Lingualism

and it was non-significant when the comparison was made between the High-SES/ESH bilinguals and the comparable groups of monolinguals (see Table 7.10).

The Hi-SES 2nd graders, unlike the 5th graders, showed a Lingualism effect, favoring MLs: $F = 12.93$, $p = 0.001$, and for children who were both Hi-SES/ESH at 2nd grade, the values were also still significant with no Bonferroni correction: $F = 7.11$, $p = 0.012$.

Table 7.10 Simple Effects of Lingualism on Narrative Total Score

| | *ML* | | *BL* | | |
Tested at	n	M (SD)	n	M (SD)	F	p
2nd grade	40	63.0 (10.5)	79	51.3 (9.9)	35.6	0.01*
5th grade	40	67.3 (7.7)	81	64.4 (8.9)	3.29	0.07
5th grade, Hi-SES only	20	70.6 (7.7)	40	67.0 (8.3)	2.59	0.11
5th grade, Hi-SES, & ESH(English & Spanish at home)	20	70.6 (7.7)	20	68.0 (8.4)	0.98	0.33

Contribution of component scores

The two component scores which comprise Narrative Total responded differently to the independent variables of the study (Table 7.11). Both showed high correlations to the Narrative Total score, and thus both contributed to the global measure. Nonetheless, the overall correlation of Language Score to Total Score, $r = 0.95$ was higher than for Story Score, $r = 0.83$, and it was consistently higher across the different Lingualism, IMS, and SES levels.

It is important, therefore, to examine both scores in analyzing the different groups' performance on the Frog Stories.

Story Score. For Story Score (see Table 7.12), with Bonferroni correction, there was a main effect for Grade, but not for SES, Lingualism, nor for any interactions. These same factors had different effects for the subcomponents of the score. There was a strong trend for the SES effect on all the scores as well as a Grade by Lingualism interaction, $F = 9.145, p = 0.003$.

The Grade effect seen in the global Story Score was most noticeable in the Sequence and Frog Story Elements subscores. The trend toward an SES effect for the global Story Score was seen as a significant effect in the

Table 7.11 Correlation of Narrative Total score with Component scores by Lingualism, SES, and IMS

	Story Score	*Language Score*
Monolinguals ($n = 80$)	0.92	0.92
SES-High ($n = 120$)	0.86	0.93
SES-Low ($n = 120$)	0.80	0.95
BL, Eng. Imm. ($n = 79$)	0.75	0.93
BL, Two-way School ($n = 81$)	0.87	0.97

Table 7.12 Main effects for Story Score and Components

	STORY		Elements		Sequence		Internal States	
	F	**p**	**F**	**p**	**F**	**p**	**F**	**p**
Grade	30.3	< 0.001	21.78	< 0.001	54.4	< 0.001	5.19	< 0.024
SES	11.7	0.0017	8.04	0.005	13.42	0.001	8.13	0.005
Lingualism	4.0	0.047	1.50	0.223	2.93	0.088	4.24	0.041

*Significant with Bonferroni correction (comparison alpha = 0.0014)

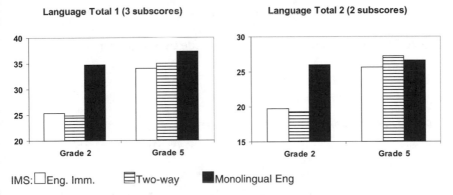

IMS: ☐Eng. Imm. ▤Two-way ■Monolingual Eng

Figure 7.4 Language Totals by School Type and Grade

Sequence subscore, and as a trend as well in the Elements and Internal States subscores.

Language Score. The main effects in English of SES, Grade, and Lingualism observed for the Language Scores were significant for both Language Total 1 (with 3 elements), $F = 34.4$, 84.8, and 56.7, respectively, and Language Total 2 (without MS Accuracy), $F = 22.5$, 62.7, and 25.8, all p *values* < 0.001 (see Figure 7.4).

As seen above for Narrative Total, there was a strong Grade by Lingualism interaction for both Language Totals (see Figure 7.5).

The two versions of the Language Score were highly correlated, $r = 0.90$ and the significance of results was rarely different when using one score instead of the other. The relative contribution of MS Accuracy to evaluations of general language performance is highlighted by the correlation of that measure with the Language Total 2, the one that did not include it. For monolinguals, the correlation was negligible, $r = -0.05$, compared to $r = 0.37$ for the bilinguals. A similar disparity was observed in the Language Total

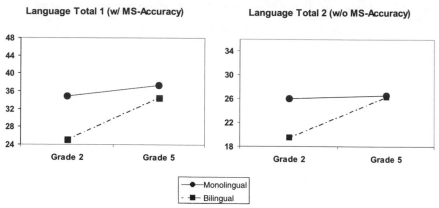

Figure 7.5 Language Scores (English), Grade by Lingualism

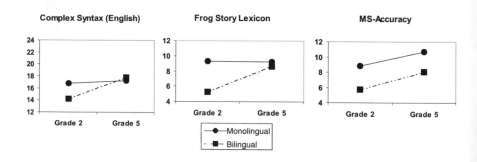

Figure 7.6 Language Score Subcomponents (English), Grade by Lingualism

1, where the correlation was 0.37 for monolinguals versus 0.73 for bilinguals. When used as part of the metric, surface well-formedness of the children's output, then, figured more heavily in the assessment of bilinguals' stories than of monolinguals'.

When one examines the subcomponents comprising the Language Total, one sees patterns of Grade by Lingualism (Figure 7.6) and by LSH (Figure 7.7).

In examining the Grade effect for the three subcomponents, one can see three different patterns of relation between the monolinguals and

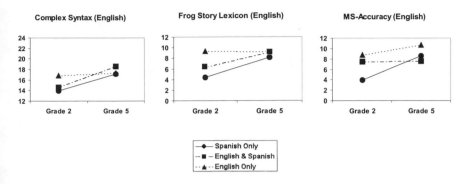

Figure 7.7 Language Score Subcomponents (English), Grade by LSH

bilinguals across grades. In Complex Syntax the 2nd grade bilinguals were well below the monolinguals, but the 5th grade bilinguals were equivalent to the monolinguals; in Lexicon, the gap narrowed but did not close, whereas in MS Accuracy, the 5th grade bilinguals were as far behind the monolinguals as the 2nd graders were. Not surprisingly, both Complex Syntax and Lexicon showed a Grade by Lingualism interaction, but MS Accuracy did not, F = 12.53, 18.41, and 0.11, $p < 0.001$, 0.001, and 0.748 respectively.

Curiously, the ESH bilinguals, unlike both the monolinguals and the OSH bilinguals, showed no change in MS Accuracy over this time period. Since these data were cross-sectional, the lack of 'improvement' may have been a cohort effect. Alternately, it may indicate that these children's language patterns in English for MS Accuracy were set by 2nd grade and then were less susceptible to being influenced by factors outside the home, or perhaps that the children were concentrating on gains with the greatest functional significance (which might be presumed to be Lexicon and Complex Syntax).

MS Accuracy alone showed a main effect of Lingualism and no interaction of Grade by Lingualism. Unlike Lexicon and Complex Syntax, grammatical well-formedness, then, appeared to be robustly different between MLs and BLs at both grades. The information in Figure 7.7 collapses across SES, but it should be noted that there were disproportionately large gains from 2nd to 5th for MLs among the Low-SES subgroup. MS Accuracy did enter into an interaction of Grade by LSH. The contrasting Grade by LSH patterns for the Language Score subcomponents are shown in Figure 7.8.

These results were paralleled by effects for the CHILDES measures (see Table 7.13 and values reported in Tables 7.2, 7.3, 7.4 and 7.5). For the Subor-

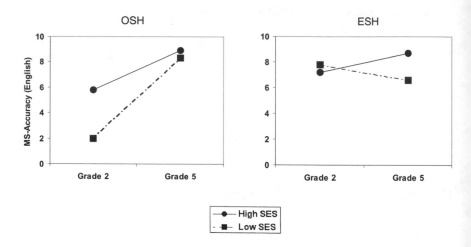

Figure 7.8 MS Accuracy (English), Grade by LSH by SES

dination Index (number of clauses per sentence) and MLU (number of words per utterance), there was also a Grade effect, but no Lingualism, LSH, or SES effect, although for SES there was a trend. For the lexical measure, Type-token ratio, there were both Grade and SES effects; for Types, a Grade effect.

Here the Type-token ratio followed the pattern for the Lexicon measure with significant effects of both Grade and SES. Subordination Index was most like the Complex Syntax measure and showed a Grade effect for Lingualism, but only a trend for SES. In general, despite statistical significance, the differences on these measures even across three grades were relatively small, and so the measures did not appear sensitive enough to characterize perceptible differences between 2nd and 5th grade stories. 'Clauses' and 'words', two basic measures of length, were particularly

Table 7.13 Main effects for 'CHILDES' measures

	Grade		*SES*	
	F	p	F	p
Subordination Index	35.58	< 0.001	6.51	< 0.011
MLU	38.41	< 0.001	6.88	< 0.009
Type-token ratio	14.25	< 0.001	22.5	< 0.001
Types	12.78	< 0.001	8.17	< 0.005

* Significant at the groupwise level, p < 0.0014

problematic: for the monolinguals, the older children's stories were superior to the younger children's, but they were 75 words and 10 clauses shorter on average. Among the bilinguals, the stories appeared to get better as they got longer, but even among bilinguals, the correlation between story quality ('Narrative Total') and length was relatively low, $r = 0.41$. While the correlation was significant, it explained less than 20% of the variance in story quality scores, so no further analyses were done with the CHILDES variables.

Differences between bilingual groups

English Scores. The six-way MANOVA showed no main effects of IMS in English for the bilinguals. Instead, LSH differences appeared more significant (Table 7.14). There were significant effects favoring the children with ESH in the Language Scores (both of them) and in the Narrative Total, but not in the Story Score. Of the subcomponents of the Language Score, there was a strong LSH Effect in Lexicon, but with the Bonferroni correction, neither the MS Accuracy nor the Complex Syntax score reached significance.

The main effect of LSH for Lexicon can be gleaned from Figure 7.7, which shows the LSH differences by Grade with ML English data for comparison. For MS Accuracy, there was an LSH by Grade interaction ($F = 23.49, p < 0.001$) and also a three-way interaction ($F = 10.21, p = 0.002*$) with LSH by Grade by SES which is graphed in Figure 7.8.

In MS Accuracy, both Hi and Low-SES groups of OSH children had higher scores at 5th grade than the 2nd grade groups. For the Low-SES children with ESH, the scores of 5th graders were lower than the scores of 2nd graders with respect to MS Accuracy. It is interesting to note that MS Accuracy showed a simple SES effect among the English monolinguals, also a decrement from 2nd to 5th grade. This difference between the LSH groups may indicate that the OSH children were still, at this stage, similar to second language learners, still improving their MS Accuracy, at both levels

Table 7.14 Home Language (LSH) effects in English Frog Story measures among Bilinguals

	F	p		F	p
Story Score	2.72	0.133	Complex Syntax	6.45	0.071
Language 1	15.36	0.000*	Lexicon	15.08	< 0.001
Language 2	10.44	0.001*	MS Accuracy	6.05	0.015
Frog Total	10.76	0.001*			

*Significant groupwise alpha (0.0033)

Table 7.15 Significant effects for Spanish Story measures

	Grade		IMS		LSH	
	F	p	F	p	F	p
Summary Scores						
Frog Total	15.64	< 0.001	9.84	0.002*		
Story Score	13.90	< 0.001	6.99	0.009		
Language Score	9.88	0.002*	7.14	0.008		
Component Scores						
Complex Syntax	22.55	< 0.001	2.20	0.141		
Lexicon	8.15	0.005	11.25	0.001*		
MS Accuracy	0.68	0.411	1.67	0.199	6.94	0.009
CHILDES Measures						
Subordination Index	11.86	0.001*	4.11	0.044		
MLU	9.85	0.002*	0	n.s.		
TTR	1.96	0.164	0.11	0.741		
Word Types**	21.86	< 0.001	2.09	0.151		

* Significant at groupwise alpha level (0.0033)
** Also in an LSH by Grade interaction, $F = 9.30$, $p = 0.003$.

of SES, whereas the ESH children, whose English was perhaps stronger to begin with, were more like the first language learners of English, showing an SES decrement.

Spanish Scores. When testing just the bilingual children with the General Linear Model, the SES effect was not significant for any of the Frog Story measures in Spanish, by contrast to the English analyses where strong SES effects pervaded the results. LSH, like SES, which showed an effect for four of the seven variables in English reported in Table 7.9, was significant (without Bonferroni correction) in Spanish only for MS Accuracy, $F = 6.94$, $p = 0.009$ (Table 7.15). Grade was a significant factor for several of the other measures, as was IMS. Thus, when other factors were held constant, Two-way schooling had a greater effect on Spanish proficiency than did the presence or relative lack of English in the home.

Figures 7.9 and 7.10 show the Spanish Narrative Total and Language Score subcomponents by Grade, IMS, and LSH, respectively.

It appears that the bilingual children in both learning situations improved in Spanish as they got older, but they did better in general in the Two-way schools. They did not appear to improve in MS Accuracy, even in

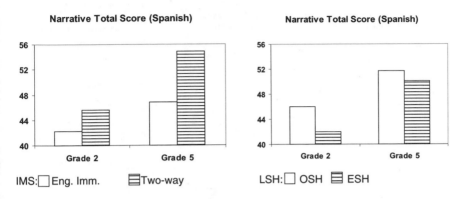

Figure 7.9 Narrative Total (Spanish), Grade by IMS and Grade by LSH

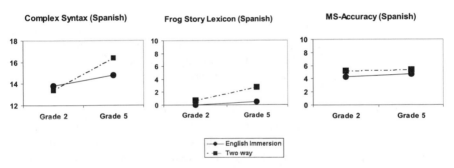

Figure 7.10 Subcomponents of Language Total Scores (Spanish), Grade by IMS

Two-way schools. Rather, IMS seemed to contribute especially to growth in Lexicon and Complex Syntax over this period. The instructional approach of the Two-way schools seemed to produce best results in the area of Lexicon and aspects of language that are tied to general intellectual development: lexical diversity and the expression of causes and effects, intentions, and complex temporal relations; in addition, positive effects were seen in the subordination index and MLU, reflecting the ability to link ideas in multiple clauses. Figure 7.9 illustrates the relative similarity of the two LSH groups at 5th grade in contrast to the relative difference between the IMS groups at 5th grade. Figure 7.9 also highlights the higher level of performance in narrative of the Two-way children relative to the English Immersion children especially at 5th grade. Figure 7.10 illustrates that it was primarily the Two-way children who showed growth across the

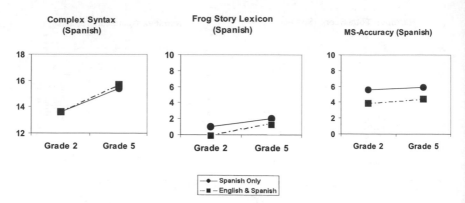

Figure 7.11 Language Score Subcomponents (Spanish), Grade by LSH

grades in Spanish for Complex Syntax and Lexicon. LSH, on the other hand, as illustrated in Figure 7.11, showed no strong effects on Complex Syntax or Lexicon. The OSH children, however, showed a notable advantage over ESH children on MS Accuracy at both grades, while MS Accuracy seemed little affected by IMS (Figure 7.10).

Following up on the one main effect of LSH, the one on MS Accuracy, it is notable that even though the differences were statistically reliable, there was considerable overlap in the two distributions, which both showed large standard deviations relative to the means for the two groups, $M = 6.27$, $SD = 4.5$ for the OSH group; $M = 7.55$, $SD = 3.3$ for the ESH group.

Within subjects results from correlation analysis

From the separation of the Frog Story measures into the two main aspects of the performance, narrative and linguistic, we can see the relation of the specific scores in one language to the same scores in the other. The correlation for the Narrative Total scores in English and Spanish was moderate, $r = 0.36$. However, some subcomponent scores showed much higher correlations than others. Correlations for selected subcomponent scores are presented in Figure 7.12, along with several additional correlations for reference and contrast, some of them based on data from the standardized tests (Chapters 4–6).

The data in Figure 7.12 suggest that Story Score and Complex Syntax correlate more highly across languages than Language Score or its subcomponents, Lexicon and MS Accuracy. On the other hand, the English Complex Syntax Score showed a significant degree of association to the Spanish Story Score (although the similar comparison within language is

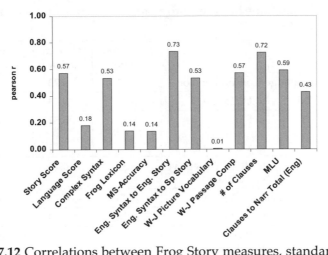

Figure 7.12 Correlations between Frog Story measures, standardized test scores, and CHILDES data (Spanish and English)

still higher, $r = 0.7$). This pattern is reminiscent of that found in Chapter 6, where literacy scores on standardized tests were highly correlated across languages while oral language scores were not so highly correlated. Literacy scores may have reflected more language-general factors because they involve general intellectual and conceptual capabilities while oral language scores may involve the learning of many individual items that are language-specific. In the case of the Frog Story data, it may be that Story Score and Complex Syntax represent relatively general capabilities that span languages, while it appears that Lexicon and MS Accuracy represent factors that need to be learned item by item in each language. While the cross-language correlations of Lexicon and MS Accuracy were very low, they were not negative, which would be one logical possibility if the two languages were in competition with each other, say for lexical storage area. Again the lack of negative correlations is consistent with the results in Chapter 6 which showed no significant negative correlations across languages.

Other objective measures, number of clauses and mean length of utterance (MLU), showed moderate correlation across languages. The correlation of number of clauses to Narrative Total was moderate, $r = 0.56$ for English and $r = 0.32$ for Spanish (not pictured). While they were both significant at the 0.01 level, they accounted for only 25% and 10% of the variance respectively in the Narrative Total scores. The correlations thus underline the need for more nuanced assessments of story quality than those quantitative measures can provide.

Table 7.16 Correlations between Frog Story measures and standardized test scores by IMS

		Eng. Imm. School	*Two-way School*	*Mono-lingual*
Story Score to Passage Comprehension		0.11	0.23	0.24
	to Dictation	0.06	0.03	0.24
	to Picture Vocabulary (production)	0.48	0.57	0.25
	to PPVT (receptive vocabulary)	0.39	0.48	0.21
Language Score to Passage Comp		0.25	0.27	0.31
	to Dictation	0.16	0.23	0.27
	to Picture Vocabulary	0.51	0.76	0.35
	to PPVT (receptive vocabulary)	0.64	0.65	0.37

Correlation analyses also addressed the question of how strongly the Frog Story measures were associated with other measures taken on the same children. Table 7.16 shows that the correlation was moderate at best (as it was for monolinguals). This indicates that the Frog Story measures gave different information from that given by the standardized scores from the Woodcock-Johnson Battery, and thus they are a useful adjunct to standardized tests in evaluating performance levels of monolingual and bilingual children. The patterns of relation were somewhat different for the bilinguals, with greater correlation for vocabulary and lower for Dictation (which may stress MS Accuracy). Correlations computed by splitting 2nd and 5th grade were very similar to these, split by IMS.

Discussion

Overall, these measures underline the multi-faceted nature of language development. With respect to the hypotheses stated in the Introduction, H1 and H3 were supported by these data; H2 was supported for Spanish, but not for English.

H1 posited that BL and ML differences would not be uniform across language behaviors. Indeed, the data showed that the Lingualism differences in favor of the monolinguals were much smaller for the narrative and discourse measures (Story Score) than for the Language Scores.

H2 posited that schooling in Spanish and English would enhance performance on complex tasks in both languages. The data indicated that bilingual children in Two-way schools showed enhanced performance in Spanish on both simple and complex language tasks. Their performance in English, however, was comparable in almost all areas to bilinguals' schooled in English Immersion, and superior in only a few domains.

H3 posited that narrative and linguistic abilities in one language would predict children's narrative and linguistic abilities in their other language. The results indicated a significant correlation between narrative skills (as indicated by the Story Score) and Complex Syntax scores across the two languages. By contrast, other language scores, MS Accuracy and Lexicon, were not reliably correlated across languages.

The bilingual children's stories exhibited age-appropriate skill in difficult tasks like creating a unified plot, motivating events through reference to internal states, and providing narrator's comments on the unfolding story. The BL children were accurate in using compound time referencing and embedded structures which distinguished their own thoughts from those of the characters. In these ways, their responses to the complex demands of the story genre were comparable to those of their monolingual peers'.

The BLs showed the greatest weakness relative to MLs in Lexicon and MS Accuracy. Except for the youngest children with the least exposure to English, who at 2nd grade were still very much like second-language learners of English, there was no implication that skill in English was negatively correlated with skill in Spanish. For the most part, Lexicon especially was low in both languages, suggesting that more time and input were needed in each language for the children to approach ML levels in vocabulary knowledge.

This is exactly what was observed. Although these are not longitudinal data, the older children among the bilinguals, the ones who, based on demographic information (Chapter 2) had more cumulative time and input in English, showed fuller lexicons than the younger children. The younger bilinguals appeared to have had, on average, less time and input in English environments than monolingual peers and the older bilingual cohorts. Measures that were low relative to those of monolinguals in 2nd grade tended to be comparable to those of monolinguals at 5th. For the most part, this Grade by Lingualism interaction on a number of measures can be traced to the lower starting point for bilinguals at the outset, and thus greater growth to reach a similar end point at 5th grade. Some of this 'catching up' might be attributed to relatively higher scores on these measures for the monolingual 2nd graders, and thus, less room for growth. But that does not appear to be the whole story. In fact (as seen in Table 7.5), simple effects when tested for Monolinguals-only showed significant grade effects, and thus growth among monolinguals, in each domain, in Story Score, in Language Score, and in the CHILDES measures. There appeared, then, to be growth in these measures over this age range for all children, but faster growth for bilinguals, as seen by the numerous Grade by Lingualism interactions.

With respect to non-significance of several simple effects, as seen, for example, in the relative equivalence of performance of High-SES children across the Lingualism groups when tested only at 5th grade, one cannot discount the possibility that the failure to find a reliable difference between Lingualism groups may have been the result of making a comparison with relatively small groups. Keeping this limitation in mind, it is worth noting that MLs showed a large advantage on the Narrative Total score at 2nd grade, but not at 5th grade. Let us reconsider the hypothesis expressed in Chapter 1, that bilingualism of the sort studied here might show its greatest advantages for English learning among children of High-SES who also had ESH. For the children in these specific subgroups, the results indicated no reliable difference on the Narrative Total between MLs and BLs at 5th grade, and this was true even if the Bonferroni correction was waived. The scores across ML and BL children were very similar among High-SES/ESH children.

Conclusions about growth drawn from these data, though, must remain tentative as they were based on a cross-sectional design. Every effort was made to equate the educational, social, and linguistic background of the participants and to sample a large enough group that individual differences in ability and volubility could be adequately randomized. Still, without longitudinal information, one cannot rule out the possibility of a cohort effect.

Further, one might question whether the findings based on the Frog Story groups are generalizable even to the larger design, much less to bilingual children in general. The difficulty of data transcription and coding of these semi-naturalistic data restricted the size of the groups to 80 bilinguals at each age, plus 4 monolingual control cells equaling another 80 children. To test the representativeness of the story subgroups with respect to the groups of 30 and 40 in the full design, the mean scores for the story groups on the Woodcock-Johnson/Muñoz and Peabody standardized measures were compared to the mean scores for the larger groups from which they were drawn. In all cells the subgroup mean was within one-third of a standard deviation of the mean for the larger group (and most were within a standard error), with no pattern as to whether one was higher or lower. Therefore, it appears that these groups adequately sampled the groups of the full design.

It is not surprising then, that the overall results are similar in their broad outline to the results from the Woodcock and Peabody measures (Chapters 4 and 5). These include, in English, main effects of SES, Grade, and Lingualism, and on some variables, a Grade by Lingualism interaction. Likewise, for the factors nested within Lingualism, there were few Frog Story differences in

English between the levels of IMS; the strongest effects were seen on some subcomponents of the Language scores from the LSH factor, favoring children with ESH. In the Spanish stories, there were no differences by IMS at 2nd grade; but by 5th grade there were differences that favored the Two-way schools, especially in Spanish Lexicon and Complex Syntax (although Spanish scores in general were considerably lower than they were in English for all groups, even those weakest in English). Notably, there were no SES effects in Spanish and surprisingly few LSH effects.

As in the standardized tests, the bilinguals were less disadvantaged with respect to the more complex narrative scores and more disadvantaged with respect to the monolinguals on the more language-specific measures (especially MS Accuracy). The largest differences between groups in the Woodcock-Johnson Batteries were found in Picture Vocabulary, a productive measure like the Frog Story, a measure that also seems to emphasize language-specific knowledge. Picture Vocabulary was also a task where a Grade by Lingualism interaction obtained (see Chapter 4).

Crucially, the Frog Story measures *add* to the information provided by the other testing of these children. Since the correlations between Frog Story measures and the standardized scores were only moderate (in the neighborhood of 0.3 for the monolinguals, cf. Table 7.16), we can be relatively confident that these data give information about different aspects of the children's performance. Unlike the standardized tests from which we must infer the details about how the different groups talk, the Frog Stories provided samples of their productive language for direct comparison.

One surprise in listening to the children's stories was how restricted their Spanish was overall, even among the children for whom Spanish was the major language of the household. Only a handful of children were so weak in Spanish as to speak it with an English accent, but many of the children with ESH found it difficult to speak Spanish for the space of the whole story, without lapsing into English for lexical items and even whole clauses. Those with OSH were more fluent in their Spanish stories, but also resorted to paraphrase for lexical gaps, avoided the subjunctive in common expressions, and made salient L2 morphosyntactic mistakes. This weakness in Spanish may have been a result of our selection criteria which stipulated that all participants had to have been born in the United States, thus perhaps restricting the range of Spanish ability in our sample. This narrowed basis for selection was intended to permit a stronger assessment of the effects of bilingualism independent of immigration. However, it eliminated from consideration the estimated 25% of the student population at each grade level who were entering the country and the Dade County school system during the time of the study and, according to information on the DCPS website, continue to enter each year in even larger numbers (http://www.dade.k12.fl.us/bfls/index.htm). This may be a group for whom native language instruction is more essential and more facilitating than for our subjects, and thus merits further research. Another possible explanation for the low Spanish scores observed in this study concerns the comparison of the contact variety of Spanish spoken in Miami by the largely bilingual Hispanic population with the dialects of Spanish spoken in the countries of origin. Even if specific elements of the language are the same, they may differ in their distribution in the speech of bilingual Spanish speakers as compared to monolingual Spanish speakers in monolingual contexts (Toribio, 2000). The effects of such differences on children's learning of the language are largely unknown.

For our subjects, the strongest educational implication of these findings is that the time spent learning in Spanish does not appear to harm the students' progress in English, but provides significant support for them in Spanish. The time spent learning Spanish in school seems to translate into learning of skills – reading, dictation, strategies for narratives – which appear available to the child in either language. But it does not seem to translate into exposure to more double-language vocabulary, for example. Vocabulary seems to be learned item by item, and has to be done in each language separately. With respect to language-specific learning of morphosyntax (such as irregular forms, or verb complement patterns), here IMS appeared to be a less potent factor than LSH. The children may have spent more time at home than at school. The effect of schooling on language-specific learning may have been weaker than that of home language because the same language-specific structures were being learned in both places, but more of the learning seems to have occurred in the home.

Importantly, the LSH effect was different for the children's two languages. English language skills were highest in children from High-SES families and ESH. IMS was a less crucial factor for English than for Spanish language development as seen in the data from this chapter, as well as Chapter 4. Two-way schooling was helpful for Spanish language development in all demographic groups, High and Low-SES, ESH and OSH.

The separate contributions of LSH, IMS, and SES background to children's language and literacy performance created a complex pattern of effects and non-effects. By using the factorial design of the larger study, which balanced the effect of each factor, we have enhanced our ability to generalize findings from the children's stories. Likewise, by expanding the performance demand on the children through the story task, we have provided an 'auditory snapshot' of each individual, to add to the perspective provided by the standardized test scores. This snapshot enriches our ability to understand what the test scores are saying and to have greater confidence in the messages they convey.

Appendix

FROG STORY CODING SHEET

Coded Subject No. _____Lang/Order _____ Coder _____ No. of Clauses _____

Part 1. Story Score (Narrative/Discourse Elements)

Each category is worth 12 points. In each column, choose the 'highest' behavior that describes the story being coded, deducting for behaviors NOT shown, according to the scale in that column.

Frog Story Elements	Sequence	Perspective/Affect	Engagement
Mentions discovery of missing frog +2 Uses mental verb+1 'looks' only	0 Picture description	–2 Uses 'here' 'there' 'now' to refer to her own reference frame (not the story's)	
+2 Initiates search	3 Gives isolated events	Poor first mention (uses pronoun right away) –1 Main characters –1 Other characters	–2 Vague or confused (in parts)
+1 Finds frog	Sequential events (some, not all)	Lapses in reference (reader must ask 'who?') –1 1 defective reference –2 2 defective references –4 5 or more	Disfluencies –2 (grave, interfere with listener's ability to follow story)
+1 Takes frog (home)	–1 for picture description –1 for irrelevant details		
(6) AVERAGE	(6) FACTUAL STORY	(6) NEUTRAL OBSERVER	(6) MATTER OF FACT TONE
+1 Articulates goal (each, up to 2)	7 Elaborated episodes	7 Ascribes intention	Attempts to be lively or engaging
+1 Articulates lack of success		8 Gives internal state info (affective statements, 1 or 2)	+1 use of 'refrain' +1 appropriate exclamations
	9 Hierarchical structure (beginning/middle/end) (highlighting of an event)	9 3 or more affective statements	+1 extensive direct speech
+4 Notes character's misperception (branch/antler or other)	12 Retrospective or prospective summary +2 for summary statement +3 for 2 or more	12 Mentions ironic perspective	Uses figures of speech +2 each (up to 3)
_____/12	_____/12	Persp: __/6 Aff: __/6 _____/12	_____/12
			Total _____/48

Part 2. Language Score

Complex Syntax		Lexicon	Morphosyntactic Accuracy
Verb Phrase	*Between Clauses*	Circle if present by name	Errors –1 each 'type', not 'token' (note word and line)
	(4) NO CONJUNCTIONS (BEYOND 'AND THEN' 'Y PUES' O 'ENTONCES'	frog jar/bottle bees (wasps)	articles pronouns prepositions
(6) NATURAL FLOW OF EVENTS English: Modals or aspectual auxiliaries +1 each (up to 3) Eng. or Spa.: Complex Ss Relative Clause or Noun Clause +1 for 2, up to 3 points Spa: Perfect Tenses +2 for one +3 for 2 or more Spa: Subjunctive +2 for one +3 for 2 or more	Causal connections/ (or intentions) +1 for 1 or 2 +2 for 3 or more Simultaneous actions ('while'/'when'– simul) +2 for 1 +3 for 2 or more Retrospective reference 'still'/'already' 'todavia' +1 each, up to 3	beehive rodent-type owl trunk (Eng) deer antlers pond/lake log cliff Other 'specific' vocabulary: Other vocabulary mistakes:	verb forms conjunctions word order other
_____/12	_____/12 Complex Syntax: _____/24	Total _____/12 (+1 for each listed word; +½ for other specific words; –½ for other mistakes (0–12 min/max)	Total: Subtract from 12 _____/12
			Total _____/48
			Total _____/96

Chapter 8

Command of the Mass/Count Distinction in Bilingual and Monolingual Children: An English Morphosyntactic Distinction

VIRGINIA C. MUELLER GATHERCOLE

The following three chapters report experiments involving morpho-syntactic elements of English and Spanish. The primary question addressed is the extent to which bilingual children follow the same processes of acquisition and the same timing in their acquisition of these elements as their monolingual peers. Central to this question is the extent to which the major variables of the core study – Instructional Method in the School (IMS), Socio-economic Status (SES), and Language Spoken in the Home (LSH) – play roles in affecting patterns or rates of acquisition. A secondary question is whether there is a difference in bilinguals' abilities with the acquisition of relatively superficial elements of the grammar (the mass/count distinction in English, gender in Spanish) and their abilities with an element attributed to Universal Grammar (UG) (*that*-trace phenomena). A comparison of bilingual and monolingual performance across these structures will help illuminate the extent to which bilingual acquisition follows paths that are similar to or different from those followed in monolingual acquisition; the extent to which school experience, SES, and LSH play a role; and the extent to which these effects are present in superficial versus purportedly universal aspects of the grammar.

The structures to be examined here are of interest because with each one, the two languages being learned by these bilinguals are vastly different. English has a mass/count distinction, Spanish does not. Spanish has a system of grammatical gender, English has natural gender. English does not allow *that*-trace structures, Spanish does. Children acquiring these two systems must develop distinct or complementary constructs in the two languages and may or may not allow their knowledge of one language to be influenced by what they know about the other.

Because of the considerable differences across the two languages, an examination of the children's acquisition of these structures allows a fine-grained account to supplement what has already been found in the core studies (Chapters 4, 5, and 6) of this project, and in other research. As suggested in Chapter 1, research has been mixed in its findings regarding the performance of bilinguals relative to their monolingual peers. Some researchers have provided evidence that bilinguals follow the same processes and timing in their acquisition of a language as their monolingual counterparts, or at least end up with grammars that resemble those of their monolingual counterparts. Just to cite a few, Oyama (1976) found that Italian immigrants to the US developed native-like pronunciation of English and native-like comprehension abilities, if they began English between the ages of 6 and 11 years. Similarly, Newport (1990) and Johnson and Newport (1989) reported that Chinese and Korean immigrants who arrived in the US at an early age (3 to 7 years) performed like their native-speaking peers on a variety of grammatical measures. And De Houwer (1990) reported that her subject learned the morphosyntax of English and Dutch in much the same fashion as monolingual learners of these languages. (See also discussion in Chapter 1 regarding educational performance and cognitive abilities in monolinguals and bilinguals.)

On the other hand, as noted in previous chapters, Umbel *et al.*, (1992) (see also Pearson *et al.*, 1993b, and Umbel and Oller, 1994) have found that while bilingual children's lexical inventories cover a full range of concepts across the two languages, their lexicons in the individual languages fall slightly short of the norms for the range of vocabulary items known by monolinguals of the same ages. Swain and Wesche (1975) reported that their bilingual subject used constructions that showed influence of one language on the other. Meisel (1986) found that his subjects differed from monolinguals for some constructs (word order and case marking), but not for others (subject-finite verb agreement). In a study of a group of adults who had immigrated to the United States as young children, Ioup (1989) found that these subjects had failed to acquire a native-like command of a variety of English structures, including aspects corresponding to Universal Grammar. Evidence suggests that bilinguals may even process certain structures in a way that is somewhere 'in between' the manner in which monolinguals in either language would process them (Hernández *et al.*, 1994). (See DeHouwer, 1990: 50–4; Singleton, 1989: 80–138, for reviews and thoughtful discussions.)

Some important recent work in this regard has been conducted by Bialystok (1991), who argues that bilingual children *necessarily* process language differently from their monolingual peers. This is especially true with regard to linguistic and metalinguistic tasks that require high levels of control and high levels of analysis. It is on these types of tasks that Bialystok has reported superior performance among bilinguals over monolinguals, even in non-linguistic problem-solving tasks (see, e.g. Bialystok & Majumder, 1998).

The goal of the three experiments in Chapters 8, 9, and 10 was to provide evidence on this question by looking in particular at constructions that are different in the two languages being learned.

General Method

In all three experiments, children were asked to judge both grammatical and ungrammatical sentences involving the structures in question. All tasks involved a puppet-correction procedure, in which the child was invited to operate a puppet that corrected a funny-talking puppet's speech.

Participants

The bilingual participants and the monolingual English-speaking participants for the three experiments were 294 of the 2nd and 5th grade participants from the Core Design. In addition, 32 2nd and 5th grade monolingual Spanish-speaking participants from Lima, Peru were tested for the Spanish portions of the experiments in Chapters 8 and 9. These Spanish-speaking participants were students at a private parochial school, and were from a middle- to upper-middle-class SES level. Thus, a total of 326 participants were tested, 148 2nd graders and 146 5th graders in Miami, and 16 2nd graders and 16 5th graders in Lima. However, 15 of the 2nd graders (all bilinguals) in Miami were dropped because they could not pass the warm-up procedure, described below. The distribution of the remaining participants according to Grade, SES, LSH, and (for bilinguals) IMS is shown in Table 8.1. The bilinguals were given four tests: mass/count (English), gender (Spanish), *that*-trace in English, and *that*-trace in Spanish. The monolinguals were given only the two tests of their language.

Procedure

The general procedure used across these experiments was a judgment and correction procedure using puppets. Children were given a grammatical or ungrammatical sentence and were asked to judge whether the sentence sounded all right. If it did not, they were to correct it. All of this was carried out through the use of one puppet who 'sometimes doesn't know how to say things right' and another (operated by the child) who helps the first puppet out. Such a procedure has been used successfully to

Table 8.1 Subjects for Morphosyntax Experiments by Group, Grade, Language Spoken at Home, and SES

Grade	Language Spoken at Home	SES	Participant Group				Total
			Mono-lingual Spanish	Two-Way Bilinguals	English Immersion Bilinguals	Monolingual English	
2	OSH	High	16	16	12		
		Low		11	14		
	ESH	High		13	15		
		Low		11	9		
	OEH	High				16	
		Low				16	
	Total		16	51	50	32	149
5	OSH	High	16	16	12		
		Low		16	16		
	ESH	High		10	13		
		Low		13	15		
	OEH	High				17	
		Low				18	
	Total		16	55	56	35	162

OSH = Only Spanish at Home; ESH = English and Spanish at Home; OEH = Only English at Home

tap children's grammatical judgments even at an early age, and at ages younger than those tested here (e.g. de Villiers & de Villiers, 1972, 1973; Gathercole, 1985a; Bialystok, 1986; see also McDaniel & Cairns, 1996, for discussion).

Before the test trials, there was a warm-up procedure. During this warm-up procedure, children were asked to judge the acceptability of sentences whose structures had nothing to do with those of the experiments. The experimenter first presented two sentences in which she modeled one puppet producing a sentence, and the correcting puppet responding 'Yes, that's good' or 'No, you should say . . . ' This was followed with five more sample sentences, for which the child was invited to operate the correcting puppet and was asked what he/she thought the correcting puppet should say. These sentences consisted of three ungrammatical and two grammatical sentences that had nothing to do with any of the structures being tested. If a child responded appropriately to four out of five of these items, and his or her corrections were of a morphosyntactic nature, the experimenter went on to the experimental task. If during these five warm-up sentences the child judged fewer than four items correctly or corrected only the semantic content of sentences, the experimenter corrected the child and went on to five more warm-up items. If the child made correct judgments about the appropriateness of at least three of these new five items, regardless of the type of correction made, the experimenter moved on to the test items. If, however, a child could not make correct judgments on at least three of this second set of warm-up sentences, that child's participation in the study was discontinued.

As noted, bilingual children were administered all four tasks (mass/count, English; gender, Spanish; *that*-trace, English; *that*-trace, Spanish), monolingual children, the two tasks of their language. The order of presentation of the tasks was balanced for the bilinguals, so that some received the two Spanish tests first, and some received the two English tests first (with the unrelated phonological translation task between the Spanish and English portions, see Chapter 11). Within language, the two tests were administered in the same order, with the *that*-trace sentences always administered second in each language. Test sentences within an experiment were administered in random order.

Mass/count experiment

This experiment examined the acquisition of the linguistic mass/count distinction in English. The goal was to explore whether bilingual children acquire the mass/count distinction, specifically as expressed with the quantifiers *much* and *many* and the nouns they modify, in a manner that is similar to that of their monolingual peers. Do bilingual children follow the same processes as those followed by monolingual children, and does the distinction emerge in the same order and at the same time as it does in monolinguals? English has a linguistic mass/count distinction, Spanish does not. Does this fact influence the process by which Spanish–English bilinguals acquire this distinction in English? In order to explore this question, let us examine the structures of these two languages in this regard.

Mass/count structures

English makes a mass/count distinction that sorts nouns and their modifiers into two groups. What are traditionally called mass nouns are those that occur only in the singular (*rice*, not *rices*), can occur in the singular preceded by *some* or no article (*some rice fell on the floor*, *rice tastes good*), and can occur with the quantifiers *much, little,* and *less* (with the singular) (*she wants that much rice, the store sold little rice this week, they sold less rice than last week*). What are traditionally called count nouns are those that can occur in the singular preceded by *a* (*a pea rolled off the table*) or in the plural preceded by _some_ or by no article (_some peas fell on the floor, peas taste good_), and can occur with the quantifiers _many_ and _few_ (with the plural) (_she wants that many peas, the store sold few peas this week_). Both types of noun can occur preceded by _the_ (_the rice, the pea, the peas_) and by other determiners, including possessive adjectives (_my rice, my pea, my peas_).

The linguistic mass-count distinction has to do with the specification of individuation through quantification. Thus, e.g. we can say '5 peas' (individuated), but not '5 rices'. The distinction is correlated, somewhat imperfectly, with an ontological distinction between objects and substances. Thus, typically, objects are named by count nouns and occur in count linguistic contexts. Objects can be described as items in the world that (1) have heterogeneous makeup, (2) have minimal parts (what 'counts' as an instance of 'X' can't be broken up and still be 'X'), (3) do not have cumulative reference (several instances of 'X' cannot be put together and still be an example of 'X'), and (4) come in individuated, countable units. Good, prototypical examples are trees, tables, and animals. Conversely, substances are typically named by mass nouns and occur in mass linguistic contexts. Substances are items that (1) have homogeneous makeup, (2) do not have minimal parts, (3) have cumulative reference, and (4) do not come in individuated, countable units. Good examples of substances are water, clay, and sand (see discussions in Pelletier, 1979).

It is an important aspect of the mass/count distinction, however, that not all referents of count nouns are necessarily items that would naturally be viewed cognitively as objects, nor are all referents of mass nouns necessarily substances. Examples are _stick, crayon_, and _sponge_ (count nouns) and _furniture, succotash_, and _money_ (mass nouns). The former are non-prototypical count nouns because they refer to items that are homogeneous and have no minimal parts; the latter are non-prototypical mass nouns because they refer to items that are heterogeneous and do have minimal parts. Nevertheless, despite their non-prototypicality, they must take the appropriate mass/count structures.

Compare this with the quite distinct structure of Spanish in which all nouns have virtually the same privileges of occurrence (see Gathercole, 1986, 1997). In Spanish, for example, any noun can generally be used in either of the contexts that distinguish mass and count nouns in English. Thus, in principle, any noun can occur in the singular or plural, and all nouns can occur with the same quantifiers. For example, one can say both (1) and (2), using the nouns _pan_ ('bread') and _mueble_ ('furniture') in both the singular and plural; similarly, the quantifiers _mucho(s)_ and _poco(s)_ can occur with both singular and plural forms of nouns, corresponding to English _much_ and _little_ in the singular and _many_ and _few_ in the plural, as in (3).

(1) Singular:
A mí me gusta el pan de Valencia.
'I like the bread from Valencia.'
Ana compró el mueble grande para el salón.
'Ana bought the large [piece of] furniture for the living room.'

(2) Plural:
Suele comprar tres panes al día.
'[S/he] usually buys three [loaves of] bread(s) per day.'
Ana compró tres muebles grandes para el salón.
'Ana bought three large [pieces of] furniture(s) for the living room.'

(3) *No tiene mucho pan.*
'[S/he] does not have a lot of bread.'
No tiene muchos panes.
'[S/he] does not have many [loaves of] bread(s).'
Tiene poco queso.
'[S/he] has little cheese.'
Tiene pocos quesos.
'[S/he] has few [types of/balls of] cheese(s).'

Note that I am not implying that Spanish speakers do not draw a *cognitive* distinction between substances and objects. It is just that their language does not *force* them to classify every nominal form into either a mass or count linguistic class.

It is helpful to draw an analogy with the distinction between grammatical and natural gender languages. In a 'grammatical gender' language, like Spanish or German, every noun is categorized into a gender class, and a competent speaker cannot use any noun without assigning it to its appropriate gender. And that assignment has only an imperfect relationship with the real-world gender of animate referents (see Gathercole & Hasson, 1995). In a 'natural gender' language, like English, on the other hand, only some nouns that refer to animate beings are marked for gender, and that marking is almost always in concord with the real-world gender of the referent.

In like manner, we could call a language like English a 'grammatical mass/count' language – every noun is marked for mass/count status, and that status has only an imperfect correlation with the ontological status of a referent (see Croft, 2001, unpublished manuscript for an alternative view within *Radical Construction Grammar*). What distinguishes mass terms from count terms is not properties of their referents, but the way they lead us to *view* referents (Bunt, 1979; Zemach, 1979). English guides the speaker-hearer in *every instance* to view a referent either as an individuated, countable object (if the label occurs in count contexts) or as an unindividuated, uncountable substance or conglomeration (if the label occurs in mass contexts).

Conversely, a language like Spanish could be called a 'natural mass/count' language. Nouns are not strictly classified as mass or count. However, one can view referents as substances or objects without being forced to do so by the syntax of the language. If one views a referent as a substance, one can refer to it and quantify it in the singular (*mucho pan*); if one views a referent as an object, one can refer to it and quantify it in the plural (*dos panes*). In such a 'natural mass/count' language, we can expect nouns for prototypical substances (sand, water) to typically occur in the singular and nouns for prototypical objects to be quantified in the plural. However, it is not the *language* that is forcing that choice.

Acquisition of mass/count

Much is known about the acquisition of the mass/count structure by monolingual children learning English. Two major questions have been addressed. One is the question of whether children approach the distinction as a syntactic one or a semantic one. In principle, it would be possible to acquire these forms as distributional co-occurrences (i.e. noun X goes with *much* and *some*; noun Y goes with *many* and *few*, and so forth) or as semantically based markers (noun Y refers to an object, so it must be a count noun; noun X refers to a substance, so it must be a mass noun). If children approached these forms semantically, one could expect them to learn the mass/count constructions either earlier or better with prototypical count and mass nouns than with non-prototypical mass and count nouns.

With regard to this first question, a considerable amount of work suggests that young children acquire this distinction as a syntactic, or distributional, phenomenon, rather than as a semantic one. Gordon (1982) examined children's use of forms like the plural, *a/some, one* and *another* and found that children's categorization was based on syntax, not semantics. Gathercole (1985a) tested whether English-speaking children are more adept at judging sentences involving *much* and *many* when those involved prototypical mass and count nouns than non-prototypical, and she found no support for this hypothesis. However, Gathercole (1985a) and Gathercole (1986) proposed that eventually children move to a higher-level semantic understanding of the mass-count distinction that does make reference to semantics. But that higher-level semantic understanding involves the nature of the quantification involved with these constructs (Gordon, 1982).

At the same time, there is evidence that among monolingual English-speaking children, even preschoolers draw on the linguistic mass/count context in which they hear a new word to determine the ontological status of its referent. In Gathercole *et al.* (1995), 3- and 4-year-olds were presented with novel stimuli with unfamiliar names and were asked to extend each new name to either an item that was of the same shape, but a different substance, as the original or an item that was of the same substance, but different shape, as the original. Participants (in the No Function conditions of that study) were able to extend the use of the new name to an item of the same shape as the original if that new name was presented with count syntax (*a blicket, blickets*), and to an item of the same substance as the original if that new name was presented with mass syntax (*some blicket, blicket*). Similarly, in a series of studies by Soja and her colleagues (Soja, 1992; Soja *et al.*, 1991), children aged 2 and 2½ were less likely to extend the name of a rigid object to a referent matching it in shape and number when the name occurred with mass syntax (*some blicket*) than with count syntax (*a blicket*), and they were more likely to extend the name of a non-solid substance to a referent matching it in shape and number when the name occurred with count syntax than with mass syntax. (See Bloom, 1994 and Carey, 1994, for discussion.)

Bloom (1994) also reports that young children are more likely to overgeneralize count syntax to *objects* that have mass names than to *substances* that have mass names. Studies have confirmed that this ability continues beyond the preschool years into the grade-school years and adulthood (Gathercole & Whitfield, 2001; Gathercole *et al.*, 1995; Rice *et al.*, 1993). It should be noted that many of these results – particularly those related to interpretations of forms containing nonsense nouns – may only indicate that children are aware of the semantics that correlates with the syntax of the MODIFIERS (*a, another, both,* and the like). Children may have developed links between modifiers and their probable types of referents, so children appear to be relying on semantic information for mass/count class. However, such children may still not have worked out that each noun is also assigned a particular mass/count status. The acquisition of the mass/count distinction requires this latter knowledge as well as the former; this mass/count classification of nouns is central to what makes a language a grammatical mass/count language instead of a natural mass/count language.

A second question that has been addressed in the literature on the acquisition of mass/count by monolinguals is the order and timing of acquisition for these constructs. There is evidence that children learn some of these constructs quite early (plural marking, use of *a, another, some,* and numerals) (Gordon, 1982; 1988), while others take much longer to acquire (e.g. the distinction between *much* and *many* and the mass and count uses of *more*) (Gathercole, 1985a, b, 1986). It appears that forms such as *a, another,* and *some* may be in place by 3 years of age; however, the understanding of the mass-count distinction in *more* is not acquired until well after 5½ years of age (Gathercole, 1985b), and a full command of the syntactic distribution of *much* and *many* is not mastered until past 8½ years of age. Furthermore, Gathercole found that children performed better on *much* and *many* when these occurred with real words than with nonsense words; that they performed better in assessing whether the noun number was correct than in assessing whether the quantifier choice was correct (consistent with Gordon's finding that noun number is learned early); and that children did better in judging and correcting sentences with *many* than they did sentences with *much*. Even at age 8½ children were allowing *much* to occur with the plural forms of count nouns (e.g. 'so much questions'; see Gathercole, 1986, for further discussion.)

These two issues that have been examined for first-language acquisition are highly relevant to our assessment of whether monolinguals and bilinguals acquire language in the same fashion. With respect to the first issue, it is not known whether bilingual children who are learning English along with another language process the mass/count distinction in a fashion that is identical to their monolingual counterparts. In particular, do bilingual children who are learning English along with a language like Spanish, which does not have a mass/count classificatory scheme for quantifiers and nouns, acquire the system based on syntactic patterning, like monolingual children do, or on the basis of semantic rules? Relevant to this question is whether bilingual children learn the two languages as autonomous systems – one with 'grammatical mass/count', the other with 'natural mass/count' – or whether there is some level of interaction between the two languages. If they learn the two languages as autonomous systems, there should be no observable difference in the process of acquisition when monolinguals and bilinguals are compared. If, on the other hand, bilingual children allow any kind of cross-comparison between the two languages, their English may be influenced by a number of factors.

First, the natural mass/count status of Spanish may lead Spanish-speaking bilinguals to prefer a semantic route to the acquisition of mass/count in English. Another potential complication for Spanish-speaking bilinguals is the fact that the quantifiers *much* and *mucho(s)* are so similar phonologically. *Mucho(s)* covers the same range of application in Spanish as is covered by both *much* and *many* in English. If bilingual children do consult back and forth between the two languages being learned, then Spanish–English bilinguals may have a prolonged period in which *much* is overgeneralized for use where *many* should occur. Since monolingual children already overgeneralize in this way, this may reinforce any suspicion on a Spanish-speaking child's part that this is a valid construct in English.

The second question concerns the timing of acquisition. Can we expect bilinguals to acquire the elements of the mass/count distinction at the same time as, and in the same order as, their monolingual counterparts? If we find a difference in the processes by which bilinguals acquire the mass/count distinction, then a difference in timing or order would not be surprising. But even if we find no difference in the processes by which bilinguals acquire this distinction, it is still possible that there could be a difference in timing. Judging from the range of variation in results obtained in previous studies of bilinguals and from the results reported in previous chapters here, it is not at all clear what the expectation in this regard should be. The following experiment explores these questions.

Method

The general method used was similar to that used in Gathercole (1985a). Children were asked to judge both grammatical and ungrammatical sentences involving *much* and *many* and to correct those that they judged to be ungrammatical. Twenty sentences were constructed in which the occurrences of *many* and *much*, of singular and plural forms of nouns, and of selected sentence frames were systematically varied. With the puppet-correction procedure, children were asked to judge whether each sentence was acceptable, and, if not, how the sentence should be worded.

Materials

Two sets of 20 sentences were drawn up. In each set (I and II), the following conditions held. First, 10 sentences involved *much*, and 10 involved *many*, with each of these quantifiers modifying each of the following 5 types of nominals twice.

A. Prototypical mass nouns: nouns that typically occur with mass quantifiers and that refer to prototypical substances. Nouns used were: *water, clay, dirt,* and *smoke*.
B. Prototypical count nouns: nouns that typically occur with count quantifiers and that refer to prototypical objects. Nouns used: *boy, finger, tree, book*.
C. Non-prototypical mass nouns: nouns that typically occur with mass quantifiers but that refer to objects that typically come in individuated, countable pieces. Nouns used: *bread, money, chalk, ice*.
D. Non-prototypical count nouns: nouns that typically occur with count quantifiers but that refer to objects with homogeneous makeup and that have no minimal parts (i.e. they can be broken up in such a way that one could still refer to the remainder with the same noun). Nouns used: *rock, noodle, crayon, stick*.
E. Flexible nouns: nouns that are standardly used with both mass and count quantifiers. Nouns used: *cake, glass, hamburger, fire*.

Each participant received each type of noun once in the singular and once in the plural with both *much* and *many*. In addition, each quantifier was modified once by one of 10 determiner patterns: *that, this, so, very, too, not . . . too, as . . . as the ghost, how* (with an interrogative sentence), Ø (with an interrogative sentence), *not . . . Ø*. The use of these determiners was distributed so that each determiner occurred once with *much* and once with *many*, and once with a singular noun and once with a plural noun. Finally, ten sentence frames were used, shown in (4), distributed with the constraint that each participant heard each sentence frame once with *much* and once with *many*, once with a singular noun, once with a plural noun, and no more than once with a given determiner.

(4) We have . . .
     The giant saw . . .
     The monster took . . .
     Grover saw . . .
     Ernie got . . .
     Mickey Mouse wanted . . .
     Big Bird had . . .
     Oscar took . . .
     He wanted . . .
     She got . . .

Examples of stimuli are shown in (5).[1]

(5) Do we have much clay?
     *The monster took that much boy.
     *Mickey Mouse wanted too many crayon.
     The giant saw as many fires as the ghost.

As noted, there were two sets of 20 sentences each. Each participant heard only the Set I or the Set II sentences. The two sets of sentences differed as follows: (1) the nouns that were used with *much* in Set I were used with *many* in Set II, and vice versa, (2) the nouns that were used in the singular in Set I were used in the plural in Set II, and vice versa, and (3) within each of the five noun types, the sentence frames and determiners that were used with *much* in Set I were used with *many* in Set II, and vice-versa.

Results

Children's responses to test sentences involved two components, judgments of sentences and corrections. These data will be reported separately.

A preliminary analysis of the data revealed no significant effects of order of testing presentation (Spanish first or English first). All analyses reported below are thus collapsed for orders of presentation.

However, preliminary tests indicated some difference by the Set of sentences (Set I vs Set II) used. There was no main effect, but Set sometimes interacted significantly with Noun Type, Noun Number, or Quantifier, when these occurred as significant effects either alone or in interaction with other major variables. These interactions appear to be related to knowledge about individual nouns. However, they occurred across all Participant Groups. For this reason, and since Set of sentences was not a major variable of the study, it will not be considered in the analyses below.

Judgments

Children's judgments were scored as being correct or incorrect. Two separate analyses were performed. The first analyzed the data for all participants, with Participant Group (Monolingual English, Bilingual Two-way, Bilingual English Immersion, Grade (2, 5), SES (High, Low), Quantifier (*much*, *many*), Noun Type (prototypical mass, prototypical count, non-prototypical mass, non-prototypical count, flexible), and Noun Number (singular, plural) treated as variables. The second analyzed these variables for the bilinguals only (Two-way and English Immersion) in combination with the variable of LSH (Only Spanish at Home [OSH], English and Spanish at Home [ESH]).

All participants

Analysis of variance revealed, first, significant main effects of Participant Group ($F(2,267) = 19.5, p < 0.0001$), Grade ($F(1,267) = 43.0, p < 0.0001$), SES ($F(1,267) = 14.5, p < 0.0002$), Quantifier ($F(1,267) = 53.0, p < 0.0001$), Noun Type ($F(4,1068) = 15.7, p < 0.0001$), and Noun Number ($F(1,267) = 46.7, p < 0.0001$). Monolinguals gave significantly more correct judgments (73.8%) than English Immersion bilinguals (68.3%), who in turn gave significantly more correct judgments than Two-way bilinguals (62.9%), Student-Newman-Keuls, $p < 0.05$. Children in the 5th grade performed better than those in the 2nd grade (72.1% vs 62.6% accuracy). Those who were in the High SES group gave more correct judgments than those in the Low SES group (70.1% vs 65.0% correct). Performance on sentences involving *many* was better than performance on sentences involving *much* (72.3% vs 62.9% accuracy). Performance on sentences involving singular nouns was better than performance on sentences involving plural nouns (71.9% vs 63.2% accuracy). Finally, performance on flexible nouns was worse (57.4% accuracy) than performance on each of the other four Noun Types (69.3% to 71.1% accuracy for each).

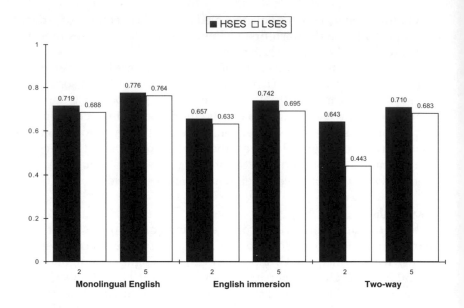

Figure 8.1 Proportion Correct Judgments by Participant Group, Grade, and SES Level

These main effects were moderated by two-, three-, and four-way interaction effects as follows. First, there were several significant interactions involving Participant Groups: Participant Group X Grade (F(2,267) = 3.7, $p < 0.03$), Participant Group X SES (F(2,267) = 3.8, $p < 0.03$), and Participant Group X Grade X SES (F(2,267) = 4.6, $p < 0.02$). Performance by Participant Group, Grade, and SES is shown in Figure 8.1. The Participant Group X Grade interaction reveals that at 2nd grade, all three groups performed significantly differently from one another (all F's (1,267) = 4.5, p's < 0.04), but at 5th grade, both bilingual groups performed significantly differently from the Monolingual English group (F's = 3.9, p's = 0.05), but not from each other. The interaction of Participant Group X SES reveals that for the Two-way bilinguals, participants from the Low SES level performed worse than those at the High SES level, F(1,267) = 22.6, $p < .0001$. The three-way interaction reveals that this latter effect was due primarily to the Two-way bilinguals at 2nd grade (High SES Two-way at 2nd grade vs Low SES Two-way at 2nd grade: F(1, 267) = 33.3, $p < 0.0001$). Thus, the worst performance was by the Low SES Two-way bilinguals at 2nd grade, but by 5th grade, this group's performance was indistinguishable from that of the other bilingual groups.

In addition, there were significant interactions involving Quantifier and

Noun Type: Quantifier X Noun Type (F(4,1068) = 35.5, p < 0.0001) and Quantifier X Noun Type X Grade (4,1068) = 7.2, p < 0.0001). See Figure 8.2. Performance was significantly better on *much* with prototypical mass and non-prototypical mass nouns than with prototypical count, non-prototypical count, and flexible nouns, and on *many* with prototypical count and non-prototypical count nouns than with prototypical mass, non-prototypical mass, and flexible nouns (all F's (1, 1068) > 11.3, p's < 0.0008). Performance on *much* with prototypical count and non-prototypical count nouns improved between Grades 2 and 5, and performance on *many* with prototypical mass and non-prototypical mass nouns improved between these two grades. Note that initially, then, in the case of mass and count nouns, children did better on those cases in which the quantifier matched the noun type – i.e. on constructs that were grammatical. It is worth commenting here that it is easier in a judgment task to perform well on grammatical forms than on ungrammatical forms. In order to do well on a grammatical sentence, participants simply have to assert that a sentence is 'OK'. To perform well on an ungrammatical sentence, a participant has to deny its acceptability, a harder task (see Bialystok, 1991). Thus, performance on ungrammatical sentences may be a better indication of children's knowledge than their performance on grammatical sentences. The fact that children initially performed better on grammatical than ungrammatical sentences is not surprising, then, given the difficulty of the tasks.

There were also significant interactions involving Quantifier and Noun Number: Quantifier X Noun Number (F(1,267) = 24.2, p < 0.0001), Quantifier X Noun Number X Participant Group (F(2,267) = 6.2, p < 0.003), and Quantifier X Noun Number X Grade (1,267) = 26.0, p < 0.0001). Figure 8.3 shows performance by Quantifier X Noun Number X Participant Group. The Quantifier X Noun Number interaction indicates that whereas the performance on *much* and *many* with singular nouns was comparable (72% for each), when these occurred with plural nouns, performance differed (*much* + plural: 53.6%, *many* + plural: 72.8%). This indicates that, in general, children were less likely to know that *much* cannot occur with plural nouns than any of the other three combinations. The interaction of Quantifier and Noun Number with Participant Group appears due to those cases in which the quantifier and noun number did not match (*much* with the plural, *many* with the singular); here the Monolingual English participants performed better than the bilinguals. The performance by Quantifier, Noun Number, and Grade was due to improvement across Grades on the ungrammatical constructs. While performance on the grammatical forms (*many* with plural nouns and *much* with singular nouns) stayed constant between 2nd and 5th grades (at 72% to 73% correct judgments throughout), performance on the ungrammatical combinations improved between 2nd and 5th

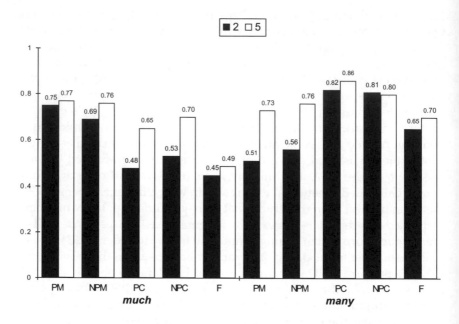

Key: PM = prototypical mass nouns, NPM = non-prototypical mass nouns, PC = prototypical count nouns, NPC = non-prototypical count nouns, F = flexible nouns

Figure 8.2 Proportion Correct Judgments by Quantifier, Noun Type, and Grade

grades: *many* with singular nouns: from 62% at 2nd grade to 81% at 5th grade, *much* with plural nouns: from 44% to 63% at the two grades, respectively.

A final set of interactions involved Noun Type: Noun Type X Noun Number (F(4,1068) = 11.1, $p < 0.0001$), Noun Type X Noun Number X Participant Group (F(8,1068) = 2.5, $p < 0.02$), Noun Type X Noun Number X SES (F(4,1068) = 2.8, $p < 0.02$), Noun Type X Noun Number X Grade X SES (F(4,1068) = 4.8, $p < 0.0008$), and Noun Type X Noun Number X Quantifier (F(4,1068) = 25.0, $p < 0.0001$).

Performance by Noun Type, Noun Number, and Participant Group is shown in Figure 8.4. While children performed similarly on singular versus plural nouns within the prototypical mass, non-prototypical mass, and flexible groups, they performed better with sentences involving prototypical count and non-prototypical count nouns that were singular than when these involved plural nouns. Within each Participant Group, performance on prototypical mass, non-prototypical mass, and flexible nouns was about

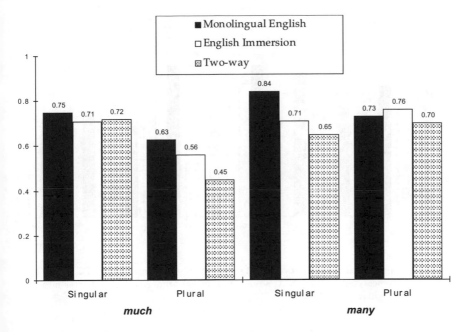

Figure 8.3 Proportion Correct Judgments by Quantifier, Noun Number, and Participant Group

equal across the sentences with singular and plural nouns; and within each group, performance on prototypical count and non-prototypical count nouns was better when the noun occurred in the singular than when it occurred in the plural. But Monolingual English participants did better than the others in judging cases in which the noun number was not appropriate for the Noun Type: mass (prototypical mass and non-prototypical mass) + plural, count (prototypical count and non-prototypical count) + singular.

Performance by Noun Type, Noun Number, and SES is shown by Group in Figures 8.5 and 8.6. The interaction of Noun Type, Noun Number, and SES was due to the fact that while the two SES levels performed similarly on singular and plural mass (prototypical and non-prototypical) nouns, on singular and plural flexible nouns, and on plural count (prototypical and non-prototypical) nouns, on singular count nouns (prototypical and non-prototypical), children from the High SES level performed better than those from the Low SES group. The interaction of these factors and Grade reveals that this effect was particular to children at 2nd grade rather than at 5th grade. Thus, the Low SES 2nd graders performed worse than the High

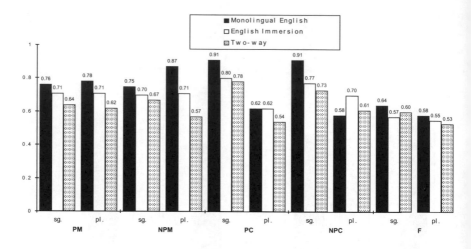

Key: PM = prototypical mass nouns, NPM = non-prototypical mass nouns, PC =
      prototypical count nouns, NPC = non-prototypical count nouns, F = flexible nouns,
      sg. = singular, pl. = plural

Figure 8.4 Proportion Correct Judgments by Noun Type, Noun Number,
and Participant Group

SES 2nd graders on singular count nouns, but by 5th grade they had closed
the gap.

The final interaction, of Noun Type X Noun Number X Quantifier, is
shown in Figure 8.7. Children performed better when mass nouns
(prototypical and non-prototypical) co-occurred with *much* than with
many, and better when count and flexible nouns (prototypical count, non-
prototypical count, and flexible) occurred with *many* than with *much*. When
count and flexible nouns occurred in the plural with *much*, performance
was particularly poor, indicating that participants judged these to be acceptable forms. That is, children generally knew that *many* does not go with
mass nouns, but they were less knowledgeable that *much* cannot occur with
plural count and flexible nouns.

Summary of judgment data findings for all participants
    There was a significant difference in performance by Participant Group,
with Monolingual English participants giving more correct judgements
than English Immersion participants, and English Immersion participants
more correct judgments than Two-way participants. This held at 2nd

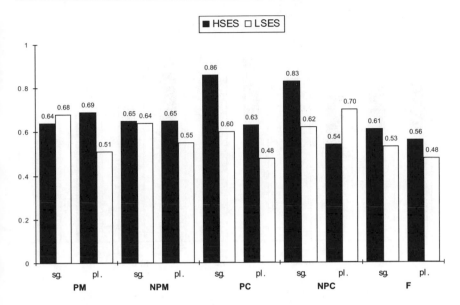

Key: PM = prototypical mass nouns, NPM = non-prototypical mass nouns, PC = prototypical count nouns, NPC = non-prototypical count nouns, F = flexible nouns, sg. = singular, pl. = plural

Figure 8.5 Proportion Correct Judgments by Noun Type, Noun Number and SES Level, 2nd grade

grade, but by 5th grade, the English Immersion and Two-way children were no longer significantly different from each other. Children from the High SES level performed better than those from the Low SES level, but this was particularly true for the Two-way bilinguals at 2nd grade, and particularly on constructs involving singular count nouns at 2nd grade. By 5th grade the Low SES children were not distinguishable from the High SES children.

Children overall performed better on *many* than on *much*, and on the singular forms than on the plural forms. Both of these results are related to the fact that children were better at knowing that *many* could not go with a singular or a mass noun than at knowing that *much* could not go with a plural or a count noun. Monolingual English participants did better on all of the ungrammatical combinations (*many* + singular, *much* + plural; count noun + singular, mass noun + plural) than the two bilingual groups.

Bilingual participants only

A second set of analyses examined only the bilinguals. These analyses

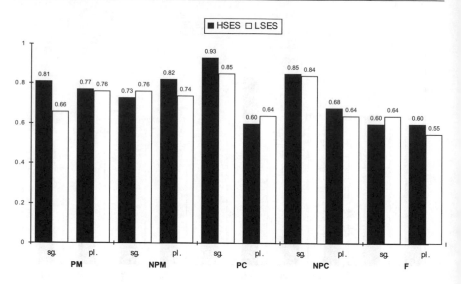

Key: PM = prototypical mass nouns, NPM = non-prototypical mass nouns, PC = prototypical count nouns, NPC = non-prototypical count nouns, F = flexible nouns, sg. = singular, pl. = plural

Figure 8.6 Proportion Correct Judgments by Noun Type, Noun Number and SES Level, 5th grade

included all of the variables mentioned above, plus that of LSH (OSH, ESH).

These analyses showed exactly the same significant results as those reported above for all participants, except for the following: First, there was no significant interaction of Quantifier X Noun Number X Participant Group, nor of Noun Type X Noun Number X Participant Group. This is consistent with the conclusion that the bilinguals from the two groups performed similarly here, and that the interactions noted above showed a difference between the Monolingual English group and the bilinguals in performance on ungrammatical combinations of quantifier plus singular or plural and on mass nouns in the singular and count nouns in the plural.

The results also showed a significant interaction of Grade X SES ($F(1,196)$ = 4.5, $p < 0.04$), and of Noun Type X Noun Number X Grade ($F(4,784) = 3.1, p$ < 0.02$). The former of these shows that at 2nd grade, there was a difference between the High and Low SES groups, $F(1,196) = 18.1, p < 0.0001$. In addition, at both SES levels, participants at 5th grade outperformed participants at 2nd grade (2H vs 5H: $F(1,196) = 9.0, p < 0.003$; 2L vs 5L: $F(1,196) = 34.8, p < 0.0001$) (see Figure 8.1). The further interaction of Grade X SES X Participant

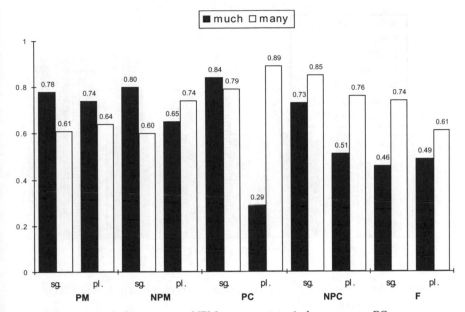

Key: PM = prototypical mass nouns, NPM = non-prototypical mass nouns, PC = prototypical count nouns, NPC = non-prototypical count nouns, F = flexible nouns, sg. = singular, pl. = plural

Figure 8.7 Proportion Correct Judgments by Quantifier, Noun Type, and Noun Number

Group revealed that the difference between SES groups at 2nd grade was primarily associated with performance of the Two-way bilinguals (see Figure 8.1).

The Noun Type X Noun Number X Grade interaction revealed that at 2nd grade, performance was better on singular nouns than on plural nouns across noun types (with a 4% to 13% difference within each noun type), but at 5th grade, performance on singular and plural nouns was similar for mass (prototypical mass and non-prototypical mass) and flexible nouns (with a 0% to 4% difference within noun types), but markedly different for count (prototypical count and non-prototypical count) nouns (singular: 88% and 82%, plural: 60% to 66%, respectively). (As noted above, there was a more complex interaction of Noun Type X Noun Number X Grade X SES, which indicated (a) that 2nd graders from the Low SES level performed poorly on mass nouns in the plural (see Figure 8.5), and (b) that High SES 2nd graders outperformed Low SES 2nd graders on singular count nouns.)

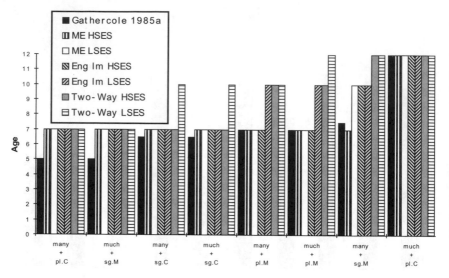

Figure 8.8 Ages at which distinct constructions reached at least 68% correct judgments, by Group and SES

Summary of judgment data for bilinguals

In addition to the results reported for the whole group, these analyses revealed that the performance of the High and Low SES bilingual groups differed at 2nd grade (but not at 5th), and that both SES groups improved in performance between 2nd and 5th grades. Finally, it is notable that there were no effects of LSH on the bilinguals' performance. (And differences by IMS were apparent at 2nd grade (English Immersion better than Two-way, especially at the Low SES level), but extinguished by 5th grade.)

It is instructive to compare these results with those reported in Gathercole (1985a). In that study, Gathercole ranked constructions for age of acquisition on the basis of the age at which accuracy reached at least 68% correct. Monolingual children were found to perform well on *many* + plural count nouns and *much* + singular mass nouns by age 5; *many / much* + singular count nouns by age 6½; *many / much* + plural mass nouns by age 7; and *many* + singular mass nouns by age 7½. *Much* + plural count nouns did not reach criterion by age 8½, the oldest children tested. Figure 8.8 compares those figures with the ages by which the participants of this study, by Group, reached the 68% criterion. (2nd graders here are shown as age 7, 5th graders as age 10.) Since the youngest age group reported here was age 7, anything that reached criterion by this age, of course, could have been acquired at a much earlier age than tested here. (Thus, those constructs that did not reach the 68% criterion by 2nd grade are most instructive.) Anything that did not reach criterion is shown as acquired at age '12', an arbitrary age chosen to represent 'beyond the ages tested'.

The information in Figure 8.8 is consistent with the findings here that the Monolingual English group outperformed the English Immersion group, which in turn outperformed the Two-way group. The role of SES level also is apparent, in that for each Participant group, the Low SES level performed more poorly than the High SES group, by achieving acquisition on certain constructs at a later age. The Low SES Two-way group lagged behind the High SES Two-way group for *many*+singular count, *much*+singular count, and for *much*+plural mass; the Low SES English Immersion group lagged behind the High SES English Immersion group for *many*+plural mass and for *much*+plural mass; and the Low SES Monolingual English group lagged behind the High SES Monolingual English group on *many*+singular mass constructions.

Corrections

Children's corrections of the sentences that they judged to be ungrammatical were examined for further information regarding the processes by which these constructs are learned. The most instructive sentences in this regard are the ungrammatical sentences. The ungrammatical sentences that are particularly instructive to examine are those for which the changes required are quite clear-cut – a change of the noun, a change of the quantifier, or both. Sentences built on prototypical mass, prototypical count, non-prototypical mass, and non-prototypical count nouns all had a single solution for correction, while sentences based on the flexible nouns allowed several options for correction (e.g. *so much cakes* could be corrected to 'so many cakes' or 'so much cake'). For this reason, only the performance on prototypical mass, prototypical count, non-prototypical mass, and non-prototypical count nouns is examined below.

One can look at children's corrections in two different ways. First, one might wish to examine the overall performance, out of all ungrammatical sentences of that type. This figure will give a snapshot view of the children's abilities in general on the various sentence types. Alternatively, one might wish to explore children's corrections relative only to those sentences that they judged to be inappropriate. This latter figure will indicate how well children perform once they recognize that there is something wrong with a sentence. In all that follows, both figures – the percentage of corrections out of all such sentences in the task (the 'absolute' percentage) and the percentage relative only to correct judgments (the percentage 'relative to judgments') are reported.

Ungrammatical sentences were divided into three correction types: those requiring a change in the noun number only, from singular to plural or vice-versa ['N-Only-Wrong'] (e.g. *The giant didn't see too much smokes, How many book did Oscar want?*), those requiring a change in the quantifier only, from *much* to *many* or vice versa ['Q-Only-Wrong'] (e.g., *She didn't get many dirt, Grover saw as much trees as the ghost*), and those requiring a change in both the quantifier and the noun number ['Q+N-Wrong'] (e.g. *He took this many waters, Big Bird had so much rock*). When a change was required for the quantifier (with either Q-Only-Wrong or Q+N-Wrong sentences), two types of response were possible. One type of response was a change from *much* to *many*, or vice versa, substituting the appropriate mass/count quantifier. A second possibility, however, was a change from one of these mass/count quantifiers to an unmarked quantifier (one that is unmarked or neutral between mass and count, 'u Q'), such as *a lot of/lots of, some, any*, and the like. The former type, substituting a mass/count quantifier, retains the complete syntactic form of the original sentence, including the determiners modifying the quantifier, e.g. 'that many clay' will be changed to 'that much clay', 'so much books' to 'so many books', and so forth. It also requires two components of knowledge – first, that the given mass/count quantifier is not appropriate, and, second, that the other mass/count quantifier is. The latter type of correction, substituting an unmarked quantifier, while leading to a grammatical sentence, does not retain the full syntactic form of the sentence (e.g. one cannot say 'that some clay' or 'so a lot of books'); furthermore, it only requires knowing that the given mass/count quantifier is not appropriate; it does not reveal whether the child knows as well that the other mass/count quantifier *is* appropriate. In all the data reported below, both types of responses are reported.

Corrections in general

Tables 8.2 to 8.4 show the percentage of correct responses broken down by type of ungrammatical sentences (N-Only-Wrong, Q-Only-Wrong, Q+N-Wrong and individual type of construct) and by Participant Group and Grade. The main percentages in each table show correct corrections out of all sentences, the 'absolute' percentage, and the percentages in parentheses show accuracy of corrections out of those sentences judged by participants to be incorrect, the percentage 'relative to judgments'. Across the three tables, the figures show a trend, first, for the Monolingual English participants to perform better than the English Immersion participants, who in turn tended to perform better than the Two-way participants, especially when the Q-Only-Wrong and Q+N-Wrong sentences were involved. (In the case of the percentage of corrections relative to correct judgments, the three groups appeared similar on the N-Only-Wrong sentences.) Second, children were more successful, in absolute percentages, at correcting the N-Only-Wrong sentences than the Q-Only-Wrong and the Q+N-

Table 8.2 Corrections of N-Only-Wrong Sentences, by Subject Group and Grade: % = number correct corrections/total opportunities (% = % correct corrections/% correct judgments)

Group	Grade	much + pl Mass N (change to much + sg Mass N)			many + sg Count N (change to many + pl Count N)			Total		Grand total
		M/C Q used	u Q used	Total	M/C Q used	u Q used	Total	M/C Q used	u Q used	
Mono English	2	49 (59)	11 (13)	60 (72)	60 (65)	10 (16)	70 (75)			
	5	47 (51)	18 (19)	65 (70)	65 (71)	15 (16)	80 (87)			
	Total							55 (62)	14 (14)	69 (76)
English Immersion	2	37 (55)	11 (17)	48 (72)	48 (66)	7 (9)	55 (75)			
	5	45 (61)	5 (7)	50 (68)	55 (64)	2 (2)	57 (66)			
	Total							46 (62)	6 (8)	52 (70)
Two-way	2	29 (71)	5 (12)	34 (83)	50 (76)	5 (7)	55 (83)			
	5	50 (70)	10 (15)	60 (85)	57 (63)	1 (1)	58 (64)			
	Total							47 (70)	5 (9)	52 (79)

Wrong sentences. When corrections relative to correct judgments only are considered, children were better at correcting one element (noun or quantifier) than two (both noun and quantifier).

Let us look at the figures in more detail. When N-Only-Wrong sentences are considered (Table 8.2), children were better overall at correcting sentences in which a count noun occurred in the singular than when a mass noun occurred in the plural. There appears to be an advantage of the Monolingual English group over the bilingual groups in the 'absolute' performance, with the Two-way bilinguals at 2nd grade having the greatest difficulty, particularly when correcting sentences involving *much* with a plural mass noun. However, when children recognized that there was a

Table 8.3 Corrections of Q-Only-Wrong Sentences, by Subject Group and Grade: % = number correct corrections / total opportunities (% = % correct corrections / % correct judgments)

Group	Grade	*many + sg Mass N* (change to much + sg Mass N)			*much + pl Count N* (change to many + pl Count N)			*Total*		*Grand total*
		M/C Q used	*u Q used*	*Total*	*M/C Q used*	*u Q used*	*Total*	*M/C Q used*	*u Q used*	
Mono English	2	28 (42)	27 (41)	55 (83)	11 (35)	16 (52)	27 (87)			
	5	27 (33)	23 (27)	50 (60)	26 (46)	24 (43)	50 (89)			
	Total							23 (39)	23 (41)	46 (80)
English Immersion	2	7 (15)	19 (40)	26 (55)	8 (24)	20 (58)	28 (82)			
	5	23 (30)	24 (32)	47 (62)	25 (49)	17 (45)	42 (94)			
	Total							16 (30)	20 (43)	36 (73)
Two-way	2	6 (17)	8 (22)	14 (39)	5 (23)	10 (45)	15 (68)			
	5	21 (34)	18 (30)	39 (64)	21 (45)	18 (38)	39 (83)			
	Total							13 (30)	14 (34)	27 (64)

problem with such sentences, they were able to correct them appropriately, regardless of group.

On sentences in which the quantifier *only* was incorrect (Table 8.3), there was again a trend, with the absolute numbers, for the Monolingual English subjects to perform better than the English Immersion subjects, who in turn were slightly ahead of the Two-way subjects. The differences across groups appeared greater at 2nd grade than at 5th grade, however. When one examines the corrections of only those sentences that were judged ungrammatical, one gains a slightly different picture. First, most children performed with a high degree of accuracy on sentences in which *much* occurred with a plural count noun (note that the Two-way bilinguals at 2nd grade still lagged behind somewhat, however). That is, although children might have

Table 8.4 Corrections of Q + N-Wrong Sentences, by Subject Group and Grade: % = number correct corrections/total opportunities (% = % correct corrections/% correct judgments)

Group	Grade	many + pl Mass N (change to much + sg Mass N)			much + sg Count N (change to many + pl Count N)			Total		Grand total
		M/C Q used	u Q use	Total	M/C Q used	u Q used	Total	M/C Q used	u Q used	
Mono English	2	28 (39)	13 (18)	41 (57)	11 (13)	0 (0)	11 (13)			
	5	30 (38)	20 (25)	50 (63)	29 (31)	13 (14)	42 (45)			
	Total							25 (30)	12 (15)	37 (45)
English Immersion	2	6 (9)	21 (33)	27 (42)	12 (16)	10 (14)	22 (30)			
	5	23 (29)	17 (22)	40 (51)	24 (29)	8 (10)	32 (39)			
	Total							16 (21)	14 (20)	30 (41)
Two-way	2	9 (18)	9 (19)	18 (37)	5 (8)	3 (5)	8 (13)			
	5	27 (36)	10 (13)	37 (49)	28 (34)	14 (17)	42 (51)			
	Total							17 (24)	9 (14)	26 (38)

performed poorly at recognizing that such sentences were ungrammatical (e.g. see corrections at 2nd grade in Table 8.3), if they did know that such sentences were inappropriate, they were generally able to correct them accurately. This contrasts with sentences in which *many* appeared with a singular mass noun. Even when looking only at those sentences that children judged to be ungrammatical, the children were much less successful in giving an appropriate correction than they were with *much* plus a plural count noun. Again, the group that had the most difficulty here was the Two-way bilingual group at 2nd grade.

On the Q+N-Wrong sentences (Table 8.4), when *many* occurred with a plural mass noun, Monolingual English children outperformed English Immersion and Two-way children, at both the 2nd and 5th grades, both in absolute percentages and percentages relative to judgments. In addition, within each group, 5th graders outperformed 2nd graders. In the case of sentences involving *much* with a singular count noun there appeared to be little difference across groups, with the English Immersion children performing the best at 2nd grade. Further, 2nd graders performed much more poorly than 5th graders, even when considering only numbers relative to judgments. Interestingly, performance on *many* with a singular mass noun (Table 8.3) appeared comparable to performance on *many* with a plural mass noun (Table 8.4), whereas performance on *much* with a plural count noun (Table 8.3) was overwhelmingly better than that on *much* with a singular count noun (Table 8.4), especially in percentages relative to judgments. The difference in performance with the count noun sentences appears to be due to the fact that a sentence with *much* + a plural count noun can only be judged incorrect on the basis of the incorrect use of *much*, while a sentence with *much* + a singular count noun can be judged incorrect on the basis of either the use of *much* or the occurrence of the noun in the singular. The data in Table 8.3 indicate that once children were able to hear that *much* + a plural count noun was faulty, they knew that it was the quantifier that was the problem. In contrast, children who judged that *much* + a singular count noun was faulty might have done so on the basis of noun number and simply corrected the form (inappropriately) to *much* + a plural count noun.

Corrections according to SES

It is also instructive to look at children's performance on corrections according to SES level. Table 8.5 shows performance by SES, Grade, and Participant Group. While the figures indicate that performance across groups by grade was comparable at the High SES level (with an advantage at 2nd grade by the Monolingual English group), at the Low SES level, the Two-way bilingual 2nd graders appeared to have had the most difficulty.

Corrections according to Language Spoken at Home

Finally, Table 8.6 shows corrections by LSH among the bilinguals. At 2nd grade, English Immersion bilinguals who came from ESH homes performed better than the other three groups at 2nd grade. However, by 5th grade, differences by LSH seemed to disappear.

Table 8.5 Corrections of all Sentences, by Subject Group and SES: % = number correct corrections/total opportunities (% = % correct corrections/% correct judgments)

Group	Grade	High SES			Low SES		
		M/C Q used	u Q used	Total	M/C Q used	u Q used	Total
Mono English	2	34 (43)	14 (19)	48 (62)	29 (41)	10 (14)	39 (55)
	5	41 (50)	12 (15)	53 (65)	35 (43)	24 (31)	59 (74)
English Immersion	2	21 (30)	17 (26)	38 (56)	18 (27)	12 (17)	30 (44)
	5	35 (45)	16 (22)	51 (67)	31 (42)	13 (19)	44 (61)
Two-way	2	25 (38)	8 (12)	33 (50)	8 (18)	6 (15)	14 (33)
	5	45 (60)	12 (16)	57 (76)	26 (37)	14 (20)	40 (57)

Table 8.6 Corrections of all Sentences, by Bilingual Participant Group, Grade, and Language Spoken at Home: % = number correct corrections/total opportunities (% = % correct corrections/% correct judgments)

Group	Grade	ESH			OSH		
		M/C Q used	u Q used	Total	M/C Q used	u Q used	Total
English Immersion	2	27 (39)	17 (25)	44 (64)	14 (21)	13 (19)	27 (40)
	5	37 (49)	13 (17)	50 (66)	28 (38)	15 (21)	43 (59)
Two-way	2	18 (32)	8 (15)	26 (47)	17 (31)	6 (11)	23 (42)
	5	38 (52)	12 (16)	50 (68)	34 (47)	13 (18)	47 (65)

Summary of data on corrections

Children's corrections appear to support many of the inferences drawn from children's judgments of the mass/count sentences. In particular, they suggest that Monolingual English children had an initial advantage over English Immersion and Two-way bilinguals, and English Immersion bilinguals had an initial advantage over Two-way bilinguals. This was particularly true when judging the appropriateness of the quantifier, not the noun number, and more pronounced at 2nd grade than at 5th grade. The effects were bound up with SES and LSH, however. Low SES, Two-way bilinguals performed more poorly at 2nd grade than any other group, and English Immersion children with ESH performed better at 2nd grade than the other bilinguals. By 5th grade, differences by SES and LSH disappeared.

Discussion

This experiment provides information on children's judgments and corrections of sentences involving the mass/count distinction, as expressed with mass and count nouns in combination with _much_ and _many_. The results are consistent with a general pattern of development in which:

(1) Children became proficient in the acceptable forms of Nouns (singular or plural) before they did so with the Quantifiers _much_ and _many_.

(2) Children became proficient in the acceptable forms of count nouns before they did so with mass nouns.

(3) Children acquired the acceptable range of usage for _many_ before they did so for _much_. In particular, children had the most difficulty with constructions involving _much_ with plural nouns, which they judged acceptable through the ages tested here.

(4) Bilingual children acquiring English in a Two-way school setting lagged behind their bilingual peers in an English Immersion setting, who in turn performed below their Monolingual English peers. This finding is consistent with the findings reported in Chapter 4, in that there were significant differences there between the performance of the three groups on the standardized tests of oral proficiency in English. The performance of Two-way bilinguals interacted significantly with their SES level, in that it was Low SES Two-way children at 2nd grade who performed the most poorly. These Two-way children caught up with their English Immersion peers, however, by 5th grade. This is also consistent with the findings in Chapter 4 suggesting that differences across groups in English abilities lessened by 5th grade.

(5) Children of a Low SES appeared to lag behind their High SES peers, es-

pecially at 2nd grade, and particularly in the Two-way group. This result is reminiscent of the High SES advantage reported for English – especially oral English – in Chapter 4.

(6) LSH appeared insignificant in children's judgments of these mass/count structures, but contributory in their ability to make grammatical corrections. English Immersion children hearing ESH at home made more grammatical corrections than English Immersion children hearing OSH at home or than either Two-way group. Those from a High SES level with ESH had the distinct advantage, those from a Low SES level with OSH, the distinct disadvantage. Again, these results are similar to those reported for English in Chapter 4, where the Low SES children with OSH performed more poorly than their counterparts from homes where both English and Spanish were spoken.

Let us examine the results of the study with regard to the questions posed at the outset. The first question was whether bilingual children learning English along with Spanish acquire the mass/count distinction in the same fashion as their monolingual peers. First, is there any evidence that bilingual children might take a semantic route to acquisition, in contrast to the syntactic route taken by monolingual children? The answer to this question appears clear. If bilinguals were using a semantic base, we would expect them to perform better overall on the prototypical mass and prototypical count nouns than on the non-prototypical mass and non-prototypical count nouns. This was not found. The only main effect of Noun Type was that all participants, including monolinguals, performed better on all M and C nouns than on flexible nouns. There was no major interaction of Participant Group and Noun Type. The only Participant Group interaction with Noun Type was the Participant Group X Noun Type X Noun Number interaction. This interaction was due to the simple fact that Monolingual English participants were ahead of the bilinguals across the board in spotting the ungrammatical combinations of quantifiers with noun number and noun type. In addition, the Noun Type X Noun Number X Grade X SES interaction revealed that the Low SES participants at 2nd grade were at a lower limit of knowledge regarding these structures, as they did not know that quantified count nouns could not occur in the singular and mass nouns could not occur in the plural. Thus, there was no evidence whatsoever that the bilinguals might be following a different route to the acquisition of these structures from their monolingual peers. Both groups appeared to acquire the mass/count distinction in English as a distributional property of structures, not a semantic property.

With regard to the second question, whether bilinguals follow a similar timing and sequence of development as the monolinguals, these data suggest a lag in development among bilinguals relative to monolinguals, and within bilinguals, among Two-way bilinguals relative to English Immersion bilinguals, and among Low SES bilinguals relative to High SES bilinguals. In addition, English Immersion bilinguals with ESH seemed to have an early advantage. But the differences were more apparent at 2nd grade, and the lower-performing groups of bilinguals appear to have been closing the gap, either fully or partially, by 5th grade. The sequence followed appears, on the whole, parallel to that followed by their monolingual counterparts, but at some delay in timing.

Is there any evidence that the bilingual children allowed the phonological similarity of *much* and *mucho(s)* to affect their acquisition of *much* and *many*? Unfortunately, this question can only be answered fully with data from children older than those tested here, because the critical construct in question, *much* plus plural count nouns, is not fully developed until beyond the ages tested here.

Thus, although there was little evidence here for a difference in the process and sequence in which bilinguals acquire the mass/count distinction, as compared with their monolingual counterparts, there was clear evidence of a lag in acquisition. Two-way bilinguals lagged behind English Immersion bilinguals, and Low SES participants lagged behind High SES participants. This conclusion is consistent with recent evidence reported in Gathercole (1997) that bilingual children show a lag behind monolingual children in their ability to rely on the mass/count structure of a sentence to determine the probable reference – substance or object – for a new label. The best explanation for this lag, and the relevance of these data for the major questions of the larger study overall, will be considered in the final Discussion section of Chapter 10 after we have reviewed the data on gender and *that*-trace structures in the next two chapters.

Note
1. Throughout these chapters, a '*' placed before a sentence indicates that the sentence is unacceptable or ungrammatical.

Chapter 9

Grammatical Gender in Bilingual and Monolingual Children: A Spanish Morphosyntactic Distinction

VIRGINIA C. MUELLER GATHERCOLE

In Chapter 8, the focus was on the acquisition of a particularly English morphosyntactic construct. In this chapter, we turn to Spanish and examine a structure particular to Spanish and not shared by English – grammatical gender.

As noted in Chapter 8, languages generally fall into two major types, those that have grammatical gender and those that have natural gender. In a natural gender language, like English, nouns that refer to humans and animate beings are sometimes distinguished on the basis of the gender of their referents. The distinction may be a matter of a choice between completely different lexical items – e.g. in English *boy* refers to males, *girl* to females, or it may be a matter of a morphological distinction – e.g. in English *mister* (for males) and *mistress* (for females) are based on the same stem. Modifiers that are used with these nouns generally do not take distinct shapes on the basis of gender (e.g. we use *the* and *small* and *happy* with both words referring to males and words referring to females); pronouns that are co-referential with these nouns may be marked for gender, but that gender is taken from the natural gender of the referent, as is generally the case for pronouns in a natural gender language (see Gathercole, 1989, for discussion of unmarked *he*, however). Nouns that do not refer to animate beings (e.g. *sand, water, chair*), and even many nouns that do (e.g. *teacher, cat*), are generally not specified in any way for gender. (For the latter type, pronoun choice may still depend on the gender of the referent, however.)

Contrast this with a grammatical gender language, like Spanish. In such a language, nouns are categorized into generally two or three classes, according to the types and forms of modifiers they may co-occur with. The use of a noun of a particular gender dictates the choice of forms – either lexically or morphologically distinct – of, e.g. articles and adjectives modifying that noun. The assignment of a noun to one gender category or another is not dependent on the natural gender of the referent. For example, German *mädchen* 'girl' is neuter. (However, there may be a tendency for nouns referring to females to be feminine and nouns for males to be masculine; see discussion in Gathercole, 1989.)

Spanish has two genders. Every noun in the language can be classified as having either masculine or feminine gender. All articles and determiners and many adjectives have distinct masculine and feminine forms. While some forms are distinguished on the basis of choice of lexical item (e.g. *el*, masculine definite article, vs *la*, feminine definite article; *mujer*, 'woman', vs *hombre*, 'man'), masculine and feminine forms are often distinguished on the basis of distinct morphological suffixes on the root (e.g. *un* 'a' (masculine) vs *una* 'a' (feminine); *pequeño* 'little' masculine, vs *pequeña* 'little' feminine; *niño* 'boy' vs *niña* 'girl'; *puerto* 'port' (masculine) vs *puerta* 'door' (feminine)). Among the morphological suffixes, there are a number of regular feminine and masculine patterns that are common to nouns, articles, and adjectives. The most regular patterns distinguish words ending in *-a* (feminine) from words ending in *-o* (masculine) (but see Klein, 1989) and Harris, 1991, and discussion in Gathercole and Hasson, 1995). For example, the nouns and modifiers in (1) and (2) are feminine, those in (3) and (4) are masculine:

-a: Feminine:

(1) *Compró una camisa blanca.*
    bought,3 sg. – a – shirt – white
    '[S/he] bought a white shirt.'

(2) *Compraron unas camisas blancas.*
    bought,3 pl. – some – shirts – white
    '[They] bought some white shirts.'

-o: Masculine:

(3) *Compró un carro nuevo.*
    bought,3 sg. – a – car – new
    '[S/he] bought a new car.'

(4) *Compraron unos carros nuevos.*
    bought,3 pl. – some – cars – new
    '[They] bought some new cars.'

According to Teschner and Russell (1984: 166–17) , nouns ending in *-a* are feminine 96.3% of the time, and nouns ending in *-o* are masculine 99.9%

of the time. Such endings thus provide very reliable cues to the gender status of a noun.

Generally when the marking of grammatical gender is as transparent as this, children have no difficulty acquiring the gender distinctions early and accurately. Children work out the agreement rules between nouns and their modifiers relatively early. Monolingual Spanish-speaking children have worked out the agreement rules between articles and nouns by 31 months of age (Hernández Pina, 1984), and are able to choose an appropriate article on the basis of the ending of a noun by 3 to 4 years of age (Cain *et al.*, 1987, Task 2) . Karmiloff-Smith (1978) found for the acquisition of French that children use 'local rules' early on, using phonological procedures for matching noun endings and modifier endings. (They later move on to semantic and syntactic procedures that make pronouns agree with co-referential noun phrases and also allow children to be flexible in the assignment of gender by taking into consideration the real-world gender of the referent.) In a study of monolingual and bilingual children from Low SES groups, Brisk (1976) found that first-grade bilinguals were comparable to or better than first-grade monolinguals in choosing an article to match the endings of real or nonsense nouns in Spanish (although it should be noted that the tasks carried out by the two groups were slightly different).

However, there are some interesting deviations from the regular patterns in Spanish, and it may take children much longer to acquire these. First, there are a large number of nouns that end in *-e*. These nouns can be either feminine or masculine:

-e: Feminine:

(5) *Salió a la calle.*
     left, 3 sg. – to – the – street
     '[S/he] went out to the street.'

-e: Masculine:

(6) *Vive en el valle.*
     lives, 3 sg. – in – the – valley
     '[S/he] lives in the valley.'

Teschner & Russell (1984: 177, 124) reported that 89.4% of *-e* words overall are masculine, but two-thirds of the most frequent *-e* words are feminine. Thus, *-e* is not a reliable cue to gender status; the child cannot readily rely on the noun ending to determine the gender of the noun in this case.

In addition, there are exceptions to the generalizations that *-a* words are feminine and take feminine modifiers and *-o* words are masculine and take masculine modifiers. First, all feminine words beginning with stressed /a/

(spelt with _a_ . . . or _ha_ . . .), such as _agua_ 'water', _águila_ 'eagle', and _ala_ 'wing', take _el_ (normally the masculine singular definite article) as the singular definite article:

(7) _El agua del río no se bebe._
the – water – from – the – river – neg. – drink, impersonal
'The water from the river cannot be drunk.'
El águila blanca se escapó de la jaula.
the – eagle – white – escaped – from – the – cage
'The white eagle escaped from the cage.'
El ángel tenía el ala rota.
the – angel – had – the – wing – broken
'The angel had a broken wing.'

A second exception is that some masculine nouns end in -_a_ and some feminine nouns end in -_o_ (either as their basic form, as for _mano_, or when some animate nouns refer to feminine referents, as _modelo_ (see Gathercole & Hasson, 1995).

(8) _Masculine_:
No entendió el problema.
neg. – understood,3 sg. – the – problem
'[S/he] did not understand the problem.'
Vieron el mapa en el coche.
saw,3 pl – the – map – in – the – car
'[They] saw the map in the car.'
Feminine:
Se metió las dos manos en el bolsillo.
put in, 3 sg. – the – two – hands – in – the – pocket
'[S/he] put both hands in his/her pocket.'
Había unas cinco modelos en el salón.
there were – some – 5 – models – in – the – living room
'There were about five models in the living room.'

The purpose of the present experiment was to examine the acquisition of these constructs by the participant groups in the larger study. Since it was expected that the regular gender patterns linking -_a_ with feminine gender and -_o_ with masculine gender would have been acquired by the ages studied here, this experiment focused on the more exceptional types of constructs described above. The main question addressed here was how bilinguals compare on the acquisition of these exceptional cases with monolinguals. A second question was whether there is any effect among the bilinguals of Instructional Method in School (IMS), Language Spoken at Home (LSH), or Socio-economic Status (SES).

Method

Linguistic stimuli

Two sets of sentences were drawn up. Each set contained 8 sentences, 4 grammatical and 4 ungrammatical. The eight sentences included two -*e* nouns (one feminine, one masculine), two -*a* nouns that were masculine, two -*o* nouns that were feminine, and two -*a* nouns that were feminine but took the article *el* because they begin with stressed /a/. One noun of each type occurred in a grammatical sentence, one in an ungrammatical sentence. The set I sentences were the following:

(9) GRAMMATICAL:

El águila blanca se escapó de la jaula.　　　[stressed initial /a/]
'The white eagle escaped from the cage.'
Dame una parte de tu bocadillo.　　　[-*e* word, feminine]
'Give me part of your sandwich.'
Había unas cinco modelos en el salón.　　　[-*o* word, feminine]
'There were about 5 models in the living room.'
Vieron el mapa en el coche.　　　[-*a* word, masculine]
'They saw the map in the car.'

(10) UNGRAMMATICAL:

El ángel tenía el ala roto.　　　[stressed initial /a/ – form
'The angel had a broken wing.'　　　should be: *el ala rota*]

Había escrito su nombre en la sobre.　　　[-*e* word, masculine –
'[S/he] had written his/her name on
the envelope.'　　　should be: *el sobre*]

Se metió los dos manos en el bolsillo.　　　[-*o* word, feminine – should
'[S/he] put both hands in his/her
pocket.'　　　be: *las dos manos*]

¿Cuál es la problema con ese señor?　　　[-*a* word, masculine –
'What is that man's problem?'　　　should be: *el problema*]

The Set II sentences were the same sentences, but with the grammaticality reversed – i.e., the grammatical sentences of Set I were changed to ungrammaticals, and the ungrammaticals of Set I to grammaticals.

Participants

Participants were the bilinguals and Monolingual Spanish monolinguals as shown in Chapter 8, Table 8.1. As noted in Chapter 8, the Monolingual Spanish monolinguals were Peruvian.[1] They came from homes in which only Spanish was spoken and attended a private, parochial school in which only Spanish was spoken. (They also took classes in English as a foreign language, however, as one of their subjects in school.) These children came from middle- and upper-middle class families, in which the fathers were professionals, but most mothers completed only high school (a common cultural practice for women in Peru).[2]

Procedure

The general procedure was as described in Chapter 8. Each participant was given one set of subjects and was asked to judge whether each sentence was acceptable. If s/he deemed any sentence unacceptable, s/he was asked to correct it.

Results

Judgments

Two major sets of analyses were performed, one comparing all participants and in which Participant Group, Grade, and Grammaticality were treated as variables, the other comparing only the bilingual participants, with SES and LSH included as variables along with the others. For each of these sets of analyses, two ANOVAs were performed; these differed according to whether *all* relevant participants were included or only those participants whose judgments were not all 'yes' or all 'no' responses. (All 'yes' or all 'no' patterns of responses might indicate that a participant is not attending to the structures or the task at hand or has no knowledge of those structures. Henceforth, these will be referred to as the 'NR participants'.) In most cases, these two analyses yielded comparable results, so the results from the former analyses will be reported. However, in those few cases in which the results differed, this will be noted.

All Participants

The first set of analyses examined Participant Group, Grade, and Grammaticality as variables. Results revealed main effects of Participant Group, $F(2,238) = 34.5$, $p < 0.0001$, and of Grammaticality, $F(1,238) = 63.1$, $p < 0.0001$. Student-Newman-Keuls analysis revealed that Monolingual Spanish participants made more correct judgments than either of the bilingual groups, $p < 0.05$ (means: Monolingual Spanish: 6.9, Two-way: 5.1, English Immersion: 4.9, out of 8). In addition, participants gave more correct responses to grammatical sentences than to ungrammatical sentences (G: 3.2, U: 2.0, out of 4).

There were interactions of Grammaticality X Participant Group, $F(2,238) = 7.9$, $p < 0.0005$, and of Grammaticality X Grade, $F(1,238) = 5.5$, $p < 0.03$.

Whereas all groups performed well on grammatical sentences (with averages of 3.2 to 3.56 correct judgments, out of 4), monolinguals outperformed both bilingual groups on ungrammaticals, Student-Newman-Keuls analysis, $p < 0.05$ (both Scheffe's S, $p < 0.0001$) (means: MS: 3.38; English Immersion: 1.69, Two-way: 1.94). The interaction of Grammaticality X Grade was due to the fact that while both grade levels performed well on grammatical sentences (2: 3.34, 5: 3.16), 5th graders performed better than 2nd graders on ungrammatical sentences (2: 1.73, 5: 2.29), $F(1,238) = 6.0$, $p < 0.02$. (This last interaction was non-significant when NR participants were eliminated from analysis.)

Because the monolingual participants all came from a middle to High SES group, it might be inappropriate to compare their performance with that of bilinguals from a Low SES group. Therefore, secondary analyses looked only at the monolinguals in comparison with the High SES bilingual participants. Results are comparable to those reported above, except that the interaction of Grammaticality X Grade becomes non-significant: Participant Group: $F(2,133) = 42.5$, $p < 0.0001$, Grammaticality: $F(1,133) = 54.0$, $p < 0.0001$, Grammaticality X Participant Group: $F(2,133) = 8.9$, $p < 0.0002$, Grammaticality X Grade: $F(1,133) = 2.7$, $p = 0.10$. (The means for the High SES bilingual participants on ungrammatical sentences were 1.4 for English Immersion subjects and 1.77 for Two-way subjects.)

Bilinguals

When only the bilinguals were examined, analyses in which Participant Group, Grade, SES, LSH, and Grammaticality were treated as variables revealed main effects of Grade, $F(1,196) = 7.0$, $p < 0.009$, and of Grammaticality, $F(1,196) = 132.2$, $p < 0.0001$. As above, 5th graders performed better than 2nd graders (2: 4.77, 5: 5.23), and performance was better on grammaticals than on ungrammaticals (G: 3.20, U: 1.82).

In addition, there were significant interactions of Grammaticality X Grade, $F(1,196) = 14.1$, $p < 0.0002$, and of Grammaticality X Participant Group X Grade X LSH, $F(1,196) = 5.7$, $p < 0.02$. The effect of Grammaticality X Grade was due to the generally better performance on ungrammaticals at 5th grade than at 2nd grade. The performance by Grammaticality, Participant Group, Grade, and LSH is shown in Figure 9.1. Performance on grammatical sentences was generally good across-the-board; however, performance on ungrammatical sentences varied according to Grade level and LSH. The four-way interaction reflects the fact that at 2nd grade, performance on ungrammaticals by the Two-way participants whose LSH was OSH was significantly better than that of the Two-way group with ESH, $F(1,204) = 5.5$, $p < 0.02$ (and nearly significantly different from both English Immersion groups: Two-way OSH vs English Immersion ESH:

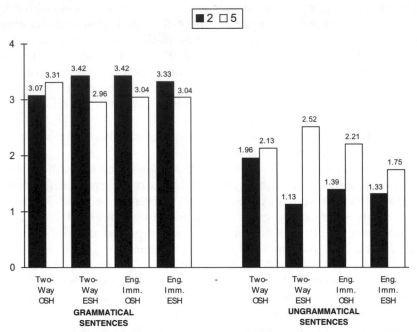

Figure 9.1 Mean correct judgments of Gender constructs by Grammaticality, Participant Group, Grade, and Language Spoken at Home, Bilinguals

F(1,204) = 3.1, p < 0.08; Two-way OSH vs English Immersion OSH: F(1,204) = 2.8, p < 0.10), but at 5th grade the English Immersion bilinguals whose LSH was ESH performed worse on ungrammaticals than the Two-way group with ESH, F(1,204) = 4.7, p < 0.03, with the other two groups performing between these two. That is, at 2nd grade, the Two-way bilinguals with OSH at home were ahead of the other bilinguals in judging ungrammaticals, but by 5th grade, the English Immersion bilinguals with ESH performed worse on ungrammaticals than their Two-way peers. (Grade and Grammaticality X Participant Group X Grade X LSH became non-significant when NR participants were eliminated from analysis.)

Summary of judgment data for Spanish gender

The results indicate that in making judgments, first, monolinguals outperformed bilinguals, especially in the identification of ungrammatical sentences. All participants were near ceiling on the judgment of grammatical sentences; only monolinguals were near ceiling on the judgment of ungrammatical sentences. In addition, 5th graders outperformed 2nd graders, especially on ungrammatical sentences. Finally, for bilinguals, LSH and IMS made a difference: at 2nd grade, Two-way bilinguals whose LSH was OSH performed better than other bilinguals in the identification of ungrammatical sentences; and at 5th grade, English Immersion bilinguals whose LSH was ESH performed worse than other bilinguals in the identification of ungrammatical sentences. There were no effects of SES.

Corrections

Children's corrections of the sentences that they judged to be ungrammatical were examined for further information regarding the process by which grammatical gender is learned. As in the case of the mass/count corrections in Chapter 8, both the 'absolute' number of corrections (number out of all opportunities) and the number 'relative to judgments' (number of correct corrections divided by number of correct judgments of ungrammaticals) will be reported.

Corrections in general and by SES

Table 9.1 shows the percentage of correct corrections by the Two-way, English Immersion, and Monolingual Spanish participants at each Grade level and by SES category. Both the absolute figures and the figures relative to judgments show an advantage in the Monolingual Spanish group over the two bilingual groups, and they suggest an advantage of the Two-way bilinguals over the English Immersion bilinguals, at both ages. However, at both Grades, the Low SES Two-way bilinguals appeared to have been ahead of the other bilingual groups.

Corrections according to Language Spoken at Home

Table 9.2 shows the two bilingual groups' performance by LSH and Grade. These correction data are consistent with the findings from the analyses of judgments. The 2nd grade Two-way bilinguals with OSH performed better than any other group at that age, and the 5th grade English Immersion bilinguals with ESH performed the worst of the children at that age.

Summary of correction data

Children's corrections appear to support many of the inferences drawn from children's judgments of the gendered sentences: Monolinguals outperformed both groups of bilinguals; 5th graders performed better than 2nd graders; and bilinguals' performance was influenced by their IMS and LSH: at 2nd grade, Two-way bilinguals with OSH at home outperformed the other bilinguals, and at 5th grade, English Immersion bilinguals with ESH at home performed worse than the other groups. That is, while Two-way bilinguals whose LSH was OSH had early success at correcting, other

Table 9.1 Corrections of ungrammatical gender constructs by Participant Group, Grade, and SES: % = number correct corrections / total opportunities (% = % correct corrections / % correct judgments)

Group	Grade	High SES	Low SES	Total
Mono Spanish	2	78 (93)	– –	78 (93)
	5	83 (98)	– –	83 (98)
English Immersion	2	15 (43)	16 (48)	16 (46)
	5	31 (65)	36 (70)	34 (68)
Two-way	2	26 (67)	39 (72)	27 (69)
	5	29 (74)	52 (84)	46 (80)

Table 9.2 Corrections of ungrammatical gender constructs by Participant Group, Grade, and Language Spoken at Home: % = number correct corrections / total opportunities (% = % correct corrections / % correct judgments)

Group	Grade	ESH	OSH	Total
English Immersion	2	15 (44)	16 (47)	16 (46)
	5	29 (65)	39 (70)	34 (68)
Two-way	2	17 (59)	36 (74)	27 (69)
	5	46 (73)	45 (85)	46 (80)

bilinguals seemed to catch up with them by 5th grade, except for English Immersion bilinguals with ESH as their LSH. In addition, children's corrections also suggest an overall advantage of the Two-way group over the English Immersion bilinguals – especially at 2nd grade – and an advantage at 5th grade of the Low SES Two-way bilinguals over the other groups.

Discussion

These results on Spanish gender reveal the following:

(1) Bilingual children learning gender in Spanish lagged behind their monolingual peers.
(2) Bilingual children with the greatest amount of Spanish input – those in Two-way schools and OSH at home – had an early advantage in learning this construct.
(3) Bilingual children with the least amount of Spanish input – those in the English Immersion schools and with ESH at home – took the longest to acquire these forms.
(4) 5th grade bilinguals (in each group) performed better than 2nd graders.
(5) SES level did not significantly affect children's judgments. However, in corrections, Low SES Two-way children may have had the advantage.

Thus, in the acquisition of Spanish gender, as in the acquisition of English mass/count, bilinguals appeared to lag behind their monolingual peers. Those bilinguals with the greatest amount of input in Spanish – those in Two-way schools and with OSH at home – appeared to have the early advantage. However, by 5th grade, the other groups appeared to be catching up with this group, except for the group with the least amount of input in Spanish, the English Immersion bilinguals with ESH at home. SES appeared to play only a minor role in children's abilities. These findings are parallel to those reported in Chapter 5 regarding performance on standardized tests for Spanish. Those data, like these, showed a monolingual advantage over bilinguals, an advantage of Two-way bilinguals over English Immersion bilinguals, and an advantage for oral tasks in the OSH group over the ESH group.

Before moving on to Experiment 3, it is instructive to examine the import of the experiments reported in Chapters 8 and 9 on our knowledge of bilinguals' acquisition. Both experiments have to do with relatively superficial aspects of the grammar, aspects which necessarily demand aspects of acquisition that proceed lexical item by lexical item. In both cases, bilinguals took longer to acquire the structures than their monolingual peers. In addition, in each case, the bilingual groups that performed the best had the greatest amount of input in the relevant language, and those who performed the worst had the least. For English mass/count, English Immersion participants did better than Two-way participants. For Spanish gender, Two-way participants with OSH at home had an early advantage over other groups, and English Immersion bilinguals with ESH at home had a late disadvantage. In addition, for English mass/count, Low SES bilinguals performed below their High SES peers. It appears this effect is related to amount of input as well. In the sample of children studied, bilinguals from the High SES group were more likely to have access to the dominant language of the community (English) than bilinguals from the Low SES group (see Chapters 2 and 4). Similarly, gender corrections suggested perhaps an advantage for the Low SES Two-way bilinguals. Again, this may well be related to amount of input these children received in Spanish relative to their High SES peers.

It should be noted that the effects of input, however, cannot necessarily be measured by a straightforward mapping between amount of input and facility with a given structure. The pattern of development observed in both the case of English mass/count and the case of Spanish gender (as well as in most of the standardized tests) shows a consistent trend in which an initial wide gap between groups is narrowed with development. This suggests that the effect of differences in exposure is most critical at *early* stages of development. This is consistent with the possibility that children need a *critical mass* of data in order to draw out generalizations governing the structures they are learning (e.g., Conti-Ramsden & Jones, 1997; Elman, May, 2000; Maratsos, 2000; Marchman & Bates, 1994). Once learners have accumulated such a critical mass, their knowledge of the structure in question becomes commensurate with that of children who had acquired that critical mass at an earlier age, and, hence, gaps that existed between groups are reduced or eliminated. This possibility and the roles of input and of a critical mass of input data will be explored further in the final Discussion section of Chapter 10.

Notes
1. I am grateful to Cecilia Montes for collecting the Peruvian data.
2. The Peruvian participants came from SES levels A and B. Levels A, B, C, etc. are defined taking into consideration several factors related to the head of the family (usually the father), but mainly to two: his profession and his monthly income. 'A' level families are those in which the father has at least a Bachelor's degree and in most cases a Master's, he is usually the director or general manager of a company, or a well-to-do lawyer or doctor; his income is no less than 2,800 dollars per month, his children attend private schools and the family spends around 450 dollars in food per month. Only 3.4% of Peruvians fall into

that group. In the case of the 'B' level families (14.4% of families in Peru), the head of the family has either gone to the university after finishing high school or gone to a technical school of some sort; the income of the family is at least 780 dollars per month. In this case, women often work but are not necessarily professionals. They might be secretaries, assistants of some type or independent workers (e.g., they may have their own small businesses).

Chapter 10

Monolingual and Bilingual Acquisition: Learning Different Treatments of that-trace Phenomena in English and Spanish

VIRGINIA C. MUELLER GATHERCOLE

The third experiment examining morphosyntactic development involved a structure that takes opposing forms in English and Spanish: – *that*-trace structures.[1] The structures in question are those involving syntactic subjects that have been extracted out of embedded clauses, as in (1) and (2), where *who/quien* acts as the subject of the embedded verb *has/tiene*.

(1) *Who do you think ___ has green eyes?*

(2) *¿Quién piensas que ___ tiene ojos verdes?*

An important difference between English and Spanish in these forms is that English does not allow the complementizer *that* (compare (1) with (3)),[2] and Spanish requires the complementizer *que* (compare (2) with (4)).

(3) **Who do you think that ___ has green eyes?*

(4) **¿Quién piensas ___ tiene ojos verdes?*

There are various syntactic approaches that have attempted to explain why languages like English do not allow an overt complementizer in such sentences. All of these syntactic theories share the position that whatever principles govern these structures, they are innate and common to all languages, or to Universal Grammar. (We shall see below that the evidence here may challenge such a position.) This, in theory, sets such structures apart from structures like mass/count and gender, because, according to the theory, knowledge of how *that*-trace structures work should be part of the innate linguistic endowment of human beings. Input should merely serve as a trigger for children to identify which type of language they are learning. Under this theoretical position, such structures should be fairly easy to learn, by both monolinguals and bilinguals. According to the Universal Grammar position, then, we might expect to find, in contrast with the differences in development between monolinguals and bilinguals for mass/count and gender, that both monolinguals and bilinguals learn these structures at the same time. Furthermore, since according to UG, input merely acts to trigger the setting or development of innate knowledge, we should find that input factors affecting quantity of input, such as Language Spoken at Home (LSH), Instructional Method in School (IMS), and Socioeconomic Status (SES), should not play a major role in the timing of development for *that*-trace structures, as they do for mass/count and gender. The purpose of this study was to explore these issues.

Background

Theoretical accounts of the phenomena in (1) to (4) attempt to explain why languages like English do not allow the extraction of subjects (like *who*) past a filled complementizer position (i.e. past an overt *that*), while languages like Spanish do. Various innate parameters or principles governing syntactic structures in Universal Grammar have been proposed. The original account for this phenomenon under UG was the postulation of a That-Trace Filter (Chomsky & Lasnik, 1977), which filtered out sequences of a complementizer (*that*) followed by an empty NP (the slot that *who* left behind). The fact that languages like Spanish do allow comparable constructions, as in (2), was thought to be linked to 'pro-drop' phenomena, or the fact that such languages typically allow sentences without overt subjects (e.g. one can say *Tiene ojos verdes* 'Has green eyes'). Researchers hypothesized that there was a cluster of properties that linked *that*-trace options with certain subject options under a 'pro-drop' or 'null subject' parameter in UG (Chomsky, 1981; Jaeggli, 1982; Jaeggli & Safir, 1989; Kenstowicz, 1989; Rizzi, 1982). English, which does not allow null subjects, also does not allow extraction through a filled Complement position, whereas Spanish, which does allow null subjects, does allow such extraction.[3] More recently, *that*-trace phenomena have been explained under a different universal principle, the Empty Category Principle (Chomsky, 1981, 1986; Lasnik *et al.*, 1984). This principle posits that an empty non-pronominal category (like a trace – i.e. what is (covertly) left behind when *who* or *quien* moves to the front of the sentence) must be in a structural position where it is governed by a 'proper governor' (Chomsky, 1986; Rizzi, 1990). Because of differences in the inflectional systems of English and Spanish, the trace in English is not 'properly governed' if there is an overt *that*, but it is in Spanish with overt *que*. (See Chomsky, 1986 and Rizzi, 1990, for details; see Gathercole & Montes, 1997, for discussion). Because the principles governing such structures are so complex and abstract, and because language is purported to be acquired very quickly and from deficient and degraded input, these principles are deemed to be innate. They might be present from birth or they may come 'on line' with maturation.

Recent work on the acquisition of English *that*-trace by young children has argued that even by preschool age, children already obey the principles governing *that*-trace structures. Thornton (1990) tested 21 children between 2;10 and 5;5 on their production of sentences involving subject and object extraction. English does not allow *that* when subjects are extracted (e.g. 'What do you think (*that) ___ eats bugs?'), but it does allow either the presence or the absence of *that* when objects are extracted (e.g. 'What do you think (that) bugs eat ___?'). Thornton reports that all but one of her subjects used complementizers at least once, and the 11 subjects who produced object extractions used complementizers more often there (25% of the time) than they did with subject extractions (18%). Furthermore, drawing on Rizzi's (1990) analysis, Thornton argues that even the children who used *that* complementizers in subject extraction were obeying the innate principles. Her explanation is that such children mistook *that* for a form that could 'properly govern' the trace, and, hence, was allowable. Thornton claims that her data, therefore, support the position that the principles governing *that*-trace are available to children by the preschool years. It should be noted, however, that eight out of these eleven children used *that* with subject extraction, and only two of these eight used *that* consistently. If Thornton were correct that these children had simply mistaken *that* for a proper governor, one could expect them to be more consistent in its overt use. Of the children who did not use *that* consistently with subject extraction, one child sometimes used *that*, sometimes medial *wh*-words, and sometimes partial movement, and the remaining five children used both *that* and the null complementizer, the latter of which they used more frequently (see Thornton 1990, Table 5). Rather than supporting the position that these children made a mistake in their analysis of *that*, these data suggest that perhaps these children simply *did not know* which complementizer was appropriate in these structures.

The present study examines children's judgments of *that*-trace sentences at ages well beyond those tested by Thornton. If native-speaking learners of English and Spanish learn the settings for *that*-trace structures by applying principles of UG, we could predict that both monolingual and bilingual children at older ages will perform well on *that*-trace structures. They should especially do better than on English mass/count and Spanish gender, both of which must necessarily involve much exposure lexical item by lexical item. If, however, children use the same learning mechanisms for the acquisition of *that*-trace structures as they do for the acquisition of mass/count and gender constructs, we can predict that results will be similar to those observed with mass/count and gender. Namely, monolinguals should perform better than bilinguals, and among bilinguals, IMS, LSH, and SES should play roles insofar as each of these affects the amount of input the children receive. That is, for English *that*-trace structures, we would expect English Immersion bilinguals with English and Spanish spoken at home (ESH) and from a High SES to have an early advantage, and for Spanish structures, we would expect Two-way bilinguals with Only Spanish spoken at home (OSH) and from a Low SES to have the early advantage.

Method

Children were again asked to judge both grammatical and ungrammatical sentences involving extraction of embedded subjects and to correct those that they judged to be ungrammatical. Four of the sentences in each language contained an overt complementizer (*that*/*que*), and four did not. With a puppet-correction procedure, children were asked to judge whether each sentence was acceptable, and, if not, how the sentence should be worded.

Materials

Two sets of eight sentences were drawn up in each language. Each participant heard only one of these sets. In each set (I and II), four sentences were grammatical, and four were ungrammatical. The Set I sentences were as follows:

English Set I:
  a. *Who did you say that came to the party?
  b. *What did John think that crashed into the tree?
  c. *Who did you think that called on the phone?
  d. *What did Mary say that fell off the shelf?
  e. Who did you say went to the baseball game?
  f. What animals did Mary think have three toes?
  g. Who did you think opened the door?
  h. What did John say was on TV?

Spanish Set I:
  a. ¿Quién dijiste que fué a México? (Who did you say that went to México?)
  b. ¿Qué pensó Juan que hizo aquel ruido? (What did John think that made that noise?)

c. ¿Quién pensaste que cantó la canción? (Who did you think that sang the song?)

d. ¿Qué dijo María que estaba en la caja? (What did Mary say that was in the box?)

e. *¿Quién dijiste tiene el pelo rubio? (Who did you say has blond hair?)

f. *¿Cuáles niños pensó María vinieron a la casa? (Which children did Mary think came to the house?)

g. *¿Quién pensaste rompió la silla? (Who did you think broke the chair?)

h. *¿Qué dijo Juan ocurrió en la escuela? (What did John say happened at school?)

The Set II English sentences were a translation of the Set I Spanish sentences, and the Set II Spanish sentences were a translation of the Set I English sentences.

Results

Children's responses to test sentences involved two components, judgments of sentences and corrections. These data will be reported separately. A preliminary analysis of the data revealed no significant effects of order of testing presentation (Spanish first or English first), nor of set of sentences (set I vs set II) on children's responses. All analyses reported below are thus collapsed for orders of presentation and sentence types.

Judgments

Children's judgments were scored as being correct or incorrect. Three major sets of analyses were performed, since language differed within participants for bilinguals, and across participants for monolinguals. The three major analyses compared (1) the performance of the two bilingual Participant Groups (Two-way, English Immersion), (2) the performance of the English-speaking Participant Groups (Monolingual English, Two-way, English Immersion), and (3) the performance of the Spanish-speaking Participant Groups (Monolingual Spanish, Two-way, English Immersion).

One final, fourth, set of analyses was conducted to compare the English monolingual participants with the Spanish monolingual participants, as a basis of comparison for the other analyses.

As with gender, for each of these analyses, two ANOVAs were performed; these differed according to whether *all* relevant participants were included or only those participants whose judgments were not all 'yes' or all 'no' responses. In most cases, these two analyses yielded comparable results, so the results from the former analyses will be reported. However, in those few cases in which the results differed, this will be noted.

The data will be examined, first, for the monolinguals, then for the monolinguals and bilinguals in each of the two languages separately, and finally for the bilinguals in the two languages.

Monolinguals

To establish a base-line comparison, the performance of the Monolingual English-speaking children and the Monolingual Spanish-speaking children was compared. Analyses of variance in which Language Group, Grade, and Grammaticality (grammatical, ungrammatical) were treated as variables revealed main effects of Language Group, $F(1,95) = 88.7, p < 0.0001$, and Grammaticality, $F(1,95) = 94.3$, $p < 0.0001$, and an interaction of Grammaticality and Language Group, $F(1,95) = 68.4$, $p < 0.0001$. These results revealed that Monolingual Spanish children performed better than Monolingual English children (means: 6.78 Monolingual Spanish vs 4.44 Monolingual English, out of 8), that children performed better on grammatical than ungrammatical sentences (3.56 vs 1.65 correct, out of 4), and that, while performance on grammatical sentences was similar across the languages (3.58 Monolingual English vs 3.5 Monolingual Spanish, out of 4), performance on ungrammatical sentences was much better in Spanish (0.87 Monolingual English vs 3.28 Monolingual Spanish, out of 4). As noted above, performance on ungrammatical sentences may be a better indication of children's knowledge than their performance on grammatical sentences; the fact that children performed better on grammatical than ungrammatical sentences is not surprising, given the difficulty of the tasks.

What is somewhat surprising, however, is the better performance of Spanish-speaking monolinguals on ungrammatical sentences over the English-speaking monolinguals.[4] This indicates that Monolingual Spanish children were more attentive to or more aware of errors in these structures than Monolingual English children were. In fact, the low performance of the English-speaking participants on ungrammatical sentences indicates that they were largely accepting such sentences as appropriate.

One difference between the Monolingual English and Monolingual Spanish children was that all Monolingual Spanish children came from a middle to High SES group, while the Monolingual English group was mixed. In order to test whether this might have affected the differences in response patterns found, only the Monolingual English participants from a High SES level were compared with the Monolingual Spanish participants. Results were comparable to those reported above. There were significant effects of Language Group: $F(1,61) = 83.7$, $p < 0.0001$, Grammaticality: $F(1,61) = 70.5, p < 0.0001$, Grammaticality X Language Group: $F(1,61) = 51.6$,

$p < 0.0001$. Thus, the differences found in performance on Spanish versus English were not an artefact of SES level. As we examine the results from all the participants below, the generality of better performance on Spanish than English will become evident, and the best explanation for this finding will be considered.

English

For all participants tested in English, ANOVAs were conducted in which Participant Group, Grade, SES, and Grammaticality were treated as variables. These analyses revealed main effects of Participant Group, $F(2,267) = 3.9, p < 0.03$, of Grade, $F(1,2647) = 17.2, p < 0.0001$, of SES, $F(1,2647) = 7.0, p < 0.009$, and of Grammaticality, $F(1,267) = 1017.7, p < .0001$, and significant interactions of Participant Group X SES, $F(2,267) = 6.9, p < 0.002$, Grade X SES, $F(1,267) = 4.8, p < 0.03$, and Grammaticality X Grade, $F(1,267) = 9.9, p < 0.002$. There were no other significant effects.

The significant main effect of Participant Group was due to the fact that the monolinguals performed significantly differently from both of the bilingual groups, Student-Newman-Keuls analysis, $p < 0.05$ (4.4 Monolingual English, 4.0 English Immersion, 4.0 Two-way, out of 8). The effect of Grade revealed that 5th graders performed significantly better than 2nd graders (4.37 vs 3.8, out of 8), and the effect of SES indicated that children from the High SES outperformed those from the Low SES (4.34 vs 3.9, out of 8). The effect of Grammaticality revealed that participants performed better on grammatical than on ungrammatical sentences (3.50 vs 0.61, out of 4).

The effect of Participant Group by SES was due to differences in performance by SES level within the Two-way group. While SES did not significantly affect performance within the Monolingual English and English Immersion groups (with averages of 4.3 to 4.50 in the ME group and of 3.87 to 4.17 in the English Immersion group), the High SES children in the Two-way group performed significantly better (4.46 correct, out of 8) than the Low SES Two-way children (3.47, out of 8), $(F(1,267) = 21.1, p < 0.0001)$.

The significant interaction of Grade X SES revealed that while the two SES groups performed similarly at 2nd grade (with means of 3.77 to 3.86), by 5th grade the High SES group outperformed the Low SES group (High SES: 4.79, Low SES: 4.0), $F(1,267) = 12.3, p < 0.0005$. (When the NR participants are removed from the analysis, the Grade X SES interaction is not significant.)

Finally, the significant interaction of Grammaticality X Grade revealed that, while both 2nd graders and 5th graders performed well on grammatical sentences (3.5 and 3.49, respectively, out of 4), the performance of 5th graders was better than that of 2nd graders on ungrammatical sentences (2nd Grade: 0.32, 5th Grade: 0.88). However, the low performance on ungrammaticals at both grades indicates that children generally judged such sentences to be grammatical. (When the NR participants are removed, the Grammaticality X Grade effect is non-significant.)

In sum, the results for English reveal that monolinguals performed better than bilinguals of either group, although the lowest performance occurred in the low SES Two-way group. In addition, 5th graders performed better than 2nd graders, although this interacted with an effect of SES, whereby only the High SES group performed better at 5th grade than at 2nd grade. In addition, the High SES bilinguals in Two-way schools performed better than their Low SES counterparts in Two-way schools. Finally, children performed better on grammatical than ungrammatical sentences; performance on ungrammaticals was poor, although it improved between 2nd and 5th grades.

Spanish

The Spanish analyses examined the effects of Participant Group, Grade, and Grammaticality on performance. Results revealed main effects of Participant Group, $F(2,238) = 26.0, p < 0.0001$, Grade, $F(1,238) = 4.2, p < 0.05$, and Grammaticality, $F(1,238) = 63.0$, $p < 0.0001$, and significant interactions of Participant Group X Grade, $F(1,238) = 3.5$, $p < .04$, Participant Group X Grammaticality, $F(2,238) = 7.2, p < 0.001$, and of Grade X Grammaticality, $F(1,238) = 8.6, p < 0.004$. There were no other significant effects. (Grade, Participant Group X Grade, and Grade X Grammaticality were not significant when NR participants were excluded, $p = 0.07$.)

Student-Newman-Keuls follow-up tests revealed that the monolinguals were significantly different from both bilingual groups, $p < 0.05$ (6.78 Monolingual Spanish vs 5.12 Two-way vs 4.88 English Immersion, out of 8). 5th graders performed better than 2nd graders (5: 5.54, 2: 4.90, out of 8): and performance was better on grammatical than ungrammatical sentences (3.30 vs 1.9, out of 4).

The significant interaction of Participant Group X Grade revealed that both bilingual groups showed a significant difference in performance by grade (Two-way: 4.6 at 2nd grade, 5.6 at 5th grade; English Immersion: 4.5 at 2nd grade, 5.2 at 5th grade), but the monolinguals did not (since they were already near ceiling by 2nd grade: 7.0 at 2nd grade, 6.56 at 5th grade) (Two-way 2nd grade vs Two-way 5th grade: $F(1, 238) = 14.6, p < 0.0002$; English Immersion 2nd grade vs English Immersion 5th grade: $F(1,238) = 6.6, p < 0.01$).

The significant effect of Participant Group X Grammaticality was similarly due to differential performance on grammaticals and ungrammaticals within each of the bilingual groups: Whereas the monolinguals performed equally well on the grammatical and ungrammatical sentences (3.5 and 3.28, respectively, out of 4), the two bilingual groups performed much better on grammatical sentences than ungrammatical ones: Two-way bilinguals: Grammatical: 3.3, Ungrammatical: 1.82, F(1,101) = 58.6, $p < 0.0001$; English Immersion bilinguals: Grammatical: 3.23, Ungrammatical: 1.65, F(1,103) = 78.0, $p < 0.0001$.

Since the Spanish monolinguals were all of a mid to High SES level, a second set of analyses was conducted with only the High SES bilinguals. Results for these groups were similar to those reported (Participant Group: F(2,133) = 25.7, $p < 0.0001$, Grade: F(1,133) = 3.8, $p < 0.054$, Grammaticality: F(1,133) = 53.7, $p < 0.0001$, Participant Group X Grade: F(2,133) = 3.4, $p < 0.04$, Participant Group X Grammaticality: F(2,133) = 8.7, $p < 0.0003$, Grade X Grammaticality: F(1,133) = 7.4, $p < 0.008$).

In sum, these analyses revealed that Monolingual Spanish participants performed better than the bilinguals of either group. Whereas the monolinguals performed well at both grades, and on both grammatical and ungrammatical sentences, the bilinguals performed better at 5th grade than at 2nd grade, and better on grammatical than on ungrammatical sentences. (We will see below that when SES and LSH are taken into consideration, the results for the bilinguals will have to be modified to reflect interactions with these factors.)

Bilinguals

Let us turn to the bilinguals' performance in the two languages. For the bilinguals, analyses in which Participant Group, Grade, SES, LSH, Language (English, Spanish), and Grammaticality were treated as variables revealed the following. First, there were main effects of Grade, F(1,196) = 36.2, $p < 0.0001$; SES, F(1,196) = 5.4, $p < 0.02$; Language, F(1,196) = 65.5, $p < 0.0001$; and Grammaticality, F(1,196) = 520.9, $p < 0.0001$. Fifth graders gave more correct responses than 2nd graders (4.84 vs 4.13, out of 8); High SES participants performed better than Low SES participants (4.62 vs 4.38); children performed better in Spanish than in English (5.0 vs 4.0, out of 8); and performance was better on grammatical than on ungrammatical sentences (3.37 vs 1.13, out of 4).

While there were no main effects of Participant Group or of LSH, these and other factors having to do with between-subject variables showed several significant interactions. First, there were interactions involving Language and SES: Language X SES, F(1,196) = 8.2, $p < 0.005$; Language X Participant Group X SES, F(1,196) = 6.1, $p < 0.02$. The performance of each Participant Group by Language and SES is shown in Figure 10.1. The significant interactions of Language with SES revealed that while children from the two SES groups did not perform significantly differently overall in Spanish (Low SES: 5.09, High SES: 4.92, out of 8), in English the Low SES participants performed much worse than the High SES group (Low SES: 3.68, High SES: 4.32), F(1, 196) = 17.4, $p < 0.0001$. However, the three-way interaction of Language X SES X Participant Group indicated that whereas in English, the Low SES Two-way children performed *worse* than either of the High SES groups and the Low SES English Immersion children performed worse than the High SES Two-way children, in Spanish, the Low SES Two-way children performed *better* than both the Low SES English Immersion children and the High SES Two-way children (English: Low SES Two-way vs High SES Two-way: F(1, 196) = 20.2, p < 0.0001; Low SES Two-way vs High SES English Immersion: F(1,196) = 10.4, p < 0.002; Low SES English Immersion vs High SES Two-way: F(1,196) = 7.2, p < 0.008; Spanish: Low SES Two-way vs Low SES English Immersion: F(1, 196) = 4.3, p < 0.04; Low SES Two-way vs High SES Two-way: F(1,196) = 4.5, p < 0.04) .

There were also several significant interactions involving the LSH: Grade X SES X LSH, F(1,196) = 4.7, p < 0.04; Language X SES X LSH, F(1,196) = 4.0, p < 0.05; Language X Grade X SES X LSH, F(1,196) = 4.9, p < 0.03. The three-way interactions can best be interpreted in the context of the four-way interaction: For English, there was no significant differences across groups at 2nd grade, but at 5th grade, the High SES groups outperformed

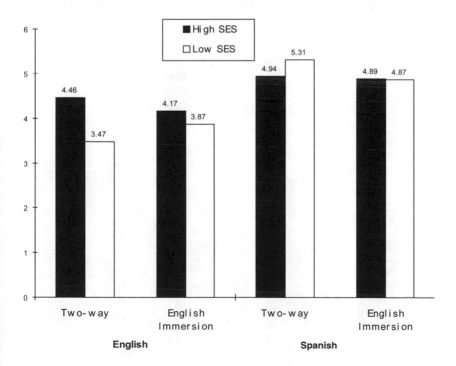

Figure 10.1 Mean number correct judgments by Participant Group, Language, and SES, Bilinguals, *that*-trace

the Low SES groups: *English*, 5th grade: High SES Only Spanish at Home vs Low SES Only Spanish at Home: F(1, 196) = 22.0, *p* < 0.0001; High SES Only Spanish at Home vs Low SES English and Spanish at Home: F(1,196) = 10.9, *p* < 0.002; High SES English and Spanish at Home vs Low SES Only Spanish at Home: F(1,196) = 15.9, *p* < 0.0001, High SES English and Spanish at Home vs Low SES English and Spanish at Home: F(1,196) = 7.3, *p* < 0.008. For *Spanish*, in contrast, while there was no significant differences across groups at 5th grade, there were at 2nd grade. Specifically, the Low SES children who had Only Spanish at Home outperformed the Low SES children with English and Spanish at Home and the High SES children with Only Spanish at Home: Low SES OSH vs Low SES ESH: F(1,196) = 12.4, *p* < 0.0005, Low SES OSH vs High SES OSH: F(1,196) = 4.7, *p* < 0.04. These results indicate that, first, in English at 2nd grade all groups performed similarly (poorly) in English, but by 5th grade each group of High SES bilinguals, regardless of LSH, outperformed each of the Low SES groups, regardless of LSH. Second, in Spanish, at 2nd grade the Low SES bilinguals with OSH at home performed better than either Low SES bilinguals with ESH or High SES bilinguals with OSH, but by 5th grade, all groups performed similarly in Spanish (see Figure 10.2).

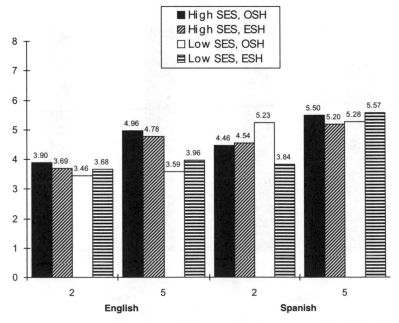

Figure 10.2 Mean number correct judgments by Language, Grade, SES, and Language Spoken at Home, Bilinguals, *that*-trace

Finally, there were a number of factors that interacted with the variable of Grammaticality: Grammaticality X LSH, F(1,196) = 5.2, p < 0.02; Grammaticality X Grade, F(1,196) = 22.2, p < 0.0001; Language X Grammaticality, F(1,196) = 103.9, p < 0.0001; Grammaticality X Language X Grade, F(1,196) = 5.8, p < 0.02; Grammaticality X Language X Participant Group X SES, F(1,196) = 5.5, p < 0.02.

The first of these reveals that on grammatical sentences, participants with English and Spanish at Home performed better than those with Only Spanish Spoken at Home (ESH: 3.46 vs OSH: 3.29, out of 4), but on ungrammatical sentences, OSH participants performed better than ESH participants (OSH: 1.25, ESH: 0.99). (When NR participants were removed from the analysis, this effect was not significant, but the interaction of Grammaticality, LSH, and SES was, F(1,156) = 5.5, p < 0.02. In this case, the advantage of ESH participants on grammatical sentences and of the OSH participants on ungrammatical sentences was limited to the Low SES level.)

The performance by Grammaticality, Language, and Grade is shown in Figure 10.3. The Grammaticality X Grade interaction reveals that, whereas both 2nd and 5th graders performed well on grammatical sentences (2:

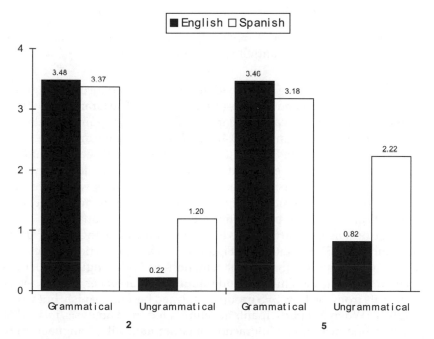

Figure 10.3 Mean number correct judgments by Grammaticality, Language, and Grade, Bilinguals, *that*-trace

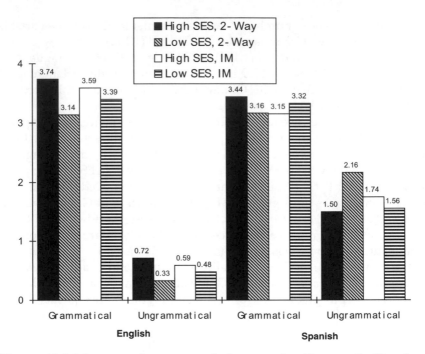

Figure 10.4 Mean number correct judgments by Grammaticality, Language, Participant Group, and SES, Bilinguals, *that*-trace

3.42, 5: 3.32, out of 4), 5th graders had more correct responses on ungrammatical sentences than 2nd graders (2: 0.71, 5: 1.52). The Grammaticality X Language interaction reveals that correct judgments on grammaticals was similar in English and Spanish (E: 3.47, S: 3.27), but on ungrammaticals was better on Spanish than on English (S: 1.73, E: 0.96). The three-way interaction of these factors reveals that the improvement in judgments on ungrammaticals in Spanish between 2nd and 5th grades was more dramatic than on ungrammaticals in English. (Again, this interaction becomes non-significant when NR participants are removed from analysis.)

The performance of participants by Grammaticality, Language, Participant Group, and SES is shown in Figure 10.4. This interaction reflects the fact that, whereas on grammatical sentences of both languages, performance across groups is similar, on ungrammatical sentences, the Two-way participants from the Low SES group performed best in Spanish, but worst in English. (When NR participants are eliminated from analysis, instead of this interaction, we find an interaction of Grammaticality, Language, SES, and LSH, $F(1,156) = 3.9$, $p < 0.05$. This result indicates that it is the participants whose LSH is OSH and who are from the Low SES group who performed best on Spanish ungrammatical sentences, and who performed the worst on English grammatical sentences.)

These results provide a complex picture of bilinguals' performance. First, overall, performance for every group was better on Spanish than on English; this was especially true with ungrammatical sentences. Fifth graders performed better than 2nd graders, especially on ungrammatical sentences, and especially ungrammatical sentences in Spanish. The group that performed best in Spanish, according to the major analyses, was the Two-way children from the Low SES group; this group also performed the worst in English. (According to the secondary analyses in which NR children were eliminated from consideration, the group that performed best in Spanish was the children from the Low SES group whose LSH was OSH; this group also performed the worst in English.) For Spanish, the Low SES participants with Only Spanish at home outperformed everyone else; but by 5th grade the other groups had caught up with this group. For English, everyone performed relatively poorly at 2nd grade, but by 5th grade, all groups except the Low SES Two-way children improved in their performance.

Summary of judgment data

The combined results on children's judgments indicate the following:

(1) Across participants performance was better on Spanish than on English.

(2) All participants performed better on grammatical sentences than on ungrammatical sentences, but it was suggested that since judging grammatical sentences presents a simpler task, the results on ungrammatical sentences may be a better measure of participants' knowledge.

(3) Participants performed better on judging ungrammatical sentences in Spanish than in English.

(4) Performance on ungrammatical sentences generally improved between 2nd and 5th grades.

For English:

(5) Monolingual English participants outperformed both Two-way and English Immersion participants, especially at the Low SES level.

(6) Bilinguals from the High SES group outperformed those from the Low SES group, especially among the Two-way bilinguals, and especially at 5th grade.

For Spanish:

(7) Monolingual Spanish participants outperformed both Two-way and English Immersion participants, especially on ungrammatical sentences.

(8) The Low SES bilinguals who came from Two-way schools, or with OSH, performed better than any other bilingual group, especially at 2nd grade.

Corrections

Children's corrections of the sentences that they judged to be ungrammatical were examined for further information regarding the processes by which these constructs are learned. Children's corrections of the ungrammatical sentences entailed the deletion of *that* when it occurred as a complementizer in English, and the insertion of *que* in those sentences in which it was missing in Spanish. As in the cases of the mass/count corrections and gender corrections in Chapters 7 and 8, both the 'absolute' percentage of corrections (number out of all opportunities) and the percentage 'relative to judgments' (number of correct corrections divided by number of correct judgments of ungrammaticals) will be reported. I will focus first on English, then on Spanish.

English

Corrections in general

Table 10.1 shows the percentage of correct corrections by the Two-way, English Immersion, and Monolingual participants at each grade level and by SES. The absolute percentages are the main figures shown, the percentages relative to judgments are shown in parentheses. For English, there is a slight advantage at 2nd grade among the Monolingual English and English Immersion participants over the Two-way participants. But at 5th grade, Two-way participants performed as well as or exceeded the performance of the other two groups of participants. These inferences must be drawn with caution, however, as the absolute numbers of correct judgments of ungrammatical sentences by all participants was quite low in English.

Corrections according to SES

The figures in Table 10.1 also show a distinct advantage among bilinguals of High SES subjects over Low SES, especially at 5th grade, but also at 2nd grade if looking at successful corrections out of sentences judged ungrammatical.

Corrections according to Language Spoken at Home

Table 10.2 shows a break-down of the bilinguals' performance by Partic-

Table 10.1 Corrections of ungrammatical *that*-trace constructs by Participant Group, Grade, and SES, by Language: % = number correct corrections / total opportunities (% = % correct corrections / % correct judgments)

Group	Grade	English			Spanish		
		High SES	Low SES	Total	High SES	Low SES	Total
Monolinguals	2	5 (43)	6 (31)	6 (35)	56 (67)	– –	56 (67)
	5	16 (61)	19 (70)	18 (65)	69 (86)	– –	69 (86)
English Immersion	2	3 (52)	1 (13)	2 (31)	11 (34)	12 (41)	11 (37)
	5	16 (64)	6 (38)	10 (52)	33 (58)	29 (63)	31 (60)
Two-way	2	1 (22)	0 (0)	0.5 (11)	8 (33)	27 (73)	15 (51)
	5	31 (99)	4 (38)	17 (78)	28 (54)	48 (71)	38 (64)

ipant Group LSH and 2nd Grade. The figures reveal no consistent picture of success for English based on LSH.

Summary, English correction data

Although the number of ungrammatical sentences judged correctly for English was very low, and it may be difficulty to discern consistencies in children's corrections, a few patterns suggest themselves. First, at 2nd grade, monolinguals performed better than the bilingual groups, but at 5th grade, at least one bilingual group (Two-way bilinguals) appears to have caught up with them. Second, High SES bilinguals were more successful in their corrections than Low SES bilinguals. Finally, there is no apparent pattern of success related to LSH. These findings are consistent with the results of the judgment data.

Spanish

Corrections in general and by SES

Table 10.1 also shows the percentage of correct corrections for Spanish

Table 10.2 Corrections of ungrammatical *that*-trace constructs by Bilingual Participant Group, Grade, and Language Spoken at Home, by Language: % = number correct corrections / total opportunities (% = % correct corrections / % correct judgments)

Group	Grade	English			Spanish		
		ESH	OSH	Total	ESH	OSH	Total
English Immersion	2	1 (26)	3 (33)	2 (31)	7 (36)	14 (38)	11 (37)
	5	14 (72)	7 (35)	10 (52)	27 (55)	35 (65)	31 (60)
Two-way	2	1 (100)	0 (0)	0.5 (11)	11 (53)	21 (53)	15 (51)
	5	14 (81)	19 (77)	17 (78)	43 (68)	35 (61)	38 (64)

by the Two-way, English Immersion, and Monolingual participants at each grade level and by SES. The figures show a distinct advantage of the monolinguals over both bilingual groups. In addition, Two-way bilinguals in the Low SES group performed better than the other bilingual groups, both at 2nd and 5th grades.

Corrections according to Language Spoken at Home

Table 10.2 shows a break-down of the bilinguals' performance on Spanish by Participant Group, LSH and Grade. Like the judgment data, these figures show an early advantage in the Two-way group from homes where Only Spanish is spoken, but that advantage gets extinguished by 5th grade.

Summary, Spanish correction data

Children's corrections in Spanish largely corresponded to what was observed in their judgments: Monolingual Spanish children performed better than Two-way children, who in turn performed better than English Immersion children. This advantage in the Two-way children was primarily located in the Low SES Two-way bilinguals, but also when Only Spanish was the LSH, this gave children an early advantage at 2nd grade.

Discussion

The results of this study on *that*-trace revealed striking differences in children's performance on Spanish versus English. Overall for *Spanish*, participants were fairly competent in judging and correcting sentences. All groups performed better in their judgments with Spanish than with English; and all groups inserted *que* in their corrections at least some of the time when it was missing. However, monolinguals performed better in their judgments and corrections than bilinguals did. Within the bilinguals, the Low SES bilinguals from Two-way schools (or in some cases with OSH , at least for judgments) were most successful at making correct judgments of Spanish sentences (especially at 2nd grade) and at correcting ungrammatical forms.

In contrast, participants appeared fairly incompetent in judging and correcting sentences in *English*. All groups regularly accepted sentences both with and without *that*. However, monolinguals performed better than both bilingual groups in judging ungrammatical sentences. Within bilinguals, the High SES group at 5th grade made more correct judgments than the Low SES group. In their corrections, Monolingual English participants appeared to be more successful than bilingual participants, but at 5th grade, Two-way bilinguals were equivalent to the monolinguals and High SES bilinguals outperformed Low SES bilinguals. LSH did not contribute in any clear way to the pattern of corrections for English.

Let us examine these results, first with regard to the initial question of the relative performance of bilinguals versus monolinguals on these structures, and, second, with regard to the best explanation for the unanticipated differences between performance in English and Spanish.

Differences across groups

In their judgments of sentences in Spanish, both Two-way participants and English Immersion participants performed worse than monolinguals, but Two-way participants from the Low SES level (or with OSH at home) performed better than other participants. In their judgments of sentences in English, the Two-way and English Immersion participants again performed worse than monolinguals, but here High SES participants performed better than Low SES participants when judging ungrammatical sentences. These general results present a picture in which bilingual participants differ significantly from their monolingual peers. Which bilingual group was more similar to the monolinguals in each language appeared to be related to the relative amount of input they received in each language. Two-way children either from a Low SES or with OSH at home appear to have heard more Spanish per day, on average, than English Immersion children or children with ESH at home; and High SES children appear to have heard a greater amount of English per day than their Low SES peers.

Corrections of ungrammatical sentences were consistent with this picture. The relative performance across groups in Spanish, with Monolingual Spanish children performing better than Low SES Two-way children, who in turn performed better than the other bilinguals, appeared directly related to the greater amount of Spanish heard by the Monolingual Spanish group relative to the bilinguals and by the Low SES Two-way group relative to the other bilingual groups. The relative performance across groups in English, with Monolingual English children performing better than High SES bilinguals, who in turn performed better than Low SES bilinguals, appeared related to the greater amount of English heard by the Monolingual English group compared with the bilingual groups, and the High SES bilinguals relative to the Low SES bilinguals. In addition, for English, children with ESH at home had a slight advantage over those with OSH. (I shall return to issues concerning SES, LSH, and input factors in the final Discussion section).

Spanish vs English

Why might it be easier for children learning Spanish to know that *que* is required in *that*-trace constructions than for children learning English to know that *that* cannot occur in such constructs? One critical difference between *que* and *that* lies in their use in structures outside of *that*-trace structures. In complement clauses in which movement has not occurred and in relative clauses, Spanish requires the use of *que*, but English allows *that* to be optional in every case except when a subject is relativized:

(1) Complement Clause
  Dijiste que Ana fué a México.
  *Dijiste ____ Ana fué a México.
  You said that Ana went to Mexico.
  You said ____ Ana went to Mexico.

(2) Relativized Direct Object
  Ana vió al hombre que enseñé en México.
  *Ana vió al hombre ____ enseñé en México.
  Ana saw the man that I taught in Mexico.
  Ana saw the man ____ I taught in Mexico.

(3) Relativized Indirect Object
  Ana vió al hombre al que le dí un caballo.
  *Ana vió al hombre al ____ le dí un caballo.
  Ana saw the man that I gave a horse to.
  Ana saw the man ____ I gave a horse to.

(4) Relativized Subject
  Ana vió al hombre que fué a México.
  *Ana vió al hombre ____ fué a México.

Ana saw the man that went to Mexico.
*Ana saw the man ___ went to Mexico.

Thus, Spanish provides the straightforward message in the input that *que* is required, while English provides model structures in which *that* is clearly optional. In English, at the very least, it appears that children have to deal with surface input that clouds the issue of whether and where *that* is required.

Another complicating factor for English is a difference between *that*-trace interrogatives and relative clause interrogatives of the type shown in (7).

(5) <u>*That*-trace</u>
   Who do you know ___ went to Mexico?
   What did you see ___ fly out the window?
   <u>Relative Clause</u>
   Who do you know ___ that went to Mexico?
   What did you see ___ that flew out the window?

In the relative clause structures, the *wh-* word has moved from a direct object position in the main clause, and the *that* (or a relative pronoun alternative such as *who* or *which*) is required. That it is required is apparent in the corresponding declarative sentences in (8):

(6) *I know a man that/who went to Mexico.*
   *I know a man ___ went to Mexico.
   I saw the bird that/which flew out the window.
   *I saw the bird ___ flew out the window.

The subtle semantic distinction between the *that*-trace sentences and the relative clause sentences may be difficult to learn and may well complicate the child's discovery of the appropriate rules governing the presence of *that* across structures.

These complex patterns governing the use of *that* in English may help explain why even at 5th grade all groups of English-speaking children are still working out the use of *that* in *that*-trace structures in English. As has been found for many structures across languages, constructs that involve relatively transparent and straightforward syntax-semantics mappings (like the Spanish use of *que*) can be learned quickly and effortlessly by children, whereas forms with more opaque and variable structures can be difficult to learn, often taking well into the school years to acquire fully (see Lieven, 1997 for an excellent discussion).

Summary

The results of this experiment provide information on the acquisition of *that*-trace structures. The results suggest, first, a lag in the acquisition of these structures by bilingual children when compared with their monolingual peers. Second, bilinguals who were enrolled in Two-way schools and who came either from Low SES or from homes in which only Spanish was spoken performed better in Spanish than either their English Immersion bilingual peers or Two-way peers who came from High SES or from homes in which both English and Spanish were spoken. In contrast, in English, bilinguals who came from a High SES level outperformed those from a Low SES level, and this was especially true for bilinguals from Two-way schools. In addition, children with ESH may have a slight advantage over those with OSH. These effects appear directly related to the amount of input each group received on a day-to-day basis in each language.

Furthermore, the results suggest that these structures were not acquired, at least in English, until an advanced age, well beyond the ages at which one might expect for a purportedly innate principle that has been hypothesized to come on line by the preschool years. The generally poor performance by all groups in English (and worse than English-speaking adults)[4] and the relatively poor performance by the bilinguals relative to the monolinguals in both languages challenge the position that children are innately endowed with principles that facilitate the easy acquisition of these structures.

Perhaps one would like to argue that some of the bilingual children had more difficulty with these structures because they had simply mis-set or mis-analyzed one language as if it were the other. Perhaps, for example, the Low SES Two-way group, those who performed best in Spanish and least well in English, applied Spanish rules directly to English structures. This hypothesis can be discounted. If these participants were doing this, we could have expected their performance on the grammatical sentences in English to be much worse than that of the other groups, and at about the same level as their performance on the ungrammatical sentences in Spanish. This was not the case. They judged 3.14 out of 4 grammatical sentences in English to be correct (compared to 3.39–3.74 in the other groups) and only 2.16 of the Spanish ungrammaticals to be incorrect. That is, they judged English sentences without *that* to be bad at most 0.86 times out of 4, while they judged Spanish sentences without *que* to be bad about 2.2 times out of 4. In addition, this group should have been much less likely to delete *that* from the ungrammatical sentences in English than the other groups. Again, this was not the case; although this group made fewer corrections of this type than High SES bilinguals, the Low SES subjects from the English Immersion group made similarly low numbers of such corrections. (See Table 10.1.)

If the Low SES Two-way group was not directly applying Spanish rules to English, perhaps they simply developed a grammar somewhere 'in between' English and Spanish and applied this to English. Again, we can rule out this possibility with the data, at least if this hypothesis would mean that this group had a single grammar that was used for both English and Spanish. If we look at the insertions and deletions of *que* and *that* by this group of participants, we find that *que* was inserted correctly in Spanish in 27% to 48% of the ungrammatical sentences (in absolute numbers; in 71% to 73% of the corrections in percentages relative to correct judgments), while *that* was inserted (inappropriately) in English only 9% of the time; similarly, *que* was never deleted (inappropriately), while *that* was deleted (correctly) 0% to 4% of the time (in absolute numbers; or 0% to 38% of the time in percentages relative to correct judgments) (see Table 10.1).

A better explanation for this group's performance than either of these hypotheses is that this group's pattern of responses was related to the input that children received. As noted above, the general differences for the Two-way and English Immersion groups with distinct SES levels and Languages Spoken at Home relative to the monolingual groups appears related to the amount of input the three groups received in the languages at hand. (See General Discussion below.)

In addition to quantity of input playing a major role here, I have suggested that the data on *that*-trace indicate that the acquisition of these structures is not accomplished in isolation from other, seemingly unrelated structures in the two languages. Other structures in which *que* and *that* occur in the two languages appear to play a crucial role in the child's acquisition of the knowledge of whether overt complementizers can occur in sentences involving subject extraction from embedded sentences. In Spanish, the obligatory presence of *que* in other complement sentences and relative clauses reinforces the obligatory presence of *que* in *that*-trace structures. In English, the optional use of *that* in other complement sentences and in all relative clauses except subject relatives, along with the subtle semantic distinction between *that*-trace structures (which disallow *that*) and interrogative subject relative structures (which require *that*), seem to make the child's discovery of the inadmissibility of *that* in *that*-trace structures a long, drawn-out process.

General Discussion

The three experiments on morphosyntactic development presented in Chapters 8, 9, and this chapter provide a complex view of the morphosyntactic development of bilinguals growing up in the context of a community like Miami. These experiments reveal the following patterns:

(1) There was a general lag in the development of morphosyntax by bilinguals relative to monolinguals. Such a lag was observed in all three experiments.

(2) However, there did not appear to be a qualitative difference in the acquisition of these structures by monolinguals versus bilinguals.

(3) When comparing bilingual groups on performance in *English*, we have observed

  (a) an early disadvantage among the Low SES bilinguals from Two-way schools and

  (b) an early advantage among bilinguals from High SES levels, or from English Immersion schools. These patterns were observed for the mass/count distinction at the 2nd grade level, and for *that*-trace at the 5th grade level (performance at the 2nd grade level was near the floor). By 5th grade for mass/count, the Low SES bilinguals had caught up with their High SES peers.

(4) When comparing bilingual groups on performance in *Spanish*, we have observed

  (a) an early advantage among Two-way bilinguals from the Low SES level or among Two-way bilinguals whose LSH was only Spanish and

  (b) a late disadvantage among English Immersion bilinguals whose LSH was both English and Spanish.

All of these results point to an important role for frequency of input, especially at the early stages, up to some 'critical mass' of data has been accumulated, in the acquisition of these structures. Let us take each of the factors of LSH, SES level, and IMS and examine them for the implications each has for input to the child.

Language Spoken at Home

The participants of this study came from three types of home: homes in which only Spanish was spoken (the Monolingual Spanish participants and some bilinguals), homes in which only English was spoken (Monolingual English participants), and homes in which both Spanish and English were spoken (some bilinguals). Considering only this factor, it appears clear that the OSH condition provided the greatest amount of input in Spanish, OEH the greatest amount in English, and ESH intermediate between the two in both languages. If input is an important factor, a participant in an OSH home should have the greatest advantage for Spanish, the greatest disadvantage for English, and vice versa for a participant in an OEH home, and intermediate between the two for a participant in a ESH home.

The results above are consistent with these predictions for Spanish:

(1) The Monolingual Spanish participants outperformed any of the others in Spanish.

(2) Among the variables that gave some bilingual participants an early advantage was OSH.
(3) Among the variables that gave some bilingual participants a late disadvantage was ESH.

With regard to English, the results were mixed: monolingual English participants outperformed any of the others in English, but bilinguals with ESH outperformed those with OSH only in their corrections of the mass/count and *that*-trace sentences.

The fact that there was not a major home language effect for English is not too surprising, in light of the generally late acquisition of the mass/count structures for *much* and *many* and of *that*-trace structures. That is, since these constructs are acquired throughout the grade school years, they are not so dependent on the language of the home. During those years, the child has access to input outside the home, including at school and in the larger community. It is difficult to know precisely how much English and Spanish children actually heard, given that parent report data are not necessarily entirely accurate. Further, we do not know how native-like the English spoken in the home might have been.

Instructional Method in School

Similarly, the participants came from three types of school: schools in which only Spanish was spoken (only for the Monolingual Spanish group), schools in which only English was spoken (the Monolingual English participants and the English Immersion bilinguals), and schools in which both Spanish and English were spoken (Two-way bilinguals). Considering only this factor, we know that Spanish-only schools provided the greatest amount of input in Spanish, English-only schools the greatest amount in English, and Two-way schools something intermediate between the two in both languages (see Chapter 3 for data on input in the English Immersion and Two-way schools). If input is an important factor, participants in Spanish-only schools should have the greatest advantage for Spanish, the greatest disadvantage for English, and vice versa for participants in English-only schools, and intermediate between the two for participants in Two-way schools.

The results above are consistent with these predictions for Spanish:

(1) The participants from only Spanish schools (the Monolingual Spanish participants) outperformed any of the others in Spanish.
(2) Among the variables that gave some bilingual participants an early advantage in Spanish was the fact that they came from Two-way schools.
(3) Among the variables that gave some bilingual participants a late disad-

vantage for Spanish was the fact that they came from English Immersion schools.

With regard to English, the results were also consistent with regard to the predictions:

(1) Among the variables that gave some bilingual participants an advantage was the fact that they came from English Immersion schools.
(2) Among the variables that gave some bilingual participants a disadvantage was the fact that they came from Two-way schools.

SES

The final factor, SES, could in theory affect performance simply because a High SES level might mean a richer environment all around – greater access to linguistic and non-linguistic stimuli and opportunities. (This richness might include more books in the home, more highly educated parents (and, hence, perhaps the child would be hearing, e.g. a richer vocabulary), more opportunities for interaction with others speaking the languages – e.g. visits to museums, more outside entertainment such as movies, and so forth (see Chapter 1).) Under this possibility, a High SES could be accompanied by a greater amount of input in whatever language is in the child's environment. For the monolinguals, one could predict that a child in the High SES category would have the advantage over the child in the Low SES category. For the bilinguals, one could predict that this would also hold, *for both languages*.

While SES did not play a major role in the performance of monolingual children, it did for bilinguals. But it did so in opposite directions for the two languages. For English, the data reported above were consistent with the prediction that higher SES conferred an advantage since:

• bilinguals who had the greatest early advantage for English were those who came from the High SES level, and
• bilinguals who had the greatest early disadvantage for English were those who came from the Low SES level.

However, the data reported above for Spanish were inconsistent with the prediction that higher SES provides an advantage: The bilinguals who had the greatest early advantage for Spanish were those of *Low SES*. This result suggests that the effect of SES cannot be attributed simply to a richer linguistic and non-linguistic environment *per se*, since, as noted, one would expect the High SES children to have the advantage for both languages. There are several factors that may have contributed to the complex relation between SES and performance in English and Spanish in these data. First, as noted in Chapters 2 and 4, data from parent questionnaires indicated that bilingual parents of High SES were more confident of their abilities in English than parents of Low SES. This may be precisely what gave the High SES children an initial advantage, and the children from the Low SES group an initial disadvantage for English. The former were probably exposed to more native-like English a greater proportion of the time than the equivalent Low SES children.

This does not help to explain the advantage of Low SES children over High SES children in Spanish. The two groups of bilingual parents rated their abilities in Spanish similarly. However, the Low SES children were most likely exposed to native-like Spanish *more often* than the High SES children, for two reasons. First, since the High SES bilingual parents were more confident about their English abilities, they may have been using English more often than the Low SES bilingual parents, giving less time for talk in Spanish. Another possible factor is that children from High SES homes may have had more opportunities for interaction with the life of the Miami community, in which both English and Spanish are used. Again, possible greater access to English among High SES children may have had the concurrent effect of proportionately less access to Spanish.

Overall predictions

Given these three factors, then, one could make the following predictions regarding relative command of English and Spanish for bilinguals in the study:

(1) The bilinguals who should have had the advantage in Spanish were those with OSH, of Low SES , and from Two-way schools. This is precisely what was found at 2nd grade for the acquisition of both gender and Spanish *that*-trace – the Two-way bilinguals with ample and consistent input in Spanish, either through living with OSH or by coming from a Low SES background, performed the best early on.

(2) The bilinguals who should have had the greatest *disadvantage* in Spanish were those with ESH, of High SES, and from English Immersion schools. In fact, it was found that the group that lagged behind the most in the acquisition of both gender and Spanish *that*-trace was the English Immersion bilinguals with ESH. However, SES did not seem to be a significant factor in this delay (except insofar as the Low SES Two-way bilinguals had the overall advantage).

(3) The bilinguals who should have had the advantage in English were those with ESH, of High SES, and from English Immersion schools. In fact, SES seemed to be the most important variable, although LSH also played a role. LSH did not appear significant in creating a general advantage for English, although it was a factor in children's performance

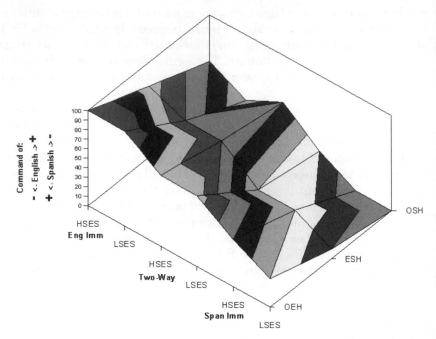

Figure 10.5 Metaphorical Topography of Effect of Input Factors (SES, Language Spoken at Home, Language Spoken at School) on Command of English and Spanish

on corrections. Since corrections entail a child's productive capacity, while judgments are more related to receptive capacities, it may be that ESH gave children an edge in production over children with OSH.

(4) The bilinguals who should have the greatest *disadvantage* in English were those with OSH, of Low SES, and from Two-way schools. In fact it was Low SES, Two-way children who had the early disadvantage in acquiring both the mass/count distinction and *that*-trace structures.

These patterns of abilities in the two languages are depicted graphically in relation to these input factors in Figure 10.5.

Frequency of input and 'critical mass'

As noted above, such effects related to frequency of input can be seen to diminish as a 'critical mass' of data is accumulated: Group differences observed in all of these studies were more apparent at 2nd grade than at 5th grade. The inference to be drawn is that by 5th grade, children in most groups had accumulated enough examples of usage on each construct to be able to draw out and generalize patterns. This possibility is consistent with growing evidence in the literature that children require a 'critical mass' of data to generate systematic, rule-governed behavior (see, e.g. Marchman & Bates, 1994 and Maratsos, 2000, in relation to normally developing monolingual children; Conti-Ramsden & Jones, 1997 and Jones & Conti-Ramsden, 1997, in relation to children with Specific Language Impairment; and Ellis & Schmidt, 1998 and Elman, May, 2000, in relation to connectionist network modeling of acquisition. See also Mägiste, 1979, for a frequency of exposure explanation for longer reaction times among bilinguals than monolinguals, and for a reduction in reaction times as exposure increases).

What counts as a 'critical mass' undoubtedly varies from construct to construct and may depend in large part on how transparent and reliable the input is in terms of form-function mappings (Lieven, 1997) and formal cues (e.g. MacWhinney, 1987 and Bates & MacWhinney, 1989). In relation to the constructs examined in these three chapters, Spanish gender, Spanish use of *que*, and English mass/count appeared more transparent and consistent than English use of *that*. Thus, with the first three types of constructions, gaps between groups at 2nd grade became less dramatic or were eliminated by 5th grade. In contrast, with English *that*-trace constructions, even at 5th grade all groups performed relatively poorly, suggesting perhaps that a greater 'critical mass' is necessary for children to work out the patterns of occurrence for *that*. (Note, paradoxically, that this is the direct opposite to what one might expect, if principles governing *that*-trace are considered to be innately endowed.) The frequency of input explanation not only applies across the different groups of bilinguals studied here, but also to comparisons of monolinguals with the bilinguals. Because monolinguals do not 'time-share' across two languages, they necessarily end up, on average, with more input data in their one language than bilinguals do in either of the two languages they are learning.

Linguistic and metalinguistic effects

Any input explanation for the findings of these studies seems to depend on the idea that frequency and quantity of exposure influences acquisition only up to the point at which the child has accumulated enough experience with a given construct to be able to draw out some generalizations. In addition, frequency effects appear more relevant to the cases of items involving *linguistic* knowledge than to items involving *metalinguistic* knowledge. Thus, across these studies, group differences were most apparent with regard to oral abilities – e.g. with vocabulary, gender, mass/count, and so forth. With tasks reliant on *metalinguistic* knowledge, on the other hand, frequency of exposure appeared less relevant than the fact of exposure to more than one system. Bialystok (Bialystok, 1986, 1988, 1991; Bialystok & Majumder, 1998) has made a very strong case arguing that bilingual children have the advantage over monolingual children precisely in those cases that demand a high level of analysis and of control of attention. The critical case in point here is reading and writing. It is clear that metalinguistic knowledge – especially phonological awareness (see, e.g. review in Goswami, 1999) – plays an important role in establishing reading readiness in children. It is not surprising, then, that the group here that had the advantage on the reading and writing tasks was the group that was the most 'balanced' in bilinguality – the Two-way bilinguals (see Chapter 4 and 5). Furthermore, it is not surprising that these tasks that involve metalinguistic awareness were the ones that showed transferability of knowledge from one language to the other (as opposed to the independence witnessed for the oral abilities in the two languages). The implication is that once a child comes to acquire the metalinguistic skills that make it possible to acquire reading and writing skills, that metalinguistic knowledge will be available for the acquisition of reading and writing in both of the languages the child knows.

The distributed characteristic

Before closing these three chapters, I would like to reflect more generally on their results in relation to two theoretical issues. One concerns the 'distributed characteristic' of bilinguals' linguistic knowledge (see Chapters 1, 4, and 5). Could the results of Chapters 8 to 10 indicating differences between monolinguals and bilinguals be explainable, at least in part, as a consequence of the distributed characteristic of bilinguals' knowledge? That is, is it possible that bilinguals' performance in each language is lower than monolinguals' simply because they have learned some things in some contexts in language A and other things in other contexts in language B? To examine this question, I find it instructive to separate the distributed characteristic of the bilingual's linguistic knowledge into two components. First, the bilingual's linguistic knowledge is distributed _across contexts_ – e.g. a child learns words _a, b,_ and _c_ in context X and words _d, e,_ and _f_ in context Y. This distributed characteristic of vocabulary knowledge is a feature of any idiolect, bilingual or monolingual – we all, for example, use different registers in speaking at home and at a job interview. Second, and relatedly, the bilingual's knowledge is distributed across languages – because language A is usually used in context X, words _a, b,_ and _c_ come from language A, and because language B is usually used in context Y, words _d, e,_ and _f_ come from language B. This aspect of the distributed nature of the bilinguals' knowledge is not shared by the monolingual, of course.

With regard to many of the linguistic features studied in this volume, one might easily expect the bilinguals' knowledge to be distributed in both of these ways. With the structures studied in Chapters 8, 9, and this chapter, the picture is less clear, however. Each of these, on the one hand, might be seen as necessarily 'distributed' across languages, in that one might argue that *all* syntactic constructs are language-specific (see, e.g. Croft, 2001). The syntactic constructs one knows in one language do not necessarily impinge on the syntactic constructs one knows in another (as I have argued for the *that*-trace data above).

The distribution *within* a given language, however, is less clear. On the one hand, it is virtually impossible to speak in English or in Spanish without using mass/count constructs and gender constructs, as well as the relevant complement structures in the language. Thus the child who is learning English or Spanish will be hearing these constructs in virtually every type of context in which he or she hears the language. On the other hand, it is true that the manner in which mass/count and gender were tested here did necessarily involve some lexical knowledge – e.g. that noun X in English is used with *much*, noun Y with *many*, and that noun X in Spanish is masculine, noun Y is feminine. Because of the distributed nature of lexical items across the bilingual's two languages, a bilingual learner may not have acquired as many of the mass and count nouns in English or as many of the relevant gendered nouns as a monolingual learner has, and this could have affected performance on these tests. Yet the results here were fully consistent with another test concerning mass/count constructs, with another group of bilingual subjects in Miami (Gathercole, 1997), and performance on that test was not reliant on knowledge of particular nouns. In that study, children's interpretations of the count structure *a X* and the mass structure *some X* as referring to objects versus substances were tested, but there, novel nouns were used. Even in that study, however, as in Chapter 8, the bilinguals were seen to lag behind their monolingual peers in the development of this more general knowledge about the mass/count distinction. Differences in performance across groups in that study would be hard to attribute to distributional properties of bilinguals' knowledge across contexts; instead, the differences can be more adequately attributed to the relative frequencies with which the children heard the constructions in question.

Possible peer effects

The other theoretical issue worth reflecting on with the results of Chapters 8, 9 and this chapter, is the influence that the absence of native-speaking peers might have had on bilinguals' development. In Chapter 4 it is pointed out that the bilinguals studied here, especially those in the Two-way schools, may have had limited access to native-speaking peers. It cannot be known without further research to what extent this may have affected the performance of children in this study.

However, additional studies in North Wales might shed some light on this question (e.g. Gathercole, Thomas, & Laporte, in press). The bilingual situation in North Wales provides an interesting comparison with the bilingual situation in South Florida. First, there are some features that the two have in common: (1) The community provides native-speaking models for both languages of the community (Spanish/English, Welsh/English), (2) both languages are commonly spoken 'on the street', in all contexts of daily life (over 70% of the population in North Wales speaks Welsh, Jones & Morris, 1997), and (3) both communities provide two types of schools, in which either two languages are used as a medium of instruction (Spanish/English, Welsh/English) or only one language is used (English in South Florida, Welsh in North Wales). (There are also some important differences, to which I will return below.)

The studies we are conducting examine children's acquisition of Welsh. They involve, among other things, the comparison of the performance of children coming from three types of home: (1) in which only Welsh is spoken; (2) in which Welsh and English have been spoken about equally since the child's birth (in some cases, these homes involve a one-parent-one-language situation, while in others, the parents are fully bilingual themselves in the two languages); and (3) in which only English is spoken. They also involve the comparison of the performance of children coming from schools in which Welsh is the medium of education versus both Welsh and English. However, the data analyzed to date come, importantly, primarily from schools in which Welsh is the medium of education. In addition, also importantly, the children from the different home-language backgrounds are *in the same schools*. Thus, they have, by necessity, the same level of access to native-speaking peers.

In some of this work, we are examining children's acquisition of grammatical gender in Welsh (Gathercole *et al.*, 2001, April-a; Gathercole *et al.*, in press), and in some children's acquisition of cues to subjects of sentences (Gathercole *et al.*, 2001, April-b). The most important comparison here, with regard to the question of the relative influence of input versus the presence of native-speaking peers is the comparison of the children from homes in which only Welsh is spoken and children from homes in which Welsh and English are spoken about equally.[5] In this work, we have found a difference in performance according to amount of exposure, similar to the differences found here and in Chapters 8 and 9: Children who come from homes in which only Welsh is spoken outperform children who come from homes in which both Welsh and English are spoken. While we are still collecting data on these issues, so the full picture is not yet available, the data examined so far suggest that frequency of input still plays a significant role when access to native-speaking peers is controlled for.

While there is not space here to explore in detail how the situation in North Wales might be different from the situation in South Florida, a number of factors suggest themselves as potentially important. These include the following: (1) Not only are native-speaking peers available to children, but also fully native-speaking adults, for both languages. Whereas in Miami, the continual influx of adult immigrants means a continual introduction of speakers whose command of English is non-native-like (and, at the same time, few non-native adult speakers of Spanish have native fluency), in North Wales, it is uncommon for adult bilingual speakers of Welsh and English to be less than native-like in the two languages. (There are also many L2 adult learners of Welsh; however, such learners would commonly speak English to children, not Welsh.) (2) A second factor that bears close examination is parents' motivations for speaking a given language or languages in the home. In Miami, the choice is often one of necessity; note, e.g. that the Low SES Spanish-speaking adults were not very confident of their English. In North Wales, in contrast, it is more commonly a matter of *choice than necessity*. Parents choose to speak only Welsh at home or both Welsh and English for political, cultural, and social reasons, not usually because they can or cannot speak English. These additional factors may well turn out to exert critical influences on the ultimate patters of linguistic development in children in North Wales.

Conclusion

These three experiments have provided information on the acquisition of morphosyntactic elements of both English and Spanish. The results of the three experiments together suggest, first, that bilingual children acquire the three constructs similarly to their monolingual peers, but at a delay. Second, the results suggest that the most important factor in determining performance by bilinguals on these three constructs is frequency of input. Frequency of input is determined by a complex interaction of the language spoken at home, the language of the school, and the SES level of the child. Finally, the results suggest that there is no qualitative difference in the acquisition of superficial aspects of the language compared with an aspect of the language that has been attributed to innate knowledge. The acquisition of *that*-trace in the two languages was affected by the same variables controlling frequency of input as the acquisition of mass/count and the acquisition of gender were. Finally, regardless of which group had an early advantage in a given language, by 5th grade, differences between groups became either lessened or eliminated totally. This suggests that, while a given group may have an early disadvantage relative to their peers in one of the languages, with time and experience they may eventually catch up with the other groups. I have suggested that the reason that the groups catch up may be that acquisition involves accumulating some critical mass of data from which the child can draw out generalizations. Once a child reaches this level at which s/he can abstract out general linguistic patterns governing a given construct, differences across children and groups become diminished or extinguished.

One major question of this volume concerns the role of SES in bilingual performance. The evidence here suggests that the role of SES is in fact quite complex. We have found in the three experiments on morphosyntactic development, as in the standardized tests, that High SES status conferred an advantage only for the acquisition of English. For the acquisition of Spanish, however, Low SES status gave children the advantage. As discussed above, this difference indicates that it is not SES level *per se*, with the educational and social advantages that that may provide, that is responsible for differences in performance. Rather, the effects appear to be related to the frequency with which children of a given SES level in the Miami setting were exposed to English versus Spanish. As argued above, children of High SES were more likely to be exposed to English more often than those of Low SES, and those of Low SES were more likely to hear Spanish more often than their High SES peers. This result is consistent with Porter's (1990) and Rossell and Baker's (1996) notion that 'time on task' is a critical factor in the acquisition of the two languages. It must be stressed that these effects are relative to the particular sample of children studied. One might expect that SES level may well affect linguistic achievements in perhaps distinct fashions in different types of setting (e.g. depending on whether bilingualism was 'additive' or 'subtractive', see Chapter 1). However, the results here indicate that SES level must always be considered when examining linguistic achievements of bilinguals.

Another issue central to the larger study is the possible interaction of the two languages in acquisition. Can a solid grounding in one language assist the acquisition of the other? The implication of the present studies is that developments in the two languages – at least those involving linguistic knowledge (as opposed to those involving metalinguistic knowledge) are largely independent. For all three studies on grammatical judgments and corrections, achievement in English was related to factors that increased a child's exposure to English, while achievement in Spanish was related to factors that increased the child's exposure to Spanish. Those who did well in Spanish were not those who did well in English, and vice versa. In fact, on the one area of language tested here in both English and Spanish, the *that*-trace structures, there was no evidence whatsoever that children were transferring knowledge of one language to structures in the other. As discussed above, this finding of independence may not apply to tasks involving metalinguistic knowledge – e.g. reading and writing. Bilinguals' knowledge of two systems may boost their metalinguistic awareness, and this then can affect their performance in both languages on these more metalinguistic tasks.

A further issue is whether children who came from Two-way schools and with both languages at home and with the advantages that High SES affords might have had the advantage in both languages. As was the case with the core studies, these three experiments did not support such a prediction. Instead, advantage in a language appeared to bear a stronger and more straightforward link with amount of exposure to that language: Two-way children, especially those from either Low SES groups or from homes with OSH, had an early disadvantage in English, at 2nd grade. (However, by 5th grade, the differences between these children and English Immersion children or those from a High SES group decreased, suggesting they may eventually catch up and be indistinguishable.) In contrast, with regard to the development of Spanish abilities, children in Two-way schools, especially from Low SES levels and with OSH at home, had an advantage in Spanish over their peers.

What were the effects of LSH on development in the two languages? The effects of LSH for these morphosyntactic constructs were more mixed. For English, LSH appeared unimportant in children's judgments, although it may have played a role in their abilities to make corrections. For Spanish, LSH may have played a more crucial role, with children with OSH having the early advantage over other groups.

In summary, all three studies in Chapters 8, 9 and this chapter suggest that bilingual children initially lagged behind their monolingual peers in linguistic development, but that they began closing the gap by 5th grade. In addition, their development in each language appeared to follow the same routes on the structures tested as those followed by their monolingual peers; thus, these studies support a position in which the two languages develop independently. I have argued here that ultimately these results are consistent with theories positing an important role for input in acquisition and positing a need for a 'critical mass' of data before a child can discover general patterns.

Notes

1. A preliminary report of the first 150 Miami participants tested for this experiment is reported in Gathercole and Montes (1997).
2. See Sobin (1987), however, for dialects that may differ in this regard.
3. In fact, Spanish requires the complementizer here, as it does elsewhere.
4. One might suggest that perhaps the monolingual children's judgments were in line with how monolingual adults might perform on these same structures.

That is, perhaps English-speaking adults would judge fewer of the ungrammatical sentences to be ungrammatical than Spanish-speaking adults. A test of 18 monolingual English-speaking adults and 16 monolingual Spanish-speaking adults who were given all set I and set II sentences of their language shows otherwise. Results reveal that there was no significant difference across groups in the mean number of correct judgments of ungrammatical sentences: English speakers correctly judged a mean of 6.8 (out of 8) and Spanish speakers correctly judged 6.1 (out of 8) ungrammatical sentences.

5. Few 'monolingual' Welsh speakers exist. Most native speakers of Welsh are bilingual in Welsh and English. Thus, the closest one can get to having 'monolingual-like' input in Welsh is in homes in which only Welsh is spoken. Children from homes in which only English is spoken are less relevant because they can be considered L2 learners of Welsh, since they typically begin learning Welsh when they start school.

Chapter 11

The Ability of Bilingual and Monolingual Children to Perform Phonological Translation

D. KIMBROUGH OLLER and ALAN B. COBO-LEWIS

Definition of Phonological Translation

In the pursuit of special relationships between bilingualism and academic capabilities within the Bilingualism Study Group (see Note 1 in Chapter 2) during the years of the research reported in this volume, considerable attention was focused on a special phonological capability of bilingual speakers. The reason for the interest was both theoretical and practical. Phonological knowledge is clearly fundamental to linguistic abilities and is predictive of reading acquisition. The question was 'do bilingual speakers have special phonological knowledge that may play a role in reading?' The study of phonological knowledge in bilingual speakers may present an important opportunity to evaluate capabilities that predict the ability to learn to read. The present chapter offers new evidence regarding relationships between reading, writing and phonological abilities that appear to be especially acute in bilingual speakers even at a very young age.

The issue of focus rests upon the ability of bilingual speakers to perform what we have called 'phonological translation' (Oller *et al.*, 1998). In a nutshell, the ability makes it possible for speakers to hear a word in one language and to render that word, not its meaning, but its phonological form, in the other language. For example, a speaker of Spanish says 'Fernando' pronouncing the name with Spanish phonetic styling; an English speaker, hearing the name, repeats it with English styling. The first pronunciation includes crisp Spanish monophthongal vowels, a tapped 'r', and no vowel nasalization. The English version, however, is translated to include new features: a retroflex 'r', a nasalized vowel between the two 'n's', and a diphthongized 'o'. Native speakers of either language recognize the Spanish rendition as Spanish and the English rendition as English, and understand that a speaker who uses the Spanish version while speaking English or vice versa either has a foreign accent, or is intentionally invoking the pronunciation style of the other language. A person who is capable of performing phonological translation in both directions can be said to be 'phonologically bilingual', and it appears that all truly bilingual speakers have this capability. Prior studies on fundamental properties of bilingualism have also addressed phonological translation (Flege & Hammond, 1994; Flege & Munro, 1994; Zuengler, 1985).

Names present a common circumstance where speakers use phonological translation when they engage in social intercourse with speakers of other languages. In business, in school, or simply on the street, persons who meet individuals of other language backgrounds are required to pronounce their names, which in many cases are introduced in the foreign language phonology, but must be rendered by monolingual speakers in their only language. Both in conversing directly with the foreign language speaker and in talking about the foreign language speaker to other persons, the monolingual new acquaintance is obliged to translate the name phonologically, or to make a potentially awkward effort at pronouncing the name in its native form. Such attempts are not only often difficult or impossible for many monolingual speakers, but in many circumstances may also seem pretentious. Thus, phonological translation is a common necessity of communication in a multilingual world. The bilingual speaker is capable of making these translations freely, and commonly is capable of choosing whether to do it or not.

Of course, names are not the only words that often require phonological translation. Linguistic borrowings (words imported from one language to another) occur frequently in all cases where there is social contact between languages. Some national organizations try to encourage their populace to resist borrowings, attempting to insist upon lexical translations that maintain a greater sense of nativeness in the home language. But often the resistance is to no avail. The French academies have managed to keep phonologically translated forms of words such as 'computer' and 'software' at bay within French usage in many formal settings, by having introduced the terms 'ordinateur' and 'logiciel' to replace them. But the French are an independently-minded lot, and while they know the academies' terms, they often say 'computer' and 'software' with a French accent that even they find humorous, given the efforts of the academies to prevent their usage. The humor is apparently attributable to a sort of delight that the French populace takes regarding its own recalcitrance, but the fact of phonological translation as a natural characteristic of languages in the context of social contact appears to run deep in all cultures. No amount of academy action can prevent it from occurring. One might say that in this regard humans are inherently recalcitrant, but another way to look at it is to conclude that humans have a tendency to use language in ways that are convenient and communicative, and so they borrow words and translate them phonologically, given that it is both convenient and communicative to do so.

When we put phonological translation under the microscope of linguistic analysis, we find that it requires recognition of the relationships between sounds in the two languages. Since the sounds of 'Fernando' produced in Spanish are clearly not sounds of English, translation requires a mapping of sounds between the two. Some mappings are more felicitous than others, and consequently there exist both good and bad phonological translations. The evidence we shall present (and see a preliminary report based on partial data from the Miami research in Oller *et al.*, 1998) indicates that some speakers are better at translating than others, and that even very young English monolingual speakers are often quite good at phonological translation from a foreign language (in this case Spanish) into their native language. Bilinguals tend to be good at it in both directions (Spanish-to-English and English-to-Spanish), but still there are notable differences among children in their abilities to perform phonological translation.

Phonological Translation and Reading

The hypothesis that drove this research initially was based on a simple suggestion: since bilingual children are obliged often to engage in phonological translation in two directions, and since phonological translation involves a mapping of phonological elements from one language to the elements of another, perhaps bilingual children are required to achieve a special sort of phonological awareness. While monolingual children might sometimes engage in phonological translation as well, they might acquire some of the same special awareness, but bilinguals might acquire more of it.

We know that phonological awareness as manifest in tasks such as rhyming or pronunciation of individual segments is highly predictive of reading abilities in young children (Bryant *et al.*, 1989; Fox & Routh, 1975; Treiman, 2000; Tunmer *et al.*, 1988). Further, it is clear that productive reading, the kind of reading that makes it possible to sound out words that have never been encountered in written form before, must include phonological decoding in languages where the writing systems are alphabetical (González, 1996; Liberman *et al.*, 1989; Treiman, 2000) as is the case for both Spanish and English. The reader must be able to map letters to sounds (phonemes or phonemic syllables), and consequently must have at least some awareness of the structure of the phonemic units of the language along with their relationships with orthographic symbols. It appears that even in languages where there is only a weak association in the writing system between phonological factors and graphological ones (as in logographic systems in languages such as Chinese or Korean [Hanja]), there are still effects of phonological awareness on reading (Cho & Chen, 1999; Shu *et al.*, 2000; Tzeng *et al.*, 1977). It also appears that the more direct the mapping between phonological and graphological elements, the faster children learn to read (see Oeney & Durgunoglu, 1997 for Turkish, or Naeslund, 1999 for German). Finally, there is growing evidence of cross-language transfer for bilinguals, such that phonological awareness for one language predicts word-decoding abilities in the other (Baum Bursztyn, 1999; Durgunoglu *et al.*, 1993).

The reasoning underlying our hypothesis can be expanded to take note of the fact that bilingual children, having to face a phonological mapping task virtually every day in phonological translation, might in fact acquire a special phonological awareness, a special capability for mapping that might produce improved reading, at least insofar as reading constitutes the productive task of phonological to graphological mapping.

In posing this hypothesis we are aware that there are numerous factors other than phonological/graphological decoding that are correlated with success in learning to read. For example, knowledge of the vocabulary and syntax of the language to be read as well as naming speed and phonological memory are clearly predictive of reading success (Manis *et al.*, 2000; Passenger *et al.*, 2000). Given this fact, it must be concluded that though phonological/graphological decoding plays an important role in reading, and even if bilingual speakers have a special leg up on decoding owing to their skills in phonological translation, it could still be the case that monolinguals might outperform bilinguals in reading within the native language of the monolinguals. The relative importance of decoding as opposed to other factors that influence reading ability simply cannot be predicted in the absence of empirical evaluation. The present research represents a step in the direction of supplying empirical evaluation of the special role that phonological translation might play in reading.

Methods

Participants

The subjects in the phonological translation research were 640 of the children who had taken the Woodcock Batteries and Peabody Picture Vocabulary tests. Each child was tested in the fifth session (see Chapter 2). The present work incorporated all the Kindergarten (K) and 2nd grade data

Table 11.1 Sample sizes for children who completed the phonological translation task

	Low SES			High SES		
	Grade			Grade		
	K	2nd	5th	K	2nd	5th
Bilinguals						
English Immersion						
Only Spanish at Home	28	21	22	13	21	13
English & Spanish at Home	24	16	19	20	11	12
Two-way Education						
Only Spanish at Home	35	22	19	19	16	29
English & Spanish at Home	14	15	24	24	18	20
Monolinguals	30	21	21	33	24	36

from Oller *et al.* (1998), but added data from the 5th grade and included data from 215 additional children.

Design

Table 11.1 presents sample sizes by Instructional Method at School (IMS), Socio-economic Status (SES), Language Spoken at Home (LSH), and Grade. Characteristics of the samples by subgrouping are detailed in Chapter 2. A variety of analysis types are provided below that were not provided in Oller *et al.* (1998).

Materials and procedures

The tests were conducted utilizing a set of commonly occurring names from Spanish and English in Miami. In training sessions, children were taught to perform phonological translation for four names in each language: Nancy, Betty, David and Arnold for English, and Rosario, Berta, Jorge, and Octavio for Spanish. When training was completed, subjects were then presented with test items for translation. The real names that were used in the test were Freddy, Victor, Jennifer, Donald, and Dorothy for English, and María, Rafael, Alicia, Teresa, and Orlando for Spanish. Subsequently, the children were presented with a set of fictitious names for translation, names that conformed to the phonotactics of each language, but which do not exist as real names (at least not commonly). With the fictitious names, subjects were given the opportunity to display their creative abilities to translate phonologically with novel names. For English the fictitious names were: Rasky, Themon (rhymes with 'demon'), Sparner, Gasil (rhymes with 'basal'), and Murdy (rhymes with 'dirty'). For Spanish the fictitious names were: Parasco, Marol, Ortaña, Cherro, and Edalfo.

In each case for both languages the fictitious names were chosen in order to offer children the opportunity to perform phonological translations with a variety of language-specific phonetic elements. Among the specific elements for English were: [θ], the 'th' in 'Themon'; [ɹ], the English retroflex 'r' as in 'Dorothy' and 'Rasky'; [ɫ], the dark 'l' as in 'Gasil'. Among the specific elements for Spanish were the trilled and tapped 'r's, [r] and [ɾ], as in 'Cherro' and 'María'; the unaspirated stop consonant as in 'Ortaña' and 'Parasco'; and the light 'l' [l] as in 'Marol' and 'Rafael'. Stress patterns in both real and fictitious names were commonly occurring ones for both languages.

The phonological translation testing occurred in a quiet room with one of the eight testers (Chapter 2), each of whom had excellent, native-like pronunciation in both languages. The elicitation was straightforward and in general easily accomplished by the testers (although some monolingual and bilingual Kindergartners and older monolinguals hesitated in attempting to translate many names, especially the fictitious ones). In order to control for order effects, the testing of Spanish-to-English and English-to-Spanish translations was counterbalanced across subjects. Experimenters were assigned randomly to subjects to the extent that it was possible given the constraints of scheduling.

Each tester was trained to administer phonological translation training and testing. The process began with instructions to the child, exemplified here for English-to-Spanish: 'We're going to play a game now. First I say a name in English, and then you say the same name in Spanish. I say "Peter" ([pʰiɾəɹ]) and you say [pitɛɾ]. I say "Emily" ([ɛməli]) and you say [emili]. OK now let's try it.' After the instructions the child was presented with the four training items for the language that the instructions had been given in, and was encouraged for each to provide a phonological translation. The experimenter gave praise if the child performed the translation, and gave hints about how to do it if not. Models were presented orally only, and orthographic representations were not used or solicited.

After the training was completed, testing began regardless of the children's level of success on the training trials. During testing no feedback was provided to the children regarding the accuracy or appropriateness of their translations. For monolingual children, the instructions were given in English for both Translation Directions (English-to-Spanish and Spanish-to-English). Bilingual subjects received instructions in Spanish for the segment of Spanish-to-English and in English for the other one. It is possible that giving the instructions in both languages may have heightened the bilinguals' tendency to perform the translations in both directions. A separate test with monolingual instructions for both directions was not given. The two segments were broken up by the separate syntax judgment tasks (see Chapters 8–10); it was hoped thus to maximally maintain the children's interest. The phonological translation tasks and training were quick, requiring only 5 to 10 minutes per child altogether.

Scoring

The scoring method was based on a three-point scale: 0 for no translation (the child pronounced the name just as it was modeled), 1 for an intermediate translation (the child translated some of the features of the word but not all of them), and 2 for perfect translation (the child translated all the features of the word appropriately). If the child refused to attempt a particular translation, the score assigned was 0. A single tester did the scoring live, on a clipboard sheet, for each session.

The scoring was complicated to some extent by the fact that several correct and appropriate translations were sometimes available, especially in the Spanish-to-English direction. For example, the Spanish name 'Rafael' [rafael] can be translated appropriately to English at least nine ways, as [ɹɑfiɛɫ], [ɹæfiɛɫ], [ɹafiɛɫ], [ɹɑfeɛɫ], [ɹæfeɛɫ], [ɹafeɛɫ], [ɹɑfaɛɫ], [ɹæfaɛɫ], [ɹafaɛɫ]. The scorers were trained to accept all these pronunciations as 'perfect' translations, but to reject pronunciations that did not include, for example, a retroflex initial consonant and a dark 'l'. Pronunciations that mixed Spanish and English elements (for example, [rafaeɫ]) were scored as 'intermediate'. Stress shifts in translation were not penalized as long as they were phonotactically permissible in the target language of the translation.

It is notable that translations from English to Spanish offered fewer correct options for translation than in the other direction. The phonemic inventory of English is larger than that of Spanish, and consequently there are more ways to render a Spanish name in English than vice versa. The different options for correct translation from English to Spanish are often based on different dialectal options (e.g. English 'Victor' can be rendered into Spanish with an initial [v] or [b], variants of the Spanish phoneme /v/). On the other hand, varying correct renderings of the Spanish name 'Rafael' are mostly based on the fact that English has more phonemic vowels than Spanish, and there are often multiple phonemic vowels of English that can be substituted for a Spanish vowel. Thus possible phonological mappings from English to Spanish tend to be many to one, while in the opposite direction, the mappings tend to be one to many.

Each overall score for a child consisted of 20 item scores, 10 for English-to-Spanish and 10 for Spanish-to-English. In each case half the item scores were for real names and half for fictitious names.

The reliability of the scoring was assessed after the fact by rescoring 15 randomly selected sessions based upon audio-tape recordings that were made during the sessions. The rescorings were done by different testers than had performed the tests in question. Average discrepancies between the two methods of scoring were less than 10% and the resulting scores correlated at 0.70. This only moderate scoring reliability may have limited the power of the statistical tests that were applied to the data, but there is no reason to believe differences among testers could have caused group effects since testers were assigned on a semirandom basis to children during testing.

Results

Analysis proceeded in three stages: (1) group means for the phonological translation data were compared across the design; (2) the magnitude of the correlations between phonological translation scores and standardized tests of language were assessed; and (3) the shape of the relationship between phonological translation and standardized tests of reading was evaluated.

Analysis of group means

In analysis of variance (ANOVA) of the phonological translation data, there were five between-subjects factors: Grade, SES, Lingualism (monolingual vs bilingual), IMS, and LSH. IMS and LSH were nested within Lingualism (i.e. only for bilingual children were there two levels on these variables). There were also two within-subjects factors: Translation Direction (Spanish-to-English vs English-to-Spanish) and Name Type (Real vs Fictitious). Because the design was unbalanced, Type III sums of squares were used.

The design yielded 59 statistical tests. Whenever there are multiple comparisons within a design, one runs the risk, unless a statistical adjustment is made, of finding some group comparisons that appear to be reliable, when in fact they are the result of chance variability across so many possible effects. In the present case, assuming statistical independence among the effects, the customary comparisonwise alpha rate of 0.05 would have yielded a groupwise Type I error rate > 95%, indicating that many apparently reliable effects would in fact be spurious results of chance in evaluation for so many comparisons. An adjustment of procedure was made so that the comparisons in the ANOVA were based on the more conservative comparisonwise alpha rate of 0.01. Under the null hy-

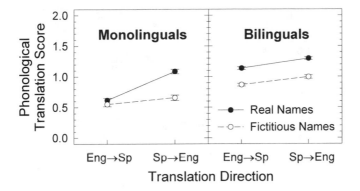

Figure 11.1 Unweighted means of phonological translation score by Lingualism, Translation Direction, and Name Type. Error bars indicate standard errors

pothesis, this criterion would yield an expected value of 0.59 Type I errors. Using this criterion, the occurrence of potential spurious effects was restricted to a statistically acceptable level. If all 59 comparisons were statistically independent, then with > 97% certainty, it can be said that no more than one Type I error would be made under the criterion that was adopted, and with > 99% certainty it can be said that no more than two Type I errors would be made.

The large sample size ($N = 640$) provided generally excellent statistical power, and some of the effects were of substantial magnitude even after the comparisonwise alpha correction. Only effects deemed significant in the light of the comparisonwise alpha criterion are reported below in the analysis of group means.

Effects excluding within-subjects factors

There was a main effect of Lingualism, $F(1, 610) = 86.41$, $p < < 0.0001$, with bilinguals outscoring monolinguals (see Figure 11.1) in every regard. The effect applied to translation of both real and fictitious names and to both Translation Directions. There was also, unsurprisingly, a main effect of Grade, $F(2, 610) = 316.30$, $p < 0.0001$, with 5th graders outscoring 2nd graders, who in turn outscored Kindergartners (see Figure 11.2). The Lingualism effect was so strong that the scores of monolingual 2nd graders were similar to those of bilingual Kindergartners, and the scores of mono-

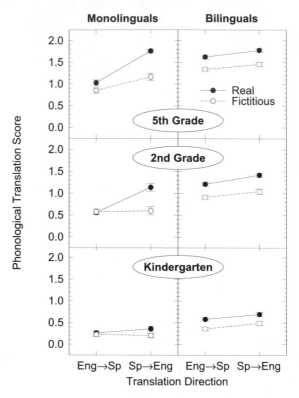

Figure 11.2 Unweighted means of phonological translation score by Lingualism, Translation Direction, Name Type, and Grade. Error bars indicate standard errors

lingual 5th graders were similar to those of bilingual 2nd graders (see Figure 11.3).

There was also a Grade × IMS interaction, $F(2, 610) = 8.52, p < 0.0003$. The interaction indicated that at K, bilinguals in Two-way education scored well below those in English Immersion (actually scoring closer to monolinguals than to bilinguals in English Immersion), but that at 2nd and 5th grade, the bilinguals in Two-way education scored at or above those in English Immersion (see Figure 11.3). The interaction is consistent with other results (see Chapters 4 and 5) suggesting cases where the bilingual children in Two-way programs began at relatively low levels of performance in K, but caught up or surpassed their English Immersion peers in later grades.

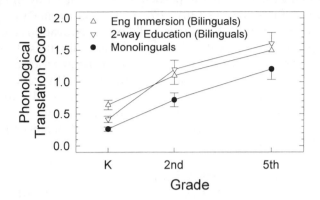

Figure 11.3 Unweighted means of bilingual children's phonological trans-lation scores, by IMS and Grade. Error bars indicate standard errors. For comparison, monolinguals' performance is also shown

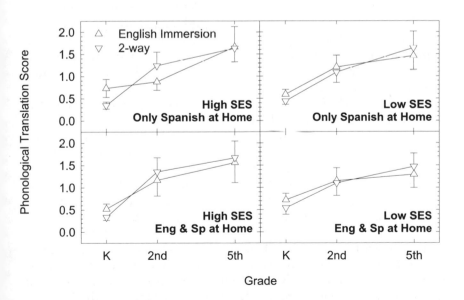

Figure 11.4 Unweighted means of phonological translation scores by SES, LSH, IMS, and Grade. Error bars indicate standard errors

This two-way interaction also participated in a four-way interaction of Grade × IMS × LSH × SES, $F(2, 610) = 2.72$, $p < 0.01$, illustrated in Figure 11.4. Regardless of SES or LSH, bilinguals in Two-way education scored below those in English Immersion at K. Among Low SES bilinguals, those in Two-way education scored similarly to those in English Immersion at 2nd grade, and slightly outscored those in English Immersion at 5th grade, regardless of LSH. Among High SES bilinguals, those in Two-way education scored above those in English Immersion at 2nd grade, especially for those with OSH, though at 5th grade, LSH and IMS made little difference to the scores of High SES bilinguals.

Effects involving within-subjects factors

There was a main effect of Translation Direction, $F(1, 610) = 145.24$, $p < 0.0001$ (it was easier for children to translate to English than to translate to Spanish), a main effect of Name Type, $F(1, 610) = 392.69$, $p < 0.0001$ (real names were translated more accurately than fictitious names), and a Translation Direction × Name Type interaction, $F(1, 610) = 42.54$, $p < 0.0001$. The interaction is best understood in the context of higher order interactions of Lingualism × Translation Direction, $F(1, 610) = 15.75$, $p < 0.0001$, and Lingualism × Translation Direction × Name Type, $F(1, 610) = 39.42$, $p < 0.0001$, illustrated in Figure 11.1. When translating fictitious names, bilinguals and monolinguals showed a similar degree of advantage for the Spanish-to-English direction. The bilinguals exhibited a similar degree of advantage for the Spanish-to-English direction for the real words, while for the monolinguals, the advantage of the Spanish-to-English direction was much larger for the real words.

This pattern can be further understood in the context of the only effect involving LSH: an LSH × Translation Direction × Name Type interaction, $F(1, 610) = 14.25$, $p < 0.0002$, illustrated in Figure 11.5. For bilinguals with ESH, the pattern was intermediate between the two alternatives illustrated in the two panels of Figure 11.1; specifically, their advantage in translating from Spanish to English was somewhat larger for real names than for fictitious names, though not as dramatically as for monolinguals, yet much more dramatically than for the bilinguals as a whole. In contrast, for bilinguals with OSH, the advantage of translating from Spanish to English was actually slightly smaller for real names than for fictitious names. This pattern may suggest either that the children with OSH did not know many of the names in English (and consequently could not benefit from that knowledge in translation), or that they were simply more inclined than the children with ESH to engage in creative phonological translation as opposed to simply recalling the phonological form for a memorized real name.

The Grade factor interacted with the within-subject factors. Specifically,

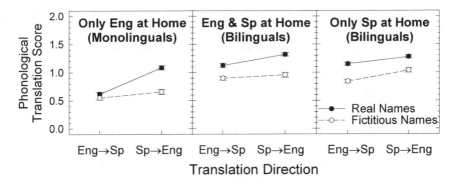

Figure 11.5 Unweighted means of phonological translation scores by LSH, Translation Direction, and Name Type. Error bars indicate standard errors. (The monolingual panel is replicated from Figure 11.1.)

there was a Grade × Translation Direction interaction, $F(2, 610) = 11.46$, $p < 0.0001$, a Grade × Name Type interaction, $F(2, 610) = 15.04$, $p < 0.0001$, and a Grade × Translation Direction × Name Type interaction, $F(2, 610) = 6.77$, $p < 0.002$. Figure 11.2 indicates that bilingual Kindergartners had advantages in translating from Spanish to English versus from English to Spanish, and in translating real names versus fictitious names, whereas monolingual Kindergartners showed only an advantage in phonological translation when the name was both real and the Translation Direction was from Spanish to English. In 2nd grade, this pattern persisted, but the effects were larger. In 5th grade, the effects remained large, and were accompanied in the monolinguals by a small advantage in translating real names even from English to Spanish.

The final effect involving the Grade factor was a Grade × Lingualism × Translation Direction interaction, $F(2, 610) = 15.26$, $p < 0.0001$, also illustrated in Figure 11.2. When data were averaged across Name Type, bilinguals at K showed a bigger advantage than monolinguals in translating from Spanish to English versus translating from English to Spanish. But at 2nd grade, bilinguals and monolinguals had nearly the same advantage, and at 5th grade, it was the monolinguals who showed the bigger advantage in translating from Spanish to English. This interaction may have depended on a general inability of monolingual Kindergartners to do much in the way of correct translation at all. However, the older monolingual children appeared to have learned to recognize many Spanish names when spoken in Spanish, and to recall the English name corresponding to each Spanish name. Consequently the monolingual children may have learned to translate lexically, by relying on memorization, a pattern that

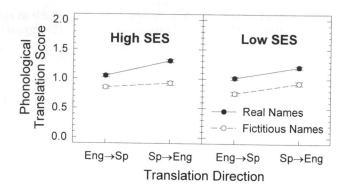

Figure 11.6 Unweighted means of phonological translation scores by SES, Translation Direction, and Name Type. Error bars indicate standard errors

would help for real names, but would not for fictitious ones. The fact that even at 5th grade the monolinguals showed only a slight (though reliable) advantage for translation of real names in the English-to-Spanish direction suggests that they found it hard to recall or produce memorized information in Spanish. Thus at 5th grade they showed maximal differentiation between English-to-Spanish and Spanish-to-English Translation Directions. Bilingual children were clearly using both strategies from K onward, relying on lexical memorization to make real translations easier than fictitious ones, but engaging in active and correct phonological translation for many of the features of fictitious names even from the age of K.

One significant effect involved SES: an SES × Translation Direction × Name Type interaction, $F(1, 610) = 13.35$, $p < 0.0003$, illustrated in Figure 11.6. For Low SES children, translating from Spanish to English showed the same advantage over translating from English to Spanish, regardless of whether the names were real or fictitious. In contrast, for High SES children, the advantage for translating from Spanish to English was small for fictitious names, but large for real names.

Correlations with measures of language proficiency

To what extent did phonological translation correlate with reading, versus other language skills, and to what extent did these correlations differ between groups and across grade? In these analyses, attention was restricted to the phonological translation of fictitious names, in order that the results not be confounded by lexical familiarity with names in both languages. In all analyses reported below, comparisonwise alphas of 0.05

were used. K data are included here even though there were cases where floor effects produced anomalies in the distribution of scores (see discussion in Chapter 5).

Cross-grade correlations with W scores

Pearson correlation coefficients were computed between scores for phonological translation of fictitious names, on the one hand, and Woodcock measures of reading, writing, and vocabulary, on the other hand. To summarize reading capabilities, a calculation was made for each child's Woodcock Basic Reading score, as the average of the Letter–Word and Word Attack W scores. (W scores derive from an item-response-theory analysis of the Woodcock scores, and are available from the Woodcock test manual. W scores on a given test are monotonically related to raw scores on the same test. Their purpose is to put scores on an interval scale. Unlike standardized scores, the W scores can be expected to increase across grade.) To summarize writing capabilities, the calculation included each child's average of Proofreading and Dictation W scores. To summarize vocabulary knowledge, the calculation combined each child's average of Oral Vocabulary, Picture Vocabulary, and Verbal Analogies W scores. Each monolingual child contributed three such W scores, and each bilingual child contributed six such W scores (three in English and three in Spanish) to the correlations, computed for English- and Spanish-language W scores separately. The advantage of using W scores over standardized scores for the Woodcock tests was that all scores were on the same scale, regardless of a child's grade. Because all scores were similarly scaled, K, 2nd grade, and 5th grade scores could be justifiably combined into a single analysis, and it could be expected that scores would rise with grade advancement.

Table 11.2 presents the correlations. The displayed confidence intervals derive from a bootstrap analysis (Efron & Tibshirani, 1993), in which the

Table 11.2 Correlations of scores for phonological translation of fictitious names with selected Woodcock-Johnson W scores (pooled across Grade)

	English			Spanish		
	Read	*Write*	*Vocab*	*Read*	*Write*	*Vocab*
Bilinguals	0.70 (0.65, 0.74)	0.67 (0.62, 0.71)	0.63 (0.58, 0.68)	0.70 (0.64, 0.74)	0.70 (0.66, 0.74)	0.63 (0.58, 0.67)
Monolinguals	0.67 (0.58, 0.75)	0.68 (0.59, 0.75)	0.64 (0.56, 0.72)			

Note. Numbers in parentheses represent endpoints of 95% confidence intervals based on 999 replications (BC$_a$method, see Efron & Tibshirani, 1993). Acceleration was estimated using the delete-20 jackknife (S-Plus, 1999: 551)

group structure was respected. That is, Subject was treated as a random factor in the bootstrap analysis, and Grade, SES, Lingualism, IMS, and LSH were each considered as fixed factors. In essence the bootstrap analysis estimated confidence intervals based on simulated reconstructions of large numbers of correlational relationships that could be projected to occur with sample sizes the same as those utilized in the real study and varying about the obtained correlational values. This method makes it possible to estimate sampling distributions, and thus to provide quantitatively specific comparisons of differences among correlations. Such quantitative comparisons are important here because the goal is to determine whether phonological translation is a better predictor of reading and or writing abilities than other measures would be.

For each group, the correlations between phonological translation of fictitious word scores and the separate W scores were similar to one another and all were quite high, ranging from 0.63 to 0.70 (see Table 11.2). Such correlations account for 39–49% of variance in the reading, writing and vocabulary measures, indicating that phonological translation was a powerful predictor of key academic abilities. The similarity among the correlations is partly a consequence of the intercorrelation among the Woodcock subtests (see Chapter 6, Tables 6.1 and 6.3). For purposes of the present research the relative magnitudes of these correlations are of potentially great interest, even though they are similar in absolute level. If phonological translation is especially closely related to reading, then the correlations with reading would be expected to be reliably higher than the correlations with writing or vocabulary. Because reading and writing in the present research were more closely associated with each other than either was with vocabulary (see Tables 6.1 and 6.3), the correlation with vocabulary would be expected to be lowest.

Direct testing of this possible pattern was pursued through bootstrap analyses in which the statistics of interest were the differences among the correlations presented in Table 11.2. Again a large number of values were computed by simulation in order to estimate the likelihood that the *relative* magnitudes of the correlations would change on resampling from the same family of correlations. The grouping structure of the dataset was respected, and 'bootstrapped confidence intervals' (BC_a method, Efron & Tibshirani, 1993) were calculated using 999 bootstrap replications and the delete–20 jackknife for estimating the acceleration parameter.

For bilinguals in English, the expected pattern obtained: the correlation with reading was slightly but significantly higher than the correlation with writing, $p < 0.05$, and the correlations with reading and writing were both significantly higher than the correlation with vocabulary, $ps < 0.05$. For bilinguals in Spanish, the correlations with reading and writing were also

Table 11.3 Correlations of scores for phonological translation of fictitious names with standardized Woodcock-Johnson Basic Reading scores and standardized Peabody Picture Vocabulary test scores (by Grade).

	English		Spanish	
	W-J Read	PPVT	W-J Read	TVIP
Bilinguals				
Kindergarten	0.20 (0.05, 0.34)	0.18 (0.03, 0.31)	0.14 (−0.01, 0.30)	0.21 (0.08, 0.34)
2nd Grade	0.32 (0.16, 0.45)	0.12 (−0.04, 0.26)	0.38 (0.24, 0.51)	0.29 (0.15, 0.44)
5th Grade	0.41 (0.27, 0.54)	0.20 (0.06, 0.37)	0.47 (0.36, 0.59)	0.44 (0.33, 0.57)
Monolinguals				
Kindergarten	0.13 (−0.12, 0.38)	−0.08 (−0.31, 0.11)		
2nd Grade	0.16 (−0.12, 0.38)	0.05 (−0.26, 0.32)		
5th Grade	0.50 (0.29, 0.67)	0.33 (0.10, 0.52)		

Note. Numbers in parentheses represent endpoints of 95% confidence intervals based on 999 replications (BC_a method, see Efron & Tibshirani, 1993). Acceleration was estimated using the delete-20 jackknife (S-Plus, 1999: 551).

both significantly higher than the correlation with vocabulary, $ps < 0.05$; however, the correlation with writing was almost identical to the correlation with reading, $p > 0.75$. For monolinguals, there were no significant differences among the correlations: the correlation with reading and the correlation with writing were very similar, $p > 0.45$, and the correlations with reading and writing were both non-significantly higher than the correlation with vocabulary, $p = 0.24$ and $p = 0.11$, respectively.

Another bootstrap analysis compared correlations of phonological translation scores with English W scores for reading, writing, and vocabulary scores between monolinguals and bilinguals [($r_{monolingual\ Eng\ read\ W}$ − $r_{bilingual\ Eng\ read\ W}$), ($r_{monolingual\ Eng\ write\ W}$ − $r_{bilingual\ Eng\ write\ W}$), and ($r_{monolingual\ Eng\ vocab\ W}$ − $r_{bilingual\ Eng\ vocab\ W}$)]. The bilinguals' correlations of reading, writing and vocabulary with phonological translation did not differ significantly from the monolinguals' correlations.

Finally, to assess Spanish versus English correlations with phonological translation, bootstrapped comparisons of the differences between English and Spanish reading, writing and vocabulary [($r_{\text{Eng read W}} - r_{\text{Sp read W}}$), ($r_{\text{Eng write W}} - r_{\text{Sp write W}}$), and ($r_{\text{Eng vocab W}} - r_{\text{Sp vocab W}}$)] were made for the bilinguals. The correlation of phonological translation with Spanish writing was slightly but significantly higher than the correlation with English writing at 5th grade. Other differences were not significant.

Within-grade correlations with standard scores

The Woodcock Oral Vocabulary, Picture Vocabulary, and Verbal Analogies tests evaluate a conglomerate of capabilities that require complex responses. Consequently, it is possible that the measures do not offer a specific assessment of vocabulary, as opposed to other abilities. Another, perhaps more precise, receptive vocabulary measure, the Peabody Picture Vocabulary Test (PPVT) and its Spanish equivalent, the Test de vocabulario en imágenes Peabody (TVIP), was also available in the study. However, the PPVT/TVIP yields only standard scores, not W scores. Thus, assessing across grade correlations between phonological translation and PPVT was not feasible. Therefore, additional analyses were conducted to compare within grade correlations between Woodcock Basic Reading *standardized* scores and phonological translation as well as correlations between PPVT/TVIP *standardized* scores and phonological translation. The correlations are presented in Table 11.3, along with their bootstrapped confidence intervals.

Additional bootstrap analyses directly tested several hypotheses. First, to compare the strength of the correlation between phonological translation and reading with the correlation with vocabulary, the differences ($r_{\text{W-J read standard}} - r_{\text{PPVT standard}}$) for the monolinguals at each grade and for the bilinguals in each language at each grade were examined. For the monolinguals, the correlation of phonological translation with reading did not differ significantly from the correlation with vocabulary at any grade (K $p = 0.1$, 2nd grade $p = 0.45$, 5th grade $p = 0.21$). For the bilinguals, the reading correlation was significantly greater than the vocabulary correlation in English at 2nd and 5th grade; other differences were not significant.

Next, growth over time was assessed by bootstrapping the change in each correlation between grades. For monolinguals, the correlation of phonological translation with reading was significantly higher at 5th grade than it was at either K or 2nd grade, and the correlation with PPVT was significantly higher at 5th grade than it was at K. For bilinguals in English, the correlation with reading was significantly higher at 5th grade than it was at K, but the correlation with PPVT did not differ significantly among the grades. For bilinguals in Spanish, the correlation with reading was significantly higher at both 2nd and 5th grades than it was at K, and the correlation with TVIP was significantly higher at 5th grade than it was at K.

Correlations between phonological translation and English reading and vocabulary scores between monolinguals and bilinguals [($r_{\text{monolingual Eng read standard}}$ − $r_{\text{bilingual Eng read standard}}$) and ($r_{\text{monolingual Eng PPVT standard}}$ − $r_{\text{bilingual Eng PPVT standard}}$)] at each grade were also examined. Bilingual Kindergartners had significantly higher correlations with their PPVT scores than did monolingual Kindergartners. No other differences were significant.

Finally, to assess Spanish versus English correlations between phonological translation and standardized test scores, the differences [($r_{\text{Eng read standard}}$ − $r_{\text{Sp read standard}}$) and ($r_{\text{Eng PPVT standard}}$ − $r_{\text{Sp PPVT standard}}$)] were bootstrapped for the bilinguals at each grade. The correlation with Spanish vocabulary was significantly higher than the correlation with English vocabulary at 5th grade; other differences were not significant.

Regression analysis

Finally, an assessment was conducted regarding the shape of the relationship between phonological translation of fictitious names and Woodcock-Johnson Basic Reading W scores for English (see Figure 11.7). Reading score was regressed on phonological translation score, Lingualism, and their interaction. The main effect of phonological translation score was highly significant, as was the main effect of Lingualism. However, their interaction was not significant ($p > 0.29$), which is indicated by the near-parallelism of the regression lines in Figure 11.7. When phonological translation score was instead regressed on Lingualism, Basic Reading W score, and their interaction, the main effects were again highly significant, and the interaction was again non-significant. Thus, for monolinguals and bilinguals with the same Basic Reading W score, the bilinguals tended to score higher in translating fictitious names. This combination of effects is expected based on the Lingualism main effect found in both this chapter's group-mean analysis of phonological translation score and Chapter 4's group-mean analysis of Woodcock-Johnson scores. But in spite of this difference in overall level, the codependence of reading score and phonological translation score was roughly the same for monolinguals and bilinguals.

Discussion

The evaluation of phonological translation provided in the present chapter suggests a variety of conclusions. First, it is clear that the bilingual children were better at phonological translation than monolinguals, even at Kindergarten (K). This result is consistent with the expectation that con-

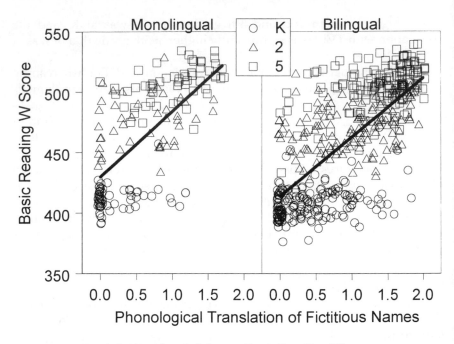

Figure 11.7 English Woodcock-Johnson Basic Reading W score versus performance in phonological translation of fictitious names. Each point represents data from a different subject. Each line represents least-squares regression equation, with slope and intercept both varying between Lingualism. Data points are jittered slightly to render overlapping points distinguishable

stant practice in phonological translation by bilinguals leads to better performance.

Second, both bilinguals and monolinguals performed phonological translation more effectively in the Spanish-to-English direction than vice versa. This result may be the result of one of two factors or a combination of them. Children in both groups may have been more comfortable speaking English (see Chapter 3), and may thus have found it easier to render words in English than Spanish. On the other hand, it may also be that it is inherently easier to translate correctly from Spanish to English than vice versa, because English has the larger phonemic and syllabic repertoire and may thus provide more correct options for Spanish-to-English translation (a one to many mapping) than in the reverse case (where the mapping tends to many to one, and fewer correct options are available for each English phoneme or syllable to be translated).

At the same time it is important to note that monolinguals showed a dramatic difference in their asymmetry on Translation Direction, since the Spanish-to-English advantage was attributable heavily to better performance on the 'real' name phonological translations. In the case of bilinguals, the advantage, though not so large, applied to translation of both real *and* fictitious names. For fictitious names the translation advantage for the Spanish-to-English direction was roughly equivalent for monolinguals and bilinguals.

Third, children in Two-way education at K trailed those in English Immersion on phonological translation, but equaled or surpassed their English Immersion peers in 2nd and 5th grades. This outcome is consistent with patterns on standardized tests where Two-way children tended to lag at K but not at later grades (see Chapter 4).

Fourth, children tended to translate the real names more effectively than the fictitious names. This outcome appears to be predictable from the fact that real names, but not fictitious ones, can be phonologically translated on a lexical basis – that is, if a name can be recognized in one language, it may be possible to recall its pronunciation in the other language as a whole word-unit, without segment-by-segment or syllable-by-syllable phonological translation. Fictitious names do not share this advantage. Since they are novel, they must be treated phonologically, not lexically. The easier phonological translation of real names was quite robust, occurring at every grade level, for children from both High and Low SES homes, and for children with both English and Spanish at home (ESH) as well as only Spanish at home (OSH).

The fact that monolingual children showed greater difficulties than bilinguals in translation of fictitious names, even in the Spanish-to-English direction, offers an indication that they tended to use lexical translation often, but had fewer resources than bilinguals when it was necessary to perform segment-by-segment or syllable-by-syllable translation, the primary elements of true phonological translation. Yet even the bilinguals appeared to use lexical translation sometimes, since their scores on real names were consistently better than on fictitious ones. Perhaps the most important advantage of the bilingual children in phonological translation was manifest on the fictitious words, where their superior abilities appear to indicate that they were more capable than monolinguals of performing the sort of phonological matching that active phonological translation requires. Consequently, it has been confirmed in the present work that bilinguals have an awareness of and ability to manipulate the relationships between phonemic and/or syllabic forms across languages that surpass those of monolinguals even in early elementary school.

It should be added that the differences seen here occurred even with a relatively simple task that can be administered in 10 minutes or less and with a relatively crude measure of phonological translation, where only a three-point scale of accuracy was used. This study represents a hopeful beginning in illustration of phonological translation abilities, but subsequent research will be needed to elaborate and refine the method, conceivably enhancing the differentiation of children who are capable and not so capable in phonological translation.

It is also possible that with a more reliable measure of phonological translation, clearer results might be obtained in correlational analysis of relations between phonological translation and reading. The correlations obtained here were not as high as in some prior studies of phonological awareness and reading (see e.g. Wagner _et al._, 1994), a fact that may be attributable to the limitation of test items (only 10 fictitious names) and relatively low reliability of scoring. Improved techniques for phonological translation evaluation would seem thus to be a worthy goal.

While both vocabulary knowledge and reading/writing measures were significantly correlated with the phonological translation measure, the bootstapping analyses from the present work illustrate that, at least in some of the analyses, phonological translation was more highly correlated with the literacy measures than vocabulary measures were. Consequently, the study hints that phonological translation may in fact be a special predictor of reading and writing.

Overall the data presented here offer encouragement for the speculation that bilingual children may have special abilities in learning to read owing to their common requirement to practice phonological translation. The correlational results as well as the bootstrapping outcomes are consistent with the idea that phonological translation practice may foster reading abilities. Bilingual children were better at phonological translation than monolinguals, and it may be notable that the standardized measures of decoding for reading (Letter–Word and Word Attack), the measures with regard to which one might expect to find most influence from phonological awareness or translation, are the ones on which the bilingual children performed best with respect to the monolingual peers in the present study (matching or exceeding their performance at 5th grade), and highest with regard to norms (exceeding the standardized mean of 100 at 5th grade in both languages, Chapters 4 and 5). Since these were the only tests where bilingual children performed so well, and since the Two-way children (the children who were best at phonological translation by 5th grade) performed especially well on them, it remains plausible to pursue the possibility that the common requirement of phonological translation in daily life had the effect of enhancing basic reading foundations in bilingual children. This suggestion is reminiscent of many reported results supporting the idea that training of phonological awareness skills can enhance reading in both normal and disordered readers (Bus & van Ijzendoorn, 1999; Gillon & Dodd, 1997; González, 1996; Gunn *et al.*, 2000; Schneider *et al.*, 1997; Schneider *et al.*, 1999), but for a contrasting view and analysis of data see Krashen (1999a, b). The results appear to supplement a growing body of information suggesting that phonological awareness skills of bilingual children as manifest in tasks such as elision, rhyming, segmentation or recognition of the linguistic origin of a word based on its phonological form are also predictive of reading abilities, even when the phonologically tested items are in one of the bilingual's languages and the reading skill is tested in the other (Arab-Moghaddam & Senechal, 2001; Baum Bursztyn, 1999; Campbell & Sais, 1995; Durgunoglu *et al.*, 1993; Francis, 1999; Jared & Kroll, 2001; Muljani *et al.*, 1998).

The data reported here show that that even in the monolinguals, correlations were high between phonological translation scores and reading. Phonological translation abilities appear, then, to play a role in reading abilities both in cases where the activity is common and obligatory (as with bilinguals) and in cases where it is less common (as with monolinguals). The fact that bilinguals are required to perform phonological translation more often than monolinguals may afford them the opportunity to profit from the experience to a greater extent, a possibility that again is suggested by the fact that bilingual children's basic reading scores in the present work were better relative to monolinguals and to norms (see Chapters 4 and 5) than their scores on any other measures.

Part 4

A Retrospective View of the Research

Chapter 12

Balancing Interpretations Regarding Effects of Bilingualism: Empirical Outcomes and Theoretical Possibilities

D. KIMBROUGH OLLER and REBECCA E. EILERS

Differing Perspectives on the Possible Value of Bilingualism

A fundamental assumption of this volume is that having command of more than one language is, in and of itself, an asset. The value can be measured in socio-cultural, economic and political terms. It may be valuable in the context of increased cognitive flexibility and metalinguistic capabilities as well (Bialystok, 1999; Cummins, 1979; Kessler & Quinn, 1980; Lindholm, 1980; Torrance et al., 1970). This volume's explicit opinion is that the study of bilingualism or second-language learning by children should not have as its sole aim the evaluation of outcomes for acquisition of the host or target language. Both languages need to be addressed. Educational strategies that may maximize functional bilingualism and bilingual literacy are seen here as more desirable than strategies that may handicap students progress in one language or the other.

The authors operationalized these assumptions, in part, by studying Miami Hispanic school children in terms of the effects of factors affecting the acquisition of both the host language, English, and the home language, Spanish. Without this balance of assessment, it seemed hard to this group of scholars to imagine how any sensible empirical evaluation of the contrasting capabilities of bilingual and monolingual speakers might be achieved. And yet, the typical pattern of research on bilingual education in the USA has been focused on evaluation of English outcomes only (see e.g. the important research of Ramírez et al., 1991c).

The research reported here cannot, of course, answer with finality the fundamental questions about the ultimate effects of bilingualism, nor can it lay to rest the confusion and anxiety that plague the public regarding optimal educational strategies for large immigrant populations in social environments such as those found in the USA. The fundamental questions that drive much of the scientific interest and that contribute to the social confusion are often too vague or too complex to admit simple answers indicating that, for example, a particular strategy of bilingual education is or is not desirable for immigrant children.

Monolingual/Bilingual Advantages and Disadvantages

A key question throughout this work has been based on simple comparisons of language and literacy performance among monolingual and bilingual children. The key results regarding comparisons among monolingual and bilingual children in English were that monolingual English children, learning only English at home and studying only English at school, generally outperformed bilingual children of all the backgrounds that were studied (with English and Spanish at home [ESH] or with only Spanish at home [OSH], with Two-way schooling or with English Immersion schooling, and regardless of Socio-economic Status [SES]). The difference favoring the monolinguals in English was especially large in oral language, smaller in literacy (see Chapter 4 for details). Differences favoring monolinguals were also seen in narrative language produced in elicited stories (Chapter 7), in grammaticality judgments regarding English sentences (Chapters 8 and 10), and grammaticality judgments regarding Spanish sentences (Chapter 9). In all these cases, differences favoring monolinguals were relatively large at Kindergarten (K) or 2nd grade, but notably smaller or absent by 5th grade, suggesting that bilingual children's abilities were improving relative to monolingual peers across the elementary school years.

Instructional Method in School for Bilingual Children

From a practical standpoint, the comparison of monolingual and bilingual outcomes may be less significant than the comparison of Instructional Methods at School (IMS). The research reported here indicated that children educated in English Immersion outperformed children in Two-way education in English for a number of standardized (Chapter 4) and probe study (Chapters 7, 8 and 10) measures. These differences were seen at the lower grades (K and/or 2nd), but were largely absent and sometimes reversed at 5th grade. Differences that favored English Immersion over Two-way education were typically much smaller than those favoring monolinguals over bilinguals. Thus, it would appear that the societal action of placing children from newly arrived immigrant families in English Immersion environments in school, presumably designed to stimulate monolingual English development, did not result in monolingual command of English by 5th grade, and notably did not produce children who significantly out-performed bilinguals educated in the more pluralistic Two-way approach in English and Spanish. In fact the evidence showed a mixed bag of out-comes, some favoring Two-way and some favoring English Immersion with respect to English command of language and literacy by the 5th grade.

The Grand Interaction Hypothesis

A note of closure seems necessary on the issue of whether some bilingual children, those assumed to have had advantages for learning English (those of High SES and ESH) might have proven to outperform monolin-gual children, while others in conditions of disadvantage might have performed more poorly (see Chapter 1, where this hypothesis is specified). The results tended to show main effects for SES (favoring children of High SES) and Language Spoken at Home (favoring children with ESH) (Chap-ters 4, 7, 8 and 10), but showed no grand interaction to confirm the idea that bilingualism might be especially beneficial in one case and detrimental in another. The possible interaction was evaluated, but its presence was not detected nor was any tendency toward a significant interaction seen.

The possibility that an interaction might be obtained under other study conditions, however, cannot be entirely ruled out. We cannot, for instance, from the present study gauge the possible role of lack of native-speaking English peers in all the bilingual schools, a factor that may have limited children's access to elaborate and well-formed English input. In addition, the presence of an ephemeral dialect, 'Spanglish', in the Miami community may have limited the bilingual children's access to full native input in English and Spanish. Finally, since study selection required that all the chil-dren who participated in the study be born in the USA , they may have had a relatively limited command of their home language when entering school and thus, they may not have been ready to profit from multilingual instruc-tion. Such factors as lack of native peers, ephemeral dialects and limited home language proficiency may or may not have played a role, but if they did, they might have masked the predicted interaction.

And as for the Outcomes in Spanish?

Regarding Spanish, the results of the research reported in this volume are clearer: Two-way education resulted in better performance in Spanish in both language and literacy, and the difference was bigger at 5th grade than at lower grades for a variety of standardized (Chapter 5) and probe study (Chapters 7, 9 and 10) measures.

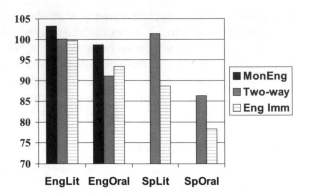

Figure 12.1 Group results in 5th grade for all standardized tests, Spanish and English (summary data on combined oral language and literacy tests from Chapters 4 and 5)

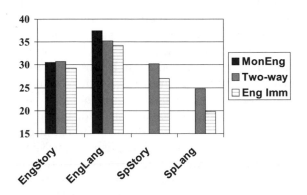

Figure 12.2 Group results in 5th grade for narrative probe study, Spanish and English (summary data on Story Scores and Language Scores from Chapter 7)

Further, the differences favoring Two-way education for Spanish at 5th grade were much larger than the inconsistent differences (where they occurred) favoring English Immersion education for English. Figures 12.1 and 12.2 illustrate this point. Note that English Immersion children showed a small advantage at 5th grade over Two-way children on the combined standardized measures of English oral language from Chapter 4, but not on the combined measures of English literacy, nor on either of the global measures of narrative from Chapter 7. In Spanish, by contrast, the differences favoring the Two-way children were large, in fact, as large or larger than differences favoring monolinguals over bilinguals in English.

Thus, it seems inevitable to conclude that Two-way education as opposed to English Immersion showed few if any long-term (across elementary school) advantages or disadvantages with regard to language and literacy in English, but that Two-way education showed significant advantages for bilingual children in acquisition of language and literacy in Spanish.

Interdependence of Languages in Bilingual Learning

A remarkable outcome of the research reported here is seen in the fact that there were many significant positive correlations between performance in Spanish and English, but absolutely no significant negative correlations between outcomes on the standardized tests across the two languages. What is at stake here is, of course, the question of interdependence (Cummins, 1979), whether the learning of one language impacts the learning of the other (positively, negatively or not at all) at the level of the individual child. Time on task (frequency of input) effects have been implicated widely in this volume regarding how much is learned in each language, especially at younger ages, so it is clear that there are costs to learning a language in terms of the amount of time or energy available to learn another. Even though the results from Chapters 4 and 5 comparing groups of children suggested the existence of some 'time on task' effects, they do not necessarily apply at the level of individual children in terms of predicting whether good performance in one language may predict good performance in the other. One might imagine that time on task effects would yield a pattern where large negative correlations would obtain across tests for the two languages – so learning English grammar well might, theoretically, be associated with particularly poor performance in learning grammar for Spanish if each of the grammatical learning tasks could be assumed to be time dependent and task independent.

The results showed no such negative correlations. In fact the interdependence across languages segregated crisply into two primary domains, one strongly positive and one weakly positive. Literacy tests showed very high and statistically reliable positive correlations across the two languages, while oral language tests showed much lower though primarily positive correlations, and no significant negative ones. The results suggest that there could be feedback from learning to read in one language that is beneficial in the learning of reading in the other. This benefit could also be the result of a 'great equalizer' effect of schooling (see the Cobo-Lewis *et al.* reasoning in Chapter 6) or of a metalinguistic characteristic of reading that tends to make reading language-general (see the Gathercole reasoning in

Chapter 10). Oral language skills on the other hand clustered together with much lower positive cross-language correlations, suggesting that at the level of the individual subject, oral skills may be acquired relatively independently across the two languages (although without discernible cross-linguistic inhibitory effects that would have been implied by negative correlations). The results of analyses in Chapter 7 also showed high positive correlations across languages for the abstract story elements of narrative reflected in the Story Score for the Frog Story, as well as the Complex Syntax measure. Pearson took special note of the apparent language-generality of these factors, while pointing to the much lower (but again non-negative) correlations across the two languages for more language-specific factors assessed in the stories (Lexicon and Morphosyntactic Accuracy), factors that appear to be acquired in an item by item fashion.

Time on Task, Frequency of Input, and the Distributed Characteristic of Bilingual Knowledge

In various ways, the data indicated that children who were exposed more consistently to a language showed advantages in the command of that language. This is a simple point, but worth making, because the effects of time on task or frequency of input are sometimes viewed as only marginally relevant in bilingualism, since many individuals do achieve command of multiple languages in spite of the costs in time to do so. Gathercole in particular (Chapter 10) emphasizes that frequency of input seemed to play a very important role in learning to command a variety of linguistic structures in the research reported here, at least up to some threshold cumulative amount (or 'critical mass', see Marchman & Bates, 1994 and Maratsos, 2000) of input. In accord with this thinking, the data in general showed, for example, that children exposed to more English (monolinguals, children in English Immersion, and bilingual children from families with ESH) did better in English than children with less English input (bilinguals, children in Two-way schools, and bilingual children from families with OSH), and that this frequency of input advantage was greatest among the younger children at K and 2nd grade. Consistent with the 'critical mass' idea, however, the frequency of input advantage diminished, often dramatically, after the presumable critical mass of input had been reached between K or 2nd grade and 5th grade; at 5th grade, then, frequency of input effects were diminished or absent.

Frequency of input effects appeared to be particularly strong for features of language that appear to be learned item by item, for example vocabulary (Chapters 4, 5 and 7) and for some of the characteristics of language-specific morphosyntax (Chapter 7). It is becoming increasingly clear that, to the extent that there are features of languages that are learned item by item, bilingual learners can come to command their two languages in ways that include disjunctions of capability – learners can acquire capabilities of expression in one language that are not acquired in the other language. The knowledge of the learner can, thus, develop a 'distributed characteristic' (see Chapter 1) where capabilities are not fully translatable by the individuals across the languages, because some kinds of knowledge tend to be coded within the individual in one language but not in the other.

The results of research in vocabulary acquisition have noted this distributed characteristic as a ubiquitous aspect of bilingualism (Ben-Zeev, 1977, 1984; Fernández *et al.*, 1992; Schaufeli, 1992; Umbel & Oller, 1994; Valdes & Geoffrion-Vinci, 1998). If one spends time learning one language in a specific environment, and another language in another environment, it may be inevitable that some information may come to be coded in one language but not the other and vice versa. A variety of results from the present volume (in particular in Chapters 4, 5, and 7) are consistent with the possibility of linguistically distributed knowledge in bilingual speakers. To the extent that the distributed characteristic is present, it complicates comparison of knowledge levels in monolingual and bilingual individuals. Tests normed with monolinguals that show low values for bilinguals may be misleading since some of the tested items that are missed by bilinguals may be items they would pass if tested in the other language. The low scores cannot be corrected by any currently known method because even if one tests in the other language, there is no known method for sensibly combining test scores from the two languages (and see J. W. Oller, *et al.*, 2000 for commentary on testing problems).

It is not clear to what extent a distributed characteristic of bilingual knowledge may apply in domains beyond vocabulary acquisition. Oller and Pearson (Chapter 1) posit the possibility that a distributed characteristic may apply to grammatical phenomena as well as to lexical ones. Gathercole (Chapter 10), however, emphasizes that many grammatical phenomena have such broad reach within languages that one cannot avoid encountering and using them regardless of social context. Still, lexicalist approaches to grammar emphasize the fact that much of syntax is lexically specific (see Cook, 1988; Haley & Lunsford, 1994, Newmeyer, 1996, and Smith, 1999 for reviews of the role of lexicalist thinking in modern linguistics). Further, as Gathercole acknowledges, there are many aspects of language-specific grammar that clearly have to be acquired item by item. For example, gender in Spanish is predictable phonologically in many cases (final 'o' indicates a masculine noun and final 'a' a feminine noun in the great majority of cases), but not in all. The other cases must be learned one by one, and leave open the possibility that a learner might not acquire knowledge of gender for some nouns precisely because those particular nouns tend to be invoked in environments where the individual typically speaks and learns English. The same idea could apply to 'mass-count' distinctions in English, where there are many words for which the mass-count status must be learned through direct exposure, and where an individual bilingual might show a weakness of grammatical knowledge of English because terms in question might pertain more to environments in which the individual tends to speak Spanish.

Even some components of presumed Universal Grammar turn out to be learned, if not item by item, at least to some extent, context by context (see Chapter 10). These facts suggest that bilingual children could show weaknesses in syntax (at least on a short-term basis) when compared with monolingual peers that are parallel with vocabulary weaknesses, and that the weaknesses could be the result of a similarly distributed characteristic of knowledge in the two languages. Evaluation of potentially distributed syntactic capabilities would seem a potentially fruitful area for future research for both theoretical reasons and from the practical standpoint that sensible language testing in the future is clearly going to have to account for the distributed characteristic of bilingual knowledge wherever it occurs.

Nevertheless, Gathercole's point seems well taken, and there remains an empirical question as to the _extent_ of generality of syntactic structures and their acquisition across languages. To the extent such structures may be locally constrained or context specific, a distributed characteristic may play a role in bilingual syntax, especially early in the learning process.

Costs and Benefits of Bilingualism

It perhaps bears noting that in spite of certain obvious advantages to speaking multiple languages, there are some necessary costs associated with their acquisition. As has been emphasized repeatedly here, lexical items tend to be learned one at a time in each language, for example. The cost is not merely seen in the time taken to reach the point of possessing two languages, but persists it appears, in subtle ways even in competent speakers. Even at the level of reaction time experiments in vocabulary, bilingual adults show slightly, but reliably delayed responses (compared to monolinguals) to presentations of printed words in either of their languages, in tasks of categorization or recognition (see Carlo, 1995, but note also Jared & Kroll, 2001). The delays apply even if words are presented in blocks by language. The result suggests that bilinguals have more linguistic space to search in memory when they are confronted with decision tasks about vocabulary than monolinguals do.

The distributed characteristic of bilingual knowledge may represent a sort of compromise achieved by default due to time constraints and differences in day-to-day environments of exposure to the two languages. The compromise is that since not every word, and perhaps not every grammatical structure, needs to be learned in both languages, the learner may acquire the two languages with limitations in each, minimizing learning costs. How significant the limitations are viewed as being, seems to depend on the perspective of the viewer. The social uniformist in the USA may see the limitations as being very significant, because the bilingual speaker may under some circumstances show weaknesses in English, while the social pluralist may see the limitations in English as minimal because the costs of having acquired a second language can be balanced against the benefits of knowing two languages and against the awareness that total capabilities in lexicalized concepts and grammatical knowledge of bilinguals may be as high (and may even be higher) than those of monolinguals.

The Narrative Results

Bilingual speakers showed themselves to have notable weaknesses in story-telling especially in Spanish (Chapter 7) in terms of linguistic expression and the details of vocabulary and grammar that implemented the telling of the Frog Story from a formal standpoint (as reflected in the Language Score, see Figure 12.2 for 5th grade summary data). At the same time, the bilingual speakers seemed to do relatively well from the standpoint of telling the stories at the level of more abstract elements of narratives (as reflected in the Story Score). To put the issue another way, it seemed the bilingual children (especially in Two-way schools) functioned fairly well in getting their story elements across, but they did it without the same level of control over the formal linguistic elements as the monolinguals.

This apparent tendency of bilinguals to manage fairly well in getting their messages across even in the context of technical linguistic disadvantage is reminiscent of the results of Pearson (1993), who found that bilingual students at the University of Miami scored statistically reliably lower on the Scholastic Aptitude Test (SAT) than their monolingual peers, but that the same bilingual students showed no disadvantage when compared with monolinguals on performance in school as measured by grade point average at the University. It would seem that bilingualism has local costs in linguistic skills, but that compensation for the limitations imposed by learning two languages is possible on the more general tasks of life (such as education), and other benefits may obtain in that an additional culture of opportunities is open to bilingual persons that is difficult for monolinguals to access.

Bilingual Learning of a Universal Grammar Feature

An intriguing question posed in this volume concerned the study of a feature of Universal Grammar that has been posited for some time to be learned by bilinguals in an all or nothing fashion, early in life (see Chapter 10). In fact the results on acquisition of *that*-trace offered no support for all-or-nothing learning. Both monolinguals and bilinguals showed a slower (and more context dependent) pattern of acquisition than one might expect given the hypothesis that the posited 'parameter' might be innately represented. Consistent with results from every other chapter in the volume, bilingual children trailed monolinguals in acquisition (especially at the younger ages), suggesting that it was largely frequency of input and learning of patterns available in the input language that accounted for the differences among groups. The idea of innate linguistic structures found no comfort in these results.

The Phonological Translation Results

Another case of a potential benefit of bilingualism that was evaluated here took stock of a special phonological activity that is required of bilinguals. Phonological translation of names and other words is required when persons move from one language to another and bring with them linguistically specific names and words. When bilinguals wish to refer to those specific names or concepts, they find themselves pressed to pronounce them in a new way ('How do you say 'Britney Spears' in Spanish?'). We reasoned that the task of phonological translation is similar to other tasks of phonological awareness in that it requires individuals to match phonological units (either phonemes or syllables) across systems. The phonological awareness tasks that are usually invoked as correlates of reading abilities in young children require matching of phonological to graphological (or orthographic) units (Bradley & Bryant, 1983; González, 1996; Tunmer *et al.*, 1988), but in phonological translation the matching is of phonological units from one language to phonological units of another. Since there is an important similarity between the two task types, we reasoned that phonological translation abilities might be predictive of reading abilities in a way that is similar to that found in studies of other phonological awareness tasks.

The results showed that, indeed, phonological translation abilities were significantly correlated with decoding abilities for written words at all grades in both languages. And the area where bilingual children (and especially the Two-way bilinguals) shone particularly brightly in group comparisons on standardized tests was word-decoding abilities (Chapters 4 and 5). It was the only area where bilingual groups outperformed (though not statistically reliably) the monolinguals, and the surprisingly high level of performance applied in reading for *both* languages. Could it be that phonological translation constitutes a training ground for skills that are especially useful in learning to read? It seems possible given these results that it does, but further research will be necessary to tie down the possible connection, a connection that is also suggested by results indicating correlations between reading skills in one of a bilingual's languages and phonological awareness or metaphonological tasks in the other (Arab-Moghaddam & Senechal, 2001; Baum Bursztyn, 1999; Campbell & Sais, 1995; Francis, 1999).

Maintaining Bilingualism in the USA

An implication that was not expected, but that pervaded the outcomes and conclusions of this research, was that Spanish appears to be losing ground rapidly in the Hispanic communities of Miami. English performance was generally better than Spanish performance on all kinds of tests, even for children who were from homes where parents reported that only Spanish was spoken, and even in Two-way schools. Data from Chapter 3 based on observations of usage of language in classrooms and hallways indicated a strong preference among Hispanic children for speaking English when given the choice, regardless of age or language background at home.

These facts provide an ironic comment on the widely held belief that Spanish is dominant in Miami and that the future of the community will be characterized by Spanish-language hegemony (or at least linguistic pluralism). It appears that even pluralistic Two-way education may, in and of itself, prove incapable of maintaining Spanish in the long term, even in this community with its powerful Spanish-language political and commercial forces. The data from our work indicate that linguistic assimilation to English is active and profound in an area where many expected to see a permanent non-English community. In fact, the work suggests that the strength of the Spanish language in Miami may be almost exclusively due to continued immigration rather than to language maintenance.

The results do suggest, however, that Two-way education can help maintain skills in Spanish, especially by building literacy in Spanish over the elementary school years, while fostering English development at a pace that is comparable to that found in English Immersion education. If an important goal of Two-way education is for children to come to speak both languages with native-like competency and with the ability to pass this capacity on as a legacy for their own children, the picture is not as bright. The relative weakness in Spanish coupled with the preference we observed for children to speak English suggests it is unlikely there will be a significant intergenerational legacy of Spanish. The image we have seen is one of a community in linguistic transition, possessing perhaps ephemeral dialects in both languages, but clearly bound toward a future of essential monolingualism in English.

Regardless of the ultimate language destiny of the greater Miami area, it is clear that Two-way education has strong advantages in an increasingly global community. If we value bilingualism, i.e. true competence in two languages, Two-way education clearly comes closer to achieving the goal than English Immersion. While it is true that all of the groups of potentially bilingual children studied here performed less well than monolingual English speakers in English, it is also true that their performance did not differ importantly by 5th grade depending on whether they were educated in English Immersion or Two-way schools. It might be concluded that there was some cost in English acquisition to having been born into a Hispanic community, but neither of the two educational methodologies was able to make up those costs; either way the monolinguals maintained some advantage. At the same time there were substantial benefits to Spanish acquisition and maintenance with Two-way education. Given that we cannot change the status of children's linguistic background entering school, it would seem important to recognize that educational practices that promote bilingualism without substantial costs to English learning should continue to be explored for their intrinsic value to society.

References

Arab-Moghaddam, N. and Senechal, M. (2001) Orthographic and phonological processing skills in reading and spelling in Persian/English bilinguals. *International Journal of Behavioral Development* 25 (2), 140–7.

August, D. and Hakuta, K. (1997) *Improving Schooling for Language-Minority Children: A Research Agenda*. Washington, DC: National Academy Press.

Baker, K. and de Kanter, A. (1981) *Effectiveness of Bilingual Education: A Review of the Literature. Final Draft Report*. Washington, DC: Office of Technical and Analytic Systems, US Department of Education.

Baker, K. and de Kanter, A. (1983) Effectiveness of bilingual education. In K. Baker and A. de Kanter (eds) *Bilingual Education: A Reappraisal of Federal Policy* (pp. 33–86). Lexington, MA: Lexington Books.

Bamberg, M. (1987) *The Acquisition of Narratives: Learning to Use Language*. Berlin: de Gruyter.

Barik, H.C. and Swain, M. (1975) Three-year evaluation of a large scale early grade French immersion program: The Ottawa study. *Language Learning* 25, 1–30.

Barik, H.C. and Swain, M. (1976a) English-French bilingual education in the early grades: the Elgin study through grade four. *Modern Language Journal* 60 (1–2), 3–17.

Barik, H.C. and Swain, M. (1976b) Primary-grade French immersion in a unilingual English-Canadian setting: The Toronto study through grade 2. *Canadian Journal of Education* 1, 39–58.

Barke, E.M. (1933) A study of the comparative intelligence of children in certain bilingual and monoglot schools in South Wales. *British Journal of Education Psychology* 3, 237–50.

Bates, E. and MacWhinney, B. (1989) Functionalism and the competition model. In B. MacWhinney and E. Bates (eds) *The Crosslinguistic Study of Sentence Processing* (pp. 3–73). Cambridge: Cambridge University Press.

Baum Bursztyn, S.E. (1999) Phonological awareness and reading ability in bilingual Native Spanish and monolingual English-speaking children. *Dissertation Abstracts International: Section B: the Sciences & Engineering* 59 (8-B), 4496.

Bentahila, A. and Davies, E.E. (1992) Convergence and divergence: Two cases of language shift in Morocco. In W. Fase, K. Jaspaert and S. Kroon (eds) *Maintenance and Loss of Minority Languages* (pp. 197–210). Amsterdam: John Benjamins Publishing.

Ben-Zeev, S. (1977) Mechanisms by which childhood bilingualism affects understanding of language and cognitive structures. In P.A. Hornby (ed.) *Bilingualism* (pp. 29–55). New York: Academic Press.

Ben-Zeev, S. (1984) Bilingualism and cognitive development. In N. Miller (ed.) *Bilingualism and Language Disability* (pp. 55–80). San Diego: College Hill Press.

Berman, R. and Slobin, D.I. (1994) *Relating Events in Narrative: A Crosslinguistic Developmental Study*. Hillsdale, NJ: Lawrence Erlbaum.

Bialystok, E. (1986) Factors in the growth of linguistic awareness. *Child Development* 57, 498–510.

Bialystok, E. (1988) Levels of bilingualism and levels of linguistic awareness. *Developmental Psychology* 24, 560–7.

Bialystok, E. (1991) Metalinguistic dimensions of bilingual language proficiency. In E. Bialystok (ed.) _Language Processing in Bilingual Children_ (pp. 113–40). Cambridge: Cambridge University Press.

Bialystok, E. (1992) Selective attention in cognitive processing: The bilingual edge. In R.J. Harris (ed.) _Cognitive Processing in Bilinguals. Advances in Psychology_ (pp. 501–13). Amsterdam, Netherlands: North-Holland.

Bialystok, E. (1999) Cognitive complexity and attentional control in the bilingual mind. _Child Development_ 70 (3), 636–44.

Bialystok, E. and Herman, J. (1999) Does bilingualism matter for early literacy? _Bilingualism_ 2 (1), 35–44.

Bialystok, E. and Majumder, S. (1998) The relationship between bilingualism and the development of cognitive processes in problem solving. _Applied Psycholinguistics_ 19 (1), 69–85.

Bloom, P. (1994) Syntax-semantics mappings as an explanation for some transitions in language development. In Y. Levy (ed.) _Other Children, Other Languages: Issues in the Theory of Language Acquisition_ (pp. 41–75). Hillsdale, NJ: Erlbaum.

Boswell, T.D. and Curtis, J.R. (1983) _The Cuban American Experience_. NJ: Rowman & Allanheld.

Bradley, L. and Bryant, P.E. (1983) Categorising sounds and learning to read: A causal connexion. _Nature_ 301, 419–21.

Brisk, M.E. (1976) The acquisition of Spanish gender by first grade Spanish-speaking children. In G.D. Keller, R.V. Teschner and S. Viera (eds) _Bilingualism in the Bicentennial and Beyond_. New York: Bilingual Press.

Brown, H.D. (1980) _Principles of Language Learning and Teaching_. Englewood Cliffs, NJ: Prentice-Hall.

Bruck, M. and Gennessee, F. (1995) Phonological awareness in young second language learners. _Journal of Child Language_ 22, 307–24.

Bryant, P.E., Bradley, L., Maclean, M. and Crossland, J. (1989) Nursery rhymes, phonological skills and reading. _Journal of Child Language_ 16, 407–28.

Bunt, H.C. (1979) Ensembles and the formal semantic properties of mass terms. In F. Pelletier (ed.) _Mass Terms: Some Philosophical Problems_ (pp. 249–77). Dordrecht: D. Reidel.

Bus, A.G. and van Ijzendoorn, M.H. (1999) Phonological awareness and early reading: A meta-analysis of experimental training studies. _Journal of Educational Psychology_ 91 (3), 403–14.

Butler, Y.G. (2000) The role of metacognition in the development of the English article system among nonnative speakers. _Dissertation Abstracts International, A (Humanities and Social Sciences): Univ Microfilms International_ 60 (8-A), 2837.

Cain, J., Weber-Olsen, M. and Smith, R. (1987) Acquisition strategies in a first and second language: Are they the same? _Journal of Child Language_ 14, 333–52.

Campbell, R. and Sais, E. (1995) Accelerated metalinguistic (phonological) awareness in bilingual children. _British Journal of Developmental Psychology_ 13 (1), 61–8.

Carey, S. (1994) Does learning a language require the child to reconceptualize the world? In L. Gleitman and B. Landua (eds) _The Acquisition of the Lexicon_ (pp. 143–67). Cambridge, MA: MIT Press.

Carlo, M.S. (1995) The effects of cross-language orthographic structure similarity on native language word recognition processes of English-Spanish bilinguals. _Dissertation Abstracts International: Section B: the Sciences & Engineering_ 55 (11-B), 5102.

Chafe, W. (1980) The deployment of consciousness in the production of a narrative. In W. Chafe (ed.) *The Pear Stories: Cognitive, Cultural, and Linguistic Aspects of Narrative Production* (pp. 9–50). Norwood, NJ: Ablex.

Chafe, W. (1982) Integration and involvement in speaking, writing, and oral literature. In D. Tannen (ed.) *Spoken and Written Language* (pp. 35–53). Norwood, NJ: Ablex.

Cho, J.-R. and Chen, H.-C. (1999) Orthographic and phonological activation in the semantic processing of Korean Hanja and Hangul. *Language & Cognitive Processes*, 14 (5–6), 481–502.

Chomsky, C. (1969) *The Acquisition of Syntax in Children from 5–10*. Cambridge, MA: MIT Press.

Chomsky, N. (1981) *Lectures on Government and Binding*. Dordrecht: Foris Publications.

Chomsky, N. (1986) *Barriers*. Cambridge: MIT Press.

Chomsky, N. and Lasnik, H. (1977) Filters and control. *Linguistic Inquiry* 8 (3), 425–504.

Christian, D. (2000) *Directory of Two-Way Bilingual Immersion Programs in the U.S.* Washington, DC: Center for Applied Linguistics. URL: http://www.cal.org/db/2way.

Collier, V. (1987) Age and rate of acquisition of second language for academic purposes. *TESOL Quarterly* 21, 617–641.

Collier, V.P. (1989) How long? A synthesis of research on academic achievement in a second language. *TESOL Quarterly* 23, 509–31.

Conti-Ramsden, G. and Jones, M. (1997) Verb use in specific language impairment. *Journal of Speech, Language and Hearing Research* 40, 1298–313.

Cook, V.J. (1988) *Chomsky's Universal Grammar: An Introduction*. Oxford: Basil Blackwell.

Croft, W. (2001) *Radical Construction Grammar: Syntactic Theory in Typological Perspective*. Oxford: Oxford University Press.

Cummins, J. (1978) Bilingualism and the development of metalinguistic awareness. *Journal of Cross-Cultural Psychology* 9, 131–49.

Cummins, J. (1979) Linguistic interdependence and the educational development of bilingual children. *Review of Educational Research* 49, 222–51.

Cummins, J. (1984) *Bilingualism and Special Education: Issues in Assessment and Pedagogy*. Clevedon: Multilingual Matters.

De Houwer, A. (1990) *The Acquisition of Two Languages from Birth: A Case Study* (Vol. xv). Cambridge: Cambridge University Press.

De La Rosa, D. and Maw, C. (1990) *Hispanic Education: A Statistical Portrait*. Washington, DC: National Council of La Raza.

de Villiers, J.G. and de Villiers, P.A. (1973) Competence and performance in child language: Are children really competent to judge? *Journal of Child Language* 1, 11–22.

de Villiers, P.A. (1991) English literacy development in deaf children: Directions for research and intervention. In J. Miller (ed.) *Research on Child Language Disorders: A Decade of Progress* (pp. 349–78). Austin, TX: Pro-ed.

de Villiers, P.A. and de Villiers, J.G. (1972) Early judgments of semantic and syntactic acceptability by children. *Journal of Psycholinguistic Research* 1, 299–310.

Deutsch, M. (1967) The role of social class in language development and cognition. In A.H. Passow, M. Goldberg and A.J. Tannenbaum (eds) *Education of the Disadvantaged* (pp. 214–24). New York: Holt, Rinehart & Winston.

Döpke, S. (1988) The role of parental teaching techniques in bilingual German-English families. *International Journal of the Sociology of Language* 72, 493–507.

Dulay, H. and Burt, M. (1978) *Why Bilingual Education? A Summary of Research Findings* (2nd edn). San Francisco: Bloomsbury West.

Dunn, L. and Dunn, L. (1981) *Peabody Picture Vocabulary Test-Revised*. Circle Pines, MN: American Guidance Service.

Dunn, L., Padilla, E., Lugo, D. and Dunn, L. (1986) *Test de Vocabulario en Imágenes Peabody – Adaptación Hispanoamericana [Peabody Picture Vocabulary Test – Latin American adaptation]*. Circle Pines, MN: American Guidance Service.

Dunn, L.M. (1987) *Bilingual Hispanic Children on the U.S. Mainland: A Review of Research on Their Cognitive, Linguistic, and Scholastic Development*. Circle Pines, MN: American Guidance Service.

Durgunoglu, A.Y., Nagy, W.E. and Hancin-Bhatt, B.J. (1993) Cross-language transfer of phonological awareness. *Journal of Educational Psychology* 85 (3), 453–65.

Efron, B. and Tibshirani, R.J. (1993) *An Introduction to the Bootstrap*. San Francisco: Chapman & Hall.

Eilers, R.E., Gavin, W.J., and Oller, D.K. (1982) Cross-linguistic perception in infancy: The role of linguistic experience. *Journal of Child Language* 9, 289–302.

Eilers, R.E., Gavin, W.J. and Wilson, W.R. (1979) Linguistic experience and phonemic perception in infancy: A cross-linguistic study. *Child Development* 50, 14–18.

Eilers, R.E., Oller, D.K. and Benito-García, C.R. (1984) The acquisition of voicing contrasts in Spanish- and English-learning infants and children. *Journal of Child Language* 11, 313–36.

Ellis, N.C. and Schmidt, R. (1998) Rules or associations in the acquisition of morphology? The frequency by regularity interaction in human and PDP learning of morphosyntax. In K. Plunkett (ed.) *Language Acquisition and Connectionism* (pp. 307–36). Hove: Psychology Press.

Elman, J. (May, 2000) *Untitled talk*. Leipzig: workshop on Building Linguistic Structure in Ontogeny.

Fase, W., Jaspaert, K. and Kroon, S. (1992) *Maintenance and Loss of Minority Languages*. Amsterdam: John Benjamins.

Fernández, M.C., Pearson, B.Z., Umbel, V.M., Oller, D.K. and Molinet-Molina, M. (1992) Bilingual receptive vocabulary in Hispanic preschool children. *Hispanic Journal of Behavioral Sciences* 14, 268–76.

Fernández, R.M. and Nielsen, F. (1986) Bilingualism and Hispanic scholastic achievement: Some baseline results. *Social Science Research* 15 (1), 43–70.

Fernandez, R.M., Paulsen, R. and Hirano-Nakanishi, M. (1989) Dropping out among Hispanic youth. *Social Science Research* 18 (1), 21–52.

Fishman, J. (1966) The ethnic group and mother tongue maintenance. In J. Fishman (ed.) *Language Loyalty in the United States*. The Hague: Mouton.

Fishman, J.A., Gertner, M.H., Lowry, E.G. and Milán, W.G. (1985) *The Rise and Fall of the Ethnic Revival: Perspectives on Language and Ethnicity*. Amsterdam: Mouton.

Flege, J.E. and Hammond, R. (1994) Mimicry of nondistinctive phonetic differences between language varieties. *Studies in Second Language Acquisition* 5, 1–17.

Flege, J.E. and Munro, M. (1994) The word unit in L2 speech production and perception. *Studies in Second Language Acquisition* 26, 381–411.

Fox, B. and Routh, D.K. (1975) Analysing spoken language into words, syllables and phonemes: A developmental study. *Journal of Psycholinguistic Research* 4, 331–42.

Francis, N. (1999) Bilingualism, writing, and metalinguistic awareness: Oral-literate interactions between first and second languages. *Applied Psycholinguistics* 20 (4), 533–61.

Frase, M., Kaufman, P. and Klein, S. (1999) *Drop-out Rates in the United States, 1997*. Washington, DC: National Center for Education Statistics, Doc. # 1999–082. URL: http://nces.ed.gov/pubsearch/pubsinfo.asp?pubid = 1999082.

Galambos, S.J. and Goldin-Meadow, S. (1990) The effects of learning two languages on levels of metalinguistic awareness. *Cognition* 34 (1), 1–56.

Galambos, S.J. and Hakuta, K. (1988) Subject-specific and task-specific characteristics of metalinguistic awareness in bilingual children. *Applied Psycholinguistics* 9 (2), 141–62.

Gale, K., McClay, D., Christie, M. and Harris, S. (1981) Academic achievement in the Milingimbi bilingual education program. *TESOL Quarterly* 15, 297–314.

Gathercole, V. (1985a) 'He has too much hard questions': The acquisition of the linguistic mass-count distinction in *much* and *many*. *Journal of Child Language* 12, 395–415.

Gathercole, V. (1985b) More and more and more about *more*. *Journal of Experimental Child Psychology* 40, 73–104.

Gathercole, V. (1986) Evaluating competing linguistic theories with child language data: The case of the mass-count distinction. *Linguistics and Philosophy* 9, 151–90.

Gathercole, V. (1989) The acquisition of sex-neutral uses of masculine forms in English and Spanish. *Applied Psycholinguistics* 10 (4), 401–27.

Gathercole, V. and Whitfield, L. (2001) Function as a criterion for the extension of new words. *Journal of Child Language* 28, 87–125.

Gathercole, V., Cramer, L., Somerville, S. and Jansen op de Haar, M. (1995) Ontological categories and function: Acquisition of new names. *Cognitive Development* 10, 225–51.

Gathercole, V. and Hasson, D. (1995) Gender marking in Spanish: Linguistic versus sociological determinants of feminine form in words for humans. In Y. Kachru and L. F. Bouton (eds) *Gender, Language and Power* (pp. 49–75). Urbana, IL: University of Illinois Press.

Gathercole, V.C. (1997) The linguistic mass/count distinction as an indicator of referent categorization in monolingual and bilingual children. *Child Development* 68 (5), 832–42.

Gathercole, V.C. and Min, H. (1997) Word meaning biases or language-specific effects? Evidence from English, Spanish, and Korean. *First Language* 17, 31–56.

Gathercole, V.C. and Montes, C. (1997) That-trace effects in Spanish- and English-speaking monolinguals and bilinguals. In A.T. Perez-Leroux and W.K. Glass (eds) *Contemporary Perspectives on the Acquisition of Spanish: Vol. 1: Developing Grammars* (pp. 75–95). Somerville, MA: Cascadilla Press.

Gathercole, V.C.M., Thomas, E. and Laporte, N. (2001, April-a) *The Acquisition of Gender in a Highly Opaque System: The Case of Welsh Mutation*. Minneapolis: Biennial Meeting of the Society for Research in Child Development.

Gathercole, V.C.M., Thomas, E. and Laporte, N. (2001, April-b) *Welsh Mutation and Cues to Subjecthood*. Minneapolis: Biennial Meeting of the Society for Research in Child Development.

Gathercole, V.C.M., Thomas, E.M. and Laporte, N. (in press). The acquisition of grammatical gender in Welsh. *Journal of Celtic Language Learning*.

Genessee, F. (1987) *Learning Through Two Languages: Studies of Immersion and Bilingual Education*. New York: Newbury House.

Gillon, G. and Dodd, B. (1997) Enhancing the phonological processing skills of children with specific reading disability. *European Journal of Disorders of Communication* 32 (2), 67–90.

Glazer, N. (1966) The process and problems of language maintenance: An integrative review. In J. Fishman (ed.) *Language Loyalty in the United States*. The Hague: Mouton.

Goldenberg, C. and Gallimore, R. (1991) Local knowledge, research knowledge, and educational change. *Educational Researcher* 20, 2–14.

González, M.J. (1996) Aprendizaje de la lectura y conocimiento fonológico: Análisis evolutivo e implicaciones educativas. (Learning to read and phonological awareness: Developmental analysis and educational implications.) *Infancia y Aprendizaje* (76), 97–107.

Gordon, P. (1982) The acquisition of syntactic categories: The case of the count/mass distinction. Ph.D. dissertation. Cambridge, MA: MIT Press.

Gordon, P. (1988) Count/mass category acquisition: Distributional distinctions in children's speech. *Journal of Child Language* 15, 109–28.

Goswami, U. (1999) Integrating orthographic and phonological knowledge as reading develops: Onsets, rimes and analogies in children's reading. In R.M. Klein and P. McMullen (eds) *Converging Methods for Understanding Reading and Dyslexia* (pp. 57–75). Cambridge, MA: MIT Press.

Grosjean, F. (1982) *Life with Two Languages*. Cambridge, MA: Harvard University Press.

Gunn, B., Biglan, A., Smolkowski, K. and Ary, D. (2000) The efficacy of supplemental instruction in decoding skills for Hispanic and non-Hispanic students in early elementary school. *Journal of Special Education* 34 (2), 90–103.

Hakuta, K. (1986) *The Mirror of Language*. New York: Basic Books.

Hakuta, K. (1987) Degree of bilingualism and cognitive ability in mainland Puerto Rican children. *Child Development* 58 (5), 1372–88.

Hakuta, K. (1994) Distinguishing among proficiency, choice, and attitudes in questions about language for bilinguals. In G. Lamberty and C.G. Coll (eds) *Puerto Rican Women and Children: Issues in Health, Growth, and Development. Topics in Social Psychiatry* (pp. 191–209). New York: Plenum Press.

Hakuta, K. and Diaz, R.M. (1985) The relationship between degree of bilingualism and cognitive ability: A critical discussion and some new longitudinal data. In K.E. Nelson (ed.) *Children's Language, Vol. 5* (pp. 319–44). Hillsdale, NJ: Lawrence Erlbaum.

Haley, M.C. and Lunsford, R.F. (1994) *Noam Chomsky*. New York: Twain Publishers.

Halliday, M.A.K. and Hasan, R. (1976) *Cohesion in English*. London: Longman Group.

Harley, B., Hart, D. and Lapkin, S. (1986) The effects of early bilingual schooling on first language skills. *Applied Psycholinguistics* 7, 295–322.

Harris, J.W. (1991) The exponence of gender in Spanish. *Linguistic Inquiry* 22, 27–62.

Hart, B. and Risley, T.R. (1981) Grammatical and conceptual growth in the language of psychologically disadvantaged children: Assessment and intervention. In M.J. Begab, H. Garber and H.C. Hayward (eds) *Psycho-social Influences in Retarded Performance: Strategies for Improving Competence* (pp. 181–98). Baltimore, MD: University Park Press.

Hart, B. and Risley, T.R. (1992) American parenting of language-learning children: Persisting differences in family-child interactions observed in natural home environments. *Developmental Psychology* 28, 1096–105.

Hart, D.J. and Lapkin, S. (1989) *French Immersion at the Secondary/Postsecondary Inter-face: Final Report on Phase I.* Toronto: OISE/Modern Language Centre. Mimeo.

Haugen, E. (1969) *The Norwegian Language in America.* Bloomington, IN: Indiana University Press.

Haugen, E. (1972) *The Ecology of Language.* Stanford, CA: Stanford University Press.

Hedberg, N.L. and Westby, C.E. (1993) *Analyzing Storytelling Skills: Theory to Practice.* Tucson, AZ: Communication Skill Builders.

Hemphill, L., Picardi, N. and Tager-Flusberg, H. (1991) Narrative as an index of communicative competence in mildly mentally retarded children. *Applied Psycholinguistics* 12, 263–79.

Hernández, A.E., Bates, E.A. and Avila, L.X. (1994) On-line sentence interpretation in Spanish-English bilinguals: What does it mean to be 'in between'? *Applied Psycholinguistics* 15, 417–46.

Hernández Pina, F. (1984) *Teorías psicosociolingüísticas y su aplicación a la adquisición del español como lengua materna.* Madrid: Siglo XXI de España Editores, S.A.

Hirano-Nakanishi, M. (1986) The extent and relevance of pre-high school attrition and delayed education for Hispanics. *Hispanic Journal of Behavioral Sciences* 8 (1), 61–76.

Hoff-Ginsberg, E. (1997) Frog stories from four-year-olds: Individual differences in the expression of referential and evaluative content. *Journal of Narrative & Life History* 7 (1–4), 223–7.

Hoff-Ginsberg, E. (1998) The relation of birth order and socioeconomic status to children's language experience and language development. *Applied Psycholinguistics* 19 (4), 603–29.

Hoff-Ginsberg, E. and Tardif, T. (1995) Socioeconomic status and parenting. In M.H. Bornstein (ed.) *Handbook of Parenting, Vol. 2: Biology and Ecology of Parenting* (pp. 161–88). Mahwah, NJ: Lawrence Erlbaum.

Huls, E. and Van de Mond, A. (1992) Some aspects of language attrition in Turkish families in the Netherlands. In W. Fase, K. Jaspaert and S. Kroon (eds) *Maintenance and Loss of Minority Languages* (pp. 100–15). Amsterdam: John Benjamins.

Hunt, K.W. (1977) Early blooming and late blooming syntactic structures. In C. Cooper and L. Odell (eds) *Evaluating Writing* (pp. 91–106): National Council of Teachers of English.

Ioup, G. (1989) Immigrant children who have failed to acquire native English. In S. Gass, C. Madden, D. Preston and L. Selinker (eds) *Variation in Second Language Acquisition* (Vol. 2, pp. 160–75). Clevedon: Multilingual Matters.

Jaeggli, O. (1982) *Topics in Romance Syntax.* Dordrecht: Foris Publications.

Jaeggli, O. and Safir, K.J. (1989) *The Null Subject Parameter.* Dordrecht: Kluwer Academic Publishers.

Jared, D. and Kroll, J.F. (2001) Do bilinguals activate phonological representations in one or both of their languages when naming words? *Journal of Memory & Language* 44 (1), 2–31.

Johnson, J. and Newport, E.I. (1989) Critical period effects in second language learning: The influence of maturational state on the acquisitions of English as a second language. *Cognitive Psychology* 21, 60–99.

Jones, K. and Morris, D. (1997) *Gender and the Welsh Language: A Research Review.* Manchester: Equal Opportunities Commission.

Jones, M. and Conti-Ramsden, G. (1997) A comparison of verb use in children with SLI and their younger siblings. *First Language* 17, 165–93.

Jones, W.R. and Stewart, W.A.C. (1951) Bilingualism and verbal intelligence. *British Journal of Psychology* 4, 3–8.

Karmiloff-Smith, A. (1978) The interplay between syntax, semantics and phonology in language acquisition processes. In R.N. Campbell and P.T. Smith (eds) *Recent Advances in the Psychology of Language*. New York: Plenum Press.

Karmiloff-Smith, A. (1981) The grammatical marking of thematic structure in the development of language production. In W. Deutsch (ed.) *The Child's Construction of Language* (pp. 121–47). London: Academic Press.

Karmiloff-Smith, A. (1986) Some fundamental aspects of language development after age 5. In P. Fletcher and M. Garman (eds) *Language Acquisition: Studies in First Language Development* (pp. 455–76). Cambridge: Cambridge University Press.

Kemper, S. (1984) The development of narrative skills: Explanations and entertainments. In S. Kuczaj (ed.) *Discourse Development* (pp. 99–124). New York and Berlin: Springer Verlag.

Kenstowicz, M. (1989) The null subject parameter in modern Arabic dialects. In O. Jaeggli and K.J. Safir (eds) *The Null Subject Parameter*. Dordrecht: Kluwer Academic Publishers.

Kessler, C. and Quinn, M.E. (1980) Positive effects of bilingualism on science problem-solving abilities. In J. E. Alatis (ed.) *Georgetown University Round Table on Languages and Linguistics 1980: Current Issues in Bilingual Education* (pp. 295–308). Washington, DC: Georgetown University Press.

Khubchandani, L. (1978) Distribution of contact languages in India. In J. Fishman (ed.) *Advances in the Study of Societal Multilingualism*. The Hague: Mouton.

Kirk, R.E. (1995) *Experimental Design: Procedures for the Behavioural Sciences* (3rd edn). Pacific Grove, CA: Brooks/Cole.

Kittel, J.E. (1959) Bilingualism and language: Non-language intelligence scores of third grade children. *Journal of Educational Research* 52, 263–68.

Klein, P.W. (1989) Spanish 'gender' vowels and lexical representation. *Hispanic Linguistics* 3, 147–62.

Krashen, S. (1999a) Effects of phonemic awareness training on delayed tests of reading. *Perceptual & Motor Skills* 89 (1), 79–82.

Krashen, S. (1999b) Training in phonemic awareness greater on tests of phonemic awareness. *Perceptual & Motor Skills* 89 (2), 412–16.

Labov, W. (1972) *Language in the Inner City*. Philadelphia: University of Pennsylvania Press.

Labov, W. and Waletzky, J. (1967) Narrative analysis: Oral versions of personal experience. In J. Helm (ed.) *Essays on the Verbal and Visual Arts* (pp. 12–44). Seattle: University of Washington Press.

Lambert, W.E. (1977) Effects of bilingualism on the individual: Cognitive and sociocultural consequences. In P.A. Hornby (ed.) *Bilingualism: Psychological, Social, and Educational Implications* (pp. 15–28). New York: Academic Press.

Lambert, W.E. (1981) Bilingualism and language acquisition. In H. Winitz (ed.) *Native Language and Foreign Language Acquisition*. New York: New York Academy of Sciences.

Lambert, W. E. and Tucker, G.R. (1972) *Bilingual Education of Children: The St. Lambert Experiment*. Rowley, MA: Newbury House.

Lapkin, S., Swain, M., Kamin, J. and Hanna, G. (1980) *Report on the 1979 Evaluation of the Peel County Late French Immersion Program, Grades 8, 9, 10. 11, and 12*. Toronto: Ontario Institute for Studies in Education.

Lasnik, H. and Saito, M. (1984) On the nature of proper government. *Linguistic Inquiry* 15 (2), 235–89.

Liberman, I.Y., Shankweiler, D. and Liberman, A.M. (1989) The alphabetic principle and learning to read. In D. Shankweiler and I.Y. Liberman (eds) *Phonology and Reading Disability* (pp. 1–33). Ann Arbor: University of Michigan Press.

Lieven, E.V.M. (1997) Variation in a crosslinguistic context. In D.I. Slobin (ed.) *The Crosslinguistic Study of Language Acquisition, Vol.5: Expanding the Contexts* (pp. 199–263). Mahwah, NJ: Lawrence Erlbaum.

Lindholm, K.J. (1980) Bilingual children: Some interpretations of cognitive and linguistic development. In K. Nelson (ed.) *Children's Language, Vol. 2* (pp. 215–66). New York: Gardner Press (J. Wiley).

Macnamara, J. (1967) The bilingual's linguistic performance – a psychological overview. *Journal of Social Issues (Special Issue on Problems of Bilingualism edited by J. Macnamara)* 23, 58–77.

MacWhinney, B. (1987) The competition model. In B. MacWhinney (ed.) *Mechanisms of Language Acquisition* (pp. 249–308). Hillsdale, NJ: Lawrence Erlbaum.

MacWhinney, B. (1995) *The CHILDES project: Tools for Analyzing Talk* (2nd edn). Hillsdale, NJ: Lawrence Erlbaum.

Mägiste, E. (1979) The competing language systems of the multilingual: A developmental study of decoding and encoding processes. *Journal of Verbal Learning and Verbal Behavior* 18, 79–89.

Malherbe, E.G. (1978) Bilingual education in the Republic of South Africa. In B. Spolsky and R. Cooper (eds) *Case Studies in Bilingual Educaiton* (Vol. 2, pp. 167–202). Rowley, MA: Newbury House.

Manis, F.R., Doi, L.M. and Bhadha, B. (2000) Naming speed, phonological awareness, and orthographic knowledge in second graders. *Journal of Learning Disabilities* 33 (4), 325–33.

Maratsos, M. (2000) More overregularizations after all: New data and discussion on Marcus, Pinker, Ullman, Hollander, Rosen & Xu. *Journal of Child Language* 27, 183–212.

Marchman, V.A. and Bates, E. (1994) Continuity in lexical and morphological development: A test of the critical mass hypothesis. *Journal of Child Language* 21, 339–66.

Martinez, E.A. (1993) *Morpho-syntactic Erosion Between Two Generational Groups of Spanish Speakers in the United States*. New York: Peter Lang.

Mayer, M. (1969) *Frog, Where Are You?* New York: Dial Books.

McDaniel, D. and Cairns, H.S. (1996) Eliciting judgments of grammaticality and reference. In D. McDaniel, C. McKee and H.S. Cairns (eds) *Methods for Assessing Children's Syntax* (pp. 233–54). Cambridge, MA: MIT Press.

Medina, M. and Escamilla, K. (1992) English acquisition by fluent- and limited-Spanish-proficient Mexican Americans in a 3-year maintenance bilingual program. *Hispanic Journal of Behavioral Sciences* 14, 252–67.

Medina, M., Saldate, S. and Mishra, S. (1985) The sustaining effects of bilingual instruction: A followup study. *Journal of Instructional Psychology* 12 (3), 132–39.

Meisel, J. (1986) Word order and case marking in early child language: Evidence from simultaneous acquisition of two first languages: French and German. *Linguistics* (Vol. 24, pp. 123–83).

Meyer, M.M. and Fienberg, S.E. (1992) *Assessing Evaluation Studies: The Case of Bilingual Education Strategies*. Washington, DC: National Academy Press.

Mujica, B. (1995) Findings of the New York City longitudinal study: Hard evidence on bilingual and ESL programs. _READ Perspectives_ 2, 7–36.

Muljani, D., Koda, K. and Moates, D.R. (1998) The development of word recognition in a second language. _Applied Psycholinguistics_ 19 (1), 99–113.

Naeslund, J.C. (1999) Phonemic and graphemic consistency: Effects on decoding for German and American children. _Reading & Writing_ 11 (2), 129–52.

Newmeyer, F.J. (1996) _Generative Linguistics: A Historical Perspective._ London: Routledge.

Newport, E.L. (1990) Maturational constraints on language learning. _Cognitive Science_ 14, 11–28.

Nielsen, F. and Fernández, R.M. (1982) _Achievement of Hispanic Students in American High Schools: Background Characteristics and Achievement._ Washington, DC: US Government Printing Office.

Ochs, E. (1985) Variation and error: A sociolinguistic approach to language acquisition in Samoa. In D.I. Slobin (ed.) _The Cross-linguistic Study of Language Acquisition_ (Vol. 1: The data, pp. 783–838). Hillsdale, NJ: Lawrence Erlbaum.

Oeney, B. and Durgunoglu, A.Y. (1997) Beginning to read in Turkish: A phonologically transparent orthography. _Applied Psycholinguistics_ 18 (1), 1–15.

Oller, D.K., Cobo-Lewis, A.B. and Eilers, R.E. (1998) Phonological translation in monolingual and bilingual children. _Applied Psycholinguistics_ 19 (2), 259–78.

Oller, D.K. and Eilers, R.E. (1982) Similarities of babbling in Spanish- and English-learning babies. _Journal of Child Language_ 9, 565–78.

Oller, D.K. and Eilers, R.E. (1983) Speech identification in Spanish- and English-learning 2-year-olds. _Journal of Speech and Hearing Research_ 26, 50–4.

Oller, D.K., Eilers, R.E., Urbano, R. Cobo-Lewis, A.B. (1997) Development of precursors to speech in infants exposed to two languages. _Journal of Child Language_ 27, 407–25.

Oller, J.W., Kim, K. and Choe, Y. (2000) Testing verbal (language) and non-verbal abilities in language minorities: A socio-educational problem in historical perspective. _Language Testing_ 17 (3), 341–60.

Orfield, G. (1986) Hispanic education: Challenges, research, and policies. _American Journal of Education_ 95, 1–25.

Osborn, J. (1968) Teaching a language to disadvantaged children. _Monographs of the Society for Research in Child Development_ 33.

Oyama, S. (1976) A sensitive period for the acquisition of a nonnative phonological system. _Journal of Psycholinguistic Research_ 5, 261–83.

Padilla, A., Lindholm, K.J., Chen, A., Durán, R., Hakuta, K., Lambert, W. and Tucker, G.R. (1991) The English-only movement: Myths, reality, and implications for psychology. _American Psychologist_ 46 (2), 120–30.

Passenger, T., Stuart, M. and Terrell, C. (2000) Phonological processing and early literacy. _Journal of Research in Reading_ 23 (1), 55–66.

Paulston, C.B. (1992) Linguistic minorities and language policies: Four case studies. In W. Fase, K. Jaspaert and S. Kroon (eds) _Maintenance and Loss of Minority Languages_ (pp. 55–79). Amsterdam: John Benjamins.

Peal, E. and Lambert, W. (1962) The relation of bilingualism to intelligence. _Psychological Monographs_ 76 (Whole No. 546).

Pearson, B.Z. (1993) Predictive validity of the SAT-Verbal scores for high-achieving Hispanic college students. _Hispanic Journal of the Behavioral Sciences_ 15, 342–56.

Pearson, B.Z. (1998) Assessing lexical development in bilingual babies and toddlers. _The International Journal of Bilingualism_ 2, 347–72.

Pearson, B.Z. and Fernández, S. (1994) Patterns of interaction in the lexical growth in two languages of bilingual infants and toddlers. *Language Learning* 44, 617–53.

Pearson, B.Z., Fernández, S. and Oller, D.K. (1993a) Lexical development in simultaneous bilingual infants: Comparison to monolinguals. *Language Learning* 43, 93–120.

Pearson, B.Z., Fernández, S.C. and Oller, D.K. (1993b) Lexical development in bilingual infants and toddlers: Comparison to monolingual norms. *Language Learning* 43 (1), 93–120.

Pearson, B.Z., Fernández, S. and Oller, D.K. (1995) Cross-language synonyms in the lexicons of bilingual infants: One language or two? *Journal of Child Language* 22, 345–68.

Pearson, B.Z. and McGee, A. (1993) Language choice in Hispanic-background junior high school students. In A. Roca and J. Lipski (eds) *Spanish in the United States: Linguistic Contact and Diversity* (pp. 91–102). Berlin: Mouton de Gruytere.

Pearson, B.Z., Navarro, A. and Mueller Gathercole, V. (1995) Assessment of phonetic differentiation in bilingual-learning infants. In D. MacLaughlin and S. McEwen (eds) *Proceedings of the Boston University Conference on Language Development* (pp. 427–38). Somerville, MA: Cascadilla Press.

Pearson, B.Z., Oller, D.K., Umbel, V.M. and Fernández, M.C. (1996, October) *The Relationship of Lexical Knowledge to Measures of Literacy and Narrative Discourse in Monolingual and Bilingual Children.* Paper presented at the Second Language Research Forum, Tucson, AZ.

Pelletier, F.J. (1979) *Mass Terms: Some Philosophical Problems.* Dordrecth: Reidel.

Pérez, L. (1986) Cubans in the United States. *Annals of the American Academy of Political and Social Sciences* 487, 126–37.

Peterson, C. and McCabe, A. (1983) *Developmental Psycholinguistics: Three Ways of Looking at a Child's Narrative.* New York: Plenum Press.

Polich, E. (1974) *Report on the Evaluation of the Lower Elementary French Immersion Program Through Grade 3.* Montreal: Protestant School Board of Greater Montreal.

Porter, R.P. (1990) *Forked Tongue: The Politics of Bilingual Education.* New York: Basic Books.

Ramírez, D.J., Yuen, S.D. and Ramey, D.R. (1991a) *Executive Summary, Final Report: Longitudinal Study of Structured English Immersion Strategy, Early-exit and Late-exit Transitional Bilingual Education Programs for Language-minority Children (Contract No. 300–87–0156).* San Mateo, CA: Aguirre International.

Ramírez, J.D., Pasta, D.K., Yuen, S.D., Billings, D.K. and Ramey, D.R. (1991b) *Final Report on the Longitudinal Study of Structured English Immersion Strategy, Early-exit and Late-exit Transitional Bilingual Education Programs for Language-minority Children (Contract No. 300–87–0156). (Vol. II).* San Mateo, CA: Aguirre International.

Ramírez, J.D., Yuen, S.D., Ramey, D.R. and Pasta, D.J. (1991c) *Final Report: Longitudinal Study of structured English Immersion Strategy, Early-exit and Late-exit Transitional Bilingual ?Education Programs for Language-minority Children (Contract No. 300–87–0156). (Vol. I).* San Mateo, CA: Aguirre International.

Rice, M.L., Cleave, P.L., Oetting, J.B. and Pae, S. (1993) *Preschoolers' Use of Syntactic Cues in Assignment of Novel Names to Unfamiliar Mass/Count Objects.* Paper presented at the biennial meeting of the Society for Research in Child Development, New Orleans, LA.

Rizzi, L. (1982) *Issues in Italian Syntax.* Dordrecht: Foris Publications.

Rizzi, L. (1990) *Relativized Minimality.* Cambridge, MA: MIT Press.

Rosenblum, T. and Pinker, S.A. (1983) Word magic revisited: Monolingual and bilingual children's understanding of the word–object relationship. *Child Development* 53, 773–80.

Rosier, P. and Farella, M. (1976) Bilingual education at Rock Point – Some early results. *TESOL Quarterly* 10, 379–88.

Rossell, C.H. and Baker, K. (1996) The effectiveness of bilingual education. *Research in the Teaching of English* 30, 7–74.

Rubin, H. and Turner, A. (1989) Linguistic awareness skills in grade one children in a French immersion setting. *Reading and Writing: An Interdisciplinary Journal* 1, 73–86.

Saer, D.J. (1923) The effect of bilingualism on intelligence. *British Journal of Psychology* 14, 25–38.

Schaufeli, A. (1992) A domain approach to Turkish vocabulary of bilingual Turkish children in the Netherlands. In W. Fase, K. Jaspaert and S. Kroon (eds) *Maintenance and Loss of Minority Languages* (pp. 117–35). Amsterdam: John Benjamins.

Schneider, W., Ennemoser, M., Roth, E. Kuespert, P. (1999) Kindergarten prevention of dyslexia: Does training in phonological awareness work for everybody? *Journal of Learning Disabilities* 32 (5), 429–36.

Schneider, W., Kuespert, P., Roth, E. and Mechtild, V. (1997) Short- and long-term effects of training phonological awareness in kindergarten: Evidence from two German studies. *Journal of Experimental Child Psychology* 66 (3), 311–40.

Scott, C. (1988) Spoken and written syntax. In M. Nippold (ed.) *Later Language Development: Ages 9 through 19* (pp. 49–95). San Diego: College-Hill.

Shu, H., Anderson, R.C. and Wu, N. (2000) Phonetic awareness: Knowledge of orthography–phonology relationships in the character acquisition of Chinese children. *Journal of Educational Psychology* 92 (1), 56–62.

Singleton, D. (1989) *Language Acquisition: The Age Factor.* Clevedon: Multilingual Matters.

Skutnabb-Kangas, T. and Toukomaa, P. (1976) *Teaching Migrant Children's Mother Tongue and Learning the Language of the Host Country in the Context of the Socio-cultural Situation of the Migrant Family (Tutkimuksia Research Reports).* University of Tampere, Finland, Department of Sociology and Social Psychology.

Slobin, D. (1973) Cognitive prerequisites for the development of grammar. In C.A. Ferguson and D.I. Slobin (eds) *Studies in Child Language Development* (pp. 175–208). New York: Holt, Rinehart & Winston.

Smith, F. (1923) Bilingualism and mental development. *British Journal of Psychology* 13, 270–82.

Smith, N. (1999) *Chomsky: Ideas and Ideals.* Cambridge: Cambridge University Press.

Smith, T. (1995) *Findings from The Condition of Education, 1995, Number 4: The Educational Progress of Hispanic Students.* Washington, DC: National Center for Education Statistics, Doc. # 95–767. URL: http://nces.ed.gov/pubsearch/pubsinfo.asp?pubid = 95767.

Smolicz, J.J. (1992) Minority languages as core values of ethnic cultures – a study of maintenance and erosion of Polish, Welsh, and Chinese languages in Australia. In W. Fase, K. Jaspaert and S. Kroon (eds) *Maintenance and Loss of Minority Languages* (pp. 277–305). Amsterdam: John Benjamins.

Snow, C. and Dickinson, D.K. (1990) Social sources of narrative skills at home and at school. *First Language* 10, 87–103.

Snow, C.E. (1995) Issues in the study of input: Fine-tuning universality, individual and devlopmental differences and necessary causes. In B. MacWhinney and P. Fletcher (eds) *NETwerken: Bijdragen van het vijfde NET symposium: Antwerp Papers in Linguistics 74* (pp. 5–17). Antwerp: University of Antwerp.

Sobin, N. (1987) The variable status of comp-trace phenomena. *Natural Language and Linguistic Theory* 5, 33–60.

Soja, N.N. (1992) Inferences about the meanings of nouns: The relationship between perception and syntax. *Cognitive Development* 7, 29–45.

Soja, N.N., Carey, S. and Spelke, E.S. (1991) Ontological categories guide young children's inductions of word meaning: Object terms and substance terms, *Cognition* 38, 179–211.

Southworth, F.C. (1980) Indian bilingualism: Some educational and linguistic implications. In V. Teller and S.J. White (eds) *Studies in Child Language and Multilingualism* (Vol. 345, pp. 121–46). New York: New York Academy of Sciences.

Stein, N.L. and Glenn, C.G. (1979) An analysis of story comprehension in elementary school children. In R.O. Freedle (ed.) *New Directions in Discourse Processing* (pp. 53–120). Norwood, NJ: Ablex.

S-Plus (1999) *S-Plus 2000: Guide to Statistics, Vol. 2.* Seattle: Mathsoft, Inc.

Swain, M. (1979) Bilingual education: Research and its implications. In C.A. Yorio, K. Perkins and J. Schacter (eds) *On Tesol '79: The Learner in Focus.* Washington, DC: Teachers of English to Speakers of Other Languages.

Swain, M. and Barik, H.C. (1976) A large scale program in French immersion: The Ottawa study through grade three. *ITL: A Review of Applied Linguistics* 33, 1–25.

Swain, M. and Lapkin, S. (1991) Additive bilingualism and French immersion education: The roles of language proficiency and literacy. In A.G. Reynolds (ed.) *Bilingualism, Multiculturalism, and Second Language Learning: The McGill Conference in Honour of Wallace E. Lambert* (pp. 203–16). Hillsdale, NJ: Lawrence Erlbaum.

Swain, M. and Wesche, M. (1975) Linguistic interaction: Case study of a bilingual child. *Language Sciences* 37, 17–22.

Tallmadge, G.K. and Wood, C.T. (1976) *User's Guide (ESEA Title I Evaluation and Reporting System).* Mountain View, CA: RMC Research Corporation.

Teschner, R.V. and Russell, W.M. (1984) The gender patterns of Spanish nouns: An inverse dictionary-based analysis, *Hispanic Linguistics* 1, 115–32.

Thomas, W.P. and Collier, V.P. (1997) *School Effectiveness for Language Minority Students.* Washington, DC: National Clearinghouse for Bilingual Education.

Thomas, W.P. and Collier, V.P. (in preparation). Research summary of study in progress: Results as of September, 1995: Language minority student achievement and program effectiveness. Fairfax, VA.: Unpublished manuscript, George Mason University.

Thornton, R.J. (1990) Adventures in long-distance moving: The acquisition of complex wh- questions. Doctoral disseration, University of Connecticut.

Toribio, A. (2000) *Verb Raising and Verbal Morphology in Spanish Language Attrition.* Boston, MA: Paper presented at the 25th Annual Boston University Conference on Language Development.

Torrance, E.P., Wu, J., Gowan, J.C. and Aliotti, N.C. (1970) Creative functioning of monolingual and bilingual children in Singapore. *Journal of Educational Psychology* 61, 72–75.

Torrance, N. and Olson, D. (1984) Oral language competence and the acquisition of literacy. In A. Pellegrini and T.D. Yawkey (eds) *The Development of Oral and Written Language in Social Contexts* (pp. 167–81). Norwood, NJ: Ablex.

Torres, J.S. and Fischer-Wylie, S.M. (1990) *Native Language Proficiency as a Predictor of LEP Students' Growth in English.* New York: Office of Research, Evaluation and Assessment, New York City Public Schools (from National Clearinghouse for Bilingual Education).

Treiman, R. (2000) The foundations of literacy. *Current Directions in Psychological Science* 9 (3), 89–92.

Troike, R. (1978) Research evidence for the effectiveness of bilingual education. *National Association for Bilingual Education Journal* 3 (1), 13–24.

Tunmer, W.E., Herriman, M.L. and Nesdale, A.R. (1988) Metalinguistic abilities and beginning reading. *Reading Research Quarterly* 23, 134–58.

Tzeng, O.J.L., Hung, D.L. and Wang, W.S.-Y. (1977) Speech recoding in reading Chinese characters. *Journal of Experimental Psychology: Human Learning and Memory* 3, 621–30.

Umbel, V.M. (1991, January) *Measuring the Receptive Vocabularies of Bilingual First, Third, and Sixth Graders.* Paper presented at the XII Symposium on Spanish and Portuguese Bilingualism, Miami, FL.

Umbel, V.M. and Oller, D.K. (1994) Developmental changes in receptive vocabulary in Hispanic bilingual school children. *Language Learning* 44, 221–42.

Umbel, V.M., Pearson, B.Z., Fernández, M.C. and Oller, D.K. (1992) Measuring bilingual children's receptive vocabularies. *Child Development* 63, 1012–20.

Valdes, G. and Geoffrion-Vinci, M. (1998) Chicano Spanish: The problem of the 'underdeveloped' code in bilingual repertoires. *Modern Language Journal* 82 (4), 473–501.

Velez, W. (1989) High school attrition among Hispanic and non-Hispanic White youths. *Sociology of Education* 62 (2), 119–33.

Veltman, C. (1983a) Anglicization in the United States: Language environment and language practice of American adolescents. *International Journal of the Sociology of Language* 44, 99–114.

Veltman, C. (1983b) *Language Shift in the United States.* Amsterdam: Mouton.

Vorih, L. and Rosier, P. (1978) Rock Point Community School: An example of a Navajo-English bilingual elementary school program. *TESOL Quarterly* 12, 263–69.

Wagner, R.K., Torgeson, J.K. and Rashotte, C.A. (1994) Development of reading-related phonological processing abilities: New evidence of bi-directional causality from a latent variable longitudinal study. *Developmental Psychology* 30, 73–87.

White, D. (1981) *Towards a Diversified Legal Profession: An Inquiry into the LSAT, Grade Inflation and Current Admissions Policies.* San Francisco: Julian Richardson Associates.

White, S. and Vanneaman, A. (1995) *NAEP FACTS: Long-Term Trends in Student Reading Performance.* Washington, DC: National Center for Education Statistics, Doc. # 98464. URL: http://nces.ed.gov/pubsearch/pubsinfo.asp?pubid = 98464.

Woodcock, R.W. (1991) *Woodcock Language Proficiency Battery: English Form – Revised.* Chicago: Riverside.

Woodcock, R.W. and Johnson, M.B. (1989) *Woodcock-Johnson Psycho-Educational Battery–Revised: Woodcock – Johnson Tests of Achievement.* Chicago: Riverside.

Woodcock, R. W. and Muñoz-Sandoval, A.F. (1995a) *Batería Woodcock-Muñoz: Pruebas de Aprovechamiento-revisada.* Chicago: Riverside.

Woodcock, R.W. and Muñoz-Sandoval, A.F. (1995b) *Woodcock Language Proficiency Battery: Spanish Form – Revised*. Chicago: Riverside.

Yoshioka, J.G. (1929) A study of bilingualism. *Journal of Genetic Psychology* 36, 473–79.

Zappert, L. and Cruz, B.R. (1977) *Bilingual Education: An Appraisal of Empirical Research*. Berkeley, CA: Bahia, Inc.

Zemach, E. (1979) Four ontologies. In F. Pelletier (ed.) *Mass Terms: Some Philosophical Problems* . Dordrecht: D. Reidel.

Zuengler, J. (1985) Identity markers in L2 pronunciation. *Studies in Second Language Acquisition* 10, 33–9.

Index